MW01688067

The Good Wines of Bordeaux

HUBRECHT DUIJKER

THE GOOD WINES OF BORDEAUX

Crus Bourgeois of the Médoc
Good St Emilions, Pomerols, Graves
and the Great Wines of Sauternes

INTRODUCTION BY
Hugh Johnson

MITCHELL BEAZLEY

Art direction: Van Sambeek Design Associates, Amsterdam
Photography: Peter van de Velde, Amsterdam and Hubrecht Duijker
Maps: Otto van Eersel
First impression 1980

English translation by Danielle de Froidmont Associates.
Translator Raymond Kaye, Editor John Gilbert.

ISBN 0 85533 472 X

Printed in the Netherlands

Typeset and prepared by T&O Graphics and Taylor Jackson Designs Ltd, Lowestoft, Suffolk

First published in the U.K. by
Mitchell Beazley London,
Artists House,
14-15 Manette Street,
London W1V 5LB

© 1980 by Het Spectrum B.V.
English translation © Mitchell Beazley Publishers 1983

All rights reserved
No part of this work may be reproduced or utilized in any form by any means, electronic or mechanical, including photocopying, recording or by any information storage and retrieval system, without prior written permission of the publishers.

For my daughter Melanie who is already very much at home in the Bordeaux châteaux.

Contents

Commonly used terms

Appellation — Short for *appellation d'origine contrôlée*, the legally protected identification of the origin of wine.
Barrique — A Bordeaux cask or barrel of about 225 litres (50 gallons; 60 US gallons).
Cave — Underground cellar.
Chai — Surface cellar characteristic of Bordeaux.
Chef de culture — Man responsible for a vineyard.
Collage — The fining (clarifying) of wine, still often done with the beaten whites of fresh eggs.
Cru — Literally 'growth'.
Cru bourgeois — Grade below that of *grand cru classé*; often wine of good, sometimes very good, quality.
Commune — French administrative district: parish.
Cuve — Fermentation vat or tank — may be of wood, concrete, steel, stainless steel, fibre-glass or other artificial material.
Cuvier, cuvierie — Area where the *cuves* stand.
Gérant — Agent, represents the owner(s) on a wine estate.
Grand cru (classé) — Château or wine included in one of the official classifications of Bordeaux and often among the élite of the region. There are classified *crus* in the Médoc, Graves, Sauternes and Saint-Emilion districts.
Maître de chai — Cellarmaster.
Mise — Bottling.
Mise en bouteilles an/du château — Bottled on the estate.
Négociant — Wine dealer or broker, or merchant.
Oenologist (enologist) — Qualified wine technician or scientist.
Régisseur — Steward or manager appointed by the owner; the *maître de chai* and the *chef de culture* work under him.
Rendement — Yield, normally expressed in hectolitres of wine per hectare (but see *Tonneau* below).
Soutirage — Drawing off; the transfer of wine to a clean cask.
Tonneau — Traditional measure used to express the yield of Bordeaux châteaux. Equal to four *barriques*, so about 900 litres (200 gallons; 240 US gallons; 100 cases).
Vignoble — Vineyard.
Vinification — The making of wine.
Viticulteur — Wine grower.

Introduction

Regular visitors to the wine regions of France soon become aware that, contrary to British folk-lore, we are not the only, nor even the most active, northern investigators of these Elysian fields. Holland and Belgium, small though they are in man-power, are rich, critical and even more fanatical followers of French wine at every level.
For several years now I have been bumping into a young Dutch writer whose reception by the (often hard-boiled) French producers has impressed me. They like him. They open their bottles, estate records, and even their homes to him. I think it is his cool candour they admire: not always the easiest attitude when tasting the grower's pride under his gaze.
Hubrecht Duijker, this cool young man, has spent the greater part of the last decade in France, methodically tasting, interviewing and photographing to make the most complete album of France and its better wine growers that anyone has yet produced. The first volumes, on Bordeaux, were rapturously received by the Bordeaux growers — not the easiest fraternity to please. The two later volumes, on Burgundy, and on the trio of Alsace, Champagne and the Loire, have had the same reception. Translated into French they have sold like buns.
Hubrecht was kind enough to tell me, when we first met five years ago in Amsterdam, that my World Atlas of Wine was his first inspiration. I am very happy, having read and profited by his books, to have sparked something so thorough, so graphic, and so enjoyable. Duijker's books are the perfect armchair journey through my favourite French provinces: the ideal appetizer to their incomparable wines.

Hugh Johnson
London

Foreword

A few years ago I wrote *The Great Wine Châteaux of Bordeaux*, a book that concentrated on the best-known châteaux and their famous, mostly red wines. It had — and still enjoys — great success. Besides the original Dutch edition, the book has been published in Germany, Great Britain, the United States and in France. To my surprise it even won awards in Bordeaux and Paris. Perhaps I should have been satisfied with this result. But as time passed I felt an increasing need to write a further book about Bordeaux. There were far too many of the better wines of the district for which up-to-date, objective information was not available.
As the title of this second book indicates, the red wines it deals with are good rather than great. *The Good Wines of Bordeaux* introduces the reader not to the *grands crus* of the Médoc but to the *crus bourgeois*. In my opinion there is a great need at present for information about this kind of wine. Many of the great Médocs have now become so expensive that most wine lovers can only allow themselves occasional indulgence in them. The *crus bourgeois*, however, still remain within the reach of many people — and their quality is often surprising.
This alone would justify the existence of a book such as this, bearing in mind, too, the wine lover who does not possess the preceding volume.
The Good Wines of Bordeaux, however, does not confine itself to the Médoc. I have also described châteaux in the Graves and Saint-Emilion that do not belong in the foremost rank, but whose quality merits attention.
In this book the reader will also encounter a range of eminent Pomerols, and I have included all the *great* Sauternes. It is my sincere hope that this work will help to extend the reputation of this latter group of marvellous, rich white wines. As Sauternes wines are not always appreciated, the growers of this district are experiencing exceptional difficulties. If in the coming years the world is not prepared to pay a more reasonable amount for these laboriously produced wines, and drink them rather more often, the future for Sauternes looks sombre.
Producing *The Good Wines of Bordeaux* has been no easy task. I have visited some 200 châteaux in the course of it and have had to taste a couple of thousand wines. I stayed in Bordeaux for about two months, visiting châteaux on five or six days a week, from early morning till dusk. The photographer Peter van de Velde followed in my footsteps during the vintage. All photographs have been specially taken for this book. I feel that Peter's great talent is abundantly clear from his brilliant material.
Obviously it would have been impossible to produce a book like this, with its 156 detailed descriptions of châteaux and 62 shorter accounts, entirely by myself. I owe a great debt of gratitude to all those who so enthusiastically helped me, including various importers and private individuals, as well as the owners of the châteaux.
A special word of thanks is due to a number of people who gave me every possible assistance and advice on the spot. There was Bruno Prats, whose hospitality I shall never forget and who, as secretary-general of the *Union des Grands Crus de Bordeaux*, enlisted the support of his members; Jean Miailhe, the dynamic, efficient and extremely helpful chairman of the *Syndicat des Crus Grands Bourgeois et Crus Bourgeois du Médoc*; my good and very expert friend, the wine merchant Herman Mostermans; that great Saint-Emilion personality Thierry Manoncourt; and the genial Christian Moueix, regarded as one of the foremost experts on Pomerol.

Hubrecht Duijker
Abcoude

Left:
The Ordonnac and Potensac cooperative in the Bas-Médoc. The Médoc has has a dozen of these collective enterprises involving some 1,500 wine growers, who own an average 12½ acres of vineyard each. In the Haut-Médoc there are cooperatives at Listrac, Pauillac, Saint-Sauveur, Cissac, Vertheuil, Saint-Estèphe and Saint-Seurin-de-Cadourne. In the Bas-Médoc there are the cooperatives of Ordonnac-Potensac, Prignac, Bégadan, Queyrac (these are combined in the Uni-Médoc organization) and Saint-Yzans-de-Médoc.

The Médoc covers about one-quarter of the total area of the Gironde département, *but has only one-twentieth of the population.*

It was Dutch hydraulic engineers who in the 17th century made considerable areas of the Médoc cultivable, straightening river banks, reclaiming and damming marshes and pools. On old maps the district around Bégadan (Bas-Médoc) was even marked as La Petite Hollande. *In fact an* 'Association des Polders de Hollande' *still functions around this commune.*

The following vintage figures from the 1970s show how greatly wine production in the Médoc can vary. Thus in 1979 more than twice as much wine was made as in 1975 or 1977.

	Cases
1974	*4,370,000*
1975	*2,940,000*
1976	*4,400,000*
1977	*2,610,000*
1978	*4,200,000*
1979	*6,085,000*

A fine Médoc tastes best at just below room temperature — 17 to 19°C (62 to 66°F).

The Medoc

The Médoc covers an area of about 880 square miles northwest of the ever-expanding city of Bordeaux. On the west it is bounded by the Atlantic Ocean, on the east by the Garonne and then the broad Gironde. The name Médoc means 'land in the middle'. In old texts it is rendered as *In Medio Aquae, Medulio* or other similar forms. For centuries the inhabitants led a difficult and impoverished existence. On the meagre soil only a little grain could be grown, mostly rye. Wine-growing would eventually bring prosperity, but not until the 18th century. Up to the end of the 15th century wine was produced only for local needs and for the city of Bordeaux. Not until the 16th century did rich merchants venture to establish wine estates of any size, at the villages of Macau and Margaux, for example. In the following century it was well-situated aristocratic families such as the Ségurs and the Pontacs who began to exploit wine properties.

It was only in 1750 that the Médoc began to fulfil its destiny as a wine region. It began to experience some prosperity and most of the wine villages built themselves a new church.

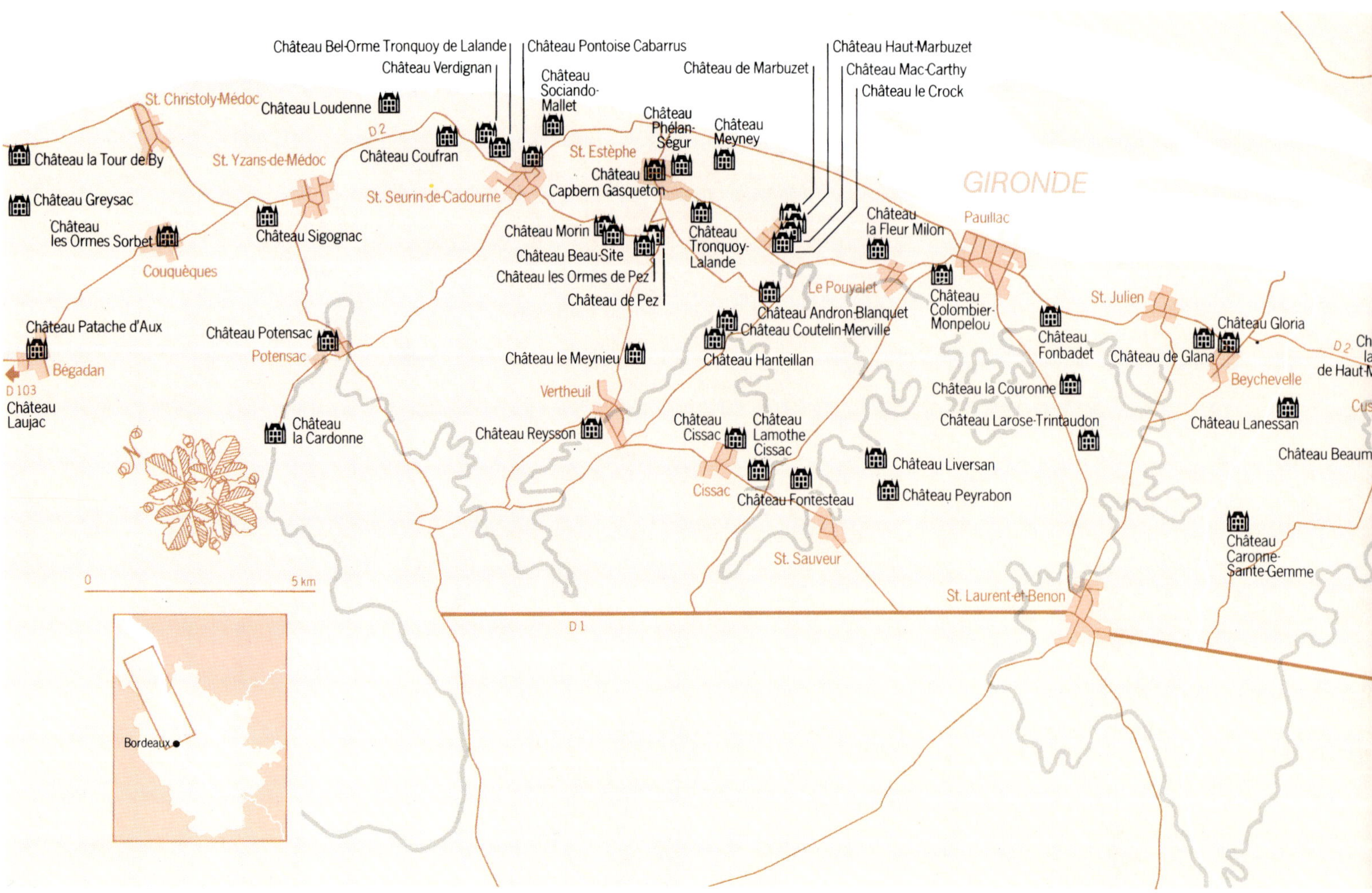

Left:
Vintage scene in Pauillac. Wine growers wait with their grapes at the local cooperative — which has one of the best reputations in the Médoc.

Below, both pages:
Map of the Médoc showing the most important communes and the location of the crus bourgeois *described in this book.*

For the Médoc and Haut-Médoc appellations there is an obligatory minimum of 10° alcohol. Haut-Médoc wines sold under commune names (Margaux, Pauillac etc.) must contain at least 10.5°.

There are six Haut-Médoc communes entitled to sell their wines under their own names. They have a combined vineyard area of 11,614 acres:

Saint-Estèphe	*2,738 acres*
Margaux	*2,632 acres*
Pauillac	*2,370 acres*
Saint-Julien	*1,843 acres*
Listrac	*1,226 acres*
Moulis	*828 acres*

Natural factors

Today about 25,000 acres of the Médoc are planted with vines. The vineyards lie in a long, narrow strip that stretches for about 50 miles between the water of the Gironde and the pine forests of the Landes. For nearly the whole of its length this strip is less than 3 miles wide. That the world's finest red wines should be produced just here is due to a unique combination of natural factors. The Médoc has an often complex, poor, usually very gravelly soil in which the vine roots have to go down deep to find nourishment. The complexities of the soil are therefore reflected in the wine. The soil also has excellent drainage while the climate, too, favours the vine. Thanks to the great water masses of sea and river, extremes of temperatures are avoided in both summer and winter. Under normal conditions, the warmth of the sun and the humidity are in perfect balance.

Grape varieties

The Cabernet Sauvignon dominates the wine landscape of the Médoc. This relatively small, concentrated grape is full of character and gives dark, full-flavoured, somewhat

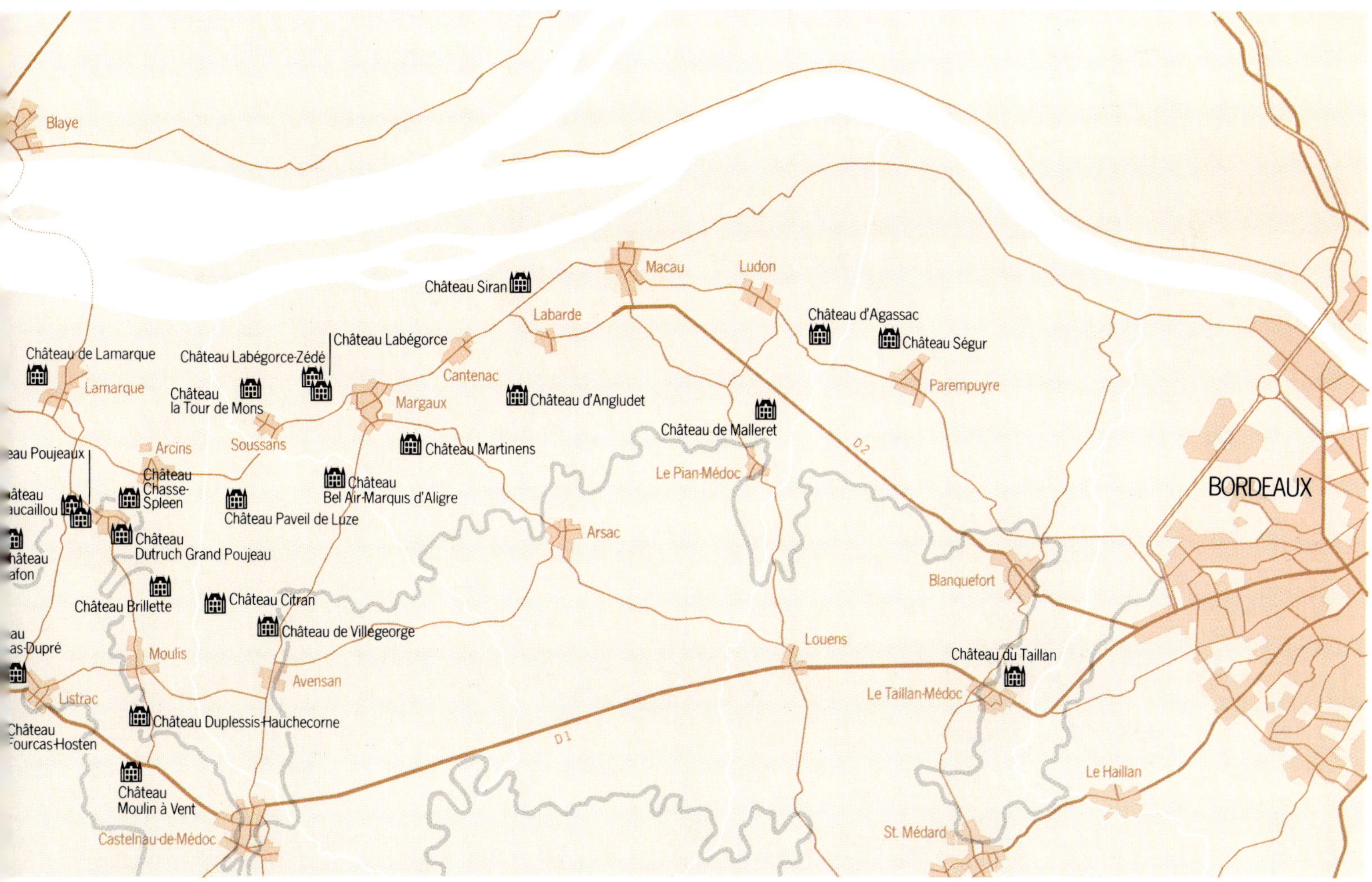

Left:
Village scene, Listrac.

Below:
Senior citizens on the terrace of the hotel-restaurant La Coquille in Pauillac.

Right:
Margaux's Maison du Vin. *This provides information about the commune and on visiting the local châteaux. An extensive selection of local wines is sold: usually various vintages of some 30 châteaux. The people of Margaux — called Marojallia by the 4th-century Roman poet Ausonius — speak French with a distinctive accent. The sheltering effect of nearby river islands gives Margaux a warmer microclimate than neighbouring villages.*

austere wines that generally need long maturation. They have a high tannin content, and in their youth often give out the scent of blackcurrants.
The Cabernet Franc is also common. Its wine is milder, more genial than that of the Cabernet Sauvignon, but has less breeding.
The Merlot is to be met with nearly everywhere. This grape produces a broad, supple wine, and is used in the Médoc to give wines from the Cabernets more substance and roundness. The Merlot is the earliest of this distinguished trio to open, followed by the Cabernet Franc and then the Cabernet Sauvignon.

Two less important and rarer varieties are the Petit Verdot (late-ripening, plenty of colour, alcohol and acidity) and the Malbec (early-ripening, not much alcohol, a lot of acid). Combining these two grapes produces a wine that is more than the sum of its parts. With its depth of colour, its subtle scent, its elegant, many-faceted taste and its long aftertaste, a good Médoc is a feast for the senses. But it has to be given the time to mature: a few seasons in the cask and then several years in the bottle.

Appellations d'origine contrôlée

The Médoc has two distinct *appellations*. The more southerly of these is the Haut-Médoc, which covers an area that begins some six miles northwest of Bordeaux, near Le Taillan and Blanquefort, and ends at the northern boundary of the commune of Saint-Seurin-de-Cadourne. The distict to the north is called simply Médoc for vinous purposes, although Bas-Médoc is the usual geographical name. The Médoc *appellation* runs as far as Saint-Vivien-de-Médoc. The Haut-Médoc *appellation* comprises some 6,400 acres with an average annual production of about 1,100,000 cases of red wine. The permitted yield is 43 hectolitres per hectare.
The Médoc *appellation* applies to about 6,700 acres producing an average of 1,200,000 cases. The permitted yield here is 45 hectolitres per hectare.
The region also has commune *appellations*. These villages all lie in the Haut-Médoc and possess some 11,700 acres of vineyard. From south to north they are Margaux, Moulis, Listrac, Saint-Julien, Pauillac and Saint-Estèphe. They produce an average of about 1,800,000 cases. The allowed yield for these village wines is 40 hectolitres per hectare. The whole Médoc region has some 1,600 wine growers.
Here are brief outlines of these six commune *appellations*.

Margaux
Because of legal difficulties and disputes Margaux did not receive its own *appellation* until 1954. Before that time the wine had to be sold as Haut-Médoc. The Margaux *appellation* covers five communes: Margaux itself (808 acres), Arsac (205 acres), Cantenac (934 acres), Labarde (287 acres), and Soussans (356 acres). With a further 42 acres lying outside these areas the Margaux *appellation* comprises 2,632 acres. The thinnest topsoil of the whole Médoc is found there, the most pebbles in the subsoil and the lowest product per hectare of all red Bordeaux. The vineyards are cut up into many small plots. Another Margaux feature is a microclimate that ripens the grapes eight to ten days earlier than in the rest of the Médoc. By and large, Margaux wines (average product 380,000 cases) have a delicate, fine personality, but exceptions to the rule occur: in the west of the commune, where there is more clay in the soil, quite firm wines are grown.

Moulis
Moulis derives its names from *moulins*, the windmills that formerly ground the local grain. This oblong commune, 7½ miles long and 1¾ to 2½ miles wide, has 828 acres of vineyard. Several of the best-known Moulis estates are concentrated in and around the hamlet of Grand Poujeaux. The average production of 130,000 cases consists of quite elegant, supple yet sinewy red wines.

Listrac
Part of this commune lies 140 feet above sea level and is thus the highest point of the Médoc. There is a beacon here. In 1914 Listrac had 3,324 acres of vineyard; now there are 1,226. Average yield is 195,000 cases. The wines are rather more robust and substantial than those of neighbouring Moulis. The village has a fine 13th-century Romanesque church.

Saint-Julien
The southern entrance to Saint-Julien (via the hamlet of Saint-Julien-Beychevelle) is appropriately marked by a gigantic wine

Left: The village of Saint-Estèphe, whose vineyards stretch over 4½ miles. The archbishopric of Bordeaux was buying Saint-Estèphe wine as early as 1369. Besides an ancient centre, the village has a modern quarter near its tiny river harbour where employees of the Shell refinery at Pauillac live. In 1970 the refinery's capacity was increased ten times, making it a noisy, smoky monstrosity that mars and pollutes the peaceful, wine-growing countryside. If only the growers had protested, it might have been built elsewhere. Thanks to Shell, Pauillac acquired its 'Château d'Huile'.

Left: Carrying home cooperative wine.

Below: Members of La Commanderie du Bontemps de Médoc et des Graves at Château Cos d'Estournel, a famous grand cru of Saint-Estèphe. From right to left: Henri Martin (Gloria, etc.); André Cazes (Lynch-Bages and Les Ormes de Pez, etc.); Herman Mostermans, of the successful export business Les Vins de Crus; Bruno Prats (Cros d'Estournel, De Marbuzet, Petit-Village, etc.); and Arlette Castéja of Tronquoy-Lalande. Although this fraternity originated in the distant past, its revival dates from 1950. Its three important celebrations are in January, June and September.

bottle. This is where some of the most splendid Médocs are made, gracious wines with a lot of suppleness and refinement. They are usually more robust than the delicate Margaux and less powerful than the Pauillacs. Saint-Julien's growers have 1,843 acres at their disposal, which produce an average of 280,000 cases.

Pauillac

With nearly 7,000 inhabitants and a monstrous Shell refinery, Pauillac is the largest and most important commune of the whole Médoc. Remarkably enough, it is without really good hotels or restaurants — which is characteristic of the Médoc. The place produces some 380,000 cases from its 2,370 acres. In many respects this wine is of excellent quality: Pauillac has no fewer than 18 of the 60 *grands crus classés* of the Médoc (including three out of the first five: Lafite-Rothschild, Mouton-Rothschild and Latour). Pauillac wine generally contains a lot of Cabernet Sauvignon, resulting in a rather sombre, deep-red colour, a blackcurrant bouquet (especially when young), and a mouth-filling, pronounced taste with power and character, depth and length of flavour.

Saint-Estèphe

With its 2,738 acres of vineyard Saint-Estèphe is the largest wine commune of the Médoc. Average annual production fluctuates around 500,000 cases. The village, known as Saint-Estèphe-de-Calon until the 18th century, has a striking, slightly bottle-shaped church tower and a pleasant *Maison du Vin* where art exhibitions are sometimes held. Saint-Estèphe has the hilliest terrain of the Médoc, and the richest soil. The wine made here is more powerful and vigorous even than Pauillac's and the complete antithesis to the delicate refinement usually met with in the Margaux.

At the end of 1977 a committee of twelve visited all the crus bourgeois *belonging to the syndicate in order to classify them. Jean Miailhe was the committee's non-voting chairman.*

The form that the committee members had to fill in listed the following points:
present status
age of estate
appellation
date of purchase by present owner
vineyard area
average age of vines
grape varieties
mode of planting
production
general condition of buildings
reception facilities
percentage of château bottling
pricing level
In addition, each member had to taste the wine and mark it out of 20 points.

Below:
The striking church of Saint-Julien. Wine accounts from the archbishopric of Bordeaux (1354, 1357, 1361, 1362, 1390) refer to the village as Sanctus Julianus. At the beginning of the 19th century the family name de Rintrac was added. A map of 1839 marks it as Saint-Julien-de-Reignac, and an ordnance map of 1875 it is simply Saint-Julien.

The Crus Bourgeois

The *grands crus classés* of the Médoc may have basked in the flattering light of recognition since 1855, but the life of the *crus bourgeois* has been difficult right from the start. They came into being, in fact, because of dissatisfaction with the 1855 classification, which placed just a few Médoc châteaux on a pedestal and left the rest undifferentiated. Obviously there were differences in the rank and file, and these became increasingly apparent as the years went by. Eventually discussions were started and in 1920 the *Syndicat des Crus Bourgeois et Bourgeois Supérieurs du Médoc* was set up. Initially this syndicate existed only in name: for 12 years, until 1932, it took no action. In that year five wine brokers, acting with the 'twofold authority' of the Bordeaux Chamber of Commerce and the Chamber of Agriculture of the Gironde, made a classification of the members of the syndicate. In the Haut-Médoc the *courtiers*, as they are termed, arrived at the following grading:
6 *crus bourgeois supérieurs exceptionnels*
100 *crus bourgeois supérieurs*
250 *crus bourgeois.*
In the Bas-Médoc they decided on:
87 *crus bourgeois.*
A total of 443 châteaux was therefore classified (although some sources give different figures). However, for many estates this tardy recognition was of little avail. The crisis years had begun, wine prices were falling, and when in 1943 two *courtiers* listed the *crus bourgeois*, only 290 châteaux remained. In 11 years some 150 wine estates had disappeared. By 1940 the syndicate of the *crus bourgeois* was defunct.

A new beginning

It was not only 1962 that the 'bourgeois' of the Médoc re-established their *syndicat* — in May of that year for the Haut-Médoc alone and in September for the whole area. The number of châteaux by this time had fallen to 110, of which 94 renewed their membership. Six new members came in later. In 1966 a committee set up by the syndicate itself granted titles to its own members. This internal classification was called a *palmarès*, literally 'prize giving'.
The result was:
18 *crus grands bourgeois exceptionnels*
44 *crus grands bourgeois*
38 *crus bourgeois.*
These ratings differed somewhat from those of 1932. This caused some confusion, particularly as the French authorities would not allow the new designations to appear on labels because the classification had been privately arranged. The 1932 terminology, which had been officially approved, was meanwhile retained by a number of châteaux. The consequence was that the labels, as displayed to the public, represented a hopelessly obsolete classification instead of the more up-to-date 1966 system.

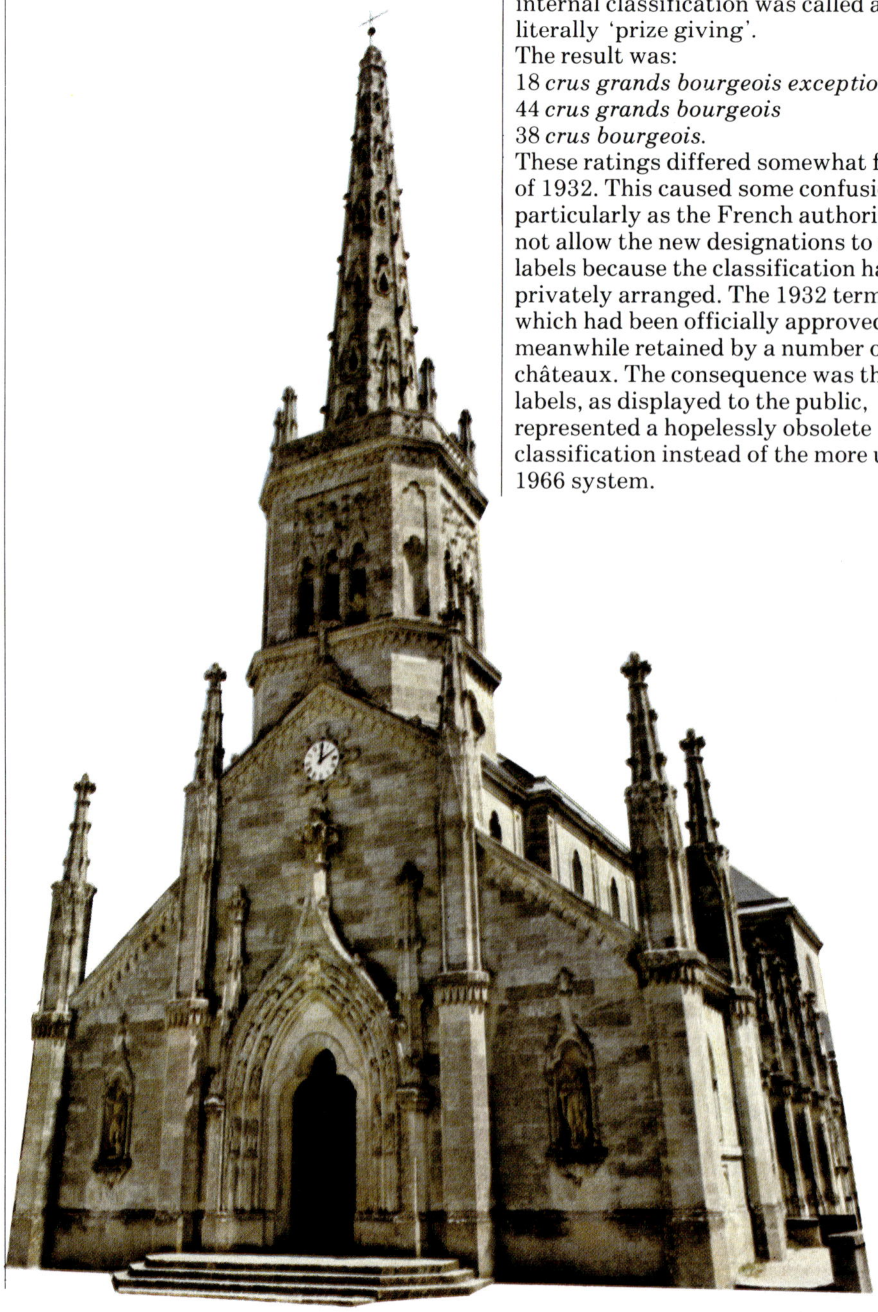

A number of crus bourgeois *belong to the prestigious Académie du Vin de Bordeaux; some are additionally members of the Union des Grands Crus de Bordeaux. In both cases this brings them into association with many* grands crus. *Members of the* bourgeois cru *syndicate in the Académie are the châteaux of Chasse-Spleen, Citran, Fourcas-Hosten, Phélan-Ségur and Poujeaux. Citran is also in the Union des Grands Crus. Gloria, Labégorce, Lanessan, Maucaillou, De Pez and Siran are* crus bourgeois *that belong to the Académie, but not to the syndicate. Lanessan and Mauccaillon have also been accepted for the Union des Grands Crus.*

Below:
View over the vines and the Gironde at the wine village of Saint-Estèphe.

Right:
This gigantic wine bottle is one of the best-known images of the Médoc. It stands by the roadside in the hamlet of Saint-Julien-Beychévelle, nearly opposite Château Gloria.

A revised version

Lack of the official recognition failed to inhibit the activities of the *Syndicat des Crus Grands Bourgeois et Crus Bourgeois du Médoc.* In 1977 it published a revised *palmarès syndical:*
18 *crus grands bourgeois exceptionnels*
41 *crus grands bourgeois*
68 *crus bourgeois.*
This gave a total of 127 châteaux — although research has convinced me that the real number was actually less than this. The *crus bourgeois* category in fact contained a number of second wines of *crus grands bourgeois (exceptionnels).*

Syndicate members work a total of about 9,100 acres in the Médoc, producing an average of some 1,890,000 cases a year.

Selection criteria

What value can be placed on the syndicate's own classification of its *crus bourgeois*? Why did it conduct its assessment behind closed doors and not call in any independent *négociants*? I discussed these questions with Jean Miailhe, the syndicate's energetic chairman, and himself a wine broker. He said that in the past practically all wine had been sold by the *courtiers*, but not now. They were not longer familiar with the wines of all

Village café in Saint-Christoly, Bas-Médoc.

In terms purely of area, the most important communes of the Haut-Médoc are: Saint-Estèphe (2,738 acres), Margaux (2,632 acres), Pauillac (2,370 acres), Listrac (1,126 acres), Saint-Seurin-de-Cadourne (1,048 acres), Saint-Laurent (882 acres), Moulis (828 acres), Saint-Sauveur (633 acres), Cussac (623 acres), Vertheuil (563 acres), Cissac (551 acres), Arcins (465 acres), Ludon (292 acres), Lamarque (274 acres), and Avensan (267 acres). The remaining six communes have less than 250 acres of vineyard.

The largest wine communes of the Bas-Médoc are: Bégadan (1,989 acres), Prignac (951 acres), Saint-Yzans-de-Médoc (828 acres), Ordonnac (549 acres), Saint-Christoly (507 acres), Blaignan (425 acres) and Saint-Germain d'Esteuil (159 acres). The other nine communes all have less than 250 acres.

the Médoc châteaux. Moreover, the *négociants* have become very chary of sticking their necks out. Miailhe told me of one well-known individual who had helped try to revise the *grand cru* classification in 1961, and who, because he was so honest, could not sell a drop of wine for the next three years. For these reasons the syndicate had been obliged to tackle the matter itself, and had begun by setting the following amended selective criteria:

Cru bourgeois The vineyard must cover at least 7 hectares (17 acres), in the Médoc, possess its own *cuverie* and make its own wine at the château. The wine has to undergo testing and approval before the classification is granted.

Cru grand bourgeois The same requirements as for *cru bourgeois*, plus the obligation to age the wine in oak casks. The wine must be of better quality than the previous category.

Cru grand bourgeois exceptionnel The same requirements as for *cru grand bourgeois*, plus the stipulation that the estate must lie in the same area as the *grands crus classés* of the Médoc (from Ludon to Saint-Estèphe). In addition the wine must be bottled at the château.

A committee of twelve

On the basis of these criteria, all the relevant châteaux were assessed in the course of 1977 by a committee of the syndicate. This consisted of six ordinary members and the six members of the administrative council. On a special form, each member gave his own assessment of the château being visited and its wine. Such matters as the vineyard (acreage, grape varieties, method of planting) were also taken into consideration, as well as the appearance of cellars and buildings. The wine received a mark out of 20. Not all the châteaux visited achieved satisfactory marks: eighteen were turn down. The châteaux that were accepted undertook to pay their membership dues in money and wine.

At time of writing, the use of the terms *grand bourgeois* and *grand bourgeois exceptionnel* on labels was still not permitted by the authorities; only the 1932 terms are allowed. I am convinced, however, that the *palmarès* of the *crus bourgeois* will gradually gain such an excellent reputation that the French legislators will have to accept this classification. The *bourgeois* intend to revise their classification again in 1987.

Differences between crus bourgeois and grands crus

How do *crus bourgeois* differ from *grands crus?* While tasting in the Médoc, it struck me that when young the better *bourgeois* came very close to *grand cru* standard. It is only after ageing in the bottle that the difference in quality really starts to show. Then you begin to note that the *crus bourgeois* generally have rather less depth, refinement and length of flavour. In most cases this has to do with the soil composition; and of course the methods employed at the châteaux are also important. However, the quality of the *crus bourgeois* has improved considerably over the last decade, and continues to do so.
Many owners are doing better financially and can now afford improved equipment, more new casks and a longer ageing period. One particular group of *bourgeois* wines is approaching, even reaching, *grand cru* level. These wines mainly come from châteaux that by purchase or exchange have acquired land from neighbouring *grands crus.* There are a few château that should have been classified in 1855 but were not — either because of a temporary decline or negligence by the owner.
Also noticeable, but quite logical, is the fact that *crus bourgeois* that are linked with a *grand cru* rank among the better wines of their category; after all, it is the same team who make the two wines, with the same expertise and the same methods. At these *bourgeois* châteaux, too, the wine usually matures in wooden casks that have come from the related *grand cru.*

One important distinction between *crus bourgeois* and *grands crus* is in the relation of price to quality. Among the *bourgeois*, which in the nature of things are generally cheaper, this seems much more realistic than among their more aristocratic fellows.

The 1977 classification

The following châteaux were classified on 29 December 1977 by the *Syndicat des Crus Grands Bourgeois et Crus Bourgeois du Médoc:*

Cru Grand Bourgeois Exceptionnel
d'Agassac (Ludon)
Andron-Blanquet (Saint-Estèphe)
Beau-Site (Saint-Estèphe)
Capbern Gasqueton (Saint-Estèphe)
Caronne-Sainte-Gemme (Saint-Laurent)
Chasse-Spleen (Moulis)
Cissac (Cissac)
Citran (Avensan)
Le Crock (Saint-Estèphe)
Dutruch-Grand-Poujeaux (Moulis)
Fourcas-Dupré (Listrac)
Fourcas-Hosten (Listrac)
Du Glana (Saint-Julien)
Haut-Marbuzet (Saint-Estèphe)
De Marbuzet (Saint-Estèphe)
Meyney (Saint-Estèphe)
Phélan-Ségur (Saint-Estèphe)
Poujeaux (Moulis)

Cru Grand Bourgeois
Beaumont (Cussac)
Bel-Orme (Saint-Seurin-de-Cadourne)
Brillette (Moulis)
La Cardonne (Blaignan)
Colombier-Monpelou (Pauillac)
Coufran (Saint-Seurin-de-Cadourne)
Coutelin-Merville (Saint-Estèphe)
Duplessis-Hauchecorne (Moulis)
La Fleur Milon (Pauillac)
Fontesteau (Saint-Sauveur)
Greysac (Bégadan)
Hanteillan (Cissac)
Lafon (Listrac)
De Lamarque (Lamarque)
Lamothe-Cissac (Cissac)
Larose-Trintaudon (Saint-Laurent)

Left:
Saint-Estèphe's Maison du Vin, *on the square facing the church. It serves mainly as a shop for the local wines. Exhibitions are held here in the summer.*

Laujac (Bégadan)
Liversan (Saint-Sauveur)
Loudenne (Saint-Yzans-de-Médoc)
Mac-Carthy (Saint-Estèphe)
De Malleret (Le Pian)
Martinens (Margaux)
Morin (Saint-Estèphe)
Moulin à Vent (Moulis)
Le Meynieu (Vertheuil)
Les Ormes de Pez (Saint-Estèphe)
Les Ormes Sorbet (Couquèques)
Patache d'Aux (Bégadan)
Paveil de Luze (Soussans)
Peyrabon (Saint-Sauveur)
Pontoise-Cabarrus (Saint-Seurin-de-Cadourne)
Potensac (Potensac)
Reysson (Vertheuil)
Ségur (Parempuyre)
Sigognac (Saint-Yzans-de-Médoc)
Sociando-Mallet (Saint-Seurin-de-Cadourne)
Du Taillan (Le Taillan)
La Tour de By (Bégadan)
La Tour du Haut-Moulin (Cussac)
Tronquoy-Lalande (Saint-Estèphe)
Verdignan (Saint-Seurin-de-Cadourne)

Cru Bourgeois
Aney (Cussac)
Balac (Saint-Laurent)
La Bécade (Listrac)
Bellerive (Valeyrac)
Bellerose (Paulillac)
Les Bertins (Valeyrac)
Bonneau (Saint-Seurin-de-Cadourne)
Le Bosq (Saint-Christoly)
Du Breuilh (Cissac)
La Bridane (Saint-Julien)
De By (Bégadan)
Cailloux de By (Bégadan)
Cap Léon Veyrin (Listrac)
Carcanieux (Queyrac)
Castéra (Cissac)
Chambert (Saint-Estèphe)
La Clare (Saint-Estèphe)
Clarke (Listrac)
La Closerie (Moulis)
De Conques (Saint-Christoly)
Duplessis-Fabre (Moulis)
Fonpiqueyre (Saint-Sauveur)
Fonréaud (Listrac)
Fort Vauban (Cussac)
La France (Blaignan)
Gallais-Bellevue (Potensac)
Grand-Duroc-Moulin (Pauillac)
Grand-Moulin (Saint-Seurin-de-Cadourne)
Haut-Bages-Monpelou (Pauillac)
Haut-Canteloup (Couquèques)
Haut-Garin (Bégadan)
Haut-Padargnac (Pauillac)
Houbanon (Prignac)
Hourton-Ducasse (Saint-Sauveur)
De Labat (Saint-Laurent)
Lamothe-Bergeron (Cussac)
Le Landat (Cissac)
Landon (Bégadan)
Larivière (Blaignan)
Lartigue de Brochon (Saint-Seurin-de-Cadourne)
Lassalle (Potensac)
Lavalière (Saint-Christoly)
Lestage (Listrac)
Mac-Carthy-Moula (Saint-Estèphe)

Monthil (Bégadan)
Moulin de la Roque (Bégadan)
Moulin Rouge (Cussac)
Panigon (Civrac)
Pibran (Pauillac)
Plantey de la Croix (Saint-Seurin-de-Cadourne)
Pontet (Blaignan)
Ramage-la-Batisse (Saint-Sauveur)
Romefort (Cussac)
La Roque de By (Bégadan)
De la Rose Maréchale (Saint-de-Cadourne)
Saint-Bonnet (Saint-Christoly)
Saint-Roch (Saint Estéphe)
Saransot (Listrac)
Soudars (Avensac)
Tayac (Soussans)
La Tour Blanche (Saint-Christoly)
La Tour du Haut-Caussan (Blaignan)
La Tour du Mirail (Cissac)
La Tour Saint-Bonnet (Saint-Christoly)
La Tour Saint-Joseph (Cissac)
Des Tourelles (Blaignan)
Vernous (Lesparre)
Vieux-Robin (Bégadan)

In this book at least one page is devoted to each *grand bourgeois exceptionnel.* Many *crus bourgeois* are mentioned in the chapter 'Other Interesting Châteaux' (pages 191-8), or as a secondary wine of a *grand bourgeois* château (see the Index, pages 199-200).

The outsiders
A number of Médoc châteaux were not classified in 1855 and have not become members of the *crus bourgeois* syndicate; yet often they make excellent wine. Joining the syndicate would further enhance their reputation, but the owners in question are not keen to do so. The most important of their reasons is that they have pinned their hopes on a revision of the *grand cru* classification that would include their wines. Accepting *bourgeois* status would be a loss of face for them. In addition, most of these estates object to the 'internal', subjective way in which the syndicate works. There was a period when the most important of the outsiders grouped themselves together as the *crus notables* and strove for inclusion in the *grands crus.* As time passed and the chances of a totally new *grand cru* classification dwindled, a number of these estates joined the *crus bourgeois:* the châteaux Chasse-Spleen, Meyney, Les Ormes de Pez, Poujeaux, Phélan-Ségur, Brillette, Peyrabon and De Lamarque are examples. I selected thirteen of the remaining unclassified châteaux, which I have visited and described:
d'Angludet (Cantenac)
Bel-Air-Marquis d'Aligre (Soussans)
La Couronne (Pauillac)
Gloria (Saint-Julien)
Labégorce (Margaux)
Labégorce-Zédé (Soussans)
Lanessan (Cussac)
Maucaillou (Moulis)
De Pez (Saint-Estèphe)
Siran (Labarde)
La Tour de Mons (Soussans)
De Villegeorge (Avensan).
With very few exceptions the wines from these châteaux are comparable at least with the best of the *crus grands bourgeois exceptionnels.*

Left:
The rear of the stately Château du Taillan.

Below left:
This fragment of wall stands in the park. It was probably once part of a monastery: du Taillan's cellar is said to have been built by monks.

Below right:
A cellar worker samples the still harsh young wine. Du Taillan produces 3,000 to 7,500 cases of red wine a year — plus a modest amount of white wine, sold as Château la Dame Blanche with the Bordeaux appellation. *The label on the latter depicts the front of Château du Taillan. La Dame Blanche is grown on 11 acres planted half with Sauvignon Blanc, half with Colombard.*

Henri-François Cruse, owner and manager of du Taillan, knows both Bordeaux and Burgundy well: he also directs the firm of Lionel Bruck/Hasenklever at Nuits-Saint-Georges. He commutes between the two regions.

Reminders of the past in the park at Château du Taillan include a 15th-century well and cannonballs from the Hundred Years' War.

Château du Taillan

Cru Grand Bourgeois
Le Taillan

If you approach the Médoc from Bordeaux, Château du Taillan is the first important estate you come to. The boundary between the Graves and Médoc districts actually crosses its land. There is a lot to see when you reach the end of the long drive. The château is a truly monumental 18th-century structure in an excellent state of preservation. It is surrounded by grounds of some 250 acres, including a vineyard, woods, and paddocks for about 300 racehorses, which are bred here. The château has the only cellar in the Médoc to be declared an historic monument: around 300 years old, it was probably built by monks.
The property was bought in 1896 by Henri Cruse and has remained in the family ever since. The present owner, Henri-François Cruse, lives in one wing of the château.

Foudres in place of casks

Château du Taillan's 40-acre vineyard is planted with Merlot (60%) and Cabernet. The grapes are fermented in concrete vats or stainless-steel tanks. After fermentation is completed, the wine is matured for a year — not in the traditional 225-litre oak *barriques*, but in much bigger *foudres.* According to Henri François Cruse, this method is used because small casks are too expensive. Furthermore, he does not consider the resulting high tannin content to be desirable: as a *cru bourgeois*, du Taillan has to be a wine that can be drunk quickly. The high Merlot content helps in this respect.

Friendly, but few subtleties

Since the 1974 vintage the wine has been bottled on the estate; before that time by the *négociant* Cruse. The 1974 did not charm me: it was a rather thin wine with a metallic taste. The 1975 was better and made a much pleasanter impression. It had a nice scent and a genial taste with some breeding and tannin. Four years after its vintage it had still not quite opened up. The 1976 seemed to be already more developed: mild in taste and scent, but without much depth or aftertaste. The 1977 had rather less substance, but its taste was not without merit. The 1978 was a wine in the manner of the 1975, with perhaps a little more suppleness. All in all, Château du Taillan is a pure, friendly but never really full-bodied Médoc, with few subtleties to claim the attention of the drinker.

Château de Malleret's vineyard receives the same careful treatment as that at Château Cantenac-Brown, which also belongs to the du Vivier family. Until 1931 vines grew close to the château, but today the plots lie out of its sight. The estate uses the brand names Château Barthez and Château Lemoyne-Nexon for its lesser qualities.

There are about 50 thoroughbreds and hunters at Château de Malleret. However, the racehorses are no longer trained here and the former gallop is now a cornfield. Count Bertrand du Vivier and his son Aalain, who assists him, are both deeply involved in French racing.

Below:
The drive up to the 18th-century château, which has an estate of 988 acres.

Far right:
The façade of Château de Malleret.

Right:
Count Bertrand du Vivier, owner of the château. Such is his enthusiasm for the chase that in the season he goes hunting twice a week if possible, on Thursdays and Sundays. He has a pack of about 80 hounds.

Château de Malleret

Cru Grand Bourgeois
Le Pian

This estate is a little world on its own. It covers a total of 988 acres, with its vineyard, cornfields, meadows and woods. As at Château du Taillan, horses are bred here, both for hunting and the racecourse. Next to the château there are splendid stables on the English model where the yearlings are kept before sale. De Malleret has been in the hands of the same family since 1827. The present owner and occupier, Comte Bertrand du Vivier, is a ***négociant***, wine maker and fanatical huntsman. It is thanks to him that Château de Malleret is again producing wine. In 1931 his father uprooted all the vines and would never hear of replanting them. Only after his death in 1958 did his son reclaim part of the former vineyard.
At present De Malleret has 146 acres of vineyard, 60% of it planted with Cabernet Sauvignon, 25% with Merlot, 10% with Cabernet Franc and 5% with Petit Verdot.

Painstaking method

The vineyard, of which a quarter lies in the Ludon commune, borders in part that of Château la Lagune. It produces between 200 and 325 *tonneaux* (approximately 20,000-32,000 cases). Fermentation takes place in steel tanks; the maturing partly in oak casks, partly in the tanks. The wine alternates between cask and tank — it is changed over every three months. One in every five casks is replaced each year. the total ageing period lasts about 18 months. Working practices at Château du Malleret are very meticulous — witness the spotless cellars. The wine is still clarified with fresh egg white, just as at the *grand cru* Cantenac-Brown, which belongs to this family.

A good Haut-Médoc

Château de Malleret's wine does not have a really pronounced character, but it is a good, balanced Haut-Médoc that does not lack firmness. At a lunch at the château the 1966 accompanied the *poulet du château*, holding its own quite decently after the power of the Cheval Blanc 1971, the great Saint-Emilion. The 1978, which in its youth had been dark purple in colour, made a great impression, with fruit and wood in its compact bouquet and an excellent taste with firmness and tannin. The 1977 was considerably lighter, and ordinarily pleasant. The bouquet of the 1976 also had fruit and wood, and its taste was mild and reasonably mouth-filling. The 1975 proved to have a lighter colour than I had expected from this marvellous year — and this was paralleled in the taste. I thought the 1978 and 1976 more representative of their vintages. Recent good years are 1979, 1981 and 1982.

For exactly the same wine as Château Ségur the name Château Ségur Fillon is used in some markets. For its simpler qualities the estate uses the brand name Domaine Boisgrand, appellation Bordeaux Supérieur.

At Ségur the vines are planted 5 feet apart; 3¼ to 4 feet is the traditional Médoc distance.

Firms that buy a lot of Ségur are Delor in Bordeaux and Coste in Langon.

Bottom left:
The unimpressive exterior of Château Ségur, with a corner of Joseph Grazioli's neat white house in the foreground. He bought the estate about 20 years ago. It is now run by his son Jean-Pierre.

Bottom right:
All Château Ségur is packed in cartons, not cases.

Below right:
The top of the stainless-steel fermentation tanks can only be reached with a ladder — here to attach a hose for transferring the grape juice.

Right:
Jean-Pierre Grazioli and his wife Véronique in their vineyard.

Château Ségur

Cru Grand Bourgeois
Parempuyre

This château is the largest wine estate of Parempuyre, a commune in the south of the Médoc. You reach it by following several signposts to the end of a little cul-de-sac. There is no real château as such — just an untidy assembly of buildings of no great beauty. In front is a comfortable white house where the owner, Joseph Grazioli, lives. He bought Ségur on his return from Morocco at the end of the 1950s. His son Jean-Pierre has now taken over the management and lives with his wife Véronique in a small house by the vineyard. Château Ségur has 82 acres of vineyard, 47% of it planted with Merlot, 27% with Cabernet Sauvignon, 20% with Cabernet Franc and 6% with Petit Verdot. The vines grow on a large plateau ringed with trees, on a subsoil that includes gravel and clay.

Modern equipment

The exterior of Château Ségur may offer little to gladden heart or eye, but inside Jean-Pierre Grazioli has everything neatly ordered. Besides a row of concrete vats stand a number of stainless-steel fermentation tanks. I saw other modern equipment, including a bottling unit and a filter, the latter used to remove any remaining impurities from the wine immediately before bottling. At Ségur the wine matures for only a short time — about three months — in oak casks and is then stored for 15 to 20 months in vats or tanks. Production fluctuates between 80 and 125 *tonneaux*. (8,000 and 12,500 cases).

Not exciting, but correct

Tasting a succession of Château Ségur vintages did not leave a wholly favourable impression. I found the wine a little dull and not particularly exciting in bouquet or taste. The 1975 was almost black in colour and had a rather 'stalky', austere bouquet and a taste with a lot of tannin and without much body. The light 1976 was already brown three years after vintage, smelled mild and tasted flat. The 1977 had more colour, but lacked fullness, subtlety and aftertaste. The 1976 was very dark in colour, had a certain stiffness and lacked roundness or fruit. Château Ségur is not a bad wine, of course, but correctness alone is not enough for a *cru grand bourgeois*.

Below:
Château d'Agassac is one of the last remaining historic buildings from the Middle Ages in the Médoc. The estate uses both bottle and 12-bottle cartons and wooden cases.

Château d'Agassac must not be confused with another Ludon property, Château Ludon-Pomiès-Agassac, which belongs to the same owners as the grand cru classé Château la Lagune. *It produces good wine, but not of the same standard as d'Agassac.*

At d'Agassac the distance between vines is even greater than at Ségur: 5¾ feet. By this means, according to Philippe Capbern-Gasqueton, quantity is sacrificed to quality.

At d'Agassac the wine is always fined with fresh egg white: usually five eggs to the cask. Occasionally the wine is also filtered.

Château d'Agassac

Cru Grand Bourgeois Exceptionnel
Ludon

The history of Château d'Agassac goes back into the mists of time. The present château was built in the 13th century on the foundations of a much older and more primitive stronghold. From 1238 it was the seat of the Seigneur d'Agassac, a notorious wastrel. A d'Agassac scandal, recorded later in the *Variétés Bordeloises* of 1784, concerned the discovery of one of the Seigneur's manservants floating dead in the moat. The nobleman was held to be responsible but, evidence being lacking, the affair was successfully hushed up.
At the end of the 16th century the estate passed to the Pomiès family, of some political fame. Right up to the present century the estate was known as Pomiès-Agassac (although the Pomiès had lost possession in the French Revolution). Wine from d'Agassac was little known outside France — except in the Netherlands, which consumed practically the entire vintage for generations.

Organic fertilizer only

Since the early 1960s the estate has belonged to the Capbern-Gasqueton family, who also own the châteaux of Capbern Gasqueton (see page 68), Calon-Ségur and Du Tertre (the latter two are *grands crus classés*). Philippe Capbern-Gasqueton runs the estate, assisted by his son Olivier. Under this new management many improvements have come about in vineyard and cellars; meanwhile the elegant château is gradually being restored. There are now 86 acres of vineyard, one-third planted with Cabernet Sauvignon, one-third with Cabernet Franc; the rest is mostly Merlot with just a little Petit Verdot. Only organic fertilizer is used: that comes from a herd of dairy cows kept on the remaining 161 acres of the estate.
The wine is fermented in lined metal tanks and then aged for at least two years in used oak casks.

Low yield

Château d'Agassac deliberately aims at a low yield. Often it is less than 35 hectolitres per hectare, although 43 hectolitres is the allowed limit. For a number of years only 20 hectolitres per hectare was produced. Such a policy is, of course, bound to improve the quality of the wine. In general, the wine from this château is nicely concentrated and complete in taste: a Haut-Médoc with less of the dour aggressiveness that makes many of the wines of the district undrinkable when young, it nevertheless has plenty of tannin. This wine will mature well in the bottle if allowed at least four or five years. Château d'Agassac seldom proves disappointing: even wine from less successful years achieves a reasonable standard.

The estate produces two other wines in addition to Siran. One with the Margaux appellation *is called Château Bellegarde, a brand that includes wine from young vines. A Bordeaux Supérieur called Château Saint-Jacques is made from a separate 37 acres.*

Grape varieties at Siran are: 50% Cabernet Sauvignon, 25% Merlot, 15% Petit Verdot and 10% Cabernet Franc.

The oldest bottle of Siran — from 1865 — is apparently in the cellars of the Parisian restaurant La Tour d'Argent.

Below:
Cherub with bunch of grapes on the steps at Siran.

Bottom:
Rear view of Siran from the park. William-Alain B. Miailhe has been sole owner since July 1978.

Far right:
Some of the buildings are soft pink in colour, just like Château Loudenne (pages 82, 83).

Right:
There are antiques all over the château, from every part of the world. In the reception hall there is a flat-bellied wine bottle bearing the name of Maarten Harpertszoon Tromp, the famous admiral of the Anglo-Dutch wars.

Château Siran

Labarde

The name Siran probably goes back to Guilhem de Siran who in 1428 swore an oath of allegiance to an abbot of a monastery in the southern Médoc. For long after that the estate was called Saint-Siran and had many illustrious owners. Since 1848, however, it has belonged to the family of which the present owner, William-Alain B. Miailhe, is a member. The château, a fairly modest building of the early 19th century, is only occasionally occupied by William-Alain or his mother. Siran is at its most beautiful in late September, when thousands of wild cyclamens bloom in the park, surrounding the trees with a shimmering carpet of pink and white. William-Alain once said to me "Siran is the cyclamens' *premier cru.*" As for the wine from his estate, he is determined to have it ranked among the *grands crus classés.* He believes that Siran's claim to this classification is justified, not only because of the quality of the wine, but also because a large part of its 62 acres of vineyard derives from the *grands crus classés* Dauzac and Giscours.

Stainless-steel tanks

In 1979 the Siran vintage was vinified in wooden fermentation vats for the last time: stainless steel was introduced in 1980. The wooden casks for the two years' maturing of the wine have been retained. About a third of these are replaced each year. The wine is clarified with fresh white of egg or with powdered albumen, and it is lightly filtered immediately before bottling. Normally the estate produces 110 to 160 *tonneaux* (11,000 to 16,000 cases) annually under the Siran name and the Margaux *appellation.* Wine from younger vines and of lesser quality is sold as Château Bellegarde, also with the Margaux *appellation.*

Remarkable quality

That Siran has a legitimate claim to *grand cru classé* status becomes obvious when you taste the wine. Its quality is remarkable. It has the hallmarks of a great Margaux, with finesse, breeding, elegance and at the same time a charming rounded quality. During a tasting of recent vintages at the château I found that I was loath to spit out the wonderful 1976! I thought the splendid 1971, and the 1970, with its seductive bouquet, were both delicious. In 1975, too, the château made a memorable wine, and the 1978, 1979, 1981 and 1982 also has great class. Even the 1977 and 1980 were good wines. One of the earlier vintages that I can heartily recommend is the 1964: a successful year for few of the châteaux of the Médoc, but at Siran they made an excellent wine.

Left:
Peter Sichel. He and his wife Diana have six children. Above the entrance to the château are the words ancien 4e grand cru*: before the French Revolution d'Angludet was among the best wines of Cantenac — as it today. This is one reason why Sichel does not feel he belongs among the* cru bourgeois *and deliberately goes his own way.*

Far left:
The salon of the château, with tapestries depicting the Spanish Riding School at Vienna. They date from the end of the 18th century and were completely restored in 1963.

Below:
The château, set on a low green hill. It dates from 1767, a date discovered on the ruins of a mill that stood here. This mill was very probably built at the same time as the château, when large establishments had to produce their own flour. The name of the estate derives from a 12th-century knight, Bertrand d'Angludet.

The estate's second wine is called Bory.

Since 1973-4 about half of all d'Angludet has gone to Britain and America.

Château d'Angludet

Cantenac

The ancient estate of Château d'Angludet lies where three communes of the Margaux *appellation* adjoin: Labarde, Arsac and Cantenac. The countryside undulates here and the vine is not so predominant as elsewhere in the district. A beautiful park stretches out in front of the low, whitewashed château with its dark-green shutters. There is an ornamental lake and ponies graze inside the white wooden fences. The whole scene suggests an English country seat rather than a wine estate — which is appropriate, since d'Angludet is occupied by a Briton, Peter A. Sichel, and his family. Sichel moved in after spending about ten years restoring the property, particularly the vineyard, in 1972. After the devastating frost of 1956 the 295-acre estate was divided into two. One half went to Château Brane-Cantenac in 1960; the other half, including the château, passed to the wine firm of Sichel in 1961 and 1963. At present 74 acres are planted with vines: 55% Cabernet Sauvignon, 35% Merlot, 8% Cabernet Franc and 2% Petit Verdot.

Increased production

The gravelly and sandy soil has ferruginous clay here and there. Production varies from 1,900 cases (1971) to 13,700 (1973), which is a good deal more than the mere 300 cases of 1961. The wine ferments in plastic-lined concrete vats. Peter Sichel would have liked to have replaced his wooden *cuves* with stainless-steel ones, but they could not be got through the cellar doors. After fermentation the wine is matured for about 20 months in vats; about 25% of them is renewed each year. The wine is clarified with gelatine and lightly filtered before bottling.

Beautiful colour

The first thing that struck me about the wines of this château was their beautiful, deep-red, vital colour. The glowing nuances tell you that taste and bouquet, too, will be subtly variegated and have a pleasing vitality. Other characteristics are an elegant personality, an uncommonly pure taste and impeccable balance. The wine has plenty of tannin for development in the bottle. Some of my favourite recent vintages are the 1975 and 1978, followed by the less concentrated 1976 (rather more reserved than might be expected of this year), and the 1974. The 1977, too, can be considered successful. The 1981 and 1982 seem very promising.

Left:
The château, in Louis Quinze style, with its chai to the left.

Below, left and right:
At Labégorce there are houses for estate workers and their families.

Château Labégorce

Margaux

There are three châteaux close together on the boundary of Margaux and Soussans with similar-sounding names: Labégorce, Labégorce-Zédé and l'Abbé-Gorsse-de-Gorsse. They once formed a single estate, that of the Abbé Gorsse. The first two are the more important both in terms of quality and quantity. Labégorce has the most outward grandeur. A rather large château, it is owned by Jean-Robert Condom, who inherited the estate from his mother, who died in 1980. I remember Madame Yvonne Condom well. When I told her that I liked the many fresh flowers in her pastel-decorated salons, she told me that she could not manage without fresh flowers. I thought this a good omen: people who like flowers seldom make a bad wine. Cellars and *cuvier* looked spotless. Everything was spick and span; even the ceiling above the cement fermentation tanks was gleaming white. Such points tell of great care taken — one of the first requirements for making good wine.

A hundred new casks

Although the estate covers 168 acres, only 74 acres of this is planted with vines. Cabernet Sauvignon, with 60%, predominates. There is a very little Petit Verdot and th rest is Merlot. The Cabernet Franc is not grown. After fermentation the wine matures for up to two years in oak casks. Jean-Robert buys about 100 new ones before each vintage, thus replacing a fifth to a sixth of the total stock each year. Labégorce produces between 10,000 and 15,000 cases annually. The larger part of the wine is sold via the firm of Dourthe, which also fines the wine (with albumin), filters it twice and bottles it.

A little too easy

I have been able to follow the Labégorce wine from the 1969 vintage. It is not a not terribly refined example of Margaux. Though made with great care and craftsmanship, it lacks the class to merit more than the epithet 'good'. Bouquet and taste are just a little too smooth, too easy, although certainly not unattractive. Labégorce is distinguished by a usually rather sombre, dark red; the mild bouquet sometimes verges on sweet and in later life is vaguely reminiscent of damp brushwood. The taste has suppleness, with often a very slightly oily quality, and a mild but full-flavoured core with sufficient alcohol. The aftertaste is respectable. I understand that Mme Condom did not join the ranks of the *crus bourgeois* because she sought *grand cru classé* status; but, in truth, Labégorce comes closer to the former standard.

Far left:
Vintage time.

Bottom left:
Owner Luc Thienpont and his cellarmaster M. Bergamin.

Bottom right:
The unpretentious château.

A tip for visitors: they collect matchboxes at the château.

The wine here is clarified with powdered albumen and lightly filtered.

Château Labégorce-Zédé

Soussans

Wine and water are closely connected at Labégorce-Zédé. This is due to Gustave Alexandre Zédé, one of Pierre Zédé's five children who in 1840 bought the larger part of the Domaine de La Bégorce. Gustave lived on the estate for part of his life and extended it, but by profession he was a naval architect and he had a special interest in submarines. In 1877 he was appointed director of France's *Constructions Navales*, and thanks to him a programme of intensive submarine development was initiated. Gustave was killed in 1891 when a torpedo charge exploded, but two years later the first French submarine was launched. It was named the *Gustave Zédé*, as is the current French deep-sea research vessel. In 1931 the last of the Zédé family sold the estate and since then it has had eight different owners. The present owner is Luc Thienpont, of Flemish birth and related to the Thienponts of the well-known Vieux Château Certan in Pomerol. Luc and his wife Annick moved into Labégorce-Zédé after their marriage in June 1979.

Gradual expansion

Labégorce-Zédé has an average annual production of 100 *tonneaux*. This is being slightly increased as the vineyard is extended from 60 to 64 acres. Grape varieties are Cabernet Sauvignon (50%), Cabernet Franc (10%), Merlot (35%), Petit Verdot (5%). Luc Thienpont has concrete fermentation vats, which also serve for ageing the wine in its second year; for its first year it is kept in used wooden casks, of which a fourth or a fifth are new.

Potential

I tasted four vintages at the château. The 1975 had a good, deep-red colour and a concentrated, not yet fully disclosed bouquet with a rather stalky tone to it. The taste had not yet opened out and contained a lot of tannin. More pleasant — but still quite harsh and young — was the 1976, a good, balanced wine. The 1977 again smelled somewhat of grape stalks, and sorely lacked the substance and suppleness of the Merlot. The 1978, tasted from the cask, struck me as mild and seemed rounder, friendlier than the preceding wines, with more fruit in the bouquet. Although Labégorce-Zédé is in every way a good wine, it lacks some charm and finesse — certainly for a Margaux. I expect, however, that Luc Thienpont, helped by his very expert relatives, will further improve the quality of Labégorce-Zédé. The 1979, 1981 and 1982 already give an indication thereof.

The type of window over the front door of the present château is a reminder that monks — of a teaching order — lived here before the fire.

Me Henri Binaud and Mme Jacques Mareilhac are the present owners of La Tour de Mons. Bertrand Clauzel, Mme Mareilhac's son, manages the concern.

Far right:
Painting of Château La Tour de Mons as it was before the fire of 1895. The lake has gone as well as the château.

Below:
Of the old château only a few fragments of wall remain, with parts of two towers and the chapel. This serves as the family vault. Not much is known of the history of La Tour de Mons: the archives were destroyed in the fire. Only a few items were saved, included the oval painting, now in the salon of the present château, of the Marquise de Mons.

Château la Tour de Mons

Soussans

Château la Tour de Mons is in Soussans, the most northerly of the five villages entitled to the Margaux *appellation.* Soussans is exceedingly small — you can go through the place almost without realizing it. Along the road there is a sign bearing the name La Tour de Mons, but the château itself is some way off, concealed from passers-by. This small plot — 6 or so acres in a *vignoble* totalling 64 acres — is separated from the rest of the estate. The estate's main vineyard lies behind the château, on raised ground surrounded by 185 acres of woodland and meadows. La Tour de Mons is a large property — and has been for centuries.

Destructive fire

The history of this wine estate began in 1289, when the original fortified dwelling was built by Jean Colomb, a prosperous citizen of Bordeaux. For a long time it served as an outer defence to the domaine of the lords of Blanquefort. It was rebuilt in the 15th century, after being destroyed in the Hundred Years' War, and in 1615 it passed into the hands of Pierre de Mons, who married the only daughter of the Baron de Soussans. The property has remained in the family to the present day. They saw La Tour de Mons created a barony in 1813, and witnessed its almost total destruction by fire in 1895. Bertrand Clauzel, who runs the estate and is the son of one of its two owners, has often heard his grandmother, who was 14 at the time, tell of the great fire.

Far right:
Bertrand Clauzel, manager since 1946, is assisted in the running of La Tour de Mons by his son Christian. The grandfather of Bertrand's wife was once notary to the famous Château Talbot in Saint-Julien. At their wedding celebrations in 1946 the pair drank the still excellent Talbot 1904.

Below:
The colour of the young wine being judged by candle flame. For serious tasting Bertrand Clauzel prefers the daylight. Indicative of his serious approach is the strip of white paint applied to the cellar wall next to the door, to provide a suitable background for assessing the colour of the wine.

The move

All that was left after this disaster was most of a 19th-century tower, part of a medieval turret, a few pieces of wall and a number of ancillary buildings, including the stables (now a cellar for bottles) and the chapel, where Bertrand's parents and ancestors are buried. The family had to move into a large house near the entrance to the estate. This house is nowadays occupied by Bertrand Clauzel and his family. Bertrand, who until 1980 was also manager at Château Cantemerle, is assisted at La Tour de Mons by Christian, one of his five sons.

Traditional methods

At La Tour de Mons, traditional working methods are employed. Here you still find the wooden fermentation vats that elsewhere in the Médoc have largely been replaced by concrete or stainless steel. They stand under an insulated ceiling on white stone piers about 3 feet high. The wine is aged, for about two years, in used oak casks. It is fined with beaten white of fresh eggs, and never filtered.

Subtly nuanced taste

During my long journey through the Médoc I was repeatedly told that La Tour de Mons makes excellent wine. The compliments came both from owners of *crus bourgeois* (who do not number this château among their members) and from *grand cru* proprietors. I largely agree with their opinion. In its youth La Tour de Mons is almost black, far from endearing — in fact rather uncompromising. But as the years go by it becomes more fragrant, supple and agreeable. A blossom-like bouquet breaks through a subtly shaded taste. One of the most enchanting wines of this château that I have drunks is the 1971. I has plenty of colour, bouquet and grace, a pleasing fullness and a disarming friendliness. The 1975 will be truly great, but some years of patience are still required. Two somewhat divergent wines are the 1977 and the 1978. In the former year night frost practically wiped out the Merlot grapes — 40% of the vineyard, the remainder comprising 45% Cabernet Sauvignon, 10% Cabernet Franc and 5% Petit Verdot. Loss of the Merlot obviously produced an almost pure Cabernet wine, with blackcurrant in the scent and an austere, tannin-filled taste. The 1978 has rather more Merlot and therefore more roundness, but this wine too will probably need nine or ten years to become more agreeable.

The need for good table wine

Honesty compels me to report that I do not regard all vintages of La Tour de Mons equally highly. The 1976 did not greatly appeal to me, nor did the 1973 or the 1966. In fact I sent this last wine — bottled in Holland and very acidic — back to my wine merchant. I did enjoy the mild maturity of the elegant 1967 and the full-flavoured 1970 — which was, however, still much too young. I also remember the Tour de Mons *vin ordinaire* that I drank at a simple family lunch at the château. When I complimented Bertrand Clauzel on this light, elegant wine he said: 'My grandfather, Pierre Dubos, told me that you should always drink good wine at table. If not, any wine you taste in the cellars after a meal is bound to taste good, and you lose your critical faculty. You need a good table wine to be able to make a good château wine.' To judge by results, the conditions is fulfilled at La Tour de Mons.

Left:
Jean-Pierre Seynat-Dulos, who followed his legal studies with a course in oenology.

Below:
This sign adorns the entrance to the château.

Bottom:
Casks in the cellar. It was the Sautter family (see main text) who in the previous century added the crown to the Martinens name. The château regularly buys used casks from grands crus such as Lascombes (recognizable from their varnish), Latour and Lafite-Rothschild.

The Martinens vineyard — no weedkiller is used here, and only organic fertilizer — lies partly in Margaux, partly in Cantenac. The estate covers 173 acres, but not all of this is vineyard.

Château Martinens

Cru Grand Bourgeois
Cantenac

According to the annals, Martinens was created by three spinster sisters called White. They built the château in 1767 and sold it nine years later. Since then the estate has had many owners, the most eminent of whom was Count Auguste François de Sautter, former chamberlain to the Emperor Napoleon, Consul-General of Tuscany and the owner of the Domaine de Beauregard in the Swiss canton of Vaud. Since 1945 Martinens has been in the hands of the Dulos family. The present owners are Mme Simone Dulos and her son Jean-Pierre Seynat-Dulos. Mme Dulos has done a great deal for the estate. When she took over in 1960 there were only 2½ acres of vineyard; today there are 74, with 12 to be added.

A preponderance of Merlot

Neither Jean-Pierre Seynat-Dulos nor his *régisseur* Robert Delile could tell me exactly in what proportions the different grape varieties grew in the vineyard. They estimated the Merlot at 55% and the Cabernet Sauvignon at about 30%. The rest is Cabernet Franc with some Petit Verdot. Annual yield varies between 18 and 85 *tonneaux.* Concrete vats are used for fermentation. The wine matures in used wooden casks for an average of 17 months. It is clarified with albumin powder and since the vintage of 1978 has been filtered before bottling.

Pleasant but not exciting

I thought the 1976 a pleasant wine without harshness or angularity. It had a soft, sultry colour. Bouquet and taste were both rather flat, without much personality. It was a characteristic Martinens: not all that exciting or memorable, but nevertheless pleasant to drink. Moreover, it had something of the elegance that characterizes many Margaux wines. The 1978 had more colour and power than the 1976 and was reasonably concentrated. In early youth the wine tasted noticeably tart; the Merlot suppleness was present only to a limited degree. I am very curious to see how this wine develops in the coming years. I also tasted the 1977: an easy, rather short-flavoured wine. My most pleasant recollections are actually of the 1970; six years after its vintage its bouquet and taste had not yet unfolded, and it had a deep, dark colour. Could it be that the character of Martinens has changed in the second half of the 1970s and become rather flat? If so it may be something to do with the fact that around 1976 the 14 year cooperation with the quality-conscious firm of Ginestet (now maintained only as a brand name) came to an end.

Left:
The château, various rooms of which are now used as cellars for the bottled wine. It lies on the southwest side of the commune of Soussans, separated from other familiar Soussans estates such as Labégorce-Zédé, La Tour de Mons and Paveil de Luze. It comes under the Margaux *appellation.*

Far left:
Owner Pierre Boyer draws the young wine from one of his concrete cuves. He only sells his wine after bottling, never en primeur.

Below:
A magnum and two ordinary bottles. The label has a certain style.

There is a stone heart with the date 1758 on the wall of one of the chais.

Château Bel-Air was the only property which the Marquis d'Aligre, who lived in Paris, owned in the Gironde.

Château Bel Air-Marquis d'Aligre

Soussans

As this château enjoys a good reputation in France, I was shocked by its appearance. The sign with the name of the château had been painted over and the buildings made a neglected, desolate impression. I began to doubt whether this really was Bel Air-Marquis d'Aligre, an estate that in 1932 had been classified as one of the six *crus bourgeois supérieurs exceptionnels.* I had, however, arrived at the right place. The owner Pierre Boyer — whose father bought the property in the 1940s — does not live in the château but in a modern house standing bleakly in the field opposite. When I tactfully asked him about the condition of the château he replied that he was not interested in visitors or publicity, and consequently there was no kind of outward show. He also said that only the wine lived in the château. Indeed, the salons appeared to be full of bottles and cases.

Traditional methods

In good years Pierre Boyer produces 40 to 50 *tonneaux* from his 42 acres. However, the yield is often lower for the vineyard is regularly affected by night frost. The wine — from roughly equal parts of Cabernet Sauvignon, Cabernet Franc, Merlot and Petit Verdot — ferments in rather grimy-looking concrete *cuves.* After fermentation the wine remains for almost a year in the *cuves* and is then matured for a further 18 months in oak casks; Boyer says that he still follows the traditional methods. Fining, therefore, is done with fresh white of egg, never a filter. He does not aim at a high yield or a large overall production. Boyer could double his vineyard area, but refuses to do so.

Below expectation

Normally this approach should result in a truly great wine, but — to my own surprise — my expectations were not fulfilled. To make quite sure that I had not been mistaken I even bought some extra bottles at Margaux's *Maison du Vin.* The result was still a supple, quite rounded and sometimes fat wine without much breeding. Even wines from great years such as 1971 and 1975 seemed rather smooth (the latter even came close to being sweet), lacking fine nuances or other memorable qualities. Bel Air-Marquis d'Aligre is certainly not a great Margaux, although it is far from being a bad one. Perhaps Pierre Boyer should seek the advice of an expert oenologist to see whether his vinification could be improved. Given his rather headstrong personality, however, I doubt whether he would ever take such a step.

Left:
Friesian dairy cows passing the main gate of the château.

Below:
Front view of Paveil de Luze, with its residential wing. Behind the château is a large park.

Far right:
Baron Geoffroy de Luze, whose ancestor, Alfred de Luze, bought the estate in 1862. In the future the baron hopes to use more new casks — he aims at 75% — for maturing his wine.

Château Paveil de Luze

Cru Grand Bourgeois
Soussans

Paveil de Luze is a large estate covering 296 acres in the communes of Soussans, Arcins, Avensan and Moulis. The château itself, long and low, with two towers and two wings, stands in the Soussans commune, as does its vineyard. The wine therefore comes under the Margaux *appellation.* The small vineyard — only 57 acres — used to be bigger: until the First World War it was almost 100 acres. The present owners, Baron Geoffroy de Luze, plans to extend it gradually to 74 acres. One of the baron's ancestors bought Château Paveil in 1862. 'De Luze' was added to 'Paveil' (derived from *pavillon*) in the present century. The Baron and his family live in the château only from May to September. In his everyday life Geoffroy de Luze — who looks like a British aristocrat, and speaks perfect English — is the commercial director of the wine firm A. de Luze in Bordeaux.

Matured in Bordeaux

The *cuvier* at Paveil de Luze contains only steel fermentation tanks. The wine remains in these after fermentation until the May following the grape harvest. It is then transported to A. de Luze for further maturing and treatment. At Bordeaux it ages in used oak casks for about 18 months. The wine is clarified with albumin and also filtered. The château's total production varies between 29 and 65 *tonneaux.*

Mild, undemanding Margaux

The basis of the wine is the juice of Cabernet Sauvignon (50%), Merlot (35%) and Cabernet Franc (15%). There is no Petit Verdot. Geoffroy de Luze told me, 'The Petit Verdot is a tremendous grape — once every ten years. It adds colour, strength and bouquet, but needs a good autumn to ripen well — which we very seldom get! We did have Petit Verdot vines, but we grubbed them up.'
The wine of Paveil de Luze struck me as somewhat lacking style and distinction. Most of the vintages I tasted left me with an impression of a mild, undemanding Margaux with no great refinement or strength of personality to offer. It is a wine that can be drunk within a few years and pleases a fairly wide public.

The Clauzel family (of Cantemerle, La Tour de Mons etc.) bought Citran in 1832. The estate was in ruins, as was the 13th-century château. The Clauzels started by cultivating the vineyard, and built the present château around 1861.

The oldest part of the vineyard — about 49 acres — lies between Paveil de Luze and the château. A later section of some 148 acres is nearer the village of Avensan. The vineyard could be extended by a further 25 acres. Vines at present are 50% Cabernet Sauvignon, 40% Merlot and 10% Cabernet Franc.

Below:
The château, used only for receptions.

Far right:
Jean Miailhe, descended from a family of wine merchants who were active in Bordeaux from 1818. William-Alain Miailhe, of Château Siran etc., is his nephew, but the two are not business associates.

Right:
Cases of Citran arranged by the entrance to the cuverie. Miailhe used the Citran 1970 to open up new markets for the château (i.e. Sweden and Canada); and 6,000 bottles of the 1972 were sold to Fauchon, the famous Paris shop. All Citran was formerly bought and sold by the firm of Cruse.

Château Citran

Cru Grand Bourgeois Exceptionnel
Avensan

Citran is an enormous estate covering no less than 988 acres. It is planted mainly with pines, poplars and acacias. Vines occupy 208 acres. In the previous century the vineyard was quite a bit bigger — 366 acres — and produced some 600 *tonneaux* annually. In this century Citran fell into decay and when in 1945 the Miailhe family took over from the Clauzels, little more than one acre of vines was left. The Miailhes have shown great drive in restoring the estate. Jean Miailhe — *gérant* until 1980 — did a lot of good work. The present owners are Jean's sister and her husband Jean Cesselin.

Stainless steel tanks

Any visitor to Citran will see that things are very well organized. The *cuvier* with its stainless-steel tanks and concrete vats looks spotless, and the same can be said of the *chai.* The château, too, which is used only for receptions, appears well maintained. The 250 to 500 *tonneaux* that Citran produces annually is mostly matured in casks, of which a third are new, for a period of about 18 months. The wine is clarified with gelatine and filtered twice.

Positive impression

I have tasted seven Citran vintages and my general impression is a positive one; the château deserved its admission on 11 March 1977 to the prestigious Académie du Vin de Bordeaux. The 1970 wine, nine years after its vinification, was not yet fully developed, had a deep, dark colour, considerable tannin and a slighty fleshy taste with the merest hint of sweetness. The 1973 proved to be a well-flavoured, pleasant wine with a mild aftertaste. The 1974 was easy, rather light and ordinarily pleasing. The 1975 had more to offer, but in my opinion it is not the equal of many other wines of that glorious year; it had not quite enough colour, strength and tannin. I was more enthusiastic about the 1976, which possessed more colour than the 1975 and had an attractive bouquet and a lively taste with roundness and elegance.

The 1977 was an unremarkable, unproblematic wine which Jean Miailhe described as 'very commercial'. The 1978 — tasted from the cask — had a dark-purple colour, concentrated fruit in the taste and a striking suppleness. It has become a good wine, and the 1979 likewise. I am under the impression that since the departure of Jean Miailhe in 1980, the wines of Citran have become slightly less distinguished, but this may be temporary.

Left:
A worker with a handful of grape stalks and pips. The grapes are fermented after these have been removed by an égrappoir, during which process the fruit is lightly crushed.

Below:
The actual château, which is no longer part of the estate, but still appears on the label.

Right:
The wine of De Villegeorge owes its class partly to the large proportion of very old vines. Some of the pickers are also quite venerable.

Merlot predominates in the vineyard, making up 60% of the grapes grown; at the turn of the century 75% were Cabernet Sauvignon.

Château de Villegeorge wine usually fetches grand cru prices.

The estate employs good-condition used casks for maturing its wine, rather than new ones. The chai can house 120 casks, not stacked but laid on the floor.

Château de Villegeorge

Avensan

It could be said that Château de Villegeorge began a new life in 1973, when it was bought by Lucien Lurton, an extremely talented and dedicated wine maker. Lucien already owned the *grands crus* Brane-Cantenac, Durfort-Vivens (both in Margaux), Climens and Doisy-Dubroca (both Barsac, see pages 162 and 164) and other properties. When he took over Lurton did not rush things or take chances. First he had the soil analyzed. To his surprise, and that of Professor Peynaud, the world-renowned oenologist, the soil was almost identical to the Margaux gravel: here then was the potential for a very good wine. Lurton bought only the vineyard and a few functional buildings, not the château itself. The cellars are not even near the château. To reach them you take a little unsurfaced track to the far side of the vineyard.

Frost damage

On one point Lurton may have made a mistake: de Villegeorge is badly troubled by frosts. From 1973 to 1982 only two really good harvests were achieved, 38 *tonneaux* in 1976 and 35 in 1979. The other years produced much less, with the approximately 2 *tonneaux* of 1977 as a dispiriting minimum. A great deal has been invested in the cellars. Steel and stainless-steel fermentation tanks were bought in and the cellar for the casks (where the wine remains for two to two and a half years) was insualted and given a gravel floor. Lurton added 15 acres of vineyard to the existing 25; it is his plan eventually to have about 50 acres. Needless to say, the wine here is made with great care and craftsmanship. Fining is done with fresh white of egg and the wine is lighty filtered just before bottling.

A most unusual Médoc

The Merlot, at 60%, dominates the vineyard here, with Cabernet Sauvignon 30% and Cabernet Franc 10%. The Merlot is unmistakably present in the wine, so much so that it is an extremely uncharacteristic Médoc. There is a markedly mild roundness to it that makes it drinkable when very young. I thought the 1973 surprisingly good, with a deep colour for its year, a ripe bouquet and a rounded taste with a racy core to it and tannin: really beautiful. The 1974 was a little lighter, had a fine bouquet of soft fruit and seemed absolutely ready five years after its vintage. The deep-coloured 1975 had subtleties in scent and taste, an excellent balance and a long aftertaste. The 1976 made a very ripe, almost 'cooked' impression in bouquet and taste (the grapes that year were picked later than those of Brane-Cantenac) and left a hint almost of sweetness. The 1977 was a light, mild wine that needs to be drunk early. The 1978, on the other hand, lingered in the mouth, was opaque in colour and seemed to promise a great deal for the coming years. 1979, 1981 and 1982 also promise well.

Ginestet used to sell 90% of Moulin à Vent under the name Château Moulin de Saint-Vincent, but this label is now used only for the estate's second, lesser, wine.

Two-thirds of the Moulin à Vent vineyard is in Moulis, with the other third in Listrac. The appellation is Moulis.

The previous owner, M. Darricarrère, is co-owner of Château Mille-Secousses in the Bordeaux district of Côtes de Bourg.

Below left:
Road sign near the entrance to the estate, along the D1.

Below right:
The château, which has not been lived in for half a century. The owner, Dominique Hessel, has his office and a reception room there, but lives with his family in Bordeaux.

Far right:
Dominique Hessel. He works hard at restoring the Moulin à Vent reputation.

Right:
The grapes are thrown into a fouloir-égrappoir, *which crushes them lightly and removes the stalks. Fermentation then takes place in one of the concrete vats on the right.*

Château Moulin à Vent

Cru Grand Bourgeois
Moulis

Chateau Moulin à Vent, the former Domaine du Moulin à Vent, was established in about 1820 by the Brun family, who remained in possession for roughly a century. The property lies on the boundary of Moulis and Listrac, along the busy D1 road that on summer days takes the Bordelais *en masse* to the beaches in the north. A lot of Château Moulin à Vent wine is therefore sold to passers-by. Until the harvest of 1974 the arrangements were different: the firm of Ginestet handled 90% of all the wine under the brand name Moulin de Saint-Vincent. The owner at that time was M. Darricarrère. Under his management the wine was matured in the concrete fermentation tanks, not wooden casks. In the latter years of this period the vineyard was rather neglected and the château received little or no attention. In 1977 Darricarrère sold the estate to Dominique Hessel, a young agricultural engineer and qualified oenologist from Libourne. At the time of my first visit Dominique had already carried out a good deal of restoration in the vineyard, the cellars and the château.

Mostly Cabernet Sauvignon

Vines are planted in 59 out of the estate's total of 77 acres. The vines are 70% Cabernet Sauvignon, 23% Merlot and 7% Petit Verdot and Malbec. Before 1993, however, M. Hessel plans to have 50% Cabernet Sauvignon, 40% Merlot and 10% Cabernet Franc. Production fluctuates from just under 55 to approximately 130 *tonneaux*. Since the 1977 vintage all wine has been matured in oak casks: Hessel uses two- to four-year-old *barriques* from Pichon-Lalande and other *grands crus*. He clarifies his wine with powdered albumen and filters it lightly just before bottling.

Distinct improvement

The investment of time and money in Château Moulin à Vent is beginning to bear fruit. The 1977 won a bronze medal at Paris, and the 1978 two golds, at Bordeaux and Blaye. I found that both these vintages had more class than the very moderate 1975 and the equally undistinguished 1976. I had to report, however, that the 1977 was a little too austere in taste, with grape stalks in the scent. Hessel admitted that he had used too much press wine; it was, after all, his first vintage. The fault was not repeated in the 1978. This wine had a good deep colour and a notable measure of tannin and blackcurrant — characteristic of a young Cabernet Sauvignon wine — in bouquet and taste. With a little more roundness and charm the wine would move up from good to very good. Hessel admitted quite openly that the wine probably consisted of 90% Cabernet Sauvignon. His Merlot vines are so old that they no longer produce very much. Replanting will gradually improve this situation, as the 1981 and 1982 show.

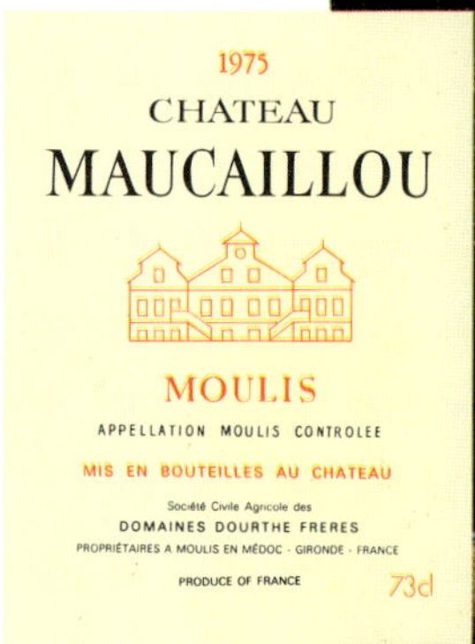

Left: The château, which dates from 1875, is occupied by Roger Dourthe (below), the man who made Maucaillou great. At 72, he sailed across the Atlantic accompanied only by his nephew, Pierre Dourthe, taking 21 days from the Azores to Barbados. Their boat was from the same designer as Sir Francis Chichester's.

Maucaillou wine is clarified with egg white and filtered once.

A few years ago, a group of Dutch wine merchants held a blind tasting of ten Médocs: nine grands crus *and Maucaillou. The Maucaillou came second, after Mouton-Rothschild.*

For the 1979 vintage, Roger Dourthe had the idea of using aseptic plugs for the wine caks, and has used them ever since. One of their advantages is that the casks do not have to be so full as is normal, and therefore the ouillage *— topping up — can be limited to once a month instead of twice a week. The wine also no longer overflows the casks when the temperature rises and the liquid expands.*

During the 1975 harvest the estate was hit by a violent hailstorm. The Merlot was already in, but about two-thirds of the Cabernet was lost. Hence the 1975 vintage is softer, less complete than you would expect a Maucaillou to be.

Château Maucaillou

Moulis

Centuries ago virtually nothing except corn was grown in the commune of Moulis — except in the area of the *mauvais cailloux*, the 'bad stones', where the soil was simply too poor. Later, however, it proved possible to cultivate the vine here successfully; for the poorer the soil the harder the plant has to work, and the better the wine. Today Château Maucaillou is one of the most renowned wine estates in central Médoc. Since 1929 it has belonged to the Dourthe family, which runs the wine firm of the same name, whose cellars and offices stand opposite the château. Roger Dourthe has since 1961 determined the Maucaillou image. He has extended the vineyard from about 49 to 106 acres (in Listrac and Lamarque as well as Moulis) and has made his wine with attention to the smallest detail.

Mostly new casks

Roger Dourthe, an agricultural engineer and how over 80, proudly showed me the impressive, tiled, fully automated *cuvier*. There is a battery of gleaming stainless-steel fermentation tanks in which temperature during fermentation can be perfectly controlled. He also showed me the large cellar full of casks, all with the vanilla-like scent of new oak. At Maucaillou the wine matures for two years in casks, 75% to 100% of which are new for each vintage. They are sealed with a special aseptic bung. After fining, filtering and bottling the wine is transferred to the large bottle cellar. Production normally amounts to 190 *tonneaux.* Grape varieties are Cabernet Sauvignon (45%), Merlot (35%), Cabernet Franc (15%) and Petit Verdot (5%).

An athletic wine

I went through a whole range of vintages with Roger Dourthe. I was already familiar with some of the wines, for my own cellar is seldom without Maucaillou. In my opinion it is an excellent wine, one that in some years — I am thinking of the 1970, 1973, 1976, 1978, 1979, 1981 and 1982 — is the equal of many *grands crus.* Maucaillou can best be described as an athletic wine of great refinement, a wine with the muscular strength not of a weightlifter but of a ballet dancer, a Nureyev. The wine usually has a deep colour, a fine, elegant bouquet and a supple, pure taste, the tannin remaining long in the mouth. Apart from the vintages already mentioned I would recommend the 1966, 1967 and 1971; the 1974 has aged into an elegant and balanced wine, while the 1977 and 1980 are somewhat lighter than usual.

Left:
Cellarmaster André Raspaud, who has been at Chasse-Spleen since 1975.

Below:
The château, built between 1840 and 1870, seen from the park. At the beginning of the 19th century Chasse-Spleen was part of Château Grand Poujeaux, one of the Médoc's oldest wine estates. Grapes were already being cultivated there at the end of the 16th century.

Régisseur *Mme Bernadette Villars read history before taking up oenology.*

The estate uses a quotation from Baudelaire's 'Spleen' in its publicity: 'J'ai plus de souvenirs que si j'avais mille ans' *(I have more memories than if I were 1,000 years old).*

A small part of Chasse-Spleen's vineyard lies in Listrac.

Chasse-Spleen was for generations the property of the Castaign family, until sold in 1906 to a German wine firm, Segnitz of Bremen. It was confiscated during the First World War, and afterwards sold at auction to Frank Lahary. His family kept it until 1976.

Some 15% of the 1978 vintage was lost during the last days of the harvest, but the remainder was so rich in tannin that the eminent oenologist. Professor Peynaud advised against using more than 50% new wooden casks, a percentage that would often normally be exceeded.

The two large modern paintings that hang in the cuvier *are rather a surprise. They are the work of the French artist Bouilly.*

Chasse-Spleen is a member of the highly respected Academie du Vin de Bordeaux, *along with many* grands crus *and the* bourgeois *châteaux Fourcas-Hosten, Gloria, Labégorce, De Pez, Phélan-Ségur, Poujeaux, Siran, Citran, Lanessan and Maucaillou. The last three are also members of the* Union des Grands Crus de Bordeaux.

Château Chasse-Spleen

Cru Grand Bourgeois Exceptionnel
Moulis

There is a tradition that Chasse-Spleen received its name from Lord Byron, who so enjoyed his stay here in 1821 that he declared it chased away spleen, i.e. ill temper or low-spirits. No one knows if the story is really true. Perhaps Byron simply drank the wine in London and gave it its nickname there. Since 1976 the estate has had three owners: the Banque de Paris et des Pays-Bas, the Société Bonniéroire Vinicole and the Société Bernard Taillan. The director of the last group, Jacques Merlaut, lives in the château from time to time. His daughter, Mme Bernadette Villars, acts as manager.

Underground cellar

The 133-acre vineyard of Chasse-Spleen is scattered over a number of plots. It is planted with 50% Cabernet (mostly Sauvignon), 40% Merlot and 10% Petit Verdot. The grapes ferment in concrete *cuves* and the wine then matures for 22 to 24 months in oak casks. At least half of these casks are replaced each vintage. They are housed in one of the few underground cellars of the Médoc, dating from 1956. Here, too, the wine is clarified cask by cask with fresh egg white. Unlike the rival Maucaillou, Chasse-Spleen wine is not normally filtered. Production varies from 200 to 300 *tonneaux*.

Consistent quality

My acquaintance with Chasse-Spleen extends over at least a dozen vintages. The wines of the 1970s in particular have struck me with their consistent quality. Even the thin 1972 was altogether acceptable. The 1974 — not an unqualified success in the Médoc — was good for its year, with a deep colour, an excellent bouquet and a decently firm taste. The 1973 offered rather more charm, colour and strength than many other Médocs of that vintage. Chasse-Spleen has no reason to be ashamed of its 1977, and the 1970, 1971, 1975, 1976, 1978 and 1979 are outstanding wines. Characteristics are plenty of colour, a firm bouquet with nuances of fruit and oak, and a substantial taste of exquisite quality. This is one of the noblest *crus bourgeois*. The first two vintages of the Eighties maintain its high standards.

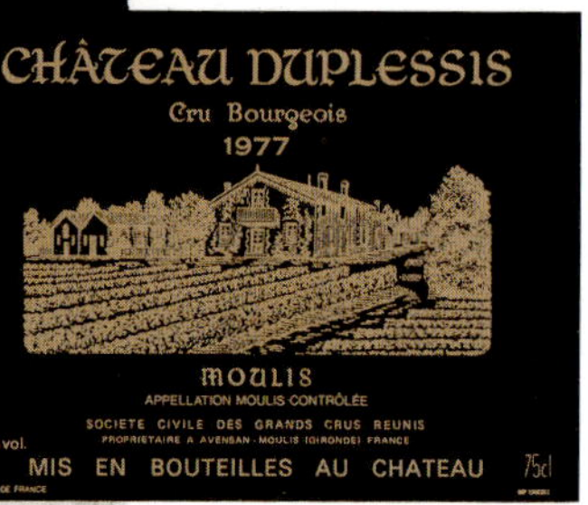

Left:
The label, which for years said only Duplessis. Now the full name is given.

Far left:
Immediately after being bottled — by a mobile unit — the wine is packed into cases.

Below:
The château, once owned by Armand Duplessis, Cardinal de Richelieu, was used as a hunting lodge. The estate made its name only last century, thanks to the efforts of the then owner, wine merchant Hauchecorne.

Château Duplessis-Hauchecorne

Cru Grand Bourgeois
Moulis

Just southwest of the village of Moulis there are two châteaux with Duplessis in their names: Duplessis-Hauchecorne, a *cru grand bourgeois*, and Duplessis-Fabre, a *cru bourgeois.* They are sometimes confused, particularly as for years Euplessis-Hauchecorne was simply labelled 'Duplessis', which left the exact origin unclear — it even suggested there was a third Duplessis. On the insistence of Duplessis-Fabre (connected with Fourcas-Dupré in Listrac), this inadequate labelling is to be abandoned and Duplessis-Hauchecorne will once again be recognizable as such. Since 1960 the estate has belonged to the *société civile* les Grands Crus Réunis. Behind this name stand the powerful Bernard Taillan and Lucien Lurton. Each of these holds half the shares, but the château is entirely run by Mestrezat-Preller, a Taillan firm. Lurton has nothing at all to do with the wine.

No shortage of space

Only part of the château is occupied, but on my first visit it was humming with activity and interest. Thanks to an enormous mobile unit, the 1977 vintage was being bottled and packed in wooden cases and then stacked in the cellar with a forklift truck. This operation did not take long: in 1977 Duplessis-Hauchecorne produced only 15 *tonneaux*, compared with the usual 60 to 100. The vineyard now covers 44 acres, planted with Cabernet Sauvignon (65%), Merlot (20%), Malbec (10%) and Petit Verdot (5%). Another 23 acres are to be planted. It struck me that the *cuvier*, with glass-lined concrete vats, and the *chais* were very large for this size of vineyard. The manager told me that this extra capacity was because a previous owner, with three other estates as well, had concentrated his winemaking here.

Rather mild and smooth

Wine from this Moulis estate is matured for about 14 months in used wooden casks and is filtered. I do not consider it a great wine, but it is by no means unsatisfactory or without flavour. Even in its early days Duplessis-Hauchecorne possesses a good deal of suppleness and the tannin present is never really astringent. The wine lacks finesse and a measure of 'bite'. It slips gently and smoothly down the throat, leaving no lasting impression behind. This does not appeal to me — but maybe it does to others, particularly if they are unaccustomed to the somewhat severe taste of the classic Médoc. For its second wine the estate uses the name Château la Morere.

Below:
Behind the present château, a pleasant country house, are the modern cellars where the wine casks are stacked three high.

Far right:
Owner François Cordonnier. At the time of writing he was still shipping some wine in casks.

Right: An old view — from 1916 — of the original château. It no longer belongs to the estate, although the adjacent cellars do.

Château Dutruch Grand Poujeaux

Cru Grand Bourgeois Exceptionnel
Moulis

About two miles from Moulis lies the hamlet of Grand Poujeaux. It is small in extent, but rich in châteaux, among them Chasse-Spleen, Poujeaux and Dutruch Grand Poujeaux. The Dutruch Grand Poujeaux estate is dispersed around the commune because although the original château was separated from the rest of the property, the adjacent cellars were not. Dividing up th property meant that the owners had to move to a house on the boundary of the commune that is now regarded as Château Dutruch Grand Poujeaux. The *cuvier* is here, and a modern hall where the wine is bottled and stored. Maturing — mostly in used casks — still takes place in the low, dark *chais* next to the old château. It is a rather disorganized situation but the owner, François Cordonnier, has adjusted to it. He took over the estate in 1967 through a family connection: his grandmother was a Dutruch.

Stainless steel introduced

Cordonnier has invested in *cuves* as well as in storage space. The first stainless-steel fermentation tanks arrived in 1979 to replace concrete vats, and more followed. After fermentation the wine matures in the cask for about 18 months, and at the end of this period it is fined with egg white. It is also filtered.
The vineyard covers 64 acres. A small piece lies directly behind the present château, the rest is in three large separate plots. In good, normal years the estate produces about 100 *tonneaux*.

Rustic elegance

While a pair of ladies labelled bottles close by I tasted several vintages in the storage area of the château. The wine is distinguished by a rather rustic elegance. Dutruch Grand Poujeaux is not a truly fine wine: there always seems to be some roughness present. With time, however, this initial roughness wears off a little. Nine years after its vintage the 1970, for example, already possessed a respectable charm. A rich or subtle bouquet should not be expected of this Moulis; the scent is pleasant but not grand. If I had to place some vintages from the late Seventies in order of preference the 1975 would come first then the 1978, 1976 and 1977.

Poujeaux wine has been drunk at the Elysée palace: when Giscard d'Estaing was elected President he ordered two consignments of it, and took four cases on a trip to Martinique.

The château's motto was coined in 1921 by Jean Theil's father. It reads:
'Je ne suis ni premier, ni second,
ni troisième
Pas même quatrième ou
cinquième
Mais je suis celui qu'on aime
Je suis, je reste Poujeaux
lui-même.'

Left:
The wine harvest in progress. Note the gravelly soil.

Below:
The late Jean Theil and his wife in front of the château. Jean's sons Philippe (production) and François (marketing) see to the running of the estate.

Right:
A bottle from the 1969 vintage. A bottle of 1953 came first in a blind tasting organized by Jean Theil in the 1960s. Its competitors were the four premiers grands crus (Mouton-Rothschild was not yet one of them). The Poujeaux came first in front of the Lafite-Rothschild.

Château Poujeaux

Cru Grand Bourgeois Exceptionnel
Moulis

Like the neighbouring Chasse-Spleen, Poujeaux was the property of the Castaign family for most of the 19th century. In 1880 the estate was divided among heirs and until the 1950s there were three Châteaux Poujeaux. Since 1957, however, they have been reunited — thanks to Jean Theil, whose father had bought one of the Poujeaux in 1921. Theil, who died in 1981, made Poujeaux wine much respected: so much so that, without recourse to publicity or sales representatives, the whole vintage can be sold directly from the château, not via the Bordeaux trade.

Seven egg-whites per cask

Poujeaux's secret lies primarily in the soil. A geologist once pointed out that the soil here is remarkably like that of Lafite-Rothschild. Furthermore, nothing is left to chance in the vinification. The wine ferments for a long time in stainless-steel, ordinary steel or concrete vats, and then matures for 18 months in oak casks. A quarter of the latter are replaced each year. Usually the wine is fined with no fewer than seven whites of egg to each cask and is lightly filtered just before bottling. Selection is rigorous during the whole vinification and maturing process: in principle, only wine from vines at least 10 years old is used for Poujeaux, and then only the best quality. Lesser wine is marketed as Château la Salle de Poujeaux — but this too is always of an attractive standard. The Poujeaux vineyard covers 124 acres; 35% of the vines are Cabernet Sauvignon, 35% are Merlot, 15% are Cabernet Franc and 15% Petit Verdot. Annual yield is between 145 and 300 *tonneaux*.

Class emerges slowly

The wine as well as the soil of Poujeaux has been compared with Lafite-Rothschild. It is said that when lunching with President Pompidou, Baron Elie de Rothschild mistook a Poujeaux 1967 for his own wine, and still would not believe it when the butler showed him the bottle. The 1967 was, in fact, a particularly gracious wine. More recent vintages of Poujeaux could less easily be confused with Lafite. They are usually dark-coloured wines, rather inaccessible when young, only beginning to reveal a certain charm after a long resting period in the bottle. Their class is irrefutable — but to experience it requires patience. Poujeaux is a classic Médoc, decently mouth-feeling and with plenty of tannin. I have a slight preference for the more supple vintages from this château, such as the 1973, 1976 and 1979, but I would also regard bottles of the very successful 1974, 1975 (with less Cabernet than usual because of hail damage, but fuller than the 1976), 1978, 1981 and 1982 as an enrichment of my cellar.

Almost all Brillette wine is sold through Viniprix en Euromarché, although Raymond Berthault set aside some for export.

Brillette's production varies from around 60 to 145 tonneaux.

The wine is always filtered once.

When Raymond Berthault took over the estate in 1976 he gave régisseur *Bertrand Bouteiller — who has held the position since 1970 — more resources in order to make a better product than ever before.*

The whole estate covers 317 acres, of which actual vineyard comprises 74 acres.

Below:
A corner of the compact château. The central part houses the cask cellar; the right wing (shown here) the cuvier*; and the left wing contains an office and living quarters.*

Right:
The late Raymond Berthault and his wife. Brillette wines do not carry his name on the label, but that of the Comte du Périer de Larsan, who owned the estate in the 19th century.

Château Brillette

Cru Grand Bourgeois
Moulis

That the Château Brillette vineyard contains a lot of gravel — always a good sign — can be deduced from its name. Brillette apparently derives from *brillance*, a reference to the reflection of the sun on the stones. Vineyard and château lie just west of the village of Moulis, on a plateau largely surrounded by woods. In the course of this century the estate has declined greatly. In about 1960 only 7½ acres of vineyard remained. Since then, however, there has been a lot of replanting. There are now 74 acres of vines, with cautious plans for 12 acres more. The rebirth of Brillette was realized by Raymond Berthault, owner from 1976. Berthault established two extremely successful chains in France: Viniprix and Euromarché. He did not acquire the vineyard for profit but as a hobby, a relaxation. He repeatedly assured me that he had only one aim at Brillette: producing the very best quality. Unfortunately, Raymond Berthault died in 1981, but his wife and son-in-law continue his work.

Professional advice

Raymond Berthault was not a man to do things by halves. As his *régisseur* he engaged the highly capable Bertrand Bouteiller, whose other responsibilities include the *grand cru* Pichon-Longueville in Pauillac. An apparatus has been installed that enables the temperature in the concrete fermentation vats to be better regulated than ever before, and there has also been investment in maintenance and repair work. After fermentation the wine — from 55% Cabernet Sauvignon vines, 40% Merlot, 5% Petit Verdot, plus other varieties — matures for 18 months in oak casks, at least one-third of which are new, on the advice of the oenologist Professor Peynaud.

Mild style, fine quality

Although I have pleasant recollections of the Brillette 1966 — a wine that will develop fully in the course of the 1980s — the vintages from 1976 onward are obviously the most interesting. I tasted three of them at the château: 1976, 1977 and 1978. The 1976 had a rich red colour, was not yet fully opened out and had an impeccable, mild and lasting taste. The 1977 was slightly thinner and lighter, but very acceptable for its year. The 1978 had a dark purplish colour going light at the edges, and revealed a markedly beautiful taste, mild and elegant. Although Château Brillette may not produce any truly great wines that burden the patience of the consumer, it does achieve a very decent quality, as the 1981 and 1982 vintages show.

Left:
Manager Henri Meunier, who has worked at Château Lafon for about a quarter of a century, although he lives at Château la Bécade. He points out that the wines of Château Lafon and Château la Bécade are in fact identical, although Lafon is a cru grand bourgeois *and La Bécade a* cru bourgeois. *The Château Lafon label is said to have been designed by Kressmann, the wine merchants, because Lafon lacked one.*

Below:
The Lafon cuvier, *where very up-to-date methods are employed.*

Lafon, like the Château Giscours and Larose-Trintaudon, has a means of heating the freshly pressed grape juice to remove the rot from the must.

By the back entrance to the château is a remnant from the past: a large dovecote.

La Bécade's vineyard covers some 50 acres; Lafon's about 40 acres.

Château Lafon

Cru Grand Bourgeois
Listrac

To reach Château Lafon you have to take a narrow, winding little road from Listrac to Cussac-le-Vieux. The château does not stand among vineyards but in woods, with a few houses around it. The owner is Jean-Pierre Théron, who also has Château de Portets in the Graves (see page 96). Théron bought Lafon at the end of the 1960s. Earlier, in 1964, he had taken over the neighbouring Château la Bécade, also in Listrac. At that time Lafon was no more than a ruin: everything had to be restored or replaced. Now a modern, compact winery is concealed behind the old façade of the château, with low, wide fermentation tanks and tall, narrow storage tanks — all of stainless steel. In addition the château has a number of concrete vats with stainless-steel hatches.

Two châteaux, one wine

Around 1970 there were 20 acres of productive vineyard and now there is twice this amount. The capacity of the *cuvier*, however, is based on a larger acreage. The manager, Henri Meunier, explained to me that Lafon also vinifies wine from Château la Bécade and, what is more, the two wines are blended. Lafon and la Bécade are, in fact, the same wine, as I can verify. When Meunier filled my glass from one of the tanks I asked him whether we were going to taste Lafon or la Bécade. "It makes no difference," was his answer. After fining in the tank, the wine is transported to la Bécade for filtering and bottling. Théron does not bottle all his wine: buyers such as Dourthe, Kressmann and Johnston bottle it themselves.

Little tannin

During my visit to Lafon I learned that the wine is not matured in casks but only in vats. The casks in the small *chai* were empty. Henri Meunier told me that a cellar for casks was being built, to be ready sometime in the 1980s. As the wine does not come in contact with wood, there is a limited tannin contents, so Lafon can usually be drunk early. The wine, from 60% Cabernet Sauvignon and 40% Malbec vines, has a mildly spicy, quite pleasant bouquet and taste, without much depth. The colour, in general, is not particularly dark. I would place the 1978 among Lafon's better vintages, and the 1976 too had a decent taste. I thought the 1975 flat; the wine seemed to have less Cabernet than usual.

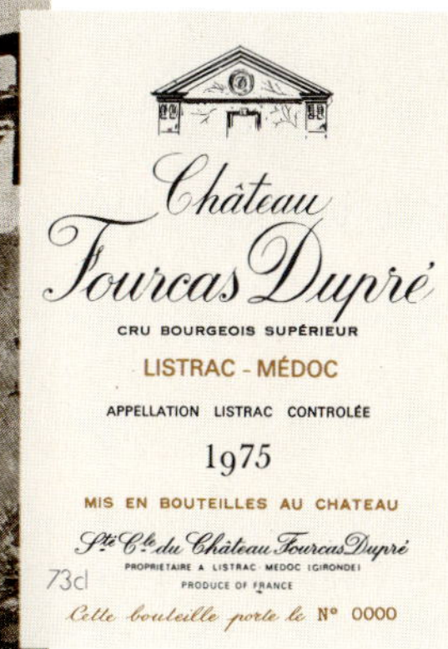

Centre left:
One of the cellars, with the estate name in large letters for traffic passing on the nearby D1.

Far left:
Guy Pagès. His brother is co-owner of La Tour de By (see page 86).

Below left:
In the neat and tidy cuverie. *The château still has its wooden vats — used occasionally for temporary storage — as well as ones made of concrete and stainless steel.*

Below right:
After fermentation, the wine is drained from the cuve. *As well as its* grand vin, *the estate produces a second wine, Bellevue Laffont, which is never exported.*

The 's' of Fourcas is always pronounced.

Château Fourcas-Dupré

Cru Grand Bourgeois Exceptionnel
Listrac

A map made by Bellegme in the 18th century, on which the Fourcas vineyard is marked, shows that wine has been made at Fourcas-Dupré for quite some time; indeed, the vineyard originated much earlier than that. 'Fourcas' is a geographical name; 'Dupré' was a 19th-century lawyer. Since 1967 the estate has been owned by a *société civile*, the shares of which are held by five persons. One of them is Guy Pagès, occupier and administrator of the château, with a 40% holding. Under his management, Fourcas-Dupré has seen much renovation and improvement in recent years. Between 1974 and 1979 not only was a completely new *cuvier* built, but also a tall *chai* where the bottles can be stacked on pallets.

Scrupulously clean

In the new cellar, fermentation is done mainly in stainless-steel tanks, although there are also wood and concrete vats. Like the rest of the facilities, this area looks spotlessly clean and perfectly maintained. The casks used at Fourcas-Dupré for maturing the wine come almost exclusively from the *premiers grands crus* Lafite-Rothschild and Margaux. They have held one wine and so are two years old. The maturation period lasts on average 18 months. The wine is fined with powdered albumen or egg gelatine. It is also filtered. The 119-acre vineyard — of which about 100 acres is actually productive — normally produces between 175 and 300 *tonneaux*.

Not a typical Listrac

According to Guy Pagès, the vineyard has less Merlot than is usual in Listrac, because of the very gravelly soil. At Fourcas-Dupré the Merlot represents 38% of the total, with 50% Cabernet Sauvignon, 10% Cabernet Franc and 2% Petit Verdot. Soil and mixture of grapes produce a wine that you might perhaps identify with communes like Cussac or Pauillac rather than Listrac. It is rather austere, none too accommodating, generally only moderate in suppleness and refinement, but of a good, reliable quality. I thought the 1970 very successful, the somewhat tart 1973 less so. The 1975, which won three gold medals in France, had a respectable depth of colour, a slightly flat but pleasant bouquet and a firm taste with a hint of sun and very ripe grapes. The 1976 was lighter in colour, more fragrant and already mature. The 1977 seemed a powerful wine with a lot of tannin, lacking somewhat in fat, with a little 'stalkiness'; but it was not unpleasant. I consider the 1978 a success: very concentrated fruit in bouquet and taste, a long aftertaste, a deep colour and excellent balance. The 1979, 1981 and 1982 also deserve a recommendation.

Left:
Robert de Crèvecoeur, director until 1982.

Far left:
The entrance to the cuverie.

Below:
The park at Fourcas-Hosten was designed in 1830 by an Englishman.

Some 50 of the 94 acres of vineyard are situated on a high-lying area near the Château Fourcas-Dupré, with the rest on lower ground nearer to the village centre.

Fourcas-Hosten has no second wine.

Between 1951 and 1971, the small amount of wine produced at Fourcas-Hosten was usually not vinified at the Château itself, but on an estate in Moulis run by the Saint-Affrique family.

Château Fourcas-Hosten

Cru Grand Bourgeois Exceptionnel
Listrac

For five generations after 1810 Fourcas-Hosten belonged to the family of the Barons de Saint-Affrique. There was even a period when there were two Fourcas-Hostens, after the estate had been divided among heirs, but in 1951 the two parts were reunited. The last generation of Saint-Affriques rather let the vineyards and cellars deteriorate. When the château passed into other hands in 1971 it had only four small concrete fermentation tanks and no cellar at all for casks. The new owners were a group of some 30 well-to-do Americans (mainly from New York and Boston), brought together by Count Arnaud de Trabuc and Phillip Towers. Money from these investors made it possible for Fourcas-Hosten to acquire nine cream-coloured metal fermentation tanks, its own *chai* and many other essential items. In addition the vineyard was replanted. It now covers 94 acres, with 50% Cabernet Sauvignon, 45% Merlot and 5% Cabernet Franc. In the coming years the percentage of Cabernet Sauvignon will be raised to between 60% and 65%.

Views of church and park

Directors of Fourcas-Hosten are Guy and Patrice Pagès of nearby Fourcas-Dupré. The uninhabited château dates from 1810. It stands opposite Listrac's 13th-century church and at the back looks out over a splendid 7½-acre park. The wine matures for a year in used oak casks, of which 25% are new; then it goes back into the *cuvés*. After filtering, the wine is bottled. The French wine firm of Nicolas generally buys 30,000 bottles a year. A lot of wine also goes to America, for obvious reasons.

Harmonious and supple

Fourcas-Hosten wine generally has good balance and a sound, supple, not too harsh taste with plenty of fruit. I consider it the most distinguished Listrac. One of my favourite recent vintages is the 1976: a vital colour, wonderful taste and a balanced whole. I have also enjoyed the 1973, which has both elegance and strength. The 1971 was still firmer, although it still had a lot of acidity and less fruit than normal. The 1975 quite simply was a great Fourcas-Hosten, the 1977 lighter than usual but nevertheless really good. The 1978 proved pure, successful, without too much tannin. I very much enjoyed the 1979 too; the 1981 and 1982 will in due time become delicious wines. The production varies between 85 and 220 *tonneaux*.

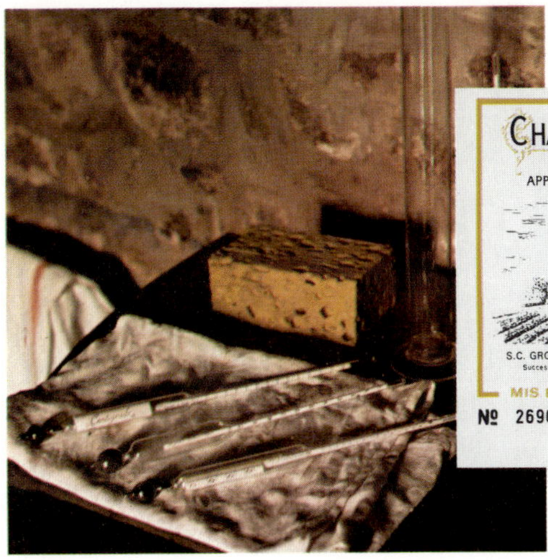

Centre left:
Meters used for testing alcoholic strength.

Far left:
Quiet work in the cellar.

Below:
The castle in its full glory.

Wine identical to De Lamarque is sometimes sold in France as Réserve des Marquis d'Evry. All of the château's wine is filtered before bottling.

Château de Lamarque

Cru Grand Bourgeois
Lamarque

Although the Médoc boasts many imposing châteaux, the castle of Lamarque is especially splendid — right out of a fairy tale. You reach it by way of a drive lined with tall trees, and a large gateway. Towers flank the main building and the walls are battlemented. The inner courtyard is a picture, with palms, flowers, a beautiful lawn and white doves. All the doors and shutters are painted wine-red. The interior of the château is also well worth seeing. It has cellars and a chapel from the 11th and 12th centuries and various rooms from the 12th and 14th. The *grand salle* is very fine, with portraits along the walls, old books in the cases and antique furniture on the valuable carpet. The castle was built about 900 years ago as a defence against the invasions via the Gironde. It achieved more or less its present form in the 14th century, but a few further alterations were made in the 17th in accordance with contemporary taste.

Reconstruction since 1963

The owner of Château de Lamarque is Mme Gromand, née Brunet d'Evry. The estate has been in the possession of her family since 1841. Her husband Roger — director of Mercedes France — has taken great pains since 1963 to make the château count for something in the Médoc, as a wine estate and not only as a historic building. He has replanted practically the entire 124-acre vineyard and has renovated the cellars. Everything has been done with the greatest care, although to my taste the décor has been rather overdone in the *cuvier*, where the concrete vats have been disguised as wood. The château's 110 to 270 *tonneaux* of wine is matured for two years in oak casks, about one-fifth of which are new.

Noticeably mild

Cabernet vines predominate in the vineyard with 70% of the total (50% Cabernet Sauvignon, 20% Cabernet Franc), followed by 25% Merlot and 5% Petit Verdot. Yet the wine did not strike me as a real Cabernet: it lacks the breeding, the austerity, the impression of blackcurrant and the generous dose of tannin. Château de Lamarque is a markedly mild, almost velvety Médoc, fairly broad in the mouth and as a rule pleasantly drinkable after only three years or so. It may not fascinate, but it is professionally made and undoubtedly agreeable. Representative good years include 1970, 1975, 1978 (which could turn out better than the 1975), 1981 and 1982, although the supple 1979, the very mild 1976 and the slightly thinner 1977 have their merits.

Left:
Laurent Poitou. His family has been at the estate for four generations.

Far left:
There is a miniature windmill in the château garden. According to Laurent Poitou, the château was named Tour du Haut-Moulin because there were the remains of an old windmill in the vineyard.

Below, centre left:
The small stone statue at the entrance to Poitou's tasting room.

Below:
The illustration on the label of Château Tour du Haut-Moulin does not give a true impression of the château's surroundings. In fact, it stands among other houses in a small street in the hamlet of Cussac-le-Vieux.

Château Tour du Haut-Moulin

Cru Grand Bourgeois
Cussac

As manager of ten wine estates in the Médoc, Laurent Poitou used to live a very busy life. But since 1982 he has devoted all his time to his own property, Château Tour du Haut-Moulin in Cussac. The château is a *maison bourgeoise,* its only striking feature a miniature wooden windmill in the garden. Poitou has a small reception cellar at the château where visitors can taste and buy, but the wine is made elsewhere. A few miles in the direction of the Gironde, along the road to the 1689 Médoc fort, are the actual cellars and the vineyard of Tour du Haut-Moulin.

The vineyard enlarged

In 1968 the vineyard covered 37 acres, today 86. Poitou was hoping to increase this to 116 acres by purchase. The vines are 50% Cabernet Sauvignon, 45% Merlot and 5% Petit Verdot. The grapes ferment in white painted concrete vats with red edges and hatches. The wine is then matured for 18 months in oak *barriques*. In principle these are not new, but Poitou tries to replace a quarter each year. Powered albumen is used for clarifying the wine, which is also filtered twice before bottling. Tour du Haut-Moulin has a good reputation. The firm of Nicolas is a regular client, taking 100 casks most years, and so is the importer Grafé-Lecocq, supplier by appointment to the Belgian court. The 1978 Tour du Haut-Moulin was offered by no fewer than 20 *négociants.*

Firm rather than fine

I have tasted and drunk various vintages in the *cuvier*, in the cellar, with Laurent Poitou, and at home I also sampled the 1960, which my host — 'mad on fruit' — poured over the strawberries. "With strawberries," he said, "you should only take a really mature wine." What the 1960 tastes like without strawberries I cannot say. However, I can give a verdict on more recent years, the 1975 and 1978, for example. Both wines were almost black in colour and their bouquets had not yet been released — although a mild, almost sweet element was beginning to break through in the 1975. Both had quite a good amount of mild tannin and a mouth-filling, somewhat 'dusty' taste with a hint of *terroir.* I thought these wines were firm rather than fine, an impression that remained unrevised after tasting other vintages.

Left:
The label shown here still bears the name of Château Beaumont's previous owner. It has now been altered.

Centre left:
Owner Bernard Soulas, who lives in the village of Eysines.

Far left:
The tall cuvier. Above the door is the date 1894.

Below:
The château, which is a copy of a small castle built by the famous French architect Mansard.

Château Beaumont

Cru Grand Bourgeois
Cussac

About the turn of the century Château Beaumont was the biggest of Cussac's wine estates. The vineyard on its plateau covered nearly 250 acres with a million vines. In the course of this century, however, Beaumont has gradually declined to just a couple of hectares in 1966. Then the estate was bought by M. and Mme de Bolivar. With limited cash and a lot of courage they reconstituted about half the vineyard. Then, in 1977, fate struck. Almost the entire crop was destroyed by frost, and not long afterwards M. de Bolivar died. His widow was forced to sell the estate and left for Venezuela. Since January 1979 Beaumont, an elegant, 19th-century building with four pointed towers, has a new and very dynamic owner, Bernard Soulas. Using his own machinery (he is also a grain farmer), he has drained the whole vineyard including the uncultivated parts, and planted a further 74 acres. He has also modernized the whole cellar complex.

No used casks

Since the harvest of 1979 Beaumont has had stainless-steel fermentation tanks, which stand in a room with an insulated, aluminium-clad ceiling. On the advice of his oenologist, Bernard Soulas uses new casks for maturing one-third of the vintage; two-thirds remains in the tanks. The wine is exchanged between cask and tank, so that all Château Beaumont comes into contact with the new oak wood during its maturing period. Soulas hopes soon to have 250 acres, the original vineyard area.

Good prospects

The Beaumont vineyard has 56% Cabernet Sauvignon vines, 36% Merlot, 7% Cabernet Franc and a tiny amount of Petit Verdot. The 1979 (of which 215 *tonneaux* were produced) was a sound, rather elegant wine in which the presence of Cabernet grapes was unmistakably perceptible. It had a nice balance and plenty of colour. The 1980 was a lighter wine, but not bad at all. Qualitywise, the most impressive vintages so far have been 1981 and 1982, wines that Bernard Soulas is justly very satisfied with. The year of 1982 also saw the biggest yield yet, 352 *tonneaux*. For its second wine the estate uses the label Château Moulin d'Arvigny.

Left:
The English-style Lanessan château, seen here from the vineyard, was built in 1878. Hubert Bouteiller, who has managed Lanessan since 1969, lives in the château with his family.

Below:
One of the treasures in the cellars: the glorious 1961.

Production figures for Lanessan, in tonneaux:
1969 — 57
1970 — 80
1971 — 30
1972 — 40
1973 — 80
1974 — 130
1975 — 100
1976 — 120
1977 — 50
1978 — 120

The estate also produces a second wine, called Comaine du Saint-Gemme. It bears the appellation *Bordeaux Supérieur and no vintage year is stated. This wine should not be confused with Château Caronne-Sainte-Gemme (discussed on page 47). The similarity in the names dates back to the time when Lanessan and Caronne-Sainte-Gemme had the same owner.*

In the 19th century the Bordelais poet Biarnez wrote:
'. . . car Lanessan mérite, qu'on lui fasse en passant une courte visite, et ce vin est bien fait pour nous affriandir'.
(. . . because Lanessan deserves a short visit on the way; that wine has been made to tempt us).

Château Lanessan

Cussac

On 17 May 1793 the wealthy shipowner Jean Delbos signed the contract that gave him possession of Château Lanessan. It was already one of the biggest estates in the Médoc and had been founded by the de Lanessan family. In the first half of the 19th century the Lanessan wine was reckoned among the best of the Médoc. The writer A. Jullien placed it in a category equivalent, in the 1855 classification, to the fourth *grands crus.;* Château Lanessan was not actually included in this classification because of the complacent attitude of the then-owner, Louis Delbos, Jean's son. Louis was also a *négociant* and could sell the Lanessan wine so easily that felt it unnecessary to submit samples for classification.

Horses and carriages

The attitude of André Delbos, Lanessan's owner from 1867 to 1909, was quite different. He invested vast sums in the estate. He had the old château completely demolished and replaced it with the present structure. This building was no doubt meant to represent the height of elegance, but it always reminds me of the kind of house in which British horror films are set. André Delbos extended the vineyard and installed a new *cuvier* on the most up-to-date principles of the day. Delbos had another pastime besides wine: horses and carriages. At the end of the 19th century Lanessan acquired its own stables (with marble mangers), English coachmen (who gave the horses English names, including Whisky), a fine collection of beautiful carriages and a saddle room where the tack was kept. The horses and the coachmen are gone, but the stables, carriages and saddle room now form the Musée du Cheval, visited by some 15,000 people a year.

Below:
Some of the carriages in the Musée du Cheval. Apart from the English mailcoach (made by Peter and Sons, of London) shown here, all the carriages are Bouteiller family heirlooms. The yellow is the family colour of the Exshaws, who owned the neighbouring Château Lachesnaye. The Bouteillers were given this carriage as a present when they bought Lachesnaye in 1961, to replace a similar one lost during the Second World War. The oldest carriage in the collection is a Phaeton from 1885.

Far right:
Immediately after picking, the grapes are pitched into a large container from where they are fed into the fouloir-égrappoir *to be lightly crushed and have their stalks removed.*

Right:
Humbert Bouteiller, whose ancestor was bouteiller *— or cellarmaster — to King Louis XIV.*

The wine of Château Lanessan is sometimes clarified with fresh egg white, sometimes with powdered albumen. The choice depends on the nature of the vintage.

The Bouteiller family

On 20 April 1907 André Delbos's daughter married Etienne Bouteiller. André died two years later and since then the Bouteillers have owned Château Lanessan. The present director is Hubert Bouteiller, who lives in the château with his family. Other Bouteiller properties are Pichon-Longueville, for which Hubert's brother Bertrand is responsible, and Lachesnaye, near Lanessan, also run by Hubert. Of these three estates Lanessan is by far the biggest. It covers 766 acres, although only 99 acres of this is planted with vines. The vineyard, however, is growing steadily: Hubert intends to expand, on the same type of soil, to 175-200 acres. He is deliberately doing this gradually, so as not to disturb the balance in the wine between old and young vines. Furthermore, expanding the vineyard too quickly would mean too intensive an enlargement programme for the *cuvier* and cellars.

Concrete vats by choice

After picking, the grapes — 70% Cabernet Sauvignon, 25% Merlot and 5% Cabernet Franc, plus some Petit Verdot — ferment in concrete vats. During the 1970s these were brought in to replace the 19th-century wooden *cuves*. Hubert Bouteiller told me that he has deliberately not gone over to stainless-steel tanks. He believes that with tanks it is the machine rather than the man that regulates the fermentation. With concrete — or wooden — *cuves* the wine maker has a greater personal contribution and therefore a deeper commitment. At Lanessan the concrete vats are lined with a hard, neutral substance. Thus the wine does not come into contact with the concrete, and cleaning the vats presents no problems.

A long period in the vat

Lanessan's annual 50 to 130 *tonneaux* of wine is matured for 18 to 30 months in (mostly) used casks. Nevertheless it has plenty of tannin and colour, which is derived from the grape skins during the long *cuvaison* — the period that the wine remains in the vat during and immmediately after fermentation. Usually this is at least three weeks: in 1977 it was 25 days, and, for some of the wine in 1978, 30 days. The wine is filtered before bottling.

Intense taste

I regard Lanessan as the prototype of the true, classic Médoc. It is a deep-coloured wine that requires a long time to lose its initial dourness — generally about ten years. The wine is intense in taste, rich in tannin and noble in nature. It is characterized by an austere, taut elegance, as I discovered in all of the vintages I tasted. Hubert Bouteiller has planted some extra Petit Verdot to give his wine a little more charm. Juice from this variety was first used in 1978; and, in fact, the wine did seem more rounded and stronger than comparable earlier years. Besides the 1978, I thought the 1976 and 1975 memorable. The 1977 had considerable merit for its year. I have also enjoyed the 1967 and the 1973, both successful for their years. Although far too young to drink, the first vintages of the Eighties were very impressive indeed.

Left:
Henri Martin, in the guise in which he is known to many: Grand Maître *of the* Commanderie du Bontemps de Médoc et des Graves. *He has also been chairman of the* Conseil Interprofessionel du Vin de Bordeaux *(CIVB), was honoured with the* Légion d'honneur, *is mayor of Saint-Julien, and co-administrator of the* premier grand cru *Château Latour.*

Below:
Bottles from the difficult 1968 vintage — when Château Gloria produced an acceptable wine. But in 1963 and 1965 nothing was produced. The château normally retains 10% to 25% of each vintage — in bottles — as a reserve.

Right:
Seven of the huge wooden casks in which the wine matures. Very occasionally new casks of the more traditional size are used for part of the wine for part of the maturing period.

The second wine, of lesser quality, is sold under Gloria's second label of Château Peymartin or under the third label, Domaine de la Croix (only wine from very young vines). There is also a fourth label, Château Haut-Beychevelle-Gloria, which is used for wine from a separate 12-acre vineyard in Saint-Julien.

Henri Martin is assisted by his son-in-law, Jean-Louis Triaud, who married Françoise Martin in 1973.

Château Gloria

Saint-Julien

Near the enormous wine bottle that announces the hamlet of Saint-Julien-Beychevelle there stands an unspectacular white house. This is Château Gloria, one of the most frequently described and discussed estates in the Médoc. The man who has given Gloria its reputation is Henri Martin. Born in 1903, he comes of a family that has been involved in the wine trade for about three centuries. His father, Alfred Martin, was a cooper and later also owned an estate called Gloria. In 1936, however, Martin senior sold the whole vineyard. He and his son turned to groceries for their livelihood. Then in 1942 Henri Martin had the opportunity of buying over 7,000 square yards of vine-growing land. Soon a new Château Gloria came into being. The property today has 86 acres of vineyard. According to Martin, there is not a single square yard that has not grown a *grand cru* — which is why he refuses to accept the status of *cru bourgeois.* Certainly, wine from Gloria commands as high a price as a fourth or fifth *grand cru classé.*

Outsize casks

The 100 to 150 *tonneaux* of wine that Gloria usually produces comes form vines 65% of which are Cabernet Sauvignon, 25% Merlot, 5% Petit Verdot and 5% Cabernet Franc. The grapes are fermented by variety and by plot in tanks of enamelled steel. A strict selection process takes place after fermentation. The wine from all the *cuves* is tasted twice, blind, once directly from the tank and once after it has been in contact with the air for a day. Wine from vines less than 10 years old will already have been removed by this stage. Only after the best *cuves* have been picked does blending begin. The wine is then matured for 16 months, not in the traditional casks but in much larger vessels containing about 1,450 gallons (1,850 US gallons) each. The process is completed by fining (with fresh white of egg) and light filtering.

Lack of unanimity

Opinions about Gloria wine differ: many praise it, others have reservations. I belong to the latter category. I find that it is a wine with a good balance, a big, full taste and an early suppleness; but it lacks the finesse, the depth and the length of flavour that would make it truly glorious. In years of concentrated wines such as 1970 and 1975, Gloria usually possesses rather less colour and compactness than might be expected. Nevertheless, it can stand comparison with any of the *crus grands bourgeois exceptionnels.* The 1970, 1973, and 1974 rather disappointed me, but I regard the 1966, 1967, 1969, 1976, 1978 and 1979 as very successful for this estate, while the 1981 and 1982 offer delicious perspectives.

Below:
The original château, seen from the vineyard, an oblong block off land, stretching from east to west.

Far right:
The extremely functional winery. Gabriel Meffre bought Du Glana in 1961.

Grape varieties are 68% Cabernet Sauvignon, 30% Merlot and 2% Cabernet Franc.

Older vintages of Du Glana should probably be avoided: I tasted the 1973 and the 1976, which were both far from inspiring.

Production in 1978 — when the wine was again vinified separately — was 120 tonneaux.

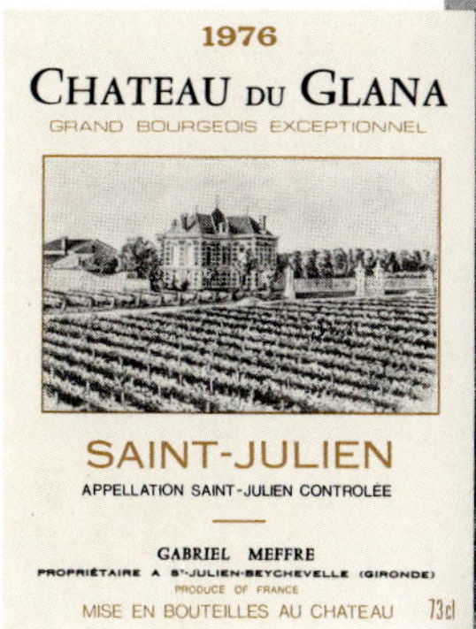

Château du Glana

Cru Grand Bourgeois Exceptionnel
Saint-Julien

This château stands next to the local football pitch in the hamlet of Saint-Julien-Beychevelle. The actual château, an unremarkable house, is occupied by a former owner and is separated from the estate. Not far from the house stands a large, unimaginative building that accommodates the cellars. The oldest part of it dates from 1968. The present owner of Château du Glana is Gabriel Meffre, who lives some 430 miles away in the Vaucluse (not to be confused with Gabriel Meffre of Gigondas). Jean Ardiley has worked as cellarmaster at du Glana since 1979. While showing me round he told a rather confusing story to the effect that the du Glana wine was not vinified separately until 1978. Before that time, I gather, the wine was made together with that from three other Meffre properties. Ardiley could offer no further clarification and I looked into the matter myself.

Irregularities

From various sources — amongst them records of a court case of June 1977 — I learned that M. Meffre was fined more than 20,000 francs for irregularities with his wines, specifically for incorrect use of vintage years and château names. The fact that in the same year Château du Glana was nevertheless admitted to the status of *cru grand bourgeois exceptionnel* shows great forgiveness on part of the selection committee.

Not very gifted

The episode of irregularities is now definitely over, and the wine of Du Glana — coming from a 110 acre vineyard — is now vinified separately in its own cellars, according to the rules. The *cuves* here are concrete and metal and together with underground tanks these also largely serve for maturing the wine. When I was there the long *chai* was far from full; there are, however, plans for gradually maturing more of the wine in the cask. The wine that goes into casks stays there for only about three months. Fining is done with powdered albumen and the wine is lightly filtered before bottling. The 1978 tasted not unpleasant but lacked breed and finesse. My impressions of subsequent vintages force me to the conclusion that du Glana is simply not one of the more gifted St-Juliens.

Centre left:
An unusual spectacle for the Médoc: a group of Spanish dancers performing in front of Larose-Trintaudon in honour of a group of Dutch wine merchants who import both Larose-Trintaudon and Rioja Marqués de Cáceres — also a Forner wine.

Far left:
Co-owner and director Elisée Forner. Two-thirds of his cuves are stainless steel, the rest concrete. The wine is clarified with powdered albumen and filtered.

Below:
Larose-Trintaudon with — naturally — roses in the garden.

Château Larose-Trintaudon

Cru Grand Bourgeois
Saint-Laurent

For years the present owners of Larose-Trintaudon, the brothers Elisée and Henrique Forner, dealt in bulk wine. Their business was established in Avignon and shipped some 9.4 million cases of wine a year. In 1965, reacting against this hectic, purely commercial existence, the brothers bought the *grand cru* Château de Camensac and one year later, after selling up their business, the *cru bourgeois* Château Larose-Trintaudon. With this latter purchase they were plunging into an uncertain adventure. The Larose-Trintaudon vineyard had not been planted for 35 years. One of the previous owners, a man named Witrus, had married a rich Texan lady. In order to keep her happy in the Médoc he had all the vines uprooted — to make way for cattle raising on a Texan scale. Everything was thought of: enormous cowsheds, automatic feeding, everything except the fact that in the Médoc summers the grass hardly grows at all! The experiment failed completely. The vines did not return to Larose-Trintaudon until 1966.

Biggest in the Médoc

With expert help the brothers began to replant on a large scale. They brought no less than 390 acres under cultivation, making Larose-Trintaudon the biggest vineyard in the whole Médoc. With their own work-force they built a *cuvier* and *chais*; and the château, which had been letting in rain for years, together with its rose garden, were completely restored. Today this extensive property is excellently equipped, with concrete and stainless-steel *cuves*, with cellars that can hold 2,600 casks, with a bottling area with perfect temperature conditions, and *égrappoirs* — machines that harvest practically all the Cabernet Sauvignon grapes. This variety accounts for 60% of the vineyard area, with 20% Cabernet Franc and 20% Merlot. Before bottling, the 425 to 765 *tonneaux* of wine matures for 15 to 21 months in casks of which about one-third are new each vintage.

Supple from the start

In spite of the astonishing scale of production, Larose-Trintaudon is a very commendable wine, and one that seems likely to improve in quality over the years, gradually approaching the level of the brothers' *grand cru* Château de Camensac, which is also in Saint-Laurent. The wine usually has a quite deep colour, a pleasant albeit not very pronounced bouquet, and a supple taste, firm and elegant, often with an impression of fruit, right from the start. The aftertaste is dominated by mild tannin. Larose-Trintaudon is a harmonious wine that thoroughly deserves the *grand* of its *bourgeois* status. I generally find it at its best after three to five years. The 1970, 1975, 1976, 1978, 1979, 1981 and 1982 were very good; and the 1971, 1972 (relatively weak), 1973, 1974, 1977 and 1980 averagely good.

Below:
The winery of Caronne-Sainte-Gemme, which produces 85 to 230 tonneaux *per year. Lesser-quality wines are marketed under the name Château de Labat; the* grand vin *is apparently also sold as Château la Grave Genestrae, Château les Sableaux or Château les Graves Cul-de-Bock.*

Far right:
The low château, surrounded by its vineyard. The owners live there only during the grape harvest.

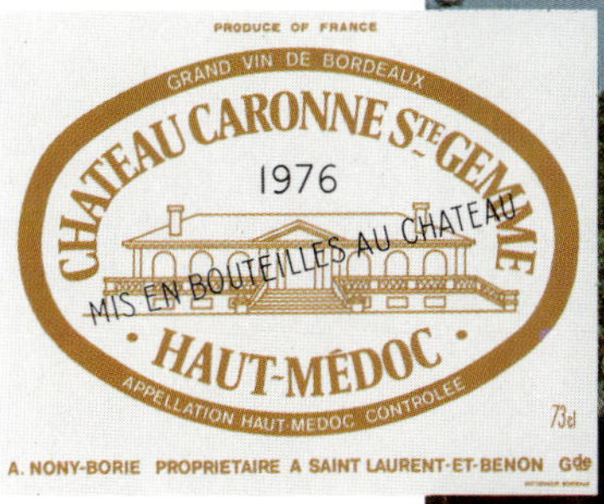

Château Caronne-Sainte-Gemme

Cru Grand Bourgeois Exceptionnel
Saint-Laurent

Caronne-Sainte-Gemme in Saint-Laurent was once part of the same estate as Château Lanessan in Cussac; it lies on the boundary of the two communes. It is approached along small, winding roads. I got thoroughly lost on my way to my first appointment at the château and arrived nearly three-quarters of an hour late. Fortunately my welcome was still cordial. The château can hardly be seen from the road, the low, white building being almost hidden by tall-growing vines. The cellars are at the opposite end of the vineyard, a somewhat disorganized group of old and not-so-old buildings around a balding patch of grass.

Old-fashioned fining

The present owner is Mme Emilie Nony-Borie, whose family has had Caronne-Sainte-Gemme since 1900. Her son Jean Nony runs the estate, which covers 370 acres, 106 of them planted with vines. The vineyard is an elongated piece of land divided by a railway line. The grape varieties are Cabernet Sauvignon (67%), Merlot (30%) and just 3% Petit Verdot. The soil is gravelly and slightly sandy. The estate has a quartet of stainless-steel *cuves* and 14 concrete ones for fermenting the wine. The wine is matured for 15 months in casks (20% new), in two long cellars, the older of which accommodates 42 casks and is blackened by vaporized alcohol. The wine is still clarified in the old-fashioned way here, cask by cask, each requiring the beaten whites of six fresh eggs.

Good, but not exceptional

In company with the *chef de culture* Robert Dalbies and the *maître de chai* Robert Creuzon, I examined a few Caronne-Saint-Gemme vintages. At first I thought that the 1976 had a hint of oxidization, but fortunately this disappeared. It was a lively, agreeable wine that seemed almost creamily mild and charming, despite the still present tannin. The 1978, drawn from the cask, offered more colour and breeding. The taste seemed to lack a little fullness and substance, and to have a tinge of green that I have not detected in other 1978 wines; but maybe I caught it at a not very flattering moment. It did not, however, lack alcohol: I would put it at 13°. If the 1978 was austere, the 1977 was more so; it was made from 90% Cabernet Sauvignon because the frost had almost completely eliminated the Merlot and Petit Verdot. With patience, however, the 1977 will become quite a pleasant wine. The 1975 was a successful vintage here but the 1971 — not very inspiring in taste and bouquet, and somewhat acidic — was less so. These and more recent vintages show that the wine of Caronne-Sainte-Gemme certainly has its merits and is of good quality, but I would not call it an exceptional *cru grand bourgeois*.

The vineyard of La Couronne used to be planted exclusively with Cabernet: two-thirds Cabernet Franc and one-third Cabernet Sauvignon. Now, however, 30% of the vines are Merlot.

Almost all of La Couronne's wine is shipped to Great Britain via Gilbey (established at Château Loudenne; see pages 82 and 83).

Château La Couronne is not a member of the crus bourgeois *syndicate.*

Bottom:
From the outside the château resembles a house, but consists, in fact, exclusively of cellars.

Below centre:
Bottles from the 1970 vintage: a delicious wine.

Far right:
The cuvier. *La Couronne also vinifies the wine of Château Haut-Batailley, a* grand cru *whose vineyard is immediately adjacent.*

Right:
Jean-Eugène Borie.

Château la Couronne

Pauillac

It may seem strange that my visit to La Couronne in Pauillac began with a lunch in Saint-Julien, but the explanation is simple. Since 1952 Jean-Eugène Borie, of the celebrated Saint-Julien *grand cru* Ducru-Beaucaillou, has managed La Couronne for his sister Mme des Brest-Borie. We lunched in Saint-Julien because La Couronne comprises only a *cuvier* and a *chai*: there is no château. Moreover, Jean-Eugène and I have known each other for years. He told me how La Couronne was founded in 1874 by Armand Lalande, the grandfather of Daniel Lawton (a well-known personality in Bordeaux). Lalande named his property Domaine de la Couronne. Obviously it did not appear in the 1855 classification; however, its wine was so good that in 1932 the estate was awarded the *cru exceptionnel* title — the only unclassified Pauillac to receive it. Coincidentally or not, that was the year La Couronne became the property of the Borie family.

Fruit, fruit, fruit!

I tasted and drank various La Couronne vintages at Ducru-Beaucaillou. The 1978 had a beautiful purple colour and was without the harshness that characterizes many young Pauillacs. My note on its bouquet read 'Fruit, fruit, fruit!': indeed, this wine was fairly bursting with fruitiness. The 1976 also lacked the usual severity and it, too, had a lot of fruit, although in a less pronounced form; the taste was supple, mild and altogether fine. La Couronne is not a typical Pauillac wine, for it is made by someone accustomed to producing a great, and always more supple, Saint-Julien. During lunch I made the acquaintance of two other La Couronne vintages. The sublime, still rather youthful 1970 started the meal, accompanying the *terrine maison* of chicken and chicken livers. The 1934, still amazingly vital, was served with the cheese.

Modest production

Although I had already visited La Couronne, Borie wanted to show me round and we drove there after the meal. The grapes — 70% Cabernet Sauvignon and 30% Merlot — are fermented in enamelled steel tanks. The wine is then matured for 16 months in used wooden casks. Fining is done with fresh egg white and there is no filtering. Borie has experimented with filters — 'but even with the lightest treatment I can always still taste something of the filter.' The quality of La Couronne makes you long for an abundant production. Unfortunately the vineyard measures only 10 acres and the yield is at most 20 *tonneaux*.
Wine from the *grand cru* Château Haut-Batailley is also vinified at La Couronne, under Borie's supervision.

The label of La Fleur Milon was designed by the Cordier firm.

André Gimenez lives in the hamlet of Mousset, just north of Le Pouyalet.

Bottom:
André Gimenez, owner of La Fleur Milon since 1955. In the background can be seen part of the arches that Gimenez had constructed in his cellars. The architect planned them as transverse arches, but Gimenez thought otherwise.

Far right:
Château La Fleur Milon is not of an impressive appearance.

Château la Fleur Milon

Cru Grand Bourgeois
Pauillac

Just north of Pauillac is the hamlet of Le Pouyalet. It has two châteaux of significance: the famous Mouton-Rothschild and the *cru grand bourgeois* La Fleur Milon. The latter is not particularly impressive. The château consists of a long, low cellar with no adjacent building. Since 1955 the owner has been the not very communicative André Gimenez. If I understood him correctly, he worked as a bricklayer for the French railways before buying the château. His parents, however, were already involved in the wine trade. Gimenez acquired the taste for wine, literally and figuratively, from a neighbour who was cellarmaster at Lafite-Rothschild and who often took him to his cellars. He is now so involved in and attached to wine that he declares, 'Le vin, c'est un amour.'

Famous neighbours

The vineyard of La Fleur Milon totals 32 acres, divided among various plots and adjoining some of the best *vignobles* in Pauillac: Lafite-Rothschild, Mouton-Rothschild, Duhart-Milon-Rothschild and Pontet-Canet. Grape varieties comprise an estimated 45% Cabernet Sauvignon, 20% Cabernet Franc and 35% Merlot. In normally good years production amounts to 45 to 60 *tonneaux*. Concrete vats are used for fermentation and the wine is matured for 18 months or so in oak casks. New casks are rarely bought. Gimenez told me that his wine is still clarified cask by cask with fresh whites of egg; the week before my visit he had bought 75 dozen eggs. He was rather vague about filtering. He had bought a filter, but it would be used little or not at all. Not only is the wine of La Fleur Milon clarified cask by cask, but this is also the mode for bottling.

Reasonably good

The few wines from La Fleur Milon that I sampled had no pronounced personality in bouquet or taste. The finishing touch seemed to be lacking in many respects: just not quite enough fruit, nuances, body, class. For me they were no more than reasonably good. It is significant that at the blind tasting — by three objective experts — for the Pauillac *appellation* the Fleur Milon 1978 scored poorly with two borderline passes (*passable*) and one average (*moyen*). A lot of La Fleur Milon is sold directly to private individuals in France. Apparently it is also marketed as Château Chantecler-Milon.

Left:
Flowerbeds in front of Fonbadet, where present owner Pierre Peyronie's great-grandfather planted the first vineyards. Mme Peyronie's own grandfather was once a director of Château Mouton-Rothschild, so the links with wine and Pauillac are both close and strong.

Below:
A Fonbadet cellar worker with three of the vintages. The wine is fined with fresh egg white — Peyronie tried other methods, but none was as good.

Right:
Although the château has a modern, horizontal Vaslin press the old traditional vertical presses are still mostly used.

Château Fonbadet

Pauillac

If you follow the château route through the Médoc from the south, you will come to a tunnel of greenery just before Pauillac. Tall, spreading trees shelter the roadway from even the fiercest summer sun. On the left here is Château Fonbadet, hidden in its park. The sound of the traffic on the road is muffled, allowing bird song to be heard. Fonbadet, a low, dazzling white 17th-century building is occupied by its owner, Pierre Peyronie. He is a quiet man who is engrossed in his wine and does not like outward show: 'I am here to make wine, not to sell it; everyone to his trade.' Fonbadet is therefore not equipped for receiving visitors. With M. Peyronie, the functional counts for much more than the visual.

A one-man operation

Pierre Peyronie attends personally to the fermentation of the grapes from his 37-acre vineyard, for his is his own *régisseur* and *maître de chai.* Some nights, when the wine is fermenting, he spends more time among the vats than in his bed. The fermentation is done in concrete vats, and there are tanks of metal and man-made materials for blending, fining and bottling. Oak casks are used for maturing the wine. About one-third of the casks are replaced each year. During or after maturing the wine is fined with fresh egg white, but not filtered. Production is usually between 50 and 85 *tonneaux.*

An astonishing vintage

The Fonbadet vineyard, scattered over the whole of the Pauillac commune, is planted with roughly 60% Cabernet Sauvignon, 19% Merlot, 15% Cabernet Franc, 4% Malbec and 2% Petit Verdot: all the important Bordeaux black grapes are there. They give an interesting, complete Pauillac, the 1978 vintage astounding everybody with its quality. At the official testing for the Pauillac *appellation*, the so-called *label,* Fonbadet ended up in the first three, with Lafite-Rothschild and Grand-Puy-Ducasse, both *grands crus.* I found it to be a compact, harmonious, fruity and deep-coloured wine: in fact, perfect. However, Fonbadet does not always produce wines of such a standard. My tasting notes for the 1976, apart from mentioning an almost opaque colour and concentrated fruit in bouquet and taste, refer to "a curious, slightly bitter aftertaste, and at the same time a little dry". The modest Peyronie does not belong to the syndicate of *cru bourgeois* growers, but his wine is the equal of most *crus grands bourgeois* and of some of the *exceptionnels.* Fonbadet has on occasion been selected (by a blind tasting) by the *Conseil Interprofessionnel du Vin de Bordeaux* to represent (anonymously) the appellation Pauillac at official functions.

Below:
Bernard Jugla behind the bar of the château's pleasant reception room. He himself devised the coat-of-arms (on bottle and case). Jugla lives at the château.

Far right:
A silver medal for the 1976 vintage awarded at the Paris agricultural show.

Right:
A handsome hearthplate with embossed wine motifs.

Château Colombier-Monpelou

Cru Grand Bourgeois
Pauillac

Colombier-Monpelou was classified as a *cru bourgeois supérieur* in 1932 and won a gold medal at Paris in 1933, but thereafter the fame and reputation of this estate declined sharply. In 1934 the owner sold the vineyard to his manager but kept the château and cellars for himself. These were in Pauillac and now serve as the headquarters of La Baronnie, Baron Philippe de Rothschild's marketing organization. The result of this separation of château and vineyard was that the grapes were processed by the Pauillac cooperative (La Rose Pauillac). Colombier-Monpelou remained a cooperative wine until 1970. The wine was, in fact, vinified separately, but the quality was not particularly good. On 1 July 1970 the estate acquired a new owner — Bernard Jugla, director and joint owner of the *grand cru* Pédesclaux — and the cooperative lost its biggest supplier. As Colombier-Monpelou had no cellars, the first year's wine was made at Pédesclaux.

New bulidings

In the middle of the 40-acre vineyard, which borders on Pontet-Canet and Pédesclaux land, stands the simple dwelling that now serves as the château. Jugla added a *cuvier*, and a cellar above and below ground. At Colombier-Monpelou, nine metal tanks are used for fermentation, and oak casks for maturing the wine. The wine remains for at least 22 months in these casks, 40% of which are replaced each year. The 30 to 75 *tonneaux* produced annually is fined with powdered albumen and not filtered.

A true, but not a great Pauillac

As far as is financially possible, Bernard Jugla works just as painstakingly here as at Château Pédesclaux. This applies to the cultivation of the vineyard as well as to the nurture of the wine. Thus the vines — 68% Cabernet Sauvignon, 18% Merlot, 6% Cabernet Franc and 5% Petit Verdot — are not treated with chemical insecticides, and no artificial fertilizers or weedkillers are used. The result is a true Pauillac: a dark-coloured, pure wine with the fruit and breeding of the Cabernet, the tannin from the oak, the discreet suppleness of the Merlot and an excellent balance. It is not a truly great wine — it has insufficient finesse, and the taste could be fuller — but it is made in a craftsmanlike way and generally offers good value for money. Part of the crop — the less successful wine — is sold under the second label, Château Grand Canyon.

Left centre:
A high-wheeled tractor bringing in the freshly picked grapes. Liversan's vineyards are 60% Cabernet Sauvignon, 20% Merlot, 10% Cabernet Franc and 10% Petit Verdot.

Far left:
Madame Peyronette, the maître de chai.

Below:
The château has antique metal wedding plaques from Germany on its façade. The tree in the foreground harbours a nest of bees.

Château Liversan

Cru Grand Bourgeois
Saint-Sauveur

With Château Liversan we come to the commune of Saint-Sauveur, a wooded district west of Pauillac. The original château remains only as an overgrown, inaccessible ruin. The building that now serves Liversan in this function is Château Fonpiqueyre; the wine from the 119-acre vineyard is sold both as Liversan and as Fonpiqueyre. Asche von Campe, a German, owns the estate, having bought it in 1971 from Mme Labeunie, a widow whose son André still works here as *régisseur.* Von Campe, an agricultural engineer, knew nothing about wine, but soon put this right by attending a course under Professor Peynaud. He takes enormous pride in the fact that Liversan has carried off gold, silver and bronze medals at various competitions since his arrival. The family lives in the 18th-century château. This is meticulously maintained — but the same cannot be said of the 7½-acre park with its planes, chestnuts, cedars, oaks and pines.

One-third matured in the cask

Liversan produces between 65 and 140 *tonneaux* of 'premier wine' and a varying amount of 'second wine' from lesser *cuves* and younger vines. The latter is marketed as Château des Moulinets or Château des Hormes. Lined concrete vats are used for fermenting the wine. About one-third of the Liversan vintages spends some months in casks and is then exchanged with the wine in the vats. In this way all the wine comes into contact with wood for about eight months of its two-year maturation period. Roughly a third of the limited number of casks are replaced each year. Until the 1976 vintage some of the wine was sold in the cask; only from 1977 was all bottling done on the estate.

A bland wine

Asche von Campe fines his wine with powdered albumen and filters it twice — after the malolactic fermentation and before bottling. After these treatments — and maturation of course — Liversan presents itself as a wine of very decent but not very exciting quality. Perfume and taste are correct, and far from unpleasant. The wine also gained an impressive number of medals and other awards. Personally, I find this wine lacking some depth, concentration and finesse. Château Liversan is not an Haut-Médoc that one selects for its enthralling personality, but that nevertheless forms a very pleasant table companion.

Left:
The château with its cellars at left. One of the château's rooms has a striking ceiling featuring musical instrument motifs, specially made for a concert attended by Queen Victoria.

Below left:
Besides the normal Peyrabon label shown here, the château has a black label for Germany and Switzerland. The same wine is also sold as Château Lapiey and Château Pierbone.

Below right:
Owner Jacques Babeau who spends half of every year at the château.

Château Peyrabon

Cru Grand Bourgeois
Saint-Sauveur

Although Peyrabon is a wine estate that has existed for a long time, and Queen Victoria once attended a concert here, it is relatively unknown. This is due to the fact that for more than a century two successive owners — Armand Roux and the Marquis de Courcelles — sold their wine exclusively to a small circle of friends and relations. Not a drop of Peyrabon was sold through the trade, not a drop was exported through the usual channels. This changed in 1958 when René Babeau bought the estate. He enlarged and restructured the vineyard and extended the hitherto restricted clientele, exporting to Germany, Switzerland, Belgium and the Netherlands and elsewhere. Since René's death in 1976 his son, Jacques Babeau, has continued this work energetically. In 1978, 49 acres of land was acquired from neighbouring Liversan — good wine-growing soil that had not been planted for 15 years. The vineyard now covers 131 acres which in a good year produce more than 200 *tonneaux.*

Making the wine

Peyrabon's wine is based on 50% Cabernet Sauvignon, 23% Cabernet Franc and 27% Merlot. During and after fermentation (in concrete vats) care is taken to ensure that the wine draws plenty of colour and tannin by remaining in contact with the grape skins. The vinification process, like the work in the vineyard, is supervised by the very capable Guy Delestrac, the *regisseur.* The wine matures for about 18 months in oak casks: a fourth of these are new each year. Fining is done with albumen and a light filtering takes place before bottling.

A striking taste

Despite the fact that Peyrabon wine is made from 73% Cabernet grapes, it is not one of those stern, hard examples of the type. Even in its youth the tannin in this wine seems to have a certain mildness. The taste is supple and quite elegant. A striking characteristic, present in various vintages I tasted, was a slight hint of *terroir* and a metallic tinge, especially in the aftertaste. It did not disturb me. There is no need to lay down Peyrabon wines for decades before they can be drunk. Of recent vintages only 1977 can be regarded as a maverick: weather conditions eliminated both the Cabernet Franc and the Merlot grapes, so that the wine was made from Cabernet Sauvignon alone.

Left:
You don't often find a Médoc château still labelling a 1967 vintage a dozen years later. But Fontesteau has many old fine vintages in store; the wine is sold directly by the owner René Léglise, not through négociants.

Below left:
The small château with its 13th-century crenellated tower. There were once two more towers on the back, but upkeep proved expensive and so they were 'shortened' some 40 years ago.

Below right:
Wooden cases are occasionally used to ship the wine, but cartons are more usual.

Right:
René Léglise in his soberly appointed château. He spends half the year here, the other half in his apartment in Bordeaux. Léglise has another small property in Saint-Sauveur, just 7 acres called Domaine d'Esteau.

Château Fontesteau

Cru Grand Bourgeois
Saint-Sauveur

Directions from the local people are essential for anyone who wants to visit Château Fontesteau. It took me quite some time to discover that the château can only be reached by taking a gravel road that starts behind the church at Saint-Sauveur, and leads you through some woods. This dusty road brings you directly to Fontesteau's only complete remaining tower, which dates from 1277 and stands against the front of the house. On the 220-acre estate, with its vineyard area of nearly 30 acres, there are some old wells. Fontesteau derives its name from these *fontaines d'eau*.

Traditional care

In 1939 Château Fontesteau was bought by René Léglise. I would like to think that this quiet, sympathetic man will still be the owner when this book goes to press, though it would not be surprising if someone of his age felt in need of a rest after more than 40 years' hard work. After picking, the grapes — 30% Cabernet-Sauvignon, 30% Cabernet Franc and 40% Merlot — are taken to the *cuvier* where they ferment in concrete vats. Maturing lasts 18 to 24 months and is done in casks. At Fontesteau new casks are only bought very occasionally. The wine is treated in a wholly traditional way during maturation and so fresh white of egg is used for fining, and there is no filtering.

Light in colour and constitution

The way in which Fontesteau makes its wine led me to expect a deep-coloured, classic Médoc rich in tannin, and consequently I was surprised when I came to taste it. Even the wine from the good year of 1975 did not have a really deep colour, and after four years there was already a degree of mildness. The 1976 was noticeably light. Obviously there was tannin present in both wines, but not a large amount. I also noted that the 1975 had a mild bouquet with some fruit, little depth, and an already quite developed, unproblematic taste without much finesse or strength (although it was slightly firmer than the light, vital 1976). The 1978 had, in the cask, distinctly more colour and more body, but I think it possible that when it has been matured it will prove to be a wine of the 1975 type. Other good vintages are 1981 and 1982. During my visit there were large stocks of bottles from the 1950s and 1960s at Fontesteau.

Left:
Inside the highly traditional cuverie *with its wooden fermenting vats. On the right is the* fouloir-égrappir *that both de-stalks and crushes the incoming fruit, which is then pumped to the vats while the stalks pile up on the floor.*

Bottom inset:
Pascal Vialard, the son of Louis; there are two daughters, Hélène and Danielle, who have their own château, La Tour du Mirail.

Below left:
The still cloudy wine is measured for alcohol.

Right:
Château Cissac with the spire of Cissac church in the background.

Cissac's second wine is called Domaine de Martigny.

Château Cissac

Cru Grand Bourgeois Exceptionnel
Cissac

As its name indicates, this château lies in the commune of Cissac, which is northwest of Pauillac. The château premises start with the cellars, immediately behind the little church at Cissac, and continue with the low, 1769 dwelling itself. Since 1940 Château Cissac has been the residence of Louis Vialard, and before that of his parents, who bought the estate in 1885. The Vialard family has worked in wine-growing for about three centuries. Ancestors of Louis were *régisseurs* at both Lafite and Latour. Louis himself makes his wine by traditional methods. His father taught him that good wine can only be made from old vines, a view that Louis has upheld: the average age of his vines is between 25 and 30 years. Château Cissac also has a *cuvier* with the classic wooden fermentation vats, which are becoming increasingly rare in the Médoc. It goes without saying that the wine is matured in oak casks.

Annual renewal

That Louis Vialard really spares no effort to make a quality wine is also indicated by the fact that at least three-quarters of the casks are replaced for each vintage — a major investment that few *crus bourgeois* are able or willing to countenance. The wine is matured for a long period: 28 to 30 months. It is, of course, fined with the beaten whites of fresh eggs and, naturally, never filtered. Bottling is scrupulously done under Louis Vialard's personal direction. Cissac's production varies from 50 to 75 *tonneaux.*

Noble taste

The soil of the 49-acre vineyard is a mixture of clay, sand and gravel. Its vines are 75% Cabernet Sauvignon, 20% Merlot and 5% Petit Verdot. The soil, the grapes, the mild Médoc climate and the craftsmanship of Vialard together produce one of the best of all *crus bourgeois*: a wine that fully deserves the designation *exceptionnel.* In good years like 1975, 1976 and 1978 Cissac is usually distinguished by a deep, glowing, vital colour, a scent in which — at least in the young wine — wood and fruit strive for precedence, and by a noble taste with nuances, elegance, tannin and suppleness, and great purity. In my opinion Cissac is an exceptionally beautiful wine, full of character, and because of its tannin it can be matured over a long period yet reveals its charm quite early. It does not possess the stern, aggressive qualities that characterize many young Pauillac and Saint-Estèphe wines. I recommend the following years without reservation: 1966, 1970, 1971, 1975 (of this one, cellarmaster Pierre Bappel exclaimed, 'Celui-là, c'est un seigneur!', and he was right), 1976, 1978, 1981 and 1982.

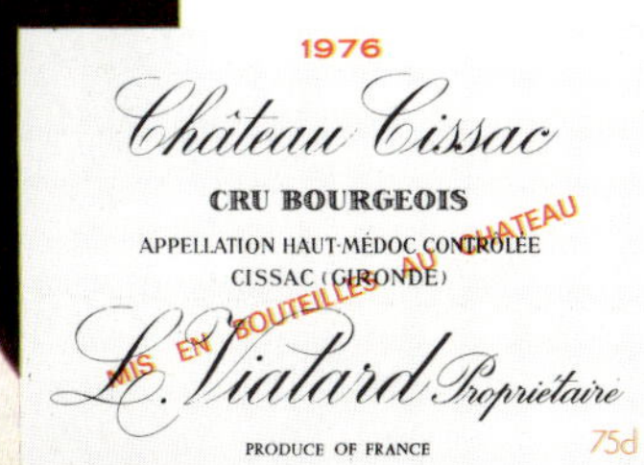

Left:
Eric Fabre, son of the owner Gabriel Fabre, in the cuvier that houses the modern, stainless-steel fermenting tanks, polished on the inside only.

Below left:
Besides its normal label, Lamothe-Cissac also has a dark purple one with golden lettering specially for the German market.

Below right: The château, dating from 1912, with its pointed towers.

All the Lamothe-Cissac wines are sold direct by the château in deals which sometimes involve Louis Vialard of Château Cissac. Louis's daughter Hélène is married to Lamothe-Cissac's owner, Gabriel Fabre. Louis Vialard has his own sales organization called French Wine Farmers with offices in London and Washington.

Lamothe-Cissac's second wine is called Château Fonsèche.

The Lamothe-Cissac property comprises some 225 acres altogether, of which 74 is vineyard. The rest is devoted to cattle-breeding and other activities.

Gabriel's son Eric has two properties of his own, Château Landat and Château Labastide, each 17 acres. Both wines are vinified at Lamothe-Cissac.

Château Lamothe-Cissac

Cru Grand Bourgeois
Cissac

Just outside the village of Cissac is a substantial, rather flamboyant *belle époque* château. This is Lamothe-Cissac, built in 1912 to replace a much simpler, lodge-like edifice. The new château did not prevent the subsequent decline of the wine and the vineyard. The depths were plumbed in 1964, when there were no vines left in cultivation. However, better days lay ahead, for in that same year the estate was acquired by the Fabre family. The Fabres quickly replanted the vineyard and there are now 86 acres in production. In 1975 they changed the name of the château to Lamothe-Cissac. Until then it had simply been called Lamothe: but since 17 other Bordeaux châteaux had this element in their names (three of them in the Médoc), customers often mistook the Fabres' wine for that of others.

Unusual fermentation tanks

The restoration of the vineyard entailed building a new *cuvier* and new cellars. Since 1968 Lamothe-Cissac has had stainless-steel tanks for fermentation — but, unusually, these are polished only on the inside, so cutting the price in half. After fermentation the wine matures for 18 months in casks. These lie in a large, tall *chai* built in 1978; a fifth of them are new for each vintage. After its year in the casks the wine spends a further six months in underground concrete tanks. It is fined with albumen and filtered before bottling. In recent years Lamothe-Cissac production has varied between 140 and 180 *tonneaux*.

More variety

The Fabres were thinking of introducing more variety in their grapes by adding some Petit Verdot to the Cabernet Sauvignon and Merlot. This they have realized: the vineyard is now planted with 65% Cabernet Sauvignon, 30% Merlot and 5% Petit Verdot. Because of this and other improvements the wine — which used to be pleasant and respectable but rather uninteresting — seems to have won in quality. It had gained some depth and finesse (although it still stays a long way behind Château Cissac). A good introduction to the improved Lamothe-Cissac form the vintages of 1979, 1981 and 1982.

Below:
The new château, completed in 1976. Wine was already being made here in the 12th century. The property used to be known as Château d'Hanteillan.

Right:
A part of the vineyards, where Hanteillan's second wine is also grown.

Hanteillan wines are fined with egg-white and slightly filtered.

The 130-foot long cellar can hold up to 500 casks; ornamentation is provided by Greek amphoras.

Château Hanteillan

Cru Grand Bourgeois
Cissac

Since 1972 this château has undergone a complete metamorphosis. The old, ruined château was demolished and replaced by a new building. The overgrown park was transformed into a garden with a broad lawn, masses of flowers, an ornamental lake and stream. The winery buildings were either renovated or replaced. The 25-acre vineyard, which had a few plots of white grapes, was extended to 173 acres. The capital for these drastic changes came from the owners who bought the estate in 1972: some of them are affiliated with the Société d'Enterprises, the biggest French construction company. This of course explains why all the building and construction work was so perfectly carried out. Many other Médoc châteaux might take Hanteillan as an example. Pierre Brion, a former member of the board of directors of the company, is the *gérant* and also a shareholder in the enterprise. He occupies an appartment in the tastefully furnished new château.

A large proportion of Merlot

The soil at Hanteillan contains some clay and so a generous percentage (40%) of Merlot has been planted. The other varieties are 48% Cabernet Sauvignon, 8% Cabernet Franc and 4% Petit Verdot. Hanteillan's production is between 115 and 310 *tonneaux*, but this will be increased in the future, since not all the new plantings are productive yet. Stainless-steel tanks are used for fermentation at Hanteillan, and oak casks (at least one-fourth of them new) for maturing the wine. The wine is fined, usually with white of egg, and lightly filtered after 16 to 24 months in the cask.

Elegant, clean Médoc

Naturally the Hanteillan vines are still quite young and not to be compared with, say, the 25- to 30-year-old plants at Château Cissac. Nevertheless, the wine already has a good deal of class. The 1976, for example, had a clear, medium-deep colour, a fine, mildly elegant fruit bouquet, and a clean taste, the grace of which was supported by the tannin from the partly new casks. I thought it a splendid wine with a good balance between wood and fruit. The 1975 and 1977 grape harvests were very small, whereas 1978 brought a normal quantity and good quality. Hanteillan will be well worth following: as the years pass and the vine roots push down further into the soil, this elegant Médoc will undoubtedly gain in depth and class. The second wine is Château Larrivaux-Hanteillan. Only half of this wine is matured in oak.

Since 1978 Château le Meynieu's output has been boosted by the addition of 7 extra acres which came into production in 1977. The 1977 harvest was a partial failure due mainly to the night frosts, and yielded a mere 18 tonneaux. *The following year's harvest gave Jacques Pedro a record 46* tonneaux.

The château's wine is fined with powdered albumen.

Below:
Château le Meynieu, built in 1858.

Bottom:
Bottling in progress.

Far right:
Jacques Pedro, wine grower and, since 1971, mayor of Vertheuil. He has two further estates in Saint-Estèphe, Château Lavillotte and Domaine de la Ronceray, together totalling some 30 acres.

Château le Meynieu

Cru Grand Bourgeois
Vertheuil

The little village of Vertheuil lies north of Cissac and west of Saint-Estèphe. Its mayor is the bearded Jacques Pedro who, like most of the 800 inhabitants, earns his living from wine. Pedro is the owner of Château le Meynieu, which lies on the northeastern side of the village, surrounded by a small, neat park. The vineyard covers 36 acres and 75% of its vines are Cabernet Sauvignon, 25% Merlot. M. Pedro has some very decided opinions about making wine. He has little faith in oenologists, only allowing them to do the chemical analyis of his wine. Pedro also told me, 'I never filter my wine. The oenologists do not agree with me on this, but I don't do it all the same.'

A long maturing time

At Le Meynieu the wine ferments in cement vats. It is then transferred to the largely underground cellar that Pedro had built in 1972, maturing for about two and a half years in used oak casks. 'I put the accent more on *conservation* than on the vinification. The wine is in contact with the wood much longer than with the cement,' says Pedro. The care taken at Le Meynieu is also shown by the way the wine is bottled and labelled. Heavy bottles and long corks are used, just as with most *grands crus.* There are normally a great many bottles in the neat concrete cellar. When I was there about 200,000, from seven different vintages, were in stock. This is not because the wine is in any way difficult to sell but results from an intelligent stock policy.

Agreeable Cabernet character

Together with Jacques Pedro I examined six vintages, and then tasted various years again at home. All in all, my opinion of Le Meynieu is definitely favourable, even though I thought the oldest wine — the 1974 — the least of them, rather lacking in length and depth. The 1975, however, was excellent: dark in colour, a first-rate distinguished bouquet and taste, and lots of tannin. The 1976 was a little milder but also very good, the 1977 proved light and amiable, the 1978 well balanced and very concentrated, and the 1982 fleshy, juicy and almost black in colour. In all the vintages, bouquet and taste had a pleasing amount of fruit and an agreeable Cabernet character.

Left:
Château Reysson, alas now totally derelict, is seen in its former slendour on the wine labels.

Below:
The Reysson cellars. The vine stalks are dumped via a conveyor belt, shown on the left in the photograph.

Bottom:
Maitre de chai *Jean Signoret inside the vast cellar. He has been at the château since 1973. Pierre Gaborias has been director since 1978; general management is in the hands of Laurent Poitou whom we met at other châteaux including Tour du Haut-Moulin (page 40).*

The Reysson property covers 500 acres in all, of which 282 are devoted to the vine. The subsoil is chiefly limestone with the odd patch of clay.

Château Reysson

Cru Grand Bourgeois
Vertheuil

The Château Reyssan label shows an elegant residence looking out over a well-groomed park. The building, however, is actually in ruins and uninhabited. Nothing is left of the park and its flower-beds are overgrown by grass. The cellars, too, were in bad shape when, in 1972, Reysson was taken over by the Grands Vignobles de Bordeaux group (see also Rayne-Vigneau in the Sauternes, page 176). The new owners totally rebuilt the interiors, leaving only the thick, ancient outer walls. Reysson has been fitted with a battery of metal fermentation tanks, painted wine-red, a modern cellar, with insulated ceiling, for the casks, and another cellar for stacking the bottles on pallets. The whole complex now makes a very good impression. Since 1980 direction has been in the capable hands of Bernadette Villars.

Expansion plans

The vineyard too has been rehabilitated and extended. When I visited the château there were 114 productive acres. This was to be increased to 150 to 175 acres in the coming years, which will raise production — now between 90 and 220 *tonneaux* — by a considerable amount. At Reysson the wine is kept in the casks for about a year. These are mostly used, four-year-old casks from Chasse-Spleen. The estate was considering buying a number of new *barriques* each year. By way of experiment one new cask was bought for the 1978 vintage. In due time the wine from it will be compared with that from the used casks. From 1978 the wine was clarified cask by cask with fresh egg white. The wine is filtered twice, after lactic acid fermentation and before bottling.

A mediocre Médoc

The 1971 is the only vintage I have tasted from before 1972. It was a rather elusive wine with an odd bouquet and taste, quite thick and hardly characteristic of the Médoc. The 1976 had a soft-red, not very deep colour, a correct, mild and somewhat flat taste, and an aftertaste with some *terroir* and dusty tannin: a good, but by no means exciting wine. The 1977 came across as almost oxidized and to me it seemed extremely poor, if not bad. I am puzzled as to why such a wine should have been bottled under the château name. I tasted the 1978 from both an old cask and from the single new one. I preferred the latter, although both wines lacked depth, strength, refinement and character. Hopefully the quality will improve under the guidance of Madame Villars. This mediocre Médoc is made from about 40% Cabernet Sauvignon grapes, 40% Merlot and 10% Petit Verdot plus Malbec.

Below:
Bottles of Haut-Marbuzet set of against a mural in the château's reception room. The label bears the motto "Qualité est ma vérité" (quality is my truth).

Bottom right:
A tractor passing the cellars.

Right:
The building that houses the offices and reception rooms of Haut-Marbuzet is not the actual château, which is to the right, out of the picture, a bright white residence occupied by Henri Duboscq. The photo shows Château MacCarthy-Moula, bought by Henri Duboscq years ago and which gives its name to a wine from a totally separate vineyard.

The Duboscqs have a third wine, called Château Chambert-Marbuzet which, together with MacCarthy-Moula covers some 32 acres of rather clayey soil in the Saint-Estèphe appellation. *Unlike Haut-Marbuzet, the other two wines are not aged in new casks, and are sold primarily to private individuals.*

At Château Haut-Marbuzet the wine ferments in concrete vats.

The demand for Haut-Marbuzet is always so huge that, according to Hervé Duboscq, there is never enough of it — one reason why the wines are hardly ever shipped to the United States.

Château Haut-Marbuzet

Cru Grand Bourgeois Exceptionnel
Saint-Estèphe

Most of the wine estates in the hamlet of Marbuzet lead a quiet life. One exception is Château Haut-Marbuzet, where cars are almost always parked in the drive. The wine from this estate is in great demand and many private individuals come here to buy their bottles. Haut-Marbuzet is also to be found in many star-spangled French restaurants, and the château claims the London Savoy and the Cunard Line as customers. The phenomenal success of Haut-Marbuzet is of comparatively recent date, for the estate was only started in 1952, by Hervé Duboscq. Through shrewd purchases he managed to assemble a total of 77 acres of wine-growing land, which now produces between 140 and 185 *tonneaux* annually. Duboscq lives in the château, a gleaming white house of little visual appeal, receiving his many visitors in the adjacent building.

Only new casks

Henri, Hervé's son, is fully involved in the work of the estate. He believes that one of the secrets of the success of Haut-Marbuzet lies in the high percentage of Merlot: 50%, with 40% Cabernet Sauvignon and 10% Cabernet Franc. This gives the wine more 'fat' from the start and makes it more agreeable than other Saint-Estèphes. However, the wine must not become too soft and gentle. That is why, according to Henri Duboscq, only new casks are used for each vintage. The tannin from the oak compensates the mildness of the Merlot grape. The new casks at Haut-Marbuzet make an impressive sight, equalled only by a few *grands crus.* They cost the château more than one million francs a year. Consequently the price of Haut-Marbuzet is around the level of the *troisième grands crus classés.*

More tannin than fruit

This dark-coloured wine is made in a craftsmanlike way, with 18 months' maturing, fining with fresh white of egg, no filtering, and bottling from the cask. So widely is it esteemed and praised that I criticize it with some diffidence. My objection to Haut-Marbuzet is that the wood, i.e. the tannin, is too strong, overwhelming the fruit. Obviously this appeals greatly to many people, but in my opinion the wood so completely dominates the wine as to suppress its true nature. The taste is almost entirely of tannin. Personally, I prefer Haut-Marbuzet in its early youth, about two years after its vintage, when the fruity taste of the young wine is still just holding its own against the power of the tannin.

Below:
In the Mac-Carthy cellars not all the wine is matured in the cask — some is aged in the vat.

Far right:
The château is approached across a gravel courtyard.

Château la Rose Marbuzet is exactly the same wine as MacCarthy.

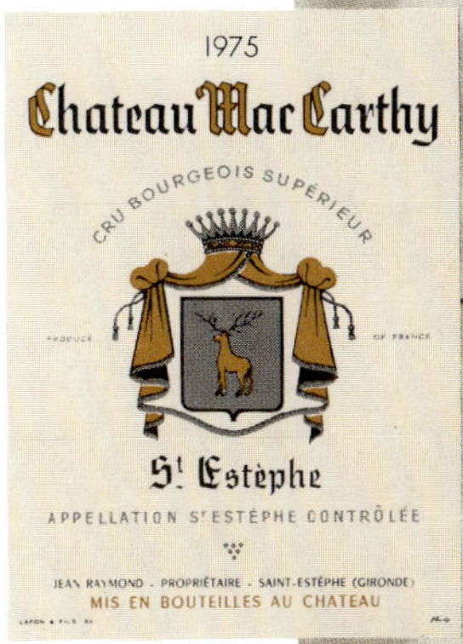

Château Mac-Carthy

Cru Grand Bourgeois
Saint-Estèphe

Château Mac-Carthy is one of the smallest properties in the hamlet of Marbuzet, yet once the whole of the district belonged to the owners of this little estate. These were the MacCarthys, who arrived from Ireland in the 18th century and became people of consequence in Bordeaux. One MacCarthy, a wine merchant, became director of the Bordeaux chamber of commerce in 1767; another attained high rank in the French navy. There is even a Rue Mac-Carthy in Bordeaux. In 1852 Château Mac-Carthy was sold to a *négociant*, Louis Raymond. His direct descendant, Jean Raymond, is the present owner. Raymond, in fact, had no great need of my visit: he does not produce a great deal of wine, and sells it without difficulty. The Mac-Carthy vineyard covers only 15 acres and normally yields 30 *tonneaux*. One exceptional years was 1977, when double this amount was harvested. However, the wine was so disappointing that Jean Raymond did not bottle it himself but sold it mainly as anonymous Saint-Estèphe.

Ancient cellar

The Mac-Carthy vineyard (two-thirds planted with Cabernet Sauvignon, one-third with Merlot) is divided into a number of separate plots, before, behind and at a distance from the château. Some of the plots border on those of *grands crus.* In fact, from the charming terrace at the rear of the château you can see Cos d'Estournel, Lafite-Rothschild and Mouton-Rothschild. At Château Mac-Carthy the wine ferments in concrete vats, and then goes into used wooden casks to mature for two years. The *chai*, with its earthen floor and wooden ceiling, could be two centuries old. Jean Raymond fines his wine with albumen ('C'est parfait') and lightly filters it just before bottling.

Mild but firm taste

I have had to limit my tasting to the 1976 and 1978 vintages. Three years after vintage the former had a reasonably deep but slightly immature colour and little bouquet. The taste seemed rather young, still with an acidic tinge, and rather thin for its year. The aftertaste was short. The 1978, tasted from the cask, made a much more positive impression. The eye encountered an almost opaque purple colour, the nose a compact, fruity bouquet, the tongue a taste characterized by a firm mildness and also fruit. If Jean Raymond succeeds in keeping and bottling these qualities, the 1978 will be a very creditable wine.

Left:
The great hall of the château is shown here. The residence is used to accommodate guests and to receive business associates of the Prats family.

Below:
The Château de Marbuzet is surrounded by a 6-acre park containing chestnut trees planted in 1904.

De Marbuzet's vineyards are planted with 56% Merlot and 44% Cabernet Sauvignon; those of Cos d'Estournel have 60% Cabernet Sauvignon, roughly 40% Merlot plus a very little Cabernet Franc.

The 1921 vintage — Merman's last — had that volatile acidity so typical of the wines of that time, but in 1979 was still surprisingly vital, and delicious with a mature Edam cheese.

Château de Marbuzet

Cru Grand Bourgeois Exceptionnel
Saint-Estèphe

There is a moral to the story of this château. At the beginning of this century M. Merman was a prosperous wine merchant, and Régina Badet a celebrated opera star. An open-air performance in Bordeaux of the opera *Bacchus Vivant* in which she sang attracted an audience of 15,000. Régina Badet became Merman's mistress and he decided to build a suitable residence for her at Marbuzet, near Saint-Estèphe, where he had a great deal of land. It had to be a real château in the Louis XVI style, similar to the Château de Rastignac (on which the White House in Washington was modelled). To raise the money, Merman sold his Château le Crock to the Cuvelier family in 1903, and building began in 1904. Château de Marbuzet was finally completed in 1914, but financial difficulties forced Merman to sell château and vineyard after only seven years. The lovely Régina had already departed. Clearly, maintaining a mistress and a Bordeaux estate can be a ruinous combination.

The Cos d'Estournel connection

At the end of 1921 Fernand Ginestet bought the Château de Marbuzet. His grandsons Jean-Marie, Yves and Bruno Prats are the present owners. Bruno, an agricultural engineer, runs the estate, as well as Cos d'Estournel, Petit-Village and the other Prats properties. The Château de Marbuzet vineyard is only 16 acres. Production ranges from 5 to 30 *tonneaux* but this is supplemented by the second wine froim Cos d'Estournel (*deuxième grand cru classé*): wine from young vines and therefore not of top quality. This brings the actual amount of wine sold as Château de Marbuzet to between 60 and 100 *tonneaux*. All the wine is vinified at Cos d'Estournel. It is fermented in lined metal tanks, matures for one year in casks that average out at four years old, is fined with fresh white of egg and is lightly filtered.

Fruit, suppleness, balance

I know Château de Marbuzet from quite a number of its vintages. What always strikes me about the wine is its clean taste and the distinct presence of fruit — often blackcurrant, indicating the use of much Cabernet Sauvignon. After about three years the wine already tastes very good. It does not contain excessive tannin, but just enough to mature well. After eight years the 1971, for example, still had something in reserve. De Marbuzet nearly always possesses excellent balance, and an agreeable suppleness. This is a pleasant wine, expertly made, that does not disappoint even in less successful years.

Below:
In 1855 the château was awarded a medal for the best-kept vineyard in the whole of the Gironde. Yet in spite of this and the fact that one of the members of the Merman family (the then owners) signed the necessary forms, the château was never classified. The steps afford a view overlooking the great park, with its palms and ornamental lake fed by a natural spring.

Far right:
Maître de chai Francis Dourthe *in his domain.*

Right:
Director Didier Cuvelier at the château's well-worn billiard table.

Château le Crock

Cru Grand Bourgeois Exceptionnel
Saint-Estèphe

If you take the little road from the *grands crus* of Cos d'Estournel and Cos Labory to the village of Saint-Estèphe, you cross a small railway line and then pass the 50-acre park of Château le Crock, forming a striking contrast to the all-pervading vines of Saint-Estèphe. The château was built around 1820 by the Merman family who had owned the land since 1788. In 1903 it was sold to the Cuvelier family (see page 62). The Cuveliers still run Le Crock but do not live there. They are based in Bordeaux, from where they also manage the *grand cru* Léoville-Poyferré in Pauillac.

Vaulted cellar

There is a dark, vaulted cellar with an earthen floor under Château le Crock where the wine spends its first year maturing, after fermenting in the white-painted concrete *cuves* used here. Beside the château there is another cellar for wine in its second year where the casks are stacked on top of one another in three tiers. About a fifth of these are new for each vintage. The wine is clarified with fresh white of egg and just before bottling, the young manager Didier Cuvelier, who has been here since 1979, filters his wine. Le Crock's annual production of about 150 *tonneaux* comes from a 77-acre vineyard. The vines there are roughly 65% Cabernet Sauvignon and 35% Merlot. Less successful wine, including that from young vines, is sold as Cru Saint-Estèphe la Croix.

Wines for laying down

At Château le Crock I became acquainted with several recent years, from the cask and from the bottle. The 1975 was distinguished by a very deep, still immature colour, an as yet unrevealed bouquet and an austere, harsh taste rich in tannin that needed much development. Clearly, it was a wine for the future. The taste started well and the aftertaste was good, but in between it was somewhat lacking in substance. I experienced exactly the same with the deep-coloured 1976, but this wine was already developed further and its bouquet was much finer. Nevertheless I felt then that it should not be drunk before 1981 or 1982. The astringent, rather aggressive 1977 had no charms for me. The 1978, however, was a very promising wine — not so concentrated in taste as many of its contemporaries but respectably strong, fruity and complete. Château le Crock is a soundly made wine that requires time; it does not slip elusively away in the mouth but, as it were, offers opposition. Good wines were also made in 1979, 1981 and 1982.

Below:
Château Morin, where visitors are definitely not welcome. Like Château Beau-Site (following page), Morin lies in the hamlet of Saint-Corbian which forms part of the Saint-Estèphe commune.

Far right:
The vineyard lies immediately behind the château, and the planting is most traditional, one vine plant per square metre.

Château Morin

Cru Grand Bourgeois
Saint-Estèphe

Morin is one of the least accessible châteaux in whole Médoc. Of some 150 properties I visited in the district, only Morin refused me entrance. A written request, an official introduction and verbal pleas were all to no avail. Maxime Sidaine, joint owner with his sister Marguérite, did not have the time to see me then, nor the following week, nor the following month — not ever. There was no point in staying. Since M. Sidaine would not answer a single question about Morin, I had to obtain my information from other sources; the wines I tasted were bought at the Maison du Vin in Saint-Estèphe. It is sad that the Sidaines should be so averse to any form of visit. Their family has owned this old wine estate (founded in 1738) since 1800, and its members have included some eminent wine growers. Among them was Dr Alibert, who enlarged the vineyard in the previous century and was much praised for his wine. One of his descendants was Paul Alibert, whose daughter married Jean Sidaine, the father of Maxime and Marguérite.

Elderly vines

The grey, inhospitable château appears only moderately well kept, but looks out over a trim park with flower-beds full of colour. Directly beyond the park is the 25-acre vineyard, two-thirds planted with Cabernet vines (mostly Sauvignon), one-third with Merlot. Most of the vines are old: their average age is between 25 and 30 years. It is undoubtedly these venerable plants that give the Morin wine many of its qualities. The *cuvier* and cellars at Château Morin are apparently not in top shape, and all the equipment is old-fashioned. Average annual production is 45 to 50 *tonneaux.*

Elegant for a Saint-Estèphe

I was able to get hold of three vintages to taste, the 1970, 1973 and 1976. In all cases it struck me that their corks were rather short, shorter than is usual with the better *crus bourgeois.* The three wines had some features in common: sombre colour, a reserved bouquet (that of the 1970 was by far the nicest), elegant taste, without a lot of tannin. In a blind tasting I would certainly place the 1976 and 1973 closer to Margaux (usually fine, gracious wines) than to Saint-Estèphe (harder and more robust). On a scale of ten I would give them seven: I rate this château's wine much higher than its hospitality.

Bottom right:
Inside the wholly classical cuvier.

Below right:
Maître de chai *Gérard Batisse has been at Château Beau-Site for around a quarter of a century.*

Far right:
The distinctive wrought-iron fencing of Beau-Site can be seen in the background at right. Beau-site should not be confused with Beau-Site-Haut-Vignoble, nor should its wine, which is a superior product, although the two properties lie immediately opposite each other. From Château Beau-Site there is a magnificent view over the vineyards of Saint-Estèphe, with the Gironde in the distance.

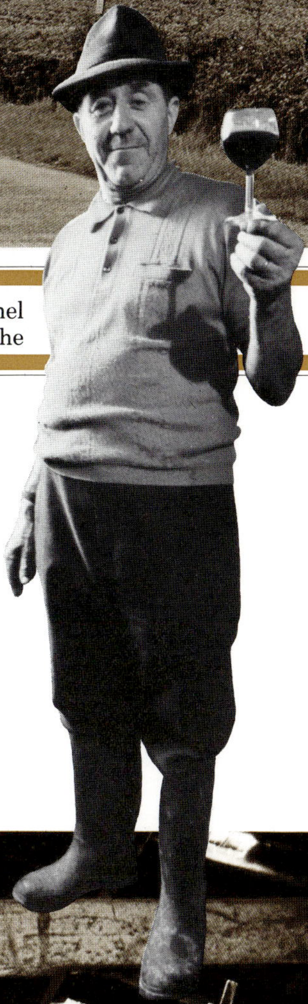

Château Beau-Site

Cru Grand Bourgeois Exceptionnel
Saint-Estèphe

In the hamlet of Saint-Corbian, west of the commune of Saint-Estèphe to which it belongs, you can recognize Beau-Site immediately from its long, imposing, wrought-iron gateway flanked by squat towers. It was intended as the entrance to a large château, which was never built. What now serves as the château is a low, ivy-covered house, home of the cellarmaster, Gérard Batisse. The only noteworthy feature is a dining room with Louis XIII furniture; business acquaintances of the wine firm of Borie-Manoux are entertained here from time to time. Since 1956 the estate has belonged to the Castéja-Borie family who control this firm as well as their wine estates. Besides Beau-Site these include Batailley, Lynch-Moussas and Haut-Bages-Monpelou in Pauillac, and Trottevieille in Saint-Emilion.

Difficult land

The vineyard of Beau-Site extends over 74 acres of clay and gravel that are difficult to work. it has about 65% Cabernet Sauvignon vines and 35% Merlot. After the harvest, the grape juice ferments in metal and wooden vats. It then matures for about 18 months in mostly used casks. A few concrete *cuves* serve for blending the wine, fining it (with albumen) and bottling. Just before the wine is bottled it goes through a filter. Production at Beau-Site seldom falls below 100 *tonneaux*, or rises above 180.

Stylish and supple

From frank conversations I learned that at Beau-Site they quite deliberately aim at a wine that is quickly drinkable. New casks are therefore hardly ever used, none of the often harsh pressed wine is added, and after fermentation the wine is in contact with the grape skins for a fairly short time. Remembering these points, I was not at all surprised that the vintages I tasted at the château were not notable for their depth, reserve, refinement or long aftertaste. However, they possessed a pleasant, quite stylish, agreeable suppleness. This accorded well with their limited tannin content and the fairly fleshy taste, so that the result was quite acceptable. I also remember the 1971 which, after eight years, had developed flawlessly into a wine that was not great but certainly delicious. Beau-Site is definitely one of the better *bourgeois* of Saint-Estèphe, but its *exceptionnel* status seems to me a little too flattering.

Below:
The château was constructed in 1850. It was here that Princess Paola of Belgium was received into the Commanderie du Bontemps du Médoc et des Graves. The property's founder, Phélan, was himself a prince, and became known as the 'prince des vignes'.

Bottom right:
Brand-new barriques ready for the new wine.

Below centre:
The amiable Guy Delon.

Right:
A group of pickers.

The Phélan-Ségur estate covers a total of 470 acres including much grazing and woodland.

Château Phèlan-Sègur

Cru Grand Bourgeois Exceptionnel
Saint-Estèphe

Phélan-Ségur came into being at the beginning of the 19th century when the progressive wine grower Phélan joined two estates together: Clos de Garramey and Ségur. Until the present century the property was known as Château Ségur-Garramey. For a long time it was owned by the Martells (the cognac family), but since 1 November 1924 it has belonged to the Delon family. Roger Delon and his son Guy hold sway at present. The Phélan-Ségur *vignoble* amounts to 128 acres and is distributed over three plots. The biggest, of 86 acres, is called Fonpetite and borders on the *grand cru* Montrose, of which it once formed part. Fonpetite is now the name of Phélan-Ségur's second wine. The two smaller plots lie next to the *grand cru* Calon-Ségur and the château itself. The latter plot is completely enclosed.

Never filtered

Phélan-Ségur's excellent location is complemented by equally exemplary wine making. The Delons leave nothing to chance and are extremely quality conscious. After picking and destalking, the grapes ferment in tanks of stainless steel or enamelled metal. The wine then matures for 12 months in the gigantic first-year *chai* with its 1,200 casks. At right angles to this cellar are the second-year *chais*. At Phélan-Ségur at least one in ten of the casks is replaced by a new one before each vintage. Only the beaten whites of fresh eggs are used here for fining — from five to seven per cask. Filters are not used at any stage. The château produces between 170 and 250 *tonneaux* a year.

Well-groomed wine

The basis of the wine is juice from Cabernet Sauvignon grapes (50%), Merlot (30%), Cabernet Franc (10%) and Petit Verdot (10%). To my mind the Merlot is always distinctly present; Phélan-Ségur does not have that hard, unapproachable quality typical of many Saint-Estéphes in their youth. It is notable for its excellent colour, its never excessive but always attractive bouquet and its taste, typical of a well-made wine, often with a hint of soft fruit (blackcurrant and cherry). Phélan-Ségur may not be one of those broad, full wines that take your nose and mouth by storm, but nevertheless it is not without strength and mettle. In its best years — 1961, 1970, 1975, 1976, 1978, 1979, 1981 — it is, in my opinion, an excellent wine; and in its merely good years — 1982 — it is still very worthwhile.

In the 1960s Château Meyney wine was also sold as Les Feuillants du Château Meyney. This label was found mainly in French shops, although a little was exported. Today this alternative name is no longer used.

Meyney has its own water tower. According to estate manager Roger Moreau the water from the tower tastes better than that from the Saint-Estèphe commune.

The oldest bottle at the château is a 1924 vintage.

Below: The low lines of Château Meyney; the main building is used exclusively for receptions. Meyney's vineyard area covers a total of 128 acres, and there are a further 52 acres of other land.

Far right: Grape pickers take a break.

Château Meyney

Cru Grand Bourgeois Exceptionnel
Saint-Estèphe

Meyney is regarded as one of the oldest of the Médoc's wine estates. Monks cultivated the first vines here, for what is now called Meyney was formerly a monastery, founded in 1662. It was known at first as the Couvent des Feuillants, later as the Prieuré des Couleys; the latter name appeared for years on the labels. It says much for the former and present owners of Château Meyney that they have left the original character of the buildings practically untouched. These form a square around a peaceful courtyard with a circular lawn and neatly raked gravel. The ivy-clad main building, which is not occupied, dates from 1662, the interconnected cellars opposite from 1666. In one of the wings you can see the tiny windows of the former cells. All the buildings are in excellent condition; the interiors, too, look immaculate. This is hardly surprising, for since 1921 Meyney has belonged to the Cordiers, a family with a well-deserved reputation for careful maintenance of their estates.

Large tuns and small casks

The grapes — 70% Cabernet Sauvignon, 24% Merlot, 4% Cabernet Franc, 2% Petit Verdot — ferment in stainless-steel or concrete *cuves*. The wine then matures for about 20 months. It spends the first year in huge wooden vessels holding about 1,100 gallons (1,320 US gallons) each. These are sealed with aseptic plugs and are very simlar to the type used at Château Gloria. For its second year the wine is transferred to traditional oak casks. At least one-quarter of these are replaced each year. Meyney's 190 to 342 *tonneaux* of wine is clarified only with fresh white of egg and is lightly filtered just before bottling.

Acid in the taste

Thanks to the world-wide efforts of the Cordier wine firm, the product of Meyney's 124-acre vineyard is very well known. I have drunk it or tasted it many times and can base my judgment on some ten different vintages. This opinion is not wholly favourable. Although Meyney usually has a deep colour, plenty of tannin and a firm constitution, it does not possess a very pronounced bouquet or character. Moreover, there is nearly always an element of acid present in the taste — sometimes slight, often distinct. A favourable exception to this rule is the long-flavoured, concentrated 1975, a superior Saint-Estèphe. Sometimes, however, the balance tips the other way. I found the 1974 (tasted blind) to be unpleasantly acidic and very disappointing. In this case the bouquet promised more than the taste could make good, as often happens with Meyney. In my view the following vintages are reasonable to good: 1960, 1962, 1966, 1970, 1971, 1973, 1976, 1977, 1978, 1979, 1980, 1981; while the 1982 will come close to the 1975 quality, if not surpass it.

Below:
A handsome Flemish tapestry adorns one of the salons of the château.

Far right:
The greyish bulk of Château Capbern Gasqueton looms just behind the Saint-Estèphe church.

Right:
Philippe Capbern Gasqueton with one of his staff. Philippe fines his wine with fresh egg white but does not usually filter it. He and his family also own the châteaux of Calon-Ségur, Du Tertre and d'Agassac (the last is described on page 17).

Château Capbern Gasqueton

Cru Grand Bourgeois Exceptionnel
Saint-Estèphe

The visitor has no problem finding this château, for it lies just behind the church in the village of Saint-Estèphe. It has been in the hands of the same family for some ten generations. The present owners are the resident Philippe Capbern Gasqueton and his two children. The grey, not very attractive château was built in 1896 on the foundations of a much smaller, lower structure. The interior made a rather melancholy impression on me: a lot of brown woodwork, dim light, autumn scenes on the walls, a black marble fireplace. The family not only make a living from their wine: they literally live right over it, for an old cellar, filled with casks and bottles runs under the house. Here the wine matures in casks for about two years. New casks are not used; most of them, however, have come from several *grand cru* and are thus well seasoned by wine.

Two plots

The vineyard consists of two plots at some distance from the château, one adjoining Calon-Ségur, the other next to Meyney. Altogether Capbern Gasqueton has 74 acres of wine land, and an area of meadow for raising cattle. Grape varieties are 40% Cabernet Sauvignon, 20% Cabernet Franc and 40% Merlot. The grapes ferment in lined steel tanks. Normal production is 90 *tonneaux*, but in 1975 the estate managed only 60 *tonneaux*. The years 1970, 1977 and 1978 also yielded much less wine than usual.

A classic Saint-Estèphe

The way in which Capbern Gasqueton wine is made results in a very classic Saint-Estèphe. It comes over as rather harsh and austere until quite a few years after its birth, and it certainly does not lack tannin. Capbern Gasqueton punishes the impatient consumer with a far from engaging taste: even wine of relatively light vintages has to be laid down for at least five years, and that from stronger years often needs ten. It is fortunate that the Merlot content is so high for otherwise the wine would remain inaccessible even longer. Too much finesse should not be expected from this Saint-Estèphe, but it fills the mouth well, definitely has character and is very soundly made. Exactly the same wine is sold, exclusively by the firm of Dourthe, under the name Le Grand Village Capbern.

Coutelin-Merville lies on the boundary between two communes, Saint-Estèphe and Cissac. The same little road that separates the two villages also marks the boundary between Coutelin-Merville and Hanteillan.

Surprisingly enough, the vineyard includes some white grapes from which the owner, Guy Estager, makes a sparkling wine under the G. Estager brand.

The château can only afford to use old casks for maturing the wine.

Below centre: Bottles of Coutelin-Merville were once transported in wooden cases, but nowadays they travel in cartons.

Below right: The grape varieties are 65% Cabernets, 30% Merlot and 5% Malbec plus Petit Verdot.

Right: Guy Estager, who is most ably assisted by his attractive wife. They live in the hamlet of Blanquet, half a mile east of the château.

Château Coutelin-Merville

Cru Grand Bourgeois
Saint-Estèphe

Coutelin-Merville is a typical example of the disastrous effect that dividing up an inheritance can have on wine estates. This estate came into existence in 1869 when the owner of Château Hanteillan (Cissac) bought land in Saint-Estèphe. This Coutelin-Merville land adjoined Hanteillan, but its grapes were vinified separately. In 1900 Hanteillan and Coutelin-Merville both went to the Estager family, remaining as a single unit until 1972 when the owner died. His three children could not agree about the division of their inheritance; two of them wanted to sell, the third did not. The result was that Hanteillan was sold that year, and Coutelin-Merville became the property of Guy Estager. He was immediately confronted with great problems. The transfer of the Hanteillan property, with all its winery buildings, took place on 15 April 1972, and since it would be impossible to construct a new *cuvier* and cellar in time for the coming vintage, where could the Coutelin-Merville grapes go? Fortunately, Hanteillan's new owner was generous enough to put fermentation tanks at Guy Estager's disposal, which gained him a few months.

Strenuous efforts

Problems were not at an end when Coutelin-Merville at last had its working buildings. Guy Estager's financial resources were strained to the limit and he could hardly afford any staff. When I visited him in 1979 he was having to drive the tractor himself, tend the 40 acres of vines with minimal help, and be his own cellarman. In addition the weather had repeatedly let him down: frost and hail hit the vineyard in 1975, 1977 and 1978, so that production fell far short of the normal 60 to 80 *tonneaux*. A direct result of these difficulties is that the château is still in need of quick cash returns and cannot allow all the wine to spend the customary two years maturing in the cask. A good deal of the vintage is sold in bulk to the trade early in the following year. The rest goes mainly to private individuals in northern France. Estager visits them all himself — yet another of his onerous tasks.

Quality could be better

Although Estager does his best to make as good a product as possible — fining with fresh egg white, and no filtering — he lacks the means, and probably the time, to achieve anything special in his wine. The 1976 and the 1978 were both somewhat flat, had an acidic tinge and seemed meagre. However, their colour was deep and their taste correct enough. I sincerely hope that Guy Estager will finally overcome his early difficulties both for his own sake and the quality of his wine. In a few years I plan to taste the Coutelin-Merville wine again, and hope to be able to revise my judgment.

Left:
Château de Pez. The property and its vineyard were bought in 1920 by Jean Bernard, uncle of the current owner Robert Dousson. In the early years, until 1932, Bernard's partner was a Dutch importer of Bordeaux wines, Jacobus Boelen.

Below left:
Robert Dousson dressed for the grape harvest.

Below centre:
Even in the poor 1972 season, Château de Pez managed to make a most respectable vintage. This was also the first year in which the Petit Verdot variety was not used.

The de Pez vineyard is one of the oldest in Saint-Estèphe, with that of the grand cru Calon-Ségur.

The second, and slightly inferior wine is called La Salle de Pez.

Blending from the various wooden fermenting vats is done when the wine has been there for six months. In other words, the vats also double as preliminary maturing casks. These wooden vats are no longer made in Bordeaux, and so Robert Dousson has them brought specially from the Cognac region.

The walls of the bottle cellar are at least five feet thick.

Château de Pez

Saint-Estèphe

Château de Pez lies in the hamlet of Pez, a small collection of houses not far from Saint-Estèphe. The origin of the estate has been traced back to 1452, but the vineyard dates from three centuries later. The first vines were planted in 1749 by the de Pontac family, at that time also owners of Château Margaux and Haut-Brion. After having a series of owners, the estate became the property of Robert Dousson in 1955. Since then its reputation has improved steadily. The vineyard consists of 57 acres of clay and lime with some gravel. The soil is naturally of such good quality that fertilizer is hardly ever needed. The vines are 70% Cabernet Sauvignon, 15% Merlot and 15% Cabernet Franc.

Wooden fermentation vats

After being picked, destalked and lightly crushed, the grapes ferment in their separate varieties and lots in the big *cuvier* with its traditional wooden vats. During fermentation Dousson keeps the temperature at 29°C or slightly lower. The wine remains in the vats for about six months. Only then is the wine from the different *cuves* blended into a homogeneous whole. Afterwards, it is transferred to oak casks for a period of at least 16 months. About 30% of the casks are new each year. The wine is clarified with whites of egg (six per cask at the end of the first year of maturing) and is never filtered.

Civilized and balanced

My many tasting notes go back to the 1945 vintage, which was of a very good colour, still vital in taste, with a firm constitution and a fairly dry aftertaste. However, because of their availability the more recent vintages are more interesting. After nine years the 1970 had developed surprisingly little: concentrated greatness in embryo. The 1971 was milder and more elegant, but also with promise for the future. The 1972 was very acceptable for its year; the 1973 stronger than many other wines of this supple, quickly drinkable vintage. For Château de Pez the 1974 was a fairly light wine; the 1975 on the other hand was dark, fruity, with a good deal of tannin — and already properly supple. The 1976 tasted agreeably vital and really full in the mouth. The 1977 was somewhat light but had its merits. There was more Merlot than usual in the 1978 (about 50%) so that alongside the breeding and the tannin from the Cabernet Sauvignon there seemed to be some extra roundness. The 1979 is a success, and the 1981 and 1982 promising. In general I regard Château de Pez as a civilized, balanced and never really harsh Saint-Estèphe of a high and reliable standard. Since 1968 all of the 80 to 160 *tonneaux* production has been sold exclusively by the firm of Gilbey.

Below:
A roaring fire of vine prunings and a final stir for the grape pickers' supper.

Far right:
The château dates from around 1790 and is partly occupied by a retired former employee. The name 'Ormes' means elms and these trees have stood on the estate for generations.

Centre right:
Jean-Michel Cazes, whose family have owned Les Ormes de Pez since 1928.

Les Ormes de Pez has no bottle cellar — the bottles are stored in Pauillac at Château Haut-Bages Avérous, a small estate (11 acres) bought by the family in 1974.

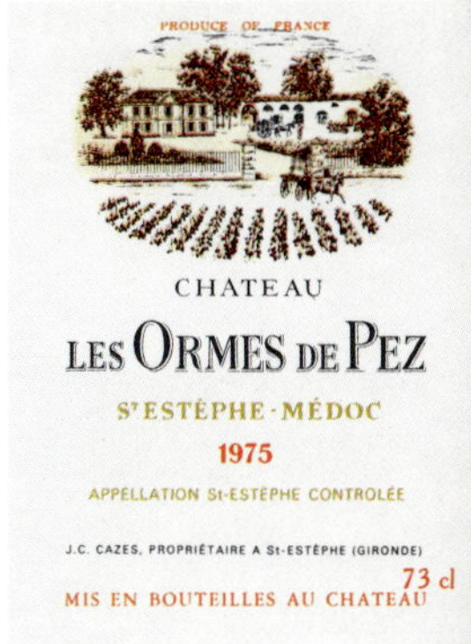

Château les Ormes de Pez

Cru Grand Bourgeois
Saint-Estèphe

The label of Château les Ormes de Pez shows, if you look closely, a romantic picture of the house, with a carriage leaving the gates. The drawing dates from the distant past but outwardly little seems to have changed: neither the façade, nor the park. But since 1981 new cellars in in use, with an impressive battery of stainless steel fermenting tanks. The *chai* is also modern. The owners are the Cazes family, also of Château Lynch-Bages in Pauillac. The team from this *grand cru* also makes the wine at Les Ormes de Pez, in a practically identical way.

Densely planted vines

The vineyard at Les Ormes de Pez covers 74 acres; the varieties planted are 55% Cabernet Sauvignon, 30% Merlot, 10% Cabernet Franc, and 5% Petit Verdot. One of the secrets of the quality of Les Ormes de Pez lies, according to Jean-Michel Cazes, in the mode of planting. The vines stand about 3 feet apart, which is less than the usual distance; on many châteaux it is several inches more. This density means that each vine bears fewer grapes — and the elements of scent and taste are therefore more concentrated, which is reflected in the wine. After fermentation the wine matures for 14 to 18 months in oak casks, mainly from Lynch-Bages and Latour. Fining is done with fresh egg white and the wine is rarely filtered. Les Ormes de Pez produces an average of 125 *tonneaux*, depending on weather conditions.

Many good qualities

Jean-Michel Cazes, a dynamic, likeable man who worked in America before becoming his father's assistant, was my guide during an extensive tasting. The oldest wine dated from 1962: mouth-filling, dark, astonishingly potent and successful. The 1966, too, had a firm taste which, like the bouquet, was beginning to show signs of ripeness. The 1967 was well advanced, but far from tired; a certain freshness was faintly discernible. The harsh, still undeveloped 1970 revealed more acid; a wine of austere colour with much in reserve and plenty of future. I thought the 1971 was disappointing for its year, being rather too acid in taste. The 1975 was brilliant, with a deep colour and a sprightly taste with a good balance, sufficient tannin and the merest hint of sweetness. The 1976, a wine with a marvellous bouquet, and ready for drinking from 1981, had a similar tinge. The 1978 tasted particularly pure, without any sweetness. It was a first-rate wine, opaque, rich in fruit, very harmonious. 1981 (dark) and 1982 (firm) show much promise. Les Ormes de Pez is never a full or fat wine, nor especially refined. But it should be ranked among the very best of the *crus grands bourgeois.*

Far left:
When I visited the château (winery buildings only — the actual château is a maison bourgeoise *occupied by a bank manager from Pauillac) my hosts had opened four recent vintages ready for me to taste.*

Below left:
François Audoy.

Below centre:
Bernard Audoy, François' son, concentrates on the still cloudy wine.

Andron-Blanquet's second wines are Château Saint-Roch and Château Blanquet. Sometimes the wine sold as Blanquet is the same as Andron-Blanquet. It varies from country to country.

Château Andron-Blanquet

Cru Grand Bourgeois Exceptionnel
Saint-Estèphe

After belonging to the same family for centuries, Château Andron-Blanquet finally changed hands in August 1971. The buyer was François Audoy from the neighbouring *grand cru* Cos Labory. The vineyards of the two châteaux adjoin in several places. Some of the Andron-Blanquet plots lie closer to Château Cos Labory than to their own château. However, Audoy does not intend to merge the two vineyards; but the location of Andron-Blanquet does have the advantage that much of the work can be combined. Altogether the vineyard area covers 37 acres, 35% of it planted with Merlot, 30% with Cabernet Sauvignon, 30% with Cabernet Franc and 5% Petit Verdot. There has been no change in these proportions since 1971.

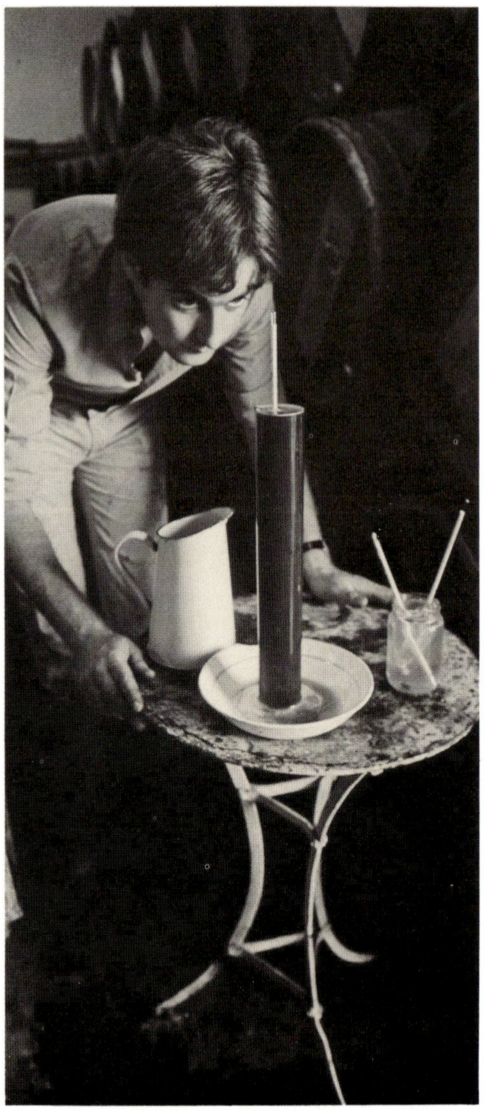

Filtered twice

At vintage time the grapes arrive in the *cuvier* with its lined concrete fermentation vats. These vats also serve in part for maturing the wine in its first year. Audoy regularly alternates the wine between casks and vats. During its second year it remains exclusively in the cask. Used casks from Cos Labory and Lafite-Rothschild are employed — stacked three high in the little cellar. Annual production varies from 30 to almost 100 *tonneaux*. In addition to being filtered twice, the wine is also cleaned by fining with albumen.

Austere taste

The first proper vintage under François Audoy was the 1973. The wine revealed less charm than might be expected from this year. I though it rather severe, with an acid tinge even after six years. The 1975 still had to open up; it had plenty of colour, and dried on the teeth. The 1976 had a beautiful colour and the beginning of mildness, a good vinous bouquet — but again a severe taste that I would have preferred to be fuller. The recently bottled 1977 was deep in colour and tasted a little acidic. In the 1978, tasted from the cask, you could distinctly smell fruit (especially blackcurrant) and it offered a slightly rounder quality than the 1975. In terms of personality, Andron-Blanquet is no charmer; nor do I regard its bouquet or taste as very endearing. It makes an austere impression and, with its lack of roundness, seems a shade meagre. However, the decidedly successful 1978 encourages me to hope that François Audoy is gradually improving the quality of his wine. The 1981 and 1982 are steps in the right direction.

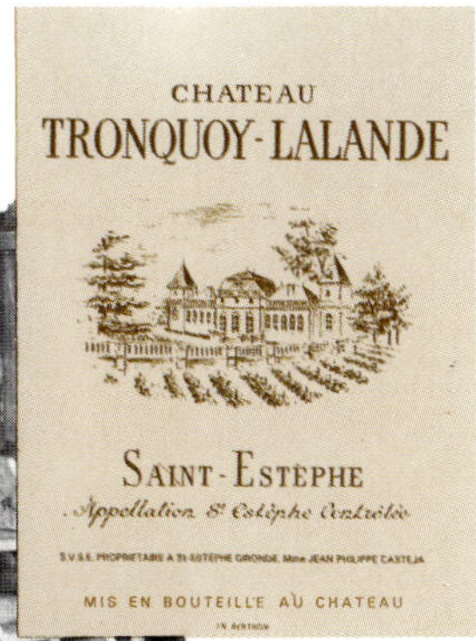

Far left:
Vintage time at Tronquoy-Lalande with the château in the background. Immediately behind it is a large 42-acre park.

Below left:
The façade of Tronquoy-Lalande, originally built in hunting lodge style; the towers were added in the 19th century.

Below right:
Arlette Castéja in her spacious salon. Her collection of Chinese plates adorns the walls of her dining room.

Château Tronquoy-Lalande

Cru Grand Bourgeois
Saint-Estèphe

When you see Château Tronquoy-Lalande today it is hard to imagine that in 1969 this proud structure was almost a ruin. Its only occupants for a long time had been the Germans and Americans in the Second World War. The walls were full of holes and covered in graffiti, the electrical fittings had gone and hardly a single pane of glass was unbroken. Now it is a comfortable place to live in, the salons are tastefully furnished and everything is shipshape. The restoration of Tronquoy-Lalande has been carried out by Jean-Philippe and Arlette Castéja. They bought the château in 1969 and did most of the renovation work entirely alone.
Tragically, Jean-Philippe died in 1973, but Arlette Castéja staunchly took over. It was no easy task. She told me that she was in a complete panic in the first year as she knew nothing about wine-making. Fortunately she was assisted by a good neighbour. In 1974 she won a gold medal with her wine at Paris, and again in 1975.

Help from Dourthe

Mme Castéja is her own *régisseur*; she employs only a *chef de culture* and a few workers. She can operate in this way because her wine is made with the help of Dourthe and sold exclusively by that firm. She has chosen this arrangement 'to keep some time for myself, including study'. The grapes — 65% Cabernet Sauvignon, 30% Merlot, 5% Cabernet Franc plus Petit Verdot — are fermented either in wooden or concrete vats. The wine is then matured for one year in casks (used ones from Dourthe) and one year in metal tanks. It is filtered just before bottling. The 40-acre vineyard produces an average of about 70 *tonneaux* a year.

A wine for laying down

One vintage that I have often drunk is the 1971. It has a sombre, dark colour, a ripe, racy bouquet, a fairly firmly constructed taste and an aftertaste with tannin, wood and a very slight burning sensation from the alcohol. The 1975 was even more potent, a real wine for laying down. The 1978 to some extent lacked the colour, firmness and tannin of the preceding vintages. It also seemed somewhat less concentrated than comparable wines from that year.
The 1980 tasted quite pleasant, with fruit. The 1981 will develop into a firmer wine, of very decent quality. In 1982 the estate produced an almost black Saint-Estèphe: vinous, firm, tannic. Tronquoy-Lalande is not a very refined or subtle wine, but one with firmness — and a usually reliable quality.

The first part of the name, Bel-Orme, means simply beautiful elm: Tronquoy-de-Lalande is the name of the widow who once owned the estate.

The Quié family are also the owners of two grands crus classés, *Rauzan-Gassies in Margaux and Croizet-Bages in Pauillac. All the wines are sold through their office in Paris where Jean-Michel Quié now lives.*

The vineyard covers 64 acres, but the estate has a further 133 acres of other land.

Below:
The château dressed for the autumn. The architect Victor Louis built the château towards the end of the 18th century. From the rear of the building the visitor has a magnificent view of the park, with the Gironde just visible through the trees.

Far right:
Inside the cellar at harvest time. The vine stalks are being packed into a bin for disposal. In the background is the fouloir-égrappoir, *a combined grape de-stalker and crusher.*

Château Bel-Orme Tronquoy de Lalande

Cru Grand Bourgeois
Saint-Seurin-de-Cadourne

I made my first visit to Bel-Orme Tronquoy de Lalande in January 1975. The estate was bought in 1936 by M. Quié, who died in 1969. The present owners, Mme Quié and her son Jean-Michel, served a delightful lunch that included *foie gras* from the Landes and *entrecôte bordelaise.* We drank their 1969, a still remarkably young wine and an excellent partner to the *foie gras.* I noted that the château itself was designed by Victor Louis, the architect of the Grand Théâtre in Bordeaux; the entrance hall is of marble and the salons are stylishly furnished. I visited the château again in the summer of 1979, when it had acquired an extra dimension from the green of the ivy and the many shady trees growing in the grounds. Mme Quié showed me round, accompanied by her manager René Sou.

In the cellars

There were busy preparation in the cellars for the coming vintage. The concrete fermentation tanks were getting a coat of paint, work was proceeding on a new 'reception area' for the incoming grapes, and so on. I always take it as a good sign when an estate attends to detail in this tidy way. The cask cellar, parallel to the *cuvier*, has an earthen floor and is constantly cool. One-fourth of the casks are new each year. The wine matures for 14 to 18 months in the wood and then for a few months in the *cuve.* Like all good bordeaux, it is transferred several times before bottling. The wine is clarified and lightly filtered before bottling. The château usually keeps a considerable stock of old vintages. I noticed good quantities of 1976, 1975, 1974 and 1971.

High tannin content

Bel-Orme wine does not possess much fruit or body, but always plenty of tannin; so much so that several years after the vintage the wine still makes a harsh, tart impression and does not taste very good. Because Jean-Michel Quié makes his wine this way, even the average vintages need keeping for ten years. Only then does a cautious smile break through — yet the wine always seems somewhat reserved. Occasionally nature helps these stubborn, dark Médocs to soften a little. Examples of more endearing vintages are the 1973, 1976, 1979 and the 1982.
The 59-acre vineyard grows Cabernet Sauvignon (30%), Cabernet Franc (30%), Merlot (30%) and Petit Verdot plus Malbec (10%). Production varies between 85 and 110 *tonneaux.*

Verdignan is the only château that Jean Miailhe wholly owns; the other estate he runs, Citran and Coufran (pages 27 and 78) are both partnerships. Verdignan's maître de chais *is Jean's son Eric who lives in a bungalow on the estate.*

Jean Miailhe claims the Verdignan soil to be very much like that of Saint-Julien.

Now and then the Verdignan wine is marketed under the name of Château Plantey de la Croix or Château la Rose Maréchale.

Bottom:
The château was begun in the 18th and completed in the 19th century — this tower is in the oldest part.

Below centre right:
Nowadays Verdignan wines are well turned-out in a bottle with a stylish label that reflects the improvement in quality since the early 1970s.

Right:
Château Verdignan bears a vague resemblance to Lafite-Rothschild.

Château Verdignan

Cru Grand Bourgeois
Saint-Seurin-de-Cadourne

'This is my Camp David,' is how Jean Miailhe describes his Château Verdignan. This busy wine grower and *négociant* takes an occasional few days off here simply to have time to think. The château, which looks a little like Lafite-Rothschild, has six comfortable bedrooms fitted and furnished to accommodate friends and business colleagues. Jean Miailhe bought Verdignan in 1972 in partnership with an associate. Since 1976 he and his children have been sole owners and have planted an extra 62 acres of vineyard. The total area is now 114 acres, planted with 60% Cabernet Suavignon, 35% Merlot and 5% Cabernet Franc. The vineyard. The total area is now 116 acres, planted with 55% Cabernet Sauvignon, 40% six miles wide here. Production in 1981 and 1982 reached 300 *tonneaux*.

His own hamlet

Verdignan's wine-making buildings are some distance from the château in the little hamlet of Cadourne, where all except two of the houses belong to Jean Miailhe. The wine ferments in stainless-steel tanks and matures in oak casks — two-year-old casks of which a fourth are new in which the wine remains for 18 to 24 months. It is fined with albumen and filtered twice.

Great improvement in quality

The quality of Verdignan rose by leaps and bounds during the 1970s. The 1970, 1971 and 1972 vintages were processed by the previous owner and produced dull, indeterminate wines. Those of 1973, 1974 and 1975 already offered more character. But Verdignan only started to be really good in 1976. Wine of this vintage had style and breed — qualities that were lacking in earlier years. I thought the 1976 had depth of colour, a certain suppleness, sufficient tannin and a sound balance. The 1977 was decidedly successful for its year, opaque, smelling of blackcurrant, and showing breeding. All it lacked was a little depth, which the 1978 had in good measure. Verdignan is never really full in flavour, but rounder and more supple than, for example, its neighbour Bel-Orme Tronquoy de Lalande. The 1979 is a very good wine, the 1980 won a gold medal in Paris, and the 1981 and 1982 look promising indeed.

Above:
This stone is set in the wall above the cellar entrance. The initials L.S. stand for Louis Simon, one of the estate's owners during the last century.

Below:
Jean Gautreau with his excellent wine.

Before the French Revolution Sociando-Mallet belonged to Guillaume de Brochon, a very influential man — there is even a street named after him in Bordeaux.

Sociando-Mallet is sometimes labelled Château la Tour de Mont, but the wine is exactly the same. The estate's second wine is called Château Lartique de Brochon. This is made from young vine plants and inferior cuves.

In addition to the vineyards of Sociando-Mallet, Jean Gautreau runs a flourishing wine business in Lesparre, which is where he lives.

Sociando-Mallet derives its unusual name from a M. Sociando and the Widow Mallet. The former was a 17th-century landowner in Saint-Seurin-de-Cadourne; Mme Mallet acquired Château Sociando around 1850 and added her name to it.

Hail destroyed a large part of the 1975 harvest, when only 30 tonneaux were picked as against 80 in 1974 and 60 in 1976. It was the first time the estate had been hit by hail since 1934, and Jean Gautreau was not insured. He is now.

Château Sociando-Mallet

Cru Grand Bourgeois
Saint-Seurin-de-Cadourne

In the Médoc it is often said that the greatest wines come from vines whose leaves look out over the Gironde and whose roots go down into gravel. Sociando-Mallet fulfils both conditions. The estate lies on the southeast side of the commune of Saint-Seurin, possesses an unrestricted view over the river and has a gravel subsoil that is almost identical to that of the *grand cru* Montrose in neighbouring Saint-Estèphe.

Despite its favoured situation, Sociando-Mallet in 1969 was a very neglected estate. Cattle were stalled in some of the buildings and there was less than 15 acres of vineyard. In that year, however, it was bought by a man obsessed by wine: Jean Gautreau, a wine merchant. He saw the potential of Sociando-Mallet and proceeded vigorously to restore it. Today Gautreau is the proud owner of 74 acres of carefully cultivated vineyard, of roomy, efficient cellars and a modest dwelling that he terms a country house rather than a château.

Great demand

From the start Jean Gautreau endeavoured to make one of the very best *crus bourgeois*; and he has succeeded. Sociando-Mallet is in great demand and among its many enthusiasts is Bordeaux's great chef Jean-Marie Amat. The wine is made from 60% 10% Cabernet Franc and is fermented partly in stainless steel, partly in lined concrete vats. It matures, for 18 to 24 months, in oak casks, half of which are new each vintage. Gautreau clarifies his wine with fresh egg white and filters it lightly before bottling. Annual production at present is 120 to 220 *tonneaux*.

A true vin de garde

Gautreau says this about his wine: 'I am against wines that are soon drinkable. I make a potent *vin de garde* and take the risk of letting the customer wait for it.' Sociando-Mallet is certainly no easy drink in its youth, although the Merlot gives it some early suppleness. Four years after its vintage the 1975 was a dark, still undeveloped wine with a very long aftertaste. It was a wine to be forgotten until 1985. The 1976 was almost opaque. There was a little vanilla in the aroma (which indicates new oak casks) and taste, a choice flavour in which the breeding and noble tannin of the Cabernet and the suppleness of the Merlot were harmoniously combined. In short, a great wine. The 1977 tasted somewhat lighter, with more acid, but could be regarded as successful for its year. The 1978 again was a splendid, generous wine, very well balanced — and suitable for long keeping. Splendid wines were also made in 1979, 1981 and 1982. In my view, Sociando-Mallet deserves to be awarded the *exceptionnel* qualification straight away — if not the status of *grand cru classé*.

Below:
Proprietor François Tereygeol whose father bought Pontoise Cabarrus and Sociando-Mallet in 1959 together with a partner. Tereygeol senior later bought the partner's share in Sociando-Mallet but subsequently sold it again, two estates apparently proving to be too much work. In 1959 Pontoise Cabarrus comprised 41 acres of vineyards of which only 12 were actually planted. Today the château has 56 acres, nearly all productive.

Far right:
At Pontoise Cabarrus the grapes have to be hoisted up into the first floor of the cellar to be fed into the fouloir-égrappoir.

Right:
Measuring the sugar content of a grape by means of a refractometer.

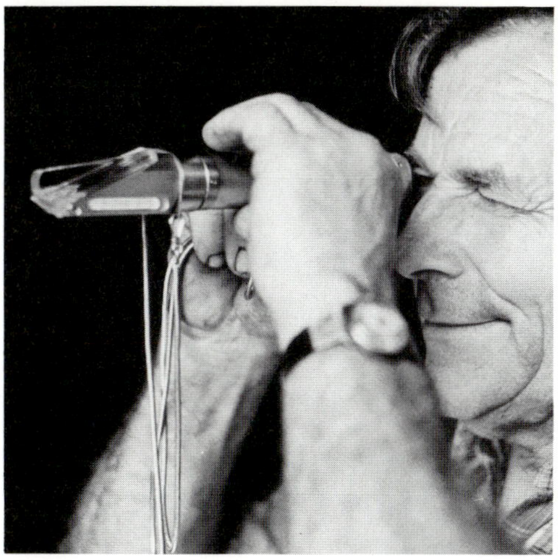

Château Pontoise Cabarrus

Cru Grand Bourgeois
Saint-Seurin-de-Cadourne

The letter N with an imperial crown appears twice on the Pontoise Cabarrus label. One of the former owners, the enormously rich Comte de Cabarrus, was a witness at the wedding of Napoleon Bonaparte and Joséphine. The imperial connection, however, does not extend beyond the label. The château and its cellars stand in a street in Saint-Seurin and certainly convey no impression of grandeur.
In 1959 the original château was separated from the estate; the former owner still lives in it. Opposite the château stands a house that one of the fomer owners of Pontoise Cabarrus donated to the commune as a home for the parish priest. However, Saint-Seurin no longer has a priest and the house stands empty. Since 1959 necessary improvements have been carried out at Pontoise Cabarrus. The wooden fermentation vats have been replaced by concrete ones and stainless-steel tanks, and the vineyard area has been increased from 30 to 56 acres. The grape varieties planted at Cabernet Sauvignon (60%), Merlot (30%), Cabernet Franc (5%) and Petit Verdot (5%).

Maturing in vat and cask

The owner of Pontoise Cabarrus is François Tereygeol, Deputy Director for Technical Affairs at the Institut National des Appellations d'Origine for the Médoc. Every day he investigates and advises châteaux — except during the grape harvest, for then Tereygeol takes time off to make his own wine. When vinification is completed he matures his wine by means of an exchange system: three months in the *cuve*, three months in the cask, then three months in the *cuve* again, and so on for a total of 18 months. He does not use new casks. The wine is cleaned by fining with albumen powder and by filtering.

Sound but not remarkable

Pontoise Cabarrus is a wine that displays neither great refinement nor disconcerting roughness: its personality comes somewhere in between. I regard it as a sound, though not remarkable Haut-Médoc. It usually has a discreet bouquet and a substantial, rather supple taste with a certain elegance and, to a limited degree, some tannin. At present Pontoise Cabarrus produces 105 to 160 *tonneaux* in normal years.

Left:
Pickers linger over wine and cheese while Coufran's maître de chai, Eric Miailhe — son of Jean — presides.

Below:
Front of the late 18th-century château, whose 500-acre estate adjoins Verdignan. Some of the 148 acres of vineyard is used to produce a second wine marketed as Les Gravilles de Château Coufran.

Right:
Jean Miailhe with a few magnums of his wine, which is matured in used casks from Mouton-Rothschild.

Château Coufran

Cru Grand Bourgeois
Saint-Seurin-de-Cadourne

Coufran could be described as an exception to a Médoc rule: as far as I know, it is one of the rare estates with a preponderance of the Merlot grape. Merlot accounts for 85% of the vines, with 10% Cabernet Sauvignon and 5% Petit Verdot Normally you would only come across such a high Merlot content in districts like Pomerol and Saint-Emilion. The man who planted this variety was Louis Miailhe, the father of Jean Miailhe who runs the estate for his family. Louis bought Coufran in1924 and replanted the neglected vineyard entirely with Merlot. Later, Jean Miailhe added some Cabernet and Petit Verdot. The vineyard covers a total of 158 acres and produces between 160 and 400 *tonneaux* a year.

Modern fermentation tanks

Since the vintage of 1974 the grapes have fermented mainly in stainless-steel tanks after they have been destalked and crushed. The château also has concrete and wooden *cuves*, but these are used almost exclusively for storage. Today the wine is matured in used oak casks for 18 months and is filtered. There was quite a long period when only part of the wine was matured in the cask. The 1973 was marketed in two versions, one that had been cask-matured and one that had not. The former was by far the better wine.
The wine at Coufran is better housed than the people. Nothing has been done to the château since the 1940s so that it now seems rather primitive as a home. Nevertheless, I had a marvellous lunch there with Jean Mialihe and his son Eric, who is in charge of vinification. The ham from Bayonne, the *pâté de campagne*, the *côte de boeuf* grilled over vine twigs and the generous series of wines soon made me forget the environment.

A commercial taste

The presence of the Merlot in Coufran wine can be distinctly tasted. In good years this is a full, almost fat wine that is pleasantly rounded within a year or two and also possesses fruit. Examples of such years are 1976, 1979, and, to an even greater extent, 1978. The Coufran bouquet usually has a fresh but mild tone. Because of the easy, accessible character of the wine, not too much should be expected by way of refinement, depth or aftertaste. Coufran leaves no memorable impression behind in either nose or mouth. It is a very pleasant, accessible Haut-Médoc, designed for those who have difficulty contending with the usually austere, rather reserved wines of this district. The vintages of 1980, 1981 and 1982 deserve attention, while the 1974, 1975 and 1977 were simply correct.

Left:
The entrance to the cellars of Château Potensac, where the wine is bottled after being lightly filtered.

Below:
Potensac church, now used to store the bottles from the château — the cellar entrance can be seen on the left. The estate was bought by the Delon family in 1870 and covers 385 acres.

Right:
Inside the wine church, which also stores bottles of Potensac's second wine, Château Lassalle.

Since the 1976 vintage exactly the same wine as Potensac has been sold under the Château Galais-Bellevue label.

Château Potensac

Cru Grand Bourgeois
Potensac

With Château Potensac we leave the Haut-Médoc for the Médoc. The landscape here becomes flatter, more monotonous. In some respects the same applies to the wine — although there are numerous Médocs of a higher quality than many Haut-Médocs; Potensac is an apt example. But this very good wine is made by the talented Michel Delon, whose *deuxième grand cru classé* Léoville-Las-Cases from Saint-Julien enjoys a tremendous reputation. Delon has invested a great deal in Château Potensac in recent years. As a result the estate has an almost completely new *cuvier* with mainly stainless-steel fermentation tanks. Michel, and earlier his father, Paul Delon, have extended the vineyard, increasing it from 17 to 124 acres, which necessitated the expansion of the cellar area. A direct consequence was that the little church of the hamlet of Potensac now belongs to the château; Paul Delon bought it in 1973 and it is used for storing bottles. The money Delon paid was spent on a complete restoration of the church at Ordonnac (to which commune Potensac belongs). So the commune ended up with one good church instead of two ruined ones, and everyone was happy.

Uniform method

As far as the facilities allow, methods at Potensac are the same as at Léoville-las-Cases and practised by the same people. The wine ferments slowly and for a long time at temperatures of 26° to 27°C at most, and it is fined with fresh egg white. The casks in which the wine is matured — for 18 to 20 months — come principally from Léoville-las-Cases. About one-fifth of them are new each year. Despite all the extensions, Château Potensac is always short of space, as indicated by the fact that in the largest *chai* the casks are sometimes stacked four high. Potensac's production does not vary greatly: the vineyard (55% Cabernet Sauvignon, 25% Merlot, 20% Cabernet Franc) is seldom affected by frost or hail; the yield is 200 to 250 *tonneaux*.

Class and balance

The Cabernet comes through strongly in the Potensac wines, with a rather austere colour, plenty of tannin and a hint of blackcurrant in bouquet and taste. The 1978, which I tasted from the cask, was simply excellent, with a deep purple colour, compact fruit and oak in the bouquet and an elegantly mouth-filling taste, also with fruit and oak, plus class and balance. It was not a 'soft' wine: bottles of Potensac must be allowed at least five years to lose their original Médoc harshness to any extent. The 1976 was also an extremely successful Potensac year — even better, in my opinion, than 1975. A truly great Potensac was made in 1982, but the 1979 and 1982 are very worthwhile too.

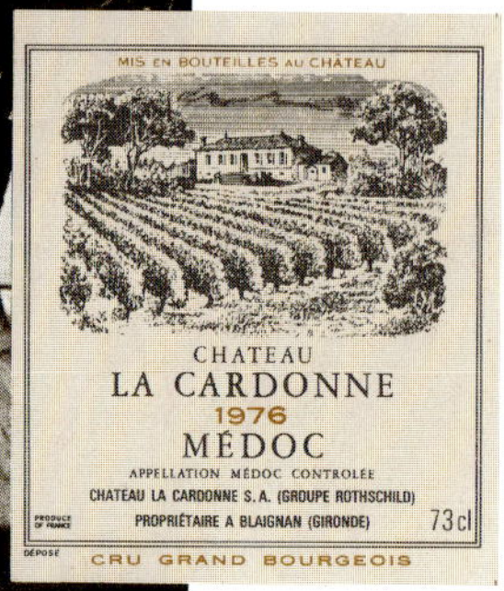

Far left:
The unoccupied château is fronted by an attractive 7-acre park. The building itself is reminiscent of Château la Lagune, a grand cru *in the commune of Ludon in the southern Médoc.*

Below:
Vintage time at La Caronne. The vineyard covered 183 acres at the time of writing, but could be extended by a further 52 acres.

For its simpler qualities the estate uses the name Château Romefort.

Château la Cardonne

Cru Grand Bourgeois
Blaignan

It is not far from Château Potensac to Château la Cardone,where the ground gradually rises to the highest plateau in the district. The 250-acre La Cardonne estate was bought in 1973 by the French Rothschild group. According to rumour, the purchase was made possible by the enormous profits then being earned by the two other wine estates owned by the group: the *grands crus* Lafite-Rothschild and Duhart-Milon-Rothschild. New brooms swept clean and there were many changes under the new regime. La Cardonne's vineyard was enlarged from 124 to 185 acres and vines were replaced. Existing buildings were restored and new ones put up; installations and equipment were replaced. Production ranges from 300 to nearly 350 *tonneaux.* This quantity may still increase, since the total potential vineyard area is 235 acres.

Hardly any casks

Since the vintage of 1978 all the wine has been fermented in reddish-brown-painted metal tanks, and it is matured in concrete *cuves.* According to manager Jean Birot, the wine only occasionally comes into contact with wooden casks, and then only for six months. (A spokesman of the Rothschild group in Paris even told me that La Cardonne was not using casks at all.) The wine — from an estimated 65% Cabernet Sauvignon, 20% Cabernet Franc and 15% Merlot — is filtered after its malolactic fermentation and before bottling.

Acceptable level

No cask maturing and two *filtrages* immediately suggests that this Rothschild wine can in no way be compared with Lafite-Rothschild and Duhart-Milon-Rothschild.

The policy at Château la Cardonne is not to aim at the highest possible quality but to produce a reasonably priced, fairly unproblematic Médoc of an acceptable standard. Expectations should not therefore be pitched too high. La Cardonne usually has a reasonably deep, clear colour, a somewhat elusive, not very distinct bouquet and a compact, slightly supple flavour that is not conspicuous for its subtlety or long aftertaste.

At one time practically all the land in the village of Couquèques was owned by a Monsieur de Sorbet, but after 1737 this large estate was split up and the wine growers of Couquèques gradually succeeded in buying land for themselves. One of them was an ancestor of Les Ormes Sorbet's present owner, Jean Boivert.

Couquèques derives its name from the word couque, which means a spiral shell. The village was formerly known as Saint-Martin-de-Couques.

Jean Boivert graduated from agricultural college and is also a qualified oenologist.

At the Les Ormes Sorbet, the wine is fined exclusively with the beaten whites of fresh eggs.

Below:
The main entrance to the château.

Right:
Jean Boivert's guests taste his wine from small glasses. the bottles bear a simple yet stylish label. He has no bottling equipment himself, and so the wine is bottled at the château by a contractor.

Château les Ormes Sorbet

Cru Grand Bourgeois
Couquèques

Château les Ormes Sorbet, in the quiet wine village of Couquèques, with its winding streets, came into being through the tenacity of one family, the Boiverts. By working hard, generation after generation, they managed to acquire so much land that Les Ormes Sorbet is now the most substantial wine estate in the village. Owner Jean Boivert — the eighth generation — possesses 49 acres and produces an annual average of 90 *tonneaux.* He may extend the vineyard eventually by a further 12 acres. First, however, the debt burden must be reduced, for the many improvements in the château, the *cuvier* and the cellars have cost a lot of money; and furthermore, Boivert has built new homes for his workers.

Half to the négociant

For fermenting the wine Boivert installed a battery of metal tanks in 1972. After fermentation the wine matures for 18 to 20 months in oak casks, of which one-third are new. Fining is done with fresh egg white and the wine is not normally filtered. Jean Boivert told me that not all the vintage is bottled at the château. Part goes in the cask to Schröder & Schyler (for the Danish importer of the wine). For years, Boivert has had a contract with these *négociants* for half his production. He sells the other half directly, mostly in and around Paris.

A classic, well-made Médoc

The vineyard of Les Ormes Sorbet contains 55% Cabernet Sauvignon vines, 35% Merlot, 5% Cabernet Franc and 5% Petit Verdot. Together these grapes give a classical, well-made Médoc with plenty of colour, tannin and breeding. The 1976 in particular struck me with its pleasing balance between Cabernet and Merlot: the harshness and firmness of the Cabernet was mitigated somewhat by the suppleness of the Merlot. By contract, the 1975 had to be made entirely from Cabernet grapes because night frost had removed the Merlot; this wine therefore tasted much more austere and unrevealing. Jean Boviert himself prefers wines of the 1976 type, and I agree with him entirely. The 1978 is comparable, but is slighty fuller. I also enjoyed the 1979, while the 1981 and 1982 are noteworthy wines. The lesser *cuves* of Château les Ormes Sorbet are sold as Château de Conques; very occasionally, in good years and in certain markets, it is exactly the same wine as Les Ormes Sorbet. Sometimes Jean Boivert makes a little rosé from young Cabernet vines, which is sold without *appellation* as Clairet des Ormes.

Château Loudenne

Cru Grand Bourgeois
Saint-Yzans-de-Médoc

When the brothers Walter and Alfred Gilbey, London wine and spirits merchants, bought Château Loudenne on 26 April 1875 it had already been a wine estate for many years. The wine of Loudenne was not, however, the main motive for the purchase; it was the château's situation close to the Gironde. The Gilbeys saw Loudenne as an ideal spot for warehousing and shipping large quantities of cheap wine. The British market was ripe for it: some years earlier the Chancellor of the Exchequer, Gladstone, had considerably reduced the duty on table wines. Loudenne was given a completely new *cuvier*, a cellar complex to accommodate 16,000 casks and 500,000 bottles, its own coopery, its own little dock, and a short railway spur leading to it. A well 1,630 feet deep was sunk, and stalls and stables for oxen and horses were built. Despite these gigantic investments, the Gilbey brothers also managed to enlarge the vineyard from about 125 to 250 acres, wishing to become wine growers as well as merchants. This development was not without problems, for not long after the purchase of Loudenne the *Phylloxera vastatrix* began its devastating onslaught on the Médoc. Despite this setback, Loudenne received a gold medal from the French government in 1887 for the best-kept

Opposite page, left:
The great cuverie at Loudenne. There is an enormous lawn in front. What the photograph does not show is the oak tree planted by former Prime Minister Edward Heath in 1975 to commemorate Château Loudenne's 100 years of British ownership.

Opposite page, right:
A sublime lunch in sublime surroundings: the dining room at Château Loudenne. On the left sits Robert Dousson of Château de Pez (whose wines have been sold by Gilbeys since 1968 on a worldwide exclusive basis), while Loudenne's hostess Marie-Christine Delorme listens attentively to the estate's oenologist Jean-Louis Camp (he worked for 11 years in Burgundy with such names as Barton & Guestier). Next to him sits Madame Dousson, flanked in turn by Joël Martin, a Gilbey employee. The late Martin Bamford, then director of Gilbey France, was absent on this occasion.

Opposite page, below:
Vintage time at Loudenne when the picking was still done by hand.

Left:
A good Loudenne is an entrancing wine — and certainly at the château itself, before a crackling open fire in one of the comfortable salons.

Below:
Loudenne again, now more in focus. They play croquet on the lawns.

The château houses a comprehensive library of wine with hundreds of old and new volumes in a variety of languages. The visitor may inspect the diaries of the Gilbey brothers themselves.

Loudenne was the first Médoc estate to use horses in place of oxen in the vineyards. For as Walter Gilbey wrote: 'Each horse does the work of two oxen, and does it much faster, so that the ploughman is compelled to be more active about his work.

Twice a week during the period leading up to harvest a few grapes are picked and examined for sugar content, etc. These samples are always taken from the same rows in the same plots. The black grapes are only picked when they have reached maximum ripeness. The white grapes are harvested just before they are fully ripe — this makes for a fresher wine.

The Loudenne Blanc label is very similar to the red wine label but is printed in gold instead of black.

Loudenne has a charming, excellently equipped tasting pavilion a little way away from the château and cellars.

vineyard in the Gironde, an award that is still commemorated on the labels.

Sublime salons

The firm of W. & A. Gilbey Ltd, now part of International Distillers and Vintners, continues to invest in Château Loudenne today. Since 1969 large amounts have been spent on 15 houses for workers, on the renovation of the Victorian *chais*, on new stainless-steel fermentation tanks, on the park with its wide lawns, on a charming museum with items of old wine-making equipment, on the vineyard and, last but not least, on the pink-painted château. Under the direction of the interior decorator Thurloe Connolly, the salons at Loudenne have been remodelled into stylish living and reception suites. Their furnishings are in sharp contrast to the often ramshackle collection of antiques that does service in most Médoc châteaux. Among the permanent residents of Loudenne are staff members of Gilbey France. From a pleasant terrace they can look out over an immaculate lawn (with croquet hoops), a small plot of vines, and the immensely broad, grey Gironde busy with shipping. There are less favoured spots in the world.

Mechanical picking

Attention to detail is not confined to externals, but extends to the wine making. Loudenne's red wine comes from a 106-acre vineyard planted with 53% Cabernet Sauvignon, 40% Merlot, and 7% Cabernet Franc. The vines are tended in exemplary fashion and are planted far enough apart for mechanical picking. At Loudenne they have found that there is no difference at all between wine from hand-gathered grapes and that from mechanically picked fruit. Trials were conducted in 1978 to discover the best out of six different harvesting machines. The grapes ferment in *cuves* of resin-coated concrete or stainless steel. Stainless-steel grills press down the *chapeau*, the cap formed mainly of skins, so that the fermenting must draws the maximum colour from it. After the fermentation process has ended the wine matures for 14 to 20 months in oak casks, a quarter of which are replaced by new ones each year.

Mild and civilized

Production of red Loudenne wine varies between 115 and 285 *tonneaux* a year. The wine is fined with powdered egg white and filtered at time of bottling. Loudenne wine seems to be born with a smile. Even in earliest youth its taste has none of the almost arrogant, unyielding character of many young Médocs. It has a certain style, a constitution that is reasonably firm if not robust, a striking purity and a correct balance. This soft, civilized Médoc lacks enough length and depth to be placed among the *exceptionnels*, but in my view it is certainly a good *cru grand bourgeois.* Some recommended years are 1970 , 1971 (ripe and relatively full-bodied), 1975 (the centennial grape harvest, a small vintage that would be ready for drinking in the early 1980s), 1976 (fairly racy and also supple), 1978 (somewhat like the 1976), and 1979 (supple, agreeable). The first reports of the 1981 and 1982 are very positive.

White wine

Loudenne produces white wine as well as red. This carries the Bordeaux *appellation* and comes from 25 acres planted with 50% Sauvignon grapes and 50% Sémillon. The yield averages around 35 *tonneaux* — which is much too little to meet the great demand. The white Loudenne, one of the few Médoc white wines, enjoys worldwide interest due not only to its scarcity but also to its excellent quality. It is a delightful, fragrant, fruity, crisp and clean-tasting dry white wine of an attractive elegance; and that cannot be said of many white Bordeaux. Loudenne Blanc ferments at relatively low temperature — 17° to 20°C — in stainless-steel tanks and is generally bottled within five months of the vintage.

Left:
Colette Bonny in working clothes, analyzing her wine — she is a qualified chemist.

Far left:
Monsieur Bonny with a magnum of the wine he has helped to create. In the 19th century, when Sigognac belonged to the Caussade-Subercaseaux family, a large part of the vintage was sold to Holland.

Below:
The château as seen from its inner courtyard, which features a well and an aviary. It is believed that the Roman Ausonius may have had a house on this spot. However that may be, there is no doubt that there was a maison noble *named Segougnac here in the 16th century.*

The estate does not officially have a second wine but it makes a simple table wine and a little rosé for its staff.

The wines are fined with fresh or powdered egg white.

Sigognac's vineyard could be extended to 150 acres.

Château Sigognac

Cru Grand Bourgeois
Saint-Yzans-de-Médoc

In the council office at Saint-Yzans there are pottery shards and other finds from the Roman period on display. These come from Château Sigognac, on whose land a Roman villa once stood. The estate with its whitewashed, almost Mediterranean-style buildings, lies just north of the village. The soil here has clay and lime. Sigognac has been through a difficult period. When Paul Grasset took over on 20 February 1964, only 9 acres of vineyard remained and trees were actually growing in some of the rooms of the château. Grasset did a lot of replanting and restoration, but he died in 1968. His wife Colette (a chemist) continued the task in exemplary fashion and has enlarged the vineyard to 111 acres. Although she remarried and is now Mme Bonny, she still sees to the vinification and administration herself. Her husband supervises the work in the vineyard and acts as Sigognac's representative.

Longer in vat than cask

At Sigognac equal proportions of Cabernet Sauvignon, Cabernet Franc and Merlot are grown and the grapes are fermented in raised concrete vats. These vats are also used for part of the maturing process. Mme Bonny exchanges the wine between vat and cask every six months in an 18-month period; it usually spends twelve months in the vat and six in the cask. New casks are hardly ever used. The wine is filtered just once, before bottling. In an abundant year production at Sigognac can reach 270 *tonneaux.* However, the vineyard is often affected by hail and frost and the vintages of 1975 and 1976, for example, produced less than 130 *tonneaux* and 1977 yielded only 66.

Light in every way

Sigognac must be reckoned among the lightweights of the *crus grands bourgeois.* Even in sunny years it is light in colour, bouquet and taste. This slender, elegant wine has little tannin and can be drunk quite soon after its vintage. These remarks are meant in no derogatory sense. I have tasted or drunk various Sigognac vintages with satisfaction, including the 1975, 1976, 1978 and 1981.

One former illustrious owner of the estate was Cardinal d'Aux, a newphew of Clement the Fifth, Archbishop of Bordeaux and later Pope, who gave his name to Château Pape Clément in the Graves region.

The total estate covers 113 acres of which 94 are currently in production. It is hoped that this will be expanded in the future.

Claude Lapalu acquired Patache d'Aux in 1964, and he is also a partner in Château la Tour de By, another estate in Bégadan (page 86).

The first cuvier at Patache d'Aux was completed on 2 August 1779 and has since been refurbished and extended several times.

Below:
Vintage time in the cuvier.

Right:
A cartload of grape stalks ready for disposal. In the background is one of the chais and the tower of Bégadan church.

Château Patache d'Aux

Cru Grand Bourgeois
Bégadan

If you drive into the village of Bégadan from the south, you will see on the left a most imposing building that looks very much like a wine château. This is exactly what it was — the original Château Patache d'Aux. Until the French Revolution it belonged to the Aux family but was then separated from the vineyard and cellars. The estate derives the first part of its name from the stagecoaches (*pataches*) that used to stop at the former Château d'Aux. The building is now a holiday home. The present Patache d'Aux estate has, perhaps not surprisingly, no actual château. The cellars are beside Bégadan's striking church, and the 'château' is an inconspicuous low building where the office is situated.

Wooden fermentation vats

Patache d'Aux (the 'x' is pronounced locally) has 94 acres of vineyard, planted with 70% Cabernet Sauvignon, 20% Merlot and 10% Cabernet Franc. The grapes ferment mainly in wooden vats: the château also has two made of concrete. The wine then matures partly in the vats, partly in casks, being rotated between the two. Owner Claude Lapalu never buys new casks, but before every vintage he replaced a quarter of the stock with two-year-old casks. The wine is pumped twice through a filter. Patache d'Aux also vinifies all the wine from another Lapalu estate: Château le Boscqu, a *cru bourgeois* from Saint-Christoly.

Full-flavoured

The 160 to 230 *tonneaux* that Patache d'Aux produces annually does not require too much patience. Claude Lapalu and his son Jean-Michel deliberately make a Médoc that is relatively soon ready for drinking and does not contain many harsh elements in its taste. It does have a fairly deep colour, a pleasant but not particuarly marked bouquet, and a full-flavoured, supple taste without a lot of subtlety. There is often a hint of fruit present in the bouquet and a suggestion of freshness in the taste. One of the best wines of the late Seventies was the 1975; after this my order of preferences would be 1978, 1979, 1976, 1974 and 1977. At the château they are very satisfied with their 1981 and 1982.

Left:
Château la Tour de By.

Below:
The old beacon tower dates from 1825 and was used until 1860.

Right:
Marc Pagès, who bought the estate with his two partners in 1965, is framed here by the labels under which his wines are sold. Moulin de la Roque is sold only to private individuals in France.

The three-star Paris restaurant Taillevent bought a whole tonneau of the 1978 vintage.

Château la Tour de By made a most acceptable wine even in the lean years of 1972 and 1977.

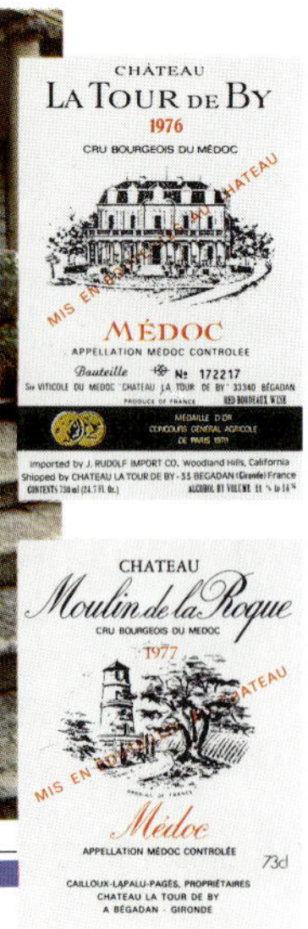

Château la Tour de By

Cru Grand Bourgeois
Bégadan

It was principally the Dutch who drained the marshes of the Médoc. The hamlet of By, in the commune of Bégadan, probably derives its name from a Dutchman who settled here long ago. I was told this by Marc Pagès who with M. Cailloux and M. Lapalu owns Château la Tour de By. This château, with its wide steps and portico, dates from 1876. It was built next to the much older and smaller Château la Roque de By, which stills stands and gives its name to the estate's second wine. The 'new' château was named after the old By beacon light, a tower built on the foundations of an old mill and now surrounded by vineyard. From the tower there is a magnificent view over the vineyard and the Gironde near by. The grape varieties planted here are Cabernet Sauvignon (65%), Merlot (33%) and Cabernet Franc (2%).

Making the wine

La Tour de By has its winery buildings some distance from the château. They are grouped around a charming courtyard where there is a 400-year-old wine press. Marc Pagès — an enthusiastic perfectionist — sees to the day-to-day management of the estate. For fermentation he uses both wooden and stainless-steel *cuves*; he clearly prefers the latter. The wine matures for 10 to 16 months in casks of which one-sixth are renewed each year. Pagès clarifies his wine with egg white in fresh or gelatined form, and filters it lightly twice (after the malolactic acid fermentation and before bottling). Great care and attention is given to all the details of the wine-making, from the specially selected *égrappoir* (destalker) to the wine cases, which all come from Libourne.

Many gold medals

At home and at the château I sampled some dozen different vintages of La Tour de By, and was very impressed by their quality. The soil in this part of the northern Médoc is made up of a gravelly crown that resembles that of Pauillac and Saint Julien. This is another reason why La Tour de By produces a remarkably good wine — as is shown by the many gold medals it has won at the Paris show. The colour of this wine varies from deep red to almost black. Its bouquet is always pure and unpretentious, with fruit (especially blackcurrant) and oak discreetly present. Its fine taste comes across as rather hard at first; the aftertaste has plenty of tannin and the balance is very sound. As a rule this wine should be kept for at least 5 years — 10-15 years if from an outstanding vintage such as 1970. Some other wines that I recommend are the 1973, 1974, 1975, 1976 (which I prefer to the 1975), 1978, 1979, 1981 and 1982 (lots of colour and class). The château produces between 275 and 400 *tonneaux* a year.

Below:
The great cuvier under whose floors Roman foundations and mosaics have been discovered.

Far right:
Laujac from the rear. A cellar runs under the entire building.

Centre right:
Bernard Cruse — his mother-in-law runs Château Corbin in Saint-Emilion (page 123).

At Laujac the wine is fined with egg gelatine and then filtered before bottling. Its second wine is marketed under the Château la Tour Coudouan label.

About 20 show jumpers are bred and trained on the estate.

Château Laujac

Cru Grand Bourgeois
Bégadan

Château Laujac was commissioned by the Cabarrus family and building started in 1810. Financial difficulties caused the planned size of the château to be reduced by half. This drastic curtailment does not show: Laujac still has imposing dimensions and perfect symmetry. In 1852 the Cruse family bought the château; this was their first wine estate. Bernard Cruse, the present owner, lives in Entre-Deux-Mers where he raises cattle, but devotes at least one day a week to Laujac.
At the beginning of this century the 798-acre estate had 348 acres of vineyard and the yield was more than 1,000 *tonneaux.* At present the vineyard measures 74 acres; Bernard Cruse hopes to enlarge it gradually to about 100 acres. Current production varies between 60 and 150 *tonneaux.* The vines grow in the higher, gravelly parts of the estate. The flat land, much of it below sea level, is used for breeding show jumpers and beef cattle, and for growing wheat and maize.

An old cuvier

The large, dark *cuvier* at Laujac is about 100 years old. Most of the fermentation vats are of wood, but there are also 11 smaller metal tanks. Both kinds are also in considerable use for maturing the wine. Normally the wine spends two-thirds of its maturation period in the vats or tanks and one-third in the casks. The time in the casks (one fourth of which are new) does not usually exceed 12 months.

Rather reserved

The grapes used in Laujac wine are 60% Cabernet Sauvignon, 25% Merlot, 10% Cabernet Franc and 5% Petit Verdot. The fruit is treated in the traditional way, including a long period in the vat, so that the wine always has a dark, strong colour. The Laujac bouquet is usually rather rarified, and still reserved even after years of maturing. The same applies to the taste: this is a fairly unforthcoming Médoc. In my view its constitution could do with filling out; the wine is often at its best from sunny, gentle years like 1976. It then becomes more full-bodied and less hard. Although it has few subtleties, Laujac nevertheless possesses a decent aftertaste. To sum up: Laujac lacks the luxury that would make it really noble, but it is a good *cru bourgeois* and a true Médoc. According to Bernard Cruse it should not be drunk before its tenth year.

Left:
Château Greysac seen from its vineyard.

Below:
Full bunches of grapes arriving at the cuverie. Vinification and blending are done under the guidance of the celebrated oenologist, Professor Peynaud.

Far right:
Baron François de Gunzburg has breathed new life into two other estates apart from Greysac: Château des Bertins in the Médoc and Château Grand-Mazerolles in Blaye. De Gunzburg ships half his Greysac to the United States.

Château Greysac

Cru Grand Bourgeois
Bégadan

Baron François de Gunzburg had already had several different careers when he bought this château in 1973. This dynamic Frenchman comes of a Parisian banking family with Russian ancestry. He has been involved in drilling for oil in America, a ski project in Alaska and the general management of Barton & Guestier, a wine firm that belongs to the Seagram group. During the eight years that de Gunzburg worked for Barton & Guestier, the turnover increased tenfold. In 1972 he decided to change from dealing in wine to making it and the following year, helped by Texan oil friends, he bought three Bordeaux châteaux. The most important of these is Greysac. De Gunzburg has enlarged the vineyard here from 37 to 138 acres, and there are plans for a further 12 acres. The baron spends two days a week in the grey-white château, and the rest of his time in Paris or in the city of Bordeaux, devoting some of it to commission work for the American market.

Three kinds of fermentation vat

The approximately 280 *tonneaux* that François de Gunzburg produces in a normal year comes from about 50% Cabernet Sauvignon, 38% Merlot, 10% Cabernet Franc and 2% Petit Verdot grapes. The fruit ferments in stainless-steel *cuves*. About 18 months is set aside for maturing in the cask. Mainly used casks are employed at Greysac; about 20% are bought new for each vintage. The wine is filtered just before bottling — how finely depends on the vintage.

Sound analyses

Baron de Gunzburg has chosen his particular kind of wine quite deliberately. He told me: 'People who buy a *cru bourgeois* want to drink it four or five years after the vintage, if not sooner. I take this into account; I am a marketing man.' He added that his wines were always 'propres et bien équilibrés' and analytically sound. The vintages I tasted were indeed honest and balanced. All of them, including the ones tasted from the cask, were noticeable for the absence of over-assertive flavours. Their taste was supple. Though they did not offer great refinement, their purity and generally attractive prices make these wines good value for money.

The Graves region encompasses 43 wine communes, although of these, only 30 or so are actually productive, and their output varies greatly from year to year. By way of example, in 1979 Graves produced 89,748 hectolitres of red wine as against a mere 31,939 in 1977. The figures for white wine were 72,931 and 25,982 hectolitres respectively.

Two of the most-visited estates in the region are the massive 14th-century fortress of Château de Roquetaillade and Château de Labrède, where the famous French politician, philosopher, writer and wine exporter Montesquieu was born in 1689 as Charles de Segondat. The wines of these two châteaux are of little importance.

Below:
A map of the Graves district. Its northern boundry actually runs north of Bordeaux through the commune of Le Taillan. In the south there are two small enclaves within the Graves territory. These are Cérons and Sauternes.

Right:
Pleasure over the new vintage at Château Ferrande.

The expansion of quarrying in the area is a regrettable development, especially since the region's gravelly soil makes such excellent wines. Most of the Bordeaux gravel pits are in this area — the 1,000 hectares of quarries in 1972 had grown to 1,600 by 1978, and the end is still not in sight. André Lurton, who owns La Louvière, leads the fight against this expansion.

Graves

There was a time when all the wine shipped as 'Bordeaux' came from Graves. This district encircles Bordeaux and the earliest vineyards were situated as close as possible to the city boundaries. In the three centuries, from 1152 to 1453, that Aquitaine — and therefore Bordeaux — belonged to the English crown, its ships carried exclusively Graves wine to England. As the years passed, Bordeaux expanded so that a number of vineyards came within its boundaries. Visiting Saint-Seurin in central Bordeaux today, it is hard to imagine this church surrounded by famous vineyards as it was in the late Middle Ages. Urbanization drove wine-growing out of the city itself, and eventually from most of the suburbs. Only a few châteaux have managed to survive, such as Haut-Brion and Les Carmes Haut Brion in Pessac, and La Mission Haut Brion Talence. As Bordeaux grew, the wine-growing areas of Graves were being extended steadily to the south, initially on the best soil up to 9 miles south of the city, then to about 30 miles along the left bank of the Garonne to Saint-Pierre-de-Mons and Saint-Pardon.

Gravel subsoil

In the Graves the vine is much less dominant than in the Médoc. Wine-growing is confined to a strip at most 9 miles wide, intermingled with small woods, meadowland and market gardens. In general the best wines are made in the northern part of the Graves (as far as the little Saucats stream just below Martillac); the soil most resembles that of the Médoc. There is a lot of gravel, or *gravier*, in the subsoil: and the name Graves derives from this. Further south the gravel content declines and the wines are often lighter and with fewer nuances. South of Le Saucats the drainage too is not so good. Relatively speaking, there is much less wine-growing land in the south than the north.

Red and white

For long the Graves was almost exclusively known for its cheap, semi-sweet white wines. These were usually sold as Graves Supérieures ('supérieure' referred only to the extra alcohol, 12° compared with 11° for the ordinary white Graves). The best Graves Blancs, however, are dry — and fortunately demand for such wines is increasing. They are made from the Sauvignon and Sémillon grapes; the Muscadelle is also permitted. Their characteristics are a natural grace, a fresh taste without assertive acids, often surprising keeping qualities and sometimes, too, fascinating nuances in the bouquet. Besides its white wines the district is increasingly producing reds: at present, in fact, more red is being made than white. The grape varieties are exactly the same as for the Médoc: Cabernet Sauvignon, Cabernet Franc, Merlot, Petit Verdot and Malbec. The minimum alcohol content for Graves Rouges is 10°. In comparison with the Médocs these wines are often more robust, slightly softer with more *terroir* , sometimes with a very light resinous aroma — and slightly less *racé*, less refined.

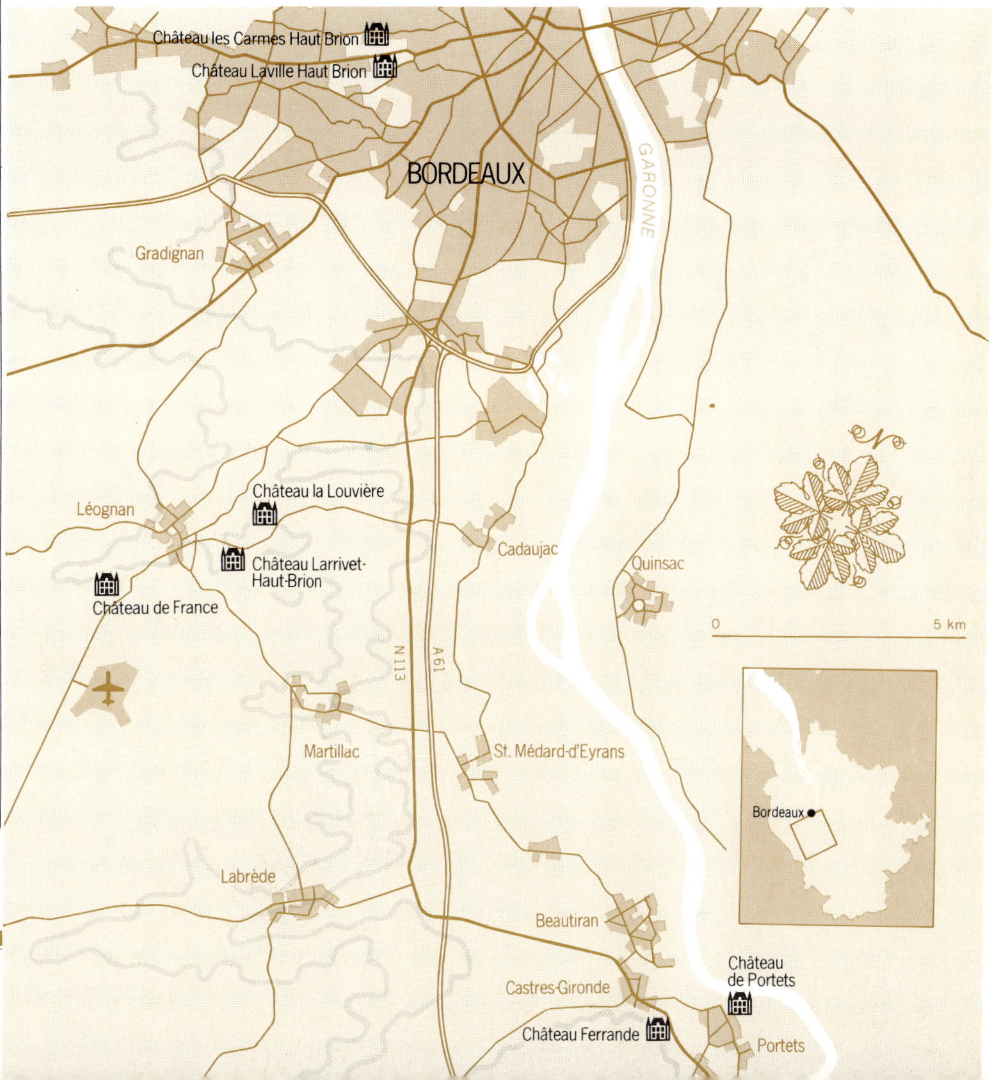

Left:
The charming château is surrounded by a handsome park with many tall trees. The park itself was designed by the celebrated landscape architect Fischer.

Below:
The vineyard of Les Carmes Haut Brion, where the vines vary in age from around 10 to 40 years. One of the pointed towers of the château is just visible in the middle background. From 1584 to the end of the 18th century — the French Revolution — the estate was the property of the Carmes Blancs, a Carmelite order.

Far right:
Philippe Chantecaille, whose grandfather built the château around 1850 and started the vineyard.

Château les Carmes Haut Brion

Pessac
Graves

Pessac, one of the Bordeaux suburbs, contains some famous châteaux, such as Haut-Brion and Pape-Clément, but many other wine estates have been swallowed up urbanization. It is to be hoped that Les Carmes Haut Brion will be spared this fate, for this estate forms an oasis of beauty and calm in the midst of urban drabness. The château, its park and its vineyard lie hidden behind a high wall. The splendid, stylishly furnished château was built in 1859 and the park is the work of the landscape gardener Fischer. The occupier and owner of Les Carmes Haut Brion is Philippe Chantecaille, chairman of the wine firm Chantecaille (the property since 1933 of the big Burgundy concern of Albert Bichot).

Small scale

Of the estate's 21 acres, 9 are planted with vines. In this small, partly walled vineyard, the grapes are often 'cooked' by the sun until almost overripe. Drainage is excellent: two days after heavy rainfall the vineyard is dry again. Even in damp years rot seldom occurs at Les Carmes Haut Brion. The vines consist of half Merlot and half Cabernet Franc; the Cabernet Sauvignon is totally absent, which you would expect in Pomerol or Saint-Emilion rather than in the Graves. The 12 *tonneaux* produced on average ferments in concrete vats. When fermentation is complete the wine is matured for about two years in used oak casks at the Chantecaille premises, where the bottling also takes place.

Class — especially in the taste

I am familiar with the wine of about eight vintages of Château les Carmes Haut Brion. Two typical features are a usually dark colour and a generally discreet and not very pronounced bouquet. It is in their taste that these red Graves show their real class. I have found them pleasant, elegant and supple — at least after about five years of bottle ageing. A wine from Les Carmes Haut Brion should never be drunk too early. The 1973 — not a particularly strong year overall — only began to taste really good in 1979. The 1971 at that time still had some reserve but was nevertheless a beautiful, complete wine, one of the best I have tasted from this château. The 1975 was also successful, given that Les Carmes Haut Brion is not notable for a really powerful taste. The 1974 was ready for drinking in 1979-80, and the fairly light 1977 should be drunk. Wines of higher quality — and deserving of patience — are the 1976, 1975, 1978, 1979, 1981 and 1982. Another characteristic of Les Carmes Haut Brion that should be mentioned is that some vintages have a slightly bitter element in the aftertaste.

The name of Laville Haut Brion was thought up by Frédéric Woltner. There is no château as such, although there is a small, ancient building between two plots of the Laville vineyard that might be the relic of some bigger complex.

The wine of Laville Haut Brion is always left to ferment out completely to eliminate all trace of sugar. The wine is vinified at La Mission Haut Brion, but the vineyards are about a quarter of a mile away on the far side of the Bordeaux-Bayonne railway line.

Below:
The wine of Laville Haut Brion set off against the chapel of Château la Mission Haut Brion.

Right:
The Woltner estates are administered by co-owner Françoise Dewavrin, seen here with her husband Francis on her left and estate manager Henri Lagardère at right. The Dewavrins live in Paris but visit Talence regularly.

Château Laville Haut Brion

Cru Classé de Graves
Talence

Laville Haut Brion, like La Mission Haut Brion and La Tour Haut Brion, belongs to the Domaines Woltner. It is situated in Talence and produces only white wine. There is no château: the grapes are vinified at La Mission Haut Brion, about a quarter of a mile away. The Laville Haut Brion vineyard was created in 1928 by Frédéric Woltner, who also gave it its name. The soil contains clay, gravel and lime, and is planted with 60% Sémillon and 40% Sauvignon vines. As the vineyard measures only 15 acres, the yield is limited: it varies from 5 *tonneaux* (1977) to about 25 *tonneaux* (1974).

Wooden casks

Henri Lagardère and his son Michel, a qualified oenologist, are responsible for vinifying the Woltner wines. After the grapes have been pressed and impurities removed from the must, the wine is left to ferment for a month in oak casks. For the whole of January the small cellar is cooled to a temperature of −5°C. This slow cold treatment prevents the formation of tartaric acid crystals. As soon as the fermentation process is completed the wine is transferred to clean wooden casks to mature for eight to ten months. Only a few of these casks are new — just enough to give the wine a hint of wood in the taste.

Right at the top

I would place Laville Haut Brion at the very top of the Bordeaux dry white wines, with Domaine de Chevalier. It has a personality entirely of its own. The Sauvignon is dominant in bouquet and taste until four to five years after vintage. Then, suddenly, the wine changes completely and the Sémillon breaks irresistibly through. The result is a golden-yellow wine that has a nutty element in the bouquet which often has something of the sweet sumptuousness of a Sauternes; the subtle delicate taste is dry and remains strongly in the mouth for some minutes.

This white Graves has an unbelievable vitality: after 15 years the 1964 was still very lively, a sublime wine. Michael Broadbent of Christie's of London confided that the 1945 Laville Haut Brion was one of the best white wines he had ever drunk in his richly experienced life. I myself have greatly enjoyed the 1971 (in 1979 this was actually still too young, too acidic of taste, but very rich in bouquet), the 1968, the very fine 1975 and the illustrious, complex 1976, which can be drunk now. Other recommended vintages are the 1954, 1966, 1967, 1969, 1970, 1978, 1979, 1980 (lighter than usual), 1981 and 1982 (a great wine with a great future).

Far left:
Owner Mme Guillemaud. Her estate is member both of the Académie du Vin de Bordeaux *and of the* Union des Grands Crus *de Bordeaux.*

Below:
Château Larrivet-Haut-Brion. The cellars are a little distance away.

In the distant past the estate was called Château de Canolle, and then Haut-Brion-Larrivet. Brion *in the local dialect means 'gravel' and the Larrivet is a stream that flows beside the estate. The* premier grand cru classé *Château Haut-Brion did not find this explanation satisfactory — the resemblance was too great. Haut-Brion-Larrivet was asked either to change its name or to substitute 'Château' by 'Domaine'. Larrivet demurred and litigation ensued. Haut-Brion won its case and Larrivet had to change its name to Château Larrivet-Haut-Brion. This was in about 1940, just when Guillemaud became the owner.*

Château Larrivet-Haut-Brion

Léognan
Graves

There was a time when Larrivet-Haut Brion was the most important estate in the commune of Léognan. For generations it covered an area of 250 acres, half of it vineyard. In 1936, however, the property was split up. The vineyard now measures 40 acres. In 1941 the estate acquired a new owner, Jacques Guillemaud. He died in 1973 and since then his widow has run the business, assisted by her cellarman Airoldi; Professor Peynaud gives oenological advice. Mme Guillemaud lives in what was formerly the estate workers' accommodation, a white, rectangular building overlooking a well-kept garden. The actual château, like the cellars, lies on the other side of a road that runs past the estate. The château is no longer part of the property and is occupied by a *collectivité*, a communal group.

A lot of red, a little white

The vineyard soil contains a great deal of gravel and is planted with Cabernet Sauvignon vines (58%), Merlot (about 37%) and Cabernet Franc and Malbec (some 5%). The proportion of Cabernet Sauvignon was increased gradually, by about 10%, during the 1970s. Both concrete and stainless-steel *cuves* are used for fermenting the wine. Mme Guillemaud hopes to go over entirely to stainless steel in the future. After its lactic acid fermentation the red wine is transferred to oak casks for about 18 months; 40% of these are replaced by new ones each year. The château also produces a very little white wine, from half Sauvignon and half Sémillon grapes. This does not go into casks and is bottled in the May following the vintage. The annual yield of white wine is no more than 2 to 5 *tonneaux*; that of the red fluctuates between 38 and 67 *tonneaux*.

Good structure

Red Larrivet-Haut-Brion is an extremely successful wine that is usually bought up quickly by the Bordeaux trade. The 1978 was a striking example: the whole vintage was sold by April 1979. In its youth the wine has a lot of fruit and a certain hardness, obviously due to the good percentage of Cabernet Sauvignon. I have never come across a fleshy or velvety Larrivet-Haut-Brion, not even when the wine was really mature. This Graves is impressive not for irresistible charm but for purity, balance and consistency of character. Keeping — for at least five years — is essential for the red wine so that it can lose its initial dourness. White Larrivet-Haut-Brion is a fragrant, mildly fresh wine that is perfectly drinkable six to eight months after bottling, but can also mature for a further five years.

Below:
Château de France seen from its vineyard, with the modern cellar complex at left. For many years — until 1974 — the wine was sold exclusively by the Calvet company.

Far right:
Besides the label shown here, there is another version with a drawing of the château.

Right:
A view of the up-to-date cuvier.

Jean-Marie Lasserre has been manager of Château de France since 1975.

The château was built in the mid-19th century.

Château de France

Léognan
Graves

Château de France at Léognan has changed owners about six times in the last 50 years, so that few of the archives remain. Practically nothing is known at the château about the origins of the estate and its name. The present owner, Bernard Thomassin, bought the estate in 1971. He lives in Paris, where he has a distillery. There has been much new planting at Château de France under his enterprising direction. In 1971 the vineyard had an area of only about 25 acres; today it is 42, plus a further 25 acres for the estate's second wine, the Bordeaux Supérieur Château Coquilles. These extensions have meant that the *cuvier* and *chais* have also had to be enlarged. Thomassin embarked on a comprehensive building programme in 1973, the last stage of which was completed in 1978. Château de France now has at its disposal the most modern, capacious cellars in the area, with 14 stainless-steel fermentation tanks, 20 other metal tanks (for the malolactic acid fermentation of the Graves wine and the maturing of the Bordeaux Supérieur), a large cellar for casks, a bottling unit and a storage area for storing bottles on pallets.

Traditional maturing

Château de France can now vinify its wine under the best possible conditions. Although fermentation is done in a very modern way in the stainless-steel tanks, the wine is matured in the traditional manner in wood for 12 months. About one-third of the stock of casks is replaced for each vintage. Château de France production fluctuates in good years around 100 *tonneaux*. The wine comes from 50% Merlot grapes, 25% Cabernet Sauvignon and 25% Cabernet Franc.

Pleasant table companion

The new installations only really started to come into use with the 1975 vintage. The wine of that year had a very deep colour with the hint of some mildness, a concentrated bouquet, and a mouth-filling, still somewhat severe taste when I tried it in 1979. In the 1976 I thought I could detect the fact that the grapes had been slightly 'cooked' in that hot, dry year; otherwise it seemed a pleasant wine, albeit a little flat and smooth. The 1978 had a deep purple colour, a good, full flavour and the blackcurrant bouquet of the Cabernet. With its good tannin content, it is becoming a very attractive wine. The 1979, 1981 and 1982 deserve attention too. Château de France is not a particularly refined wine, but thanks to its deep colour and very correct, quite firm taste, it makes a an enjoyable table companion.

Left:
André Lurton produces some 44 tonneaux of white and 114 tonneaux of red wine at la Louvière.

Below:
The rear elevation of the château, whose great hall has a painted ceiling showing the wife of a former owner (and a mayor of Bordeaux) as an angel whose eyes follow the visitor through the room. The entrance hall ceiling is decorated with trompe l'oeil *painting in various shades of grey by the Flemish artist Lonsing.*

Far right:
The grapes are delivered to the cuvier by tipper tractor.

Château la Louvière

Léognan
Graves

A member of the Bordeaux *parlement*, the Carthusian order, a mayor of Bordeaux, a mayor of Léognan — these have been some of the more illustrious owners of La Louvière. The château is one of the most imposing in the Graves. It reminded me of a smaller version of the famous Château Margaux inthe Médoc, for this 1795 building, too, has a stone staircase flanked by carved heraldic animals, leading to the main entrance and a tall portico with columns. But whereas Margaux was designed by a pupil of Victor Louis, who built the Bordeaux Grand Théâtre, La Louvière was the work of the master himself. Unfortunately the château was long neglected. However, the present dynamic owner, André Lurton, who bought it in 1965, is busy restoring it to its former glory. Lurton, who owns other estates, comes from an old wine-growing family. His brother Lucien's responsibilities include Brane-Cantenac, de Villegeorge and Climens.

Stainless steel for the white

La Louvière comprises 118 acres of vineyard, about 80 acres being planted with black grapes and the rest with white. The red wine, from 80% Cabernet Sauvignon and 20% Merlot, is fermented in *cuves* of concrete or steel. The white, from 85% Sauvignon and 15% Sémillon, goes into stainless steel for fermentation. La Louvière Rouge matures for one year in oak casks, one-third of them new, and then for roughly one more year in tanks. The white wine is sometimes matured in casks, but the duration depends on demand. Lurton likes to bottle his La Louvière Blanc within a year of the vintage.

More Merlot for the red

My impression from nine vintages is that this wine is gradually becoming less hard. From 1970 to 1975 it had a lot of tannin and a rather austere taste, but from 1976 the tannin seemed to have been reduced and the character of the wine was more congenial. I thought the 1978, even after only one year, was already enchanting. André Lurton confirmed this impression: for some years he has been increasing the proportion of the mild-tasting Merlot, and is aiming at 40%. A truly great wine was made in 1982; it belongs perhaps among the five best red Graves of that year.
The white wines are distinguished by a very pale colour with the merest tinge of green, a mildly fresh bouquet and a clean, similarly mildly fresh taste. Here too you can recognize the hand of the master, for these wines are produced with exceptional care.

Left:
The cellars of Château Ferrande, where M. Bortoletto has been maître de chai *since 1969. His boss Marc Teisseire also manages five other estates, including La Tour Martillac and Le Tuquet.*

Below:
M. Bortoletto stands proudly before his inner sanctum. Ferrande also makes a second wine called Château Lognac (red only).

Right:
Front view of the small château whose name derives from the French word ferrant, *'farrier'. In the Graves region there is a château called Ferran and Ferrand occurs three times in other districts.*

Château Ferrande

Castres
Graves

In selecting Graves châteaux for inclusion in this book Ferrande was an obvious choice from the start. it is one of the two non-*crus classés* to belong to the Union des Grands Crus de Bordeaux (the other was Larrivet-Haut-Brion). The estate received this honour thanks to Henri Delnaud, who bought it in 1954. Assisted by his manager Marc Teisseire, who arrived in 1955, Delnaud expanded Ferrande and also improved the quality of its wines. The vineyard was enlarged from 32 to 106 acres and the cellars were totally renovated. Henri Delnaud died in 1970 but his good work is being continued by his heirs, who live during the summer in the delightful château: a 'Chartreuse' style of building, typical of the district, with a small pointed turret on top.

Majority of red

Ferrande produces both red and white Graves. The red comes from 84 acres planted with Cabernet Sauvignon (40%), Merlot (40%) and Cabernet Franc (20%). Both concrete and stainless-steel vats are in use for fermentation. The red wine matures for about 18 months in oak casks, of which about 10% are replaced each year.
White grapes are grown on 22 acres planted with 60% Sémillon, 35% Sauvignon and 5% Muscadelle. The white wine is not matured in the wood but is bottled from the vats six months after the vintage.

Style and balance

I tasted some of the wines with the cellarmaster in the big *chai* where no fewer than 700 casks can be stored. It struck me that the red nearly always had a sound bouquet, very pure, pleasant, with some fruit, and more refined than sumptuous. Its taste combined the stylishness of the Cabernet with the suppleness of the Merlot. The wines were not lacking in tannin, so although they are drinkable relatively early, they can keep well — certainly strong years like 1975, 1978 and 1982. Wines such as the light 1977 and 1980 have a shorter life. All the wines excellently balanced the elements of colour, bouquet, taste and aftertaste. Although red Ferrande may not be a really rich or deep wine, its style, purity, soft nature and good balance are delightful. The white wine, too, is good, immediately enticing with its Sauvignon bouquet with plenty of fruit, and its gently fresh taste. I find that white Ferrande tastes most delicious two years after the vintage. White production varies from 23 to 32 *tonneaux*; red amounts to between 77 and 165 *tonneaux*.

Below:
The great inner courtyard of an estate that covers a total of 110 acres and is run by eight permanent staff including maître de chai (since 1959) Roger Martin. Owner Jean-Pierre Théron lives at the château.

Right:
Part of the vineyard with the Garonne in the distance.

Far right:
Grape picker in stone.

Château de Portets

Portets
Graves

The present Château de Portets was built in the 19th century on the foundations of a 16th-century castle, which was traditionally occupied by the most powerful man of the locality. Strategically placed on the edge of the village of Portets, not far from the Garonne, it was frequently the scene of fighting. In one such skirmish in the mid-17th century,the current lord, the Duc d'Epernon, was defeated by a force from Bordeaux that came up by river, and that was the end of the original castle. In what form it existed from then until the 19th century is not clear. The annals report that Napoleon and his entourage visited Château de Portets on 31 July 1808. Bonaparte was returning from Spain and lunched at the castle; what wine he drank is not recorded. Perhaps it was his Burgundy Chambertin, which he often diluted with water. After his short stay at Portets, the emperor rode on to Bordeaux, where he was ceremonially received.

The grape varieties

The present owner of the estate is the engineer and oenologist Jean-Pierre Théron, who also has properties in the Médoc (see Château Lafon, page 36). He grows both red and white Graves and his 80-acre vineyard is roughly equaly divided between black and white grapes. The red wine, from two-thirds Merlot and one-third Cabernet Sauvignon, ferments in concrete vats and then matures for 18 months in used oak casks. The white wine, with two-thirds Sémillon and one-third Sauvignon as its basis, is bottled in the spring following the vintage and is not matured in wood. The total production from Château de Portets varies between 40 and 75 *tonneaux*.

An accessible red Graves

Château de Portets produces a respectable dry white Graves, but not one of any great subtlety. It has quite a pronounced Sémillon bouquet and a mildly fresh taste with a hint of rusticity. The estate's red enjoys a much better reputation, and I have tasted it more frequently. It is not a wine to tax the buyer's patience for too long: often it is ready for drinking after about three years. Its colour is usually of an adequate depth but is never really concentrated or opaque. Its bouquet seems rather flat, sometimes even a little insubstantial, as in the 1976. The taste parallels this closely: not especially compact, with a soft suppleness quite early (not surprising, given the Merlot content) and a hint of *terroir.* The total picture is that of a sound, easily accessible red Graves without a great deal of subtlety or personality. Jean-Pierre Théron has much success with it.

Left:
Looking eastward from the walls of Saint-Emilion.

Below:
A map of the Saint-Emilion district. It comprises a thousand or so estates all tightly packed one against the other. Saint-Emilion itself is surrounded by satellite districts: Montagne-Saint-Emilion, Parsac-Saint-Emilion, Saint-Georges-Saint-Emilion (these three may sell their wines as Montagne-Saint-Emilion), Lussac-Saint-Emilion and Puisseguin-Saint-Emilion.

Right:
The town itself has many pleasant little wine shops full of bottled temptation.

Saint-Emilion

Saint-Emilion attracts between 200,000 and 300,000 visitors a year; in the Gironde *Département* only the city of Bordeaux and the resort of Arcachon exceed this number. The little town is especially busy at weekends. The car parks near the town walls are full, queues form outside places of interest, the many wine shops do a roaring trade and the confectioners sell the local delicacy of *macarons* in vast quantities. Many visitors conclude their walk through the town with a glass of refreshing sparkling wine, which is served in the 600-year-old Couvent des Cordeliers and produced in the cellars below.

Local monuments

The touristic success of Saint-Emilion is easily explained. This little wine town has a unique collection of monuments and the atmosphere of the distant past pervades all its narrow, uneven streets. The town was named after the Breton saint Aemilianus who died in 767. He lies buried in the catacombs beside the *église monolithe*, a remarkable church carved out of the rock, a task that took 400 years. (For a while, after the French Revolution, a saltpetre factory was set up inside the church.) Conspicuous inside the 1¼-mile-long town walls is Saint-Emilion's most important defensive structure: the Château du Roy, a tall, square tower with walls six to seven feet thick. Every year from this tower the *ban des vendanges* is proclaimed, after which the grape harvest can begin.

Heavy demand, much wine

The central square of Saint-Emilion formerly served as the timber market. There used to be many woods around the town. Today, however, trees are a rarity in this wine district; generally they are only to be found immediately around the various châteaux. Apart from these patches of woodland, the grape dominates the landscape completely. Practically every available plot of ground is planted with vines and other crops are

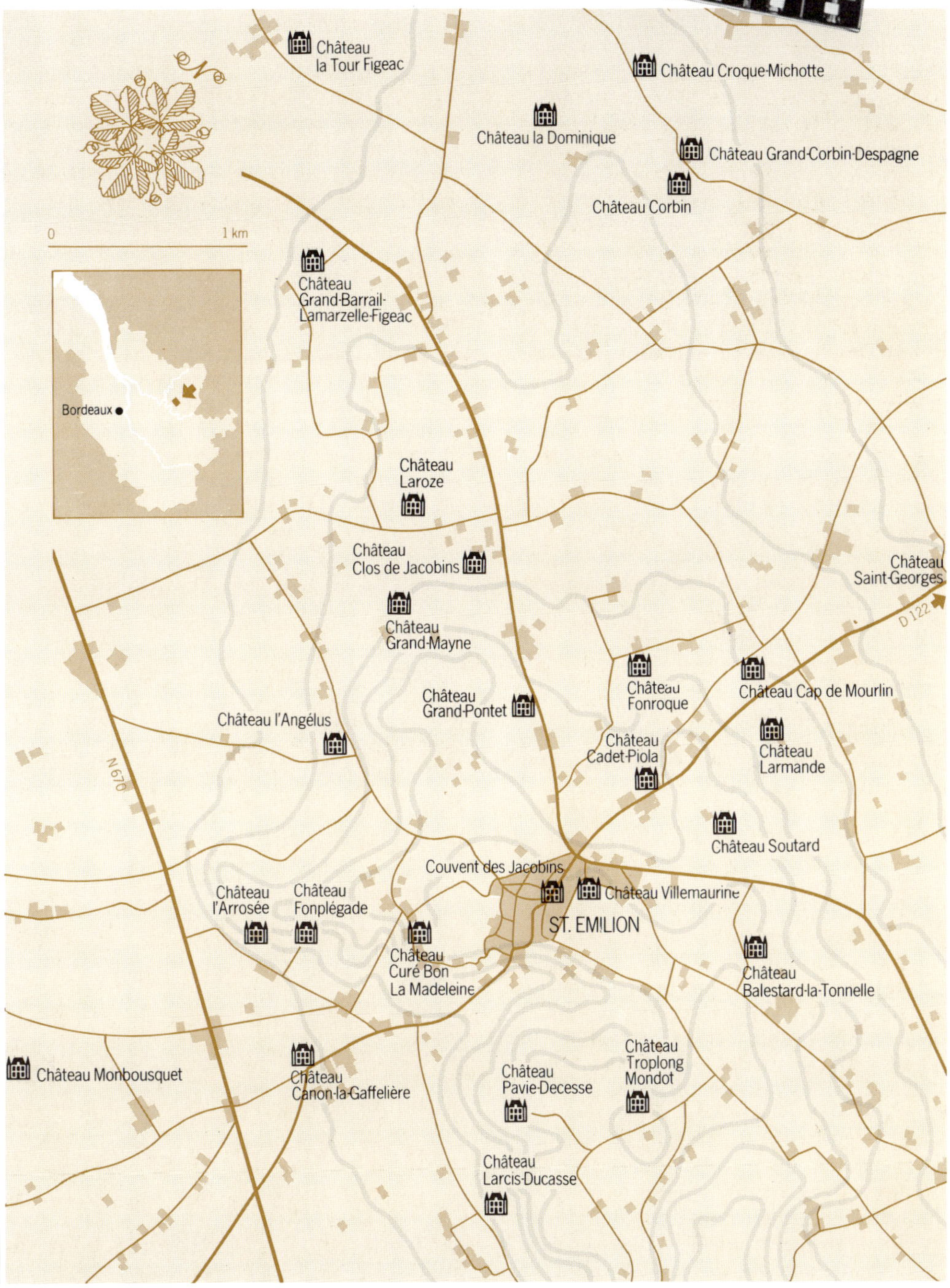

Saint-Emilion wines pure and simple must have a minimum alcohol content of 11°; the grands crus *and higher qualities must have at least 11.5°.*

In order to test for grand cru *status, (usually in June), samples are taken at the candidate châteaux by two people: an official and a wine merchant. One of these samples is then tasted by a jury consisting of a wine merchant, a grower and a wine broker, who may accept or reject the wine, or reserve judgment on it. The first two decisions are final, but if judgment has been reserved the second sample is tasted by a second jury whose decision must be accepted. Wines rejected by the panel may not be sold as* grands crus, *but may bear the Saint-Emilion* appellation

Right:
Grandes Murailles, just outside Saint-Emilion. This was once the north wall of a Gothic chapel that formed part of a monastery destroyed during the Hundred Years' War. The wines of Grandes Murailles are described in the chapter 'Other Châteaux of Interest'.

Below:
The houses of Saint-Emilion are all very old: the whole town has been listed as an ancient monument.

Some Saint-Emilions have a dairy-like aroma occasionally reminiscent of yoghurt.

hardly ever seen. This situation has undoubtedly contributed hugely to Saint-Emilion's commercial prosperity. Thanks to the many thousands of visitors and an effective public relations campaign, Saint-Emilion is one of the best-known Bordeaux wines. Moreover, supply of the wine is sufficient to meet the heavy demand: average production is around 2,200,000 cases a year. In the record year of 1979 the figure was nearly 3,200,000, 550,000 cases more than the combined yield of the Médoc communes of Margaux, Moulis, Listrac, Saint-Julien, Pauillac and Saint-Estèphe.

Friendly and approachable

The personality of Saint-Emilion wine has also contributed much to its popularity. Essentially, the wine is more rounded and supple, sooner drinkable and more easily approachable and 'open' than, for example, the Médocs. This is due to the predominance of the Merlot grape. The Cabernet Franc, known locally as the Bouchet, is the prevalent Cabernet here, and gives friendlier wines than the Cabernet Sauvignon. This choice of grape varieties is, of course, related to the soil types of the district. Saint-Emilion's most important area of plateau (The *côtes*) is made up of a thick stratum of limestone; and here the Cabernet Sauvignon yields a rather uninteresting wine in large quantities but with little alcohol. This grape is therefore planted only to make a modest contribution to the Saint-Emilion bouquet. Not all the local wine-growing is done on the *côtes*. The district also has a broad area of sand (incorrectly called *graves*, because only a small part of it has concentrated gravel), and a plain stretching to the Dordogne. Because of these contrasting soils there are many different types of Saint-Emilion. The ideal of a good, firm, generous and yet subtle Bordeaux is by no means always realized in practice, particularly as some growers regard quantity as more important than good quality; after all, by reason of the great demand, they can easily sell even mediocre wines at fairly high prices.

Grand cru: a devalued term

It is useful and important to know that in Saint-Emilion the term *grand cru* is not a guarantee of quality. This is discussed further in the following pages and in the chapter entitled 'Other interesting châteaux' (pages 191-8). It arises from the fact that the wine growers of Saint-Emilion managed to obtain permission from the Institut National des Appellations d'Origine to designate all their better wines as *grands crus*. This was a shrewd move, as the term *grand cru* has an almost magical effect on the wine lover, and consequently on the wine importer and the price. What need was there, after all, for a group of *crus bourgeois*, as in the Médoc? Saint-Emilion was thus allowed three categories of *grands crus*:
premiers grands crus classés (A and B)
grands crus classés
grands crus
The first two titles were to be valid for ten years, the third for just one wine of one vintage. In theory, *grand cru* without the *classé* was a designation merited by every château — a system that was apparently logical and democratic. In practice, however, the term *grand cru* has been greatly devalued because, in the eyes of most consumers, one *grand cru* is equal to another. When the Saint-Emilion classification was carried out in 1954, a host of new wines from this district suddenly sprang up to claim parity with the *grands crus classés* of the Médoc, although often this was not justified on grounds of quality.
It is significant that the Médoc, with some 25,000 acres of vineyard at present, has 61 *grands crus classés* whereas Saint-Emilion, with 13,000 acres, comfortably exceeds 300 *grands crus* (all categories) in good years! It is true that the Saint-Emilions have to pass a test before receiving their titles, but given the very divergent qualities that are sold as *grands crus* (*classés*), it may be wondered what criteria the tasting committees apply. The Saint-Emilion classification should

Left:
The 220-foot tower of the church of Saint-Emilion. The lowest part of the tower dates from the 12th century and is Romanesque; the middle section is 14th-century Gothic. The spire was added in the 15th century.

Below:
Sunday afternoon in the Couvent des Cordeliers. Beneath these historic ruins lie cellars where a fresh sparkling wine is made under the name of Clos des Cordeliers, an ideal refreshment for day trippers after a walk through the fascinating old town. The wine is frequently enjoyed with freshly baked macarons made to a centuries-old local recipe.

Right:
The latest vintage is earnestly discussed.

The Saint-Emilion classification is reviewed every ten years — at least that is the theory. A slightly revised classification was due at the end of 1980 (this should have come out in 1979) and the next revision should appear in 1990.

Today Saint-Emilion is a single-crop district, with the grape dominating all agricultural life. But things were not always that way. When Château Grand-Mayne was run by Jean-Pierre Nony's grandmother between 1914 and 1920, only 36 out of a total of some 220 acres were used to grow grapes. The rest was devoted to grain, which explains why Saint-Emilion once had many mills.

The limestone soil in the côtes is 15-20 feet deep in places.

therefore not be trusted too blindly; and the same must be said of the Jurade seal. The regional wine fraternity, the Jurade de Saint-Emilion, used to reward the best wines, which were given a numbered label with a seal. Today, however, the Jurade seal is available to all châteaux who are entitled to the *grand cru* designation in the relevant year (on condition that 10 centimes per label goes to the Jurade). In short, Saint-Emilions should be chosen with great care.

The Saint-Emilion crus classés

The following is the official classification for the Saint-Emilion district.

Premiers grands crus classés A
Ausone
Cheval Blanc

Premiers grands crus classés B
Beauséjour
Beauséjour Duffau-Lagarosse
Belair
Canon
Clos Fourtet
Figeac
La Gaffelière
Magdelaine
Pavie
Trottevieille

Grand crus classés
l'Angélus***
l'Arrosée***
Balestard-la-Tonnelle***
Bellevue*
Bergat
Cadet-Bon
Cadet-Piola***
Canon-la-Gaffelière***
Cap de Mourlin (Veuve Jean Capdemourlin)***
Cap de Mourlin (Jacques Capdemourlin)***
La Carte
Le Châtelet
Chauvin
La Clotte**
La Clusière
Corbin***
Corbin-Michotte*
Côte Baleau*
La Couspade
Coutet
Le Couvent
Couvent des Jacobins***
Croque-Michotte***
Curé-Bon La Madeleine***
Dassault
La Dominique***
Faurie de Souchard**
Fonplégade***
Fonroque***
Franc-Mayne**
Grand-Barrail-Lamarzelle-Figeac***
Grand-Corbin**
Grand-Corbin-Despagne***
Grand-Mayne***
Grandes Murailles**
Grand-Pontet***
Guadet-Saint-Julien**
Haut-Corbin
Haut-Sarpe**
Clos des Jacobins***
Jean-Faure
Laniote**
Larcis-Ducasse***
Lamarzelle
Larmande***
Laroze***
Clos la Madeleine**
Matras
Mauvezin
Moulin du Cadet**
l'Oratoire
Pavie-Decesse***
Pavie-Macquin
Pavillon-Cadet
Petit-Faurie-de-Soutard**
Le Prieuré
Ripeau
Saint-Georges Côte Pavie**
Clos Saint-Martin*
Sansonnet
La Serre*
Soutard***
Tertre Daugay**
La Tour du Pin Figeac (A. Moueix)**
La Tour du Pin Figeac (Bélivier)*
La Tour Figeac***
Trimoulet**
Trois Moulins
Troplong Mondot***
Villemaurine***
Yon-Figeac*

Grands crus classés Marked with three asterisks (***) have entries of their own in this book. The châteaux marked with two asterisks (**) are briefly described in the chapter 'Other interesting châteaux' (pages 191-8). Those marked with one asterisk (*) are briefly mentioned in this chapter. See also the Index (pages 199-200). In addition, all the *premiers grands crus classés* are described in the author's book *The Great Châteaux of Bordeaux.*

Left:
The side entrance to the château.

Below:
The courtyard of Larcis-Ducasse with its ancient well.

Far right:
Manager Philippe Dubois was born at the château.

Below the label:
This stamp is taken from a 1922 label and is still used on the Larcis-Ducasse cases.

Château Larcis-Ducasse is a member of two prestigious associations, the Académie du Vin de Bordeaux and the Union des Grands Crus de Bordeaux.

Château Larcis-Ducasse

Grand Cru Classé
Saint-Emilion

Château Larcis-Ducassis lies at the foot of a 330-feet-high plateau southeast of the town of Saint-Emilion. The vineyard borders on the *premier grand cru classé* Pavie. Most of the 27-acre vineyard is situated on a fairly steep slope, which makes it difficult and expensive to work. Some of it is even inaccessible to a caterpillar tractor, and if it rains hard a good deal of soil is always washed downhill. As manager Philippe Dubois observed: 'You have to fight nature here to make wine.' But because the site is so steep, it enjoys a slightly higher average temperature than other vineyards in Saint-Emilion.

For about a century the estate has been the property of the Gratiot family. The present owner is Mme Hélène Gratiot-Alphandery, who lectures in psychology at the University of Paris. Her son Jacques, the director of a cosmetics company, looks after the business side of Larcis-Ducasse and visits the château once a month.

Wooden vats only for maturing

Behind the château, a fine *maison bourgeoise* from 1830, are the cellars with their cement fermentation vats. Larcis-Ducasse also has wooden vats, but these are only used for maturing and storing the wine. The château hardly uses traditional oak casks at all. The wine stays in the vats for from 18 to 30 months; exactly how long depends on the wine itself. Jacques Gratiot regards 50 *tonneaux* as a normal yield for Larcis-Ducasse, but in years such as 1976, 1977 and 1978, less than 35 *tonneaux* was produced. The vineyard is planted with 50% Merlot vines, 30% Cabernet Franc and 20% Cabernet Sauvignon.

A long-distance runner

The wine of Larcis-Ducasse rather resembles a long-distance runner: sinewy but spare. It matures very well, but seldom surprises the drinker with its generous taste and still less with its subtleties. Its colour is deep but never black, its bouquet pleasant (often with some fruit), but never exuberant, its taste good but rarely excellent. The best Larcis-Ducasse I have drunk was the 1970. I found the 1974 somewhat disappointing; the 1975 was not quite up to many other *grands crus classés* of that year (and its aftertaste left a slight burning sensation); the 1977 appeared a little light, and the 1978 lacked some class. Nevertheless, Larcis-Ducasse is by no means a bad Saint-Emilion. You just wish that it filled the mouth in a more ample, and yet finer manner.

From 1948 to 1951 the château's director, Jean-Paul Valette, lived in the Dutch province of Zeeland where he studied milk production. He also spend some time working in Friesland before moving to Chile where he met his wife. After South America came Saint-Emilion.

The celebrated oenologist Professor Emile Peynaud acts as consultant to both Château Pavie and Château Pavie-Decesse, both of which are members of the Union des Grands Crus de Bordeaux.

Far right:
The shutters are always closed, for the château, built around 1890, is unoccupied.

Below:
Pavie-Decesse seen from its vineyards high above the plain of Saint-Emilion.

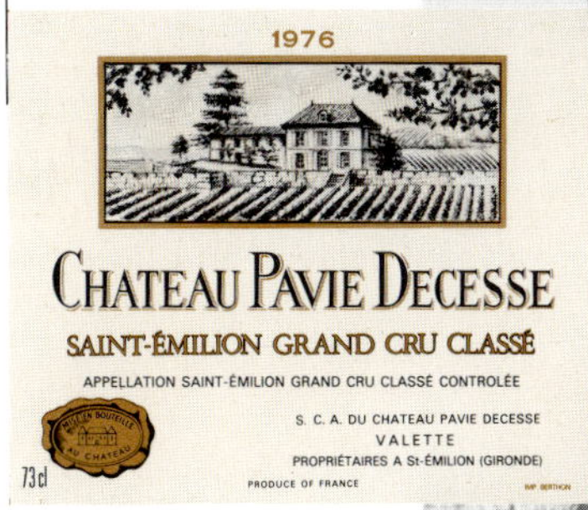

Château Pavie-Decesse

Grand Cru Classé
Saint-Emilion

In 1971 Pavie-Decesse was taken over by the Valette family, who are also at Château Pavie. Since then a great deal has been invested in the estate. Alterations have been made in the vineyard. There has been replanting; pruning methods identical to those at Château Pavie have been introduced; and all other processes have been geared to the production of quality. This was very necessary, for the reputation of Pavie-Decesse had seriously declined, as had the yield: in 1971 it was only 16 hectolitres per hectare, whereas the norm would be twice this figure. The cellars, too, have been transformed. In 1973 director Jean-Paul Valette added three large stainless-steel fermentation tanks to the existing cement vats. In the new tanks the temperature is thermostatically controlled during fermentation. Finally, the grey-white château (then unoccupied) was given a large reception hall on the first floor.

High situation

After fermentation the wine matures for 22 months in oak casks, a third of which are replaced each year. As Pavie-Decesse lies about 260 feet up, on the edge of a plateau and above Pavie, the wind often blows strongly, turning the wine in the vats temporarily cloudy; even so, it is not filtered. Fining is done with powdered albumin. The château is chronically short of space for storing bottles of wine. As a result a stone quarry a few hundred yards up on the plateau has been fitted out for the purpose. The storage space is needed because of the château's sales policy. Since 1976, Jean-Paul Valette has kept back a third of the vintage for bottle ageing.

A severe Saint-Emilion

Pavie-Decesse is a wine that benefits greatly from bottle ageing — unlike many other Saint-Emilions. It needs longer to develop, even in comparison with the Pavie with its higher classification; and Pavie-Decesse is rather harder, less fine. None of the recent Pavie-Decesse vintages has seemed to me to be particularly charming, generous or nicely rounded. Indeed, it is rather severe, with a potential that remains, as it were, locked up for a long time, and usually a colour that is dark and hard — a Saint Emilion, perhaps, for Médoc drinkers. The 9-acre vineyard consists of 55% Merlot vines, 25% Cabernet Franc and 20% Cabernet Sauvignon — although from my tasting I would have expected a greater percentage of the last-named variety. Recommended vintages are the 1978 and 1975, and the 1976 was very good. 1979, 1981 and 1982 promise well. Production varies from about 18 to nearly 50 *tonneaux*.

Far left:
Just a small part of the extensive cellars of Troplong Mondot.

Below left:
Bottles of the very pleasant 1973 vintage.

Below right:
A view of the château with its circular tower.

Right:
Claude Valette with one of his dogs.

Yet another member of the Union des Grands Crus de Bordeaux, Château Troplong Mondot utilizes a specials 'soft' égrappoir *which crushes the grapes only slightly.*

Château Troplong Mondot

Grand Cru Classé
Saint-Emilion

The concrete water tower just behind Château Troplong Mondot stands on the highest piece of ground in Saint Emilion. Fortunately the tower is largely hidden by trees, so that it does not spoil the view. The château, with its white walls and shutters, looks out over its 72-acre vineyard, with the steeple of the Saint-Emilion church in the distance. Château Troplong Mondot was built in 1745 by Raymond de Sèze who, during the Revolution, had the dubious honour of defending Louis XVI at his trial. The estate was then called Mondot. Later Troplong, President of the Senate under Napoleon III, added his name to it. The present owner is Claude Valette, whose grandfather bought Troplong Mondot in 1936. He is related to Jean-Paul Valette who runs Pavie and Pavie-Decesse.

Ample premises

Production at Troplong Mondot sometimes reaches 140 *tonneaux*, as in 1976; its *cuvier* and cellars are therefore unusually big for Saint-Emilion. The château has eight stainless-steel fermentation tanks with centralized temperature control. There are also some concrete vats, glazed on the inside. The wine is matured in the traditional manner for about 18 months in oak casks (some one-third of them new for each vintage). With 65% of the total the Merlot dominates the vineyard, followed by about 15% Cabernet Sauvignon, nearly 10% Cabernet Franc and 10% Malbec.

A balanced wine

Troplong Mondot enjoys an excellent reputation, especially in Belgium, which takes about two-thirds of the vintage. The 1964 was among the best wines of Saint-Emilion and did brilliantly at many tastings. The 1966, too, was outstanding. The total picture to emerge from tasting the vintages of the last decade is of a balanced wine with a not particularly pronounced, delicate bouquet and a reasonably full, quite elegant taste, often with a respectable amount of fruit. It struck me that the wines up to and including 1975 seemed to have rather more tannin than the later vintages. During my visit, Claude Valette confirmed this impression. He told me that Troplong Mondot was being made somewhat more supple than previously, when it was often not fully ready for drinking before ten years. However, this little extra suppleness has not essentially changed the character of the wine. In my view Troplong Mondot is not conspicuous for luxury or refinement, but it is a good, pleasant Saint-Emilion. I would count as my favourite among the Seventies vintages the 1970, 1971, 1975 1976 (powerful, with no less than 12.8° alcohol) and the quite concentrated 1978.

Far left:
Cellarmaster Georges Gresta has been with the estate for a quarter of a century.

Below:
Front view of the chateau, which dates from around 1850.

Château Canon-la-Gaffelière

Grand Cru Classé
Saint-Emilion

If you drive from the south into Saint-Emilion, you pass Canon-la-Gaffelière; the château stands near the point where the approach road to the town runs alongside the railway line. Officially, Canon-la-Gaffelière is one of the *côtes* estates of Saint-Emilion — although with the exception of one or two plots the vineyard is completely flat. It covers 47 acres and grows 60% Merlot, 35% Cabernet Franc and 5% Cabernet Sauvignon. Since 1971 the estate has had German owners — at present the three Counts von Neipperg, who live in Germany, not far from Heilbronn, in Schwaigern, where they also have wine properties. The manager of Canon-la-Gaffelière is Michel Boutet, who lives at Château Peyreau.

Rotation between tank and cask

In 1974 Canon-la-Gaffelière acquired a completely new *cuvier* with an impressive battery of stainless-steel fermentation tanks. This new building is larger than the residential part of the original château. The new tanks also serve for maturing the wine. Boutet works a rotational system, so that the wine spends three months in the tanks, three months in the casks, then three months in the tanks again, and so on. The total maturation period lasts at least 6 and not more than 24 months. Half of the casks are replaced by new ones each year.

Firm and supple

At Canon-la-Gaffelière the aim is not a classic *vin de garde,* a wine for laying down, but a Saint-Emilion for people to enjoy quite quickly. This is why the wine is not exclusively matured in the cask — that would give it too much tannin. A firm suppleness in the taste is characteristic of Canon-la-Gaffelière. It lacks depth, and certainly refinement, yet it is by no means without merit, particularly if it still possesses its youthful élan and fruitiness. In 1979 I thought the 1976, for example, was already charming (although it obviously had still to lose some tannin) and I also tasted the fruity, successful 1977 with pleasure. On the other hand, I considered the 1970 already too mature and the 1971 was in no way representative of that extraordinary Saint-Emilion year. The average yield at Canon-la-Gaffelière is 100 *tonneaux.* Wine from Château la Mondotte, a 10-acre estate belonging to the Von Neippergs, is also vinified in the cellars here.

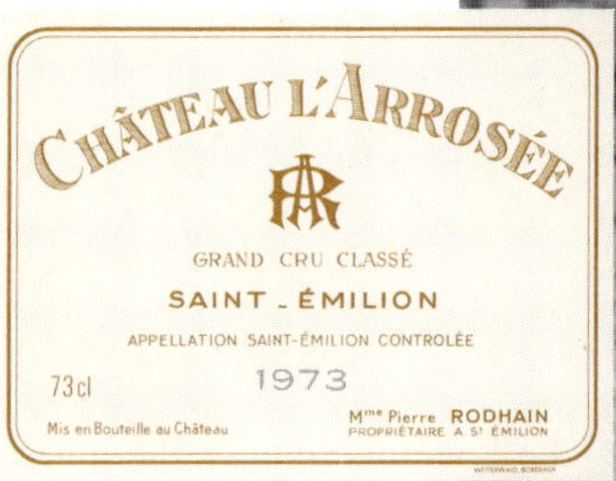

Left:
François Rodhain runs l'Arrosée which belongs, strictly speaking, to his mother. Income is provided by the estate itself and by grapes that are sold to the Saint-Emilion cooperative. The latter are taken from lower-lying vineyards.

Bottom:
The tiny château tucked away among the vines. The vineyard rises steeply behind the building.

Below right:
L'Arrosée is occupied by a family of wine growers who work for François Rodhain.

The estate's averge yield is 50 tonneaux. Its name is derived from the French verb arrosser, *which means to water or sprinkle. There are three natural springs on the property.*

Grape harvest at l'Arrosée is usually later than at other Saint-Emilion châteaux — ten days later in 1977, which explains the astonishing quality of this particular vintage.

Rodhain plans to level the steepest parts of his vineyard when replanting time comes around, to make them accessible for tractors. Till then, however, working by horse must continue.

Château l'Arrosée

Grand Cru Classé
Saint-Emilion

In the 19th century Château l'Arrosée enjoyed an outstanding reputation. Under Napoleon III it was the property of his minister and adviser Pierre Magne. L'Arrosée wine was served at the Imperial court and Napoleon even slept once at the château. However, for much of the present century l'Arrosée led an inconspicuous existence; from 1933 to 1966 the estate formed part of the Saint-Emilion cooperative. All the grapes were processed there and the château itself possessed neither *cuvier* nor cellar. In addition, the present owner's grandfather gave away l'Arrosée land to the cooperative; some of the buildings now stand there. Membership of the cooperative did l'Arrosée's reputation no good at all. Even today the château is one of the least-known of the *grands crus classés*, although in terms of quality it has much to offer.

Steep slope

The 25-acre vineyard of l'Arrosée, planted with 50% Merlot grapes, 35% Cabernet Sauvignon and 15% Cabernet Franc, lies against a steep slope. Part of the ground can only be worked with a horse. The château at the foot of the slope is, in fact, no more than a farmhouse. François Rodhain rents l'Arrosée from his mother and lives a few hundred yards away in a big house near the busy Libourne-Bergerac road. Methods at l'Arrosée are very traditional, with cement *cuves* for fermentation and oak casks for maturing the wine. It remains in the casks for from one to two and a half years. Used casks from Château Cheval Blanc are often bought for this purpose.

A concentrated, great wine

L'Arrosée has a sheltered, south-facing vineyard and Rodhain is always one of the last growers to harvest. His grapes are therefore picked at optimal ripeness. Some of the vines are quite ancient, dating from 1920. These factors, together with the classical vinification, produce a concentrated, dark wine with a great deal of power and class; in my opinion, it is the best in Saint-Emilion, deserving the status of *premier grand cru classé.* I thought the 1978 was splendid: deep-coloured, full-flavoured, with a certain finesse, plenty of fruit and a long aftertaste. The 1977, too, was excellent for its year, with a striking amount of fruit in bouquet and taste. The 1964 was equally fabulous; Rodhaim vinified a small part of that vintage himself. When I visited the château, nearly every nook and cranny was filled with bottles. This will quickly change if the world discovers l'Arrosée.

Left:
Three handsome old labels.

Far left:
The modest château, which its wall sundial. The cellars are in the rock wall with the white grille door.

Below left:
The maître de culture and his wife, who occupy a part of the château.

Below right:
Owner Maurice Landé and his son, Bertrand.

The Château has the only vineyard actually in Saint-Emilion itself: about one-third of an acre right next to the Couvent des Cordeliers.

Château Curé Bon La Madeleine

Grand Cru Classé
Saint-Emilion

From the end of the 15th century the Bon family of Saint-Emilion owned land on the great wine-growing area southwest of the town, but it was not until the beginning of the 19th century that vines were planted on it. The man who took the initiative in this was the parish priest in the family, *le curé* Bon. His wine soon became famous. It could hardly be otherwise, for the vineyard was surrounded on all sides by renowned estates: Ausona, Belair, Canon and Magdelaine. The priest left the vineyard to his nephew Camille Lapelleterie, who decided to call it Curé Bon La Madeleine. His uncle had never built himself a real château. The simple house, beside his vineyard, still contains personal mementoes, such as letters, Bibles, furniture and a silver wine taster.

A damp rock cellar

The present owners of Château Curé Bon are Maurice Landé and his son Bertrand. They sell tableware and have a shop in Libourne. Their vineyard measures only 12 acres and is planted with Merlot (80%) and Cabernet Franc plus a little Malbec (20%). In good years the yield is 20 to 25 *tonneaux*. The wine ferments in cement vats. After fermentation is complete, the wine is left for a few months and then transferred to wooden vats, where it matures for 18 to 24 months. Between one-sixth and one-fifth of the casks are replaced each year. They stand in a damp, partially underground cellar hewn out of the rock.

A monumental wine

The wine from Curé Bon La Madeleine is one of the most monumental of Saint-Emilions. Take, for example, the 1976, which I have tasted many times: a splendidly deep colour, a broad bouquet rich in fruit, a complex, luxurious taste, and a mild, lingering aftertaste. In my view it is a great wine which at a blind tasting I would, strangely enough, associate with Pomerol rather than Saint-Emilion. In less glorious years, too, the Curé Bon is often splendid; examples are the 1972, the 1974 and the 1977. I also have very good recollections of the 1978, which I tasted from the vat in the company of the Landés. It was a formidable wine, almost black, with a great deal of fruit. It had 12.7° of alcohol and in the course of the 1980s it is undoubtedly going to impress its consumers. Father Bon would be content.

Far left:
Armand Moueix, the owner, tasting his wine. He and his wife live at the château.

Below:
An imposing view up the drive of Château Fonplégade with its tall cedars.

Right:
A small part of the immaculately maintained and rather hilly vineyard.

Most Fonplégade wine is shipped to Britain and Belgium; other major customers include the United States, Holland and Denmark.

Château Fonplégade

Grand Cru Classé
Saint-Emilion

Fonplégade is one of the most illustrious châteaux of Saint-Emilion; a real château, built in the mid-19th century, flanked on both sides by angular, pointed towers. Since 1953, Fonplégade has belonged to Armand Moueix (not to be confused with Jean-Pierre or Christian Moueix of the firm of Jean-Pierre Moueix). Château and vineyard are, like Château l'Arrosée, on the steep southern slope of Saint-Emilion's most important *côte*. The château looks down towards the lower-lying land and, in the distance, Entre-Deux-Mers and the Saint-Emilion cooperative. Two tall cedars stand in front of the building and on all sides the vines form a blanket of green. Beside the château there is a large orangery, used by the firm of A. Moueix for receptions.

Used casks

In total the vineyard covers 44 acres, planted half with Cabernet Sauvignon, half with Cabernet Franc. After picking, the grapes ferment in cement vats. The wine then stays in oak casks for about 15 months. For each vintage about one-third of the casks are renewed. These casks are used for two vintages and then passed on either to the *négociant* firm of A. Moueix, or to third parties. The wine is still clarified with fresh egg white. Fonplégade production varies from about 46 to 114 *tonneaux*, as in 1978 and 1982 respectively.

Robust taste

Although the name Fonplégade is derived from a group of fountains on the estate, there is nothing watery about the wine. Fonplégade's better years have a deep colour, quite a robust taste and a decent amount of alcohol. They are not exuberant, joyous wines, nor are they conspicuous for their refinement; and in my experience they have not been exceptional in their bouquets. Despite these critical remarks, Fonplégade can be a very good wine, with roundness notwithstanding its power, a certain elegance and plenty of fruit. In quality it is clearly superior to the bulk of Saint Emilions — and thus deserves its place among the classified *crus*. It should be remembered, too, that the estate's sheltered position means that in less sunny years its wine is a little firmer than the products of many other châteaux.

Far left:
Leaded, stained-glass windows in the reception hall at the Couvent des Jacobins.

Below:
The entrance (left) and gardens of the château, which is in Saint-Emilion itself.

The family of Alain Borde's wife became owners of the Couvent des Jacobins in 1901, when the vineyard comprised a mere 10 acres.

There is an ancient quarry beneath the château, then 24 steps below that is another huge room used as the bottle cellar.

The estate's second wine is sold as Château Beau-Mayne.

The vines grow in two types of soil: one sandy, the other clayey (with a very heavy blue clay).

Couvent des Jacobins

Grand Cru Classé
Saint-Emilion

Couvent des Jacobins was the only estate in Saint-Emilion where the owner received me in a grey pinstripe suit: at that time Alain Borde was still a notary as well as a wine maker. He and his mother-in-law, the very experienced *négociant* Mme Joinaud, run this ancient estate. The Dominican monastery was built in the 13th century. It was the gift of Edmund, called Crouchback, the Duke of Lancaster and governor of Aquitaine, and second son of King Henry III of England. This new *couvent* replaced an earlier one that was outside the town walls and therefore indefensible. All that remains of the earlier house is a wall on the edge of a vineyard, Les Grandes Murailles. The monks of the Couvent des Jacobins made such good wine that it was served at the English court. Alain Borde continues this tradition of quality by producing an excellent wine.

Immaculately maintained

Everything on this estate exudes perfection. The residence and the garden are immaculately maintained, the *cuvier* with its concrete and stainless steel vats is spotless, the underground cellars have even floors and are nicely lit. The reception hall is one of the most tasteful in Saint-Emilion. What was once the monastery bakehouse was converted into a beautiful hall in 1974, with walls stripped to the stonework, a window with leaded panes, some religious objects (including a Bible of 1685) and facilities for wine tasting. Alain Borde told me a lot about his wine. The vineyard lies near l'Angélus and Grand-Mayne and comprises three plots totalling 23 acres. The vines are 65% Merlot, 25% Cabernet Franc, 9% Cabernet Sauvignon and 1% Malbec. Production ranges from 5 to 45 *tonneaux*. Selection is very rigorous and wine from young vines is vinified separately. The wine is matured first in wooden casks, 20% of them new, and then for several years in the bottle: Borde does not want to sell his wine too young for the simple reason that it needs time to develop.

Complete and balanced

Although I found the Couvent des Jacobins 1971 to be somewhat over-strong, with too much alcohol, the more recent vintages greatly impressed me. They had a dark, rather sombre colour and a taste that perfectly combined body, roundness, breeding, tannin, fruit and suppleness in the right proportions: complete and balanced wines. The concentrated 1975 promised much, the 1976 was a real charmer, the 1977 had surprising body and substance (only 5 *tonneaux* of it after selection!), the 1978 was firm and beautiful, the 1979, 1981 and 1982 most promising. Anyone tasting these wines will know what Alain Borde meant when he said: 'I do not live *from* the Couvent des Jacobins but *for* the Couvent des Jacobins.'

Left:
Bottles of Villemaurine pictured in front of the retail shop which is open on Saturdays and Sundays. The actual château is in the background.

Below left:
Casks of wine in the great cellars.

Below right:
One of the entrances to the cellar complex, which lies 25 to 30 feet below ground level.

Right:
The original château, built in 1893.

Château Villemaurine

Grand Cru Classé
Saint-Emilion

The history of Château Villemaurine goes back to the 8th century, when the Moors were invading France. A Moorish troop was camped just outside Saint-Emilion to protect the army's rear. The people of Saint-Emilion called this spot the Ville Maure and from this the later form Villemaurine was derived. Robert Giraud, a *négociant* by profession, has owned the estate since 1970 — except for the château itself, where a physiotherapist lives and works. According to Giraud, many improvements have been made since he took over. In the 20-acre vineyard the percentage of Cabernet Sauvignon has been increased to 30% (the rest is Merlot), a salesroom has been opened opposite the château and a great deal of interior work done, particularly in the underground cellars. Villemaurine has the biggest rock cellar in Saint-Emilion, big enough to lose yourself in. Giraud hopes to be able to entertain 1,000 people at a time here; and of course this is where the wine matures in casks.

The 22 to 50 *tonneaux* that the château normally produces ferments in stainless steel vats. The wine then develops for about 26 months in oak casks. Sometimes, according to Giraud, half of these casks are replaced by new ones. It is hard to tell in this damp cellar, for many of the casks are covered with mould.

Disappointing quality

The relatively high percentage of Cabernet Sauvignon, and the total absence of Cabernet Franc, make Villemaurine a rather atypical Saint-Emilion. The 1978 was much harder than other comparable Saint-Emilions of that year. It was a wine with a lot of colour, power and tannin. As Robert Giraud finds that his wine requires a considerable time for bottle ageing, he gave me the 1970, 1971 and 1972 as representative vintages to taste. The 1972 had a good deep colour, with a vague hint of vanilla in the bouquet (usually a sign that new oak has been used) and a somewhat meagre, rough taste that lacked charm and refinement. The 1971 did not appeal to me at all. It had a rather grudging bouquet, and a fairly tart taste. The 1970 did not enchant me either: in the reasonably full flavour I tasted both a tinge of sweetness and again a dash of acidity. Bearing in mind the many gold medals Château Villemaurine carried off in the previous century, it would seem that the potential for a really great wine is here. It is to be hoped that this potential will be better employed in the future.

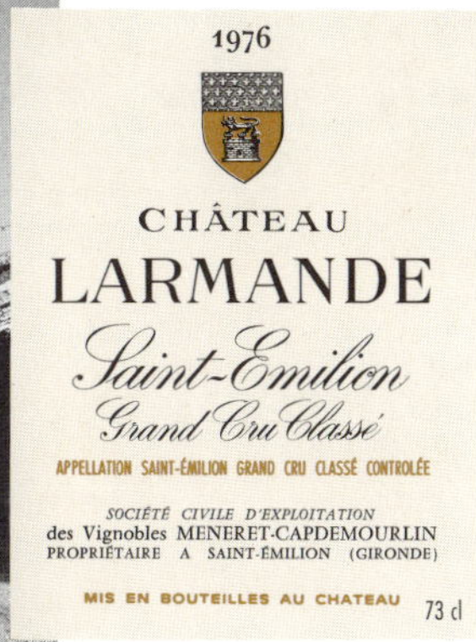

Far left:
The modest château; bottles are kept in its cellar in Saint-Emilion.

Below:
Larmande's vineyard produced very good vintages in 1974 and 1975.

Right:
Creeping vines being sprayed; this is never done to the grapevines.

Larmande's second wine is called Château des Templiers. Larmande belongs to the Union des Grands Crus de Bordeaux.

Château Larmande

Grand Cru Classé
Saint-Emilion

Château Larmande is a rising star in the firmament of the *grands crus classés*. This old vineyard, where vines have grown since the 16th century, lies in the north of the Saint-Emilion district. In general the soil here produces wines that are fairly firm and require time for full development. Larmande's own vineyard area increased from 28 acres in 1975 to 45.5 acres in 1982. The total yield now can reach more than 100 *tonneaux*. The Mèneret-Capdemourlin family owns Château Larmande. Jean Mèneret looks after the commercial aspects of the wine, his son Philippe is responsible for the oenological side. Philippe told me that proportions of the different grape varieties will gradually be changed. In 1979 the proportions were 60% Merlot, 25 to 30% Cabernet Franc and 10 to 15% Cabernet Sauvignon; the percentage of the Cabernet Franc is now 35%, that of the Cabernet Sauvignon 5%.

Considerable investments

There is no actual château in the Larmande estate — just a few houses dotted around the cellars. The Mènerets themselves live in the town of Saint-Emilion. However, the wine is well accommodated at Larmande. Since the vintage of 1975 the estate has had a brand-new *cuvier*, with gleaming stainless-steel fermentation tanks. In addition, new casks have been used since 1978 for maturing the wine — a third of the total. These considerable investments make it clear that Larmande is going all out for the production of quality wine.

A sturdy wine

One of the vintages tasted was the 1978. It had a dark colour, a rather reserved nose and a firm taste with quite some tannin. The rounded quality that you experience in many Saint-Emilions was almost absent. Larmande develops more slowly than many other Saint-Emilions. The maturation period is always less than two years: thus the 1976 matured for about 17 months, the 1977 just under 13 months. This 1977 was good for its year: rather lighter than the 1978, but with strength and class. Earlier vintages from Larmande gave me an impression of how the wine may develop. Eight years after its vintage, the 1971 was deep-coloured, with a full and mild flavour. The 1970 came over as younger and more compact, but had a lot of taste and a good balance. Altogether, Larmande is a well-made, characterful Saint-Emilion that certainly rewards those who patiently await its development.

Left:
Joint owners Maurice Jabiol (left) and son Alain. Their second wine is the simple Saint-Emilion Chevaliers de Malte. In addition they market the grand cru classé Faurie de Souchard (see page 196), bottles of which are seen maturing in the cave cellar of Cadet-Piola (at right).

Below:
The entrance to Cadet-Piola, whose name is emblazoned in large letters on the roof.

At Cadet-Piola there are trenches hacked out of the rock, as can be seen at Châteaux Soutard and Bellevue. These were made by the Romans to plant their vines 2000 years ago.

Château Cadet-Piola

Grand Cru Classé
Saint-Emilion

The drawing on the Cadet-Piola label would lead you to expect not only a château but an extensive vineyard, a park and some rather frivolous occupants into the bargain. The reality is quite different. Cadet-Piola has no château, the vineyard covers only 17 acres, there is no park, and the owners are two hard-working, friendly men, Maurice Jabiol and his son Alain. This little estate lies immediately north of the town of Saint-Emilion, on a 250-foot hill. The rocky ground is covered by a layer of soil only 8 inches thick in some places. Beneath the vineyard stretch vaulted cellars where in a damp half-light, the wine matures in casks and bottles.

Long-established quality

There is a long tradition of thorough, very serious work at Cadet-Piola. This is clear, for example, from the position accorded the estate in the 19th century in *Bordeaux et ses vins.* It ranked seventh among Saint-Emilion châteaux in 1864 and 1874, eighth in 1881 and 1885, and sixth in 1893. Today, too, its wine can be rated among the best Saint-Emilions. The yield varies between 18 and 40 *tonneaux* annually. The grapes ferment in concrete and stainless steel vats. The wine is then matured in oak casks for 12 to 18 months. A quarter of these casks are replaced by new ones each year. For the first year the wine ages in its casks above ground and for the second year goes into the underground cellar. The Jabiols fine their wine with fresh white of egg. The basis of Cadet-Piola wine is 51% Merlot grapes, 28% Cabernet Sauvignon, 18% Cabernet Franc and 3% Malbec. Insecticides are never used in the vineyard.

Generous bouquet and taste

The first thing that you notice about the Cadet-Piola wines is their dark colour. Only the 1976 did not quite conform in this respect — the Jabiols assured me that its colour would improve in the bottle; this was in 1979. Another characteristic is a generous, full and broad taste that remains in the mouth for a long time. The bouquet has the same generosity, sometimes (as in the tremendous 1969) with a certain creaminess. Together these elements make this a formidable wine, a great Saint-Emilion. Two of the best of the recent vintages are the 1975 and the 1979; probably neither will show its qualities to greatest advantage until ten years after their vintage. The 1976 is milder, more immediately charming, yet not lacking in substance and tannin. The pleasantly rounded 1977 has its virtues, while the 1981 and 1982 are both very impressive. Cadet-Piola surely deserves a place among the *premiers grands crus classés* of Saint-Emilion.

Left:
The front of Château Soutard, which gets its name from the Southards, a family of English origin.

Below left:
Cases of Soutard. The wine is bottled by gravity.

Bottom right:
Comte Jacques des Ligneris, who has worked at Soutard since 1945.

Below right:
François des Ligneris in the château's private cellar. A qualified architect, François now devotes all his time to helping his father.

Right:
The great hall runs the full width of the château.

Château Soutard

Grand Cru Classé
Saint-Emilion

My first visit to Soutard was made during the brilliant late summer of 1970. In a most hospitable manner, Comte Jacques des Ligneris let me taste various excellent years, including 1966, 1964, 1948 and 1945. Since then I have always had a certain affection for Château Soutard, which has been strengthened by later vintages and subsequent visits. The château is about 200 years old, with large rooms and old furniture. It was built as a summer residence for the Soutard family. In the past the vineyard covered about 125 acres. Later the property was divided into three, Soutard retaining 54 acres. Over the years this has been planted with an increasing proportion of Merlot, which now accounts for 60%, with 35% Cabernet Franc grapes and 5% Cabernet Sauvignon.

Not obsessed with profit

During the vintage and the fermentation of the wine the Count and his son François supervise everything personally, day and night ('C'est un travail de passion!'). The grapes ferment in vats of stainless steel or concrete. The wine is then transferred to oak casks, of which about one-third are replaced every year. The maturation period is sometimes longer than the usual 18 months: for example, the greater part of the 1976 vintage was only bottled in May 1979. About this the Comte des Ligneris remarked: 'We are not obsessed with profit. If we think that the wine needs a long time to mature, then that is what happens.' Another Soutard feature is the stringent selection procedure that is applied. Only the best wine bears the Soutard name. The rest is sold as Saint-Emilion *tout court* under the Clos de la Tonnelle name.

A distinguished wine

Almost 35 years after its vintage I renewed my acquaintance at Soutard with the 1945. The wine was still beautiful, with the scent of autumn leaves, of mushrooms. Its colour was once described as the 'varnish of a Stradivarius'. I told the Count that I thought it a very great wine, to which he replied 'C'est amusant' — the understatement of that year. Will the 1975 Soutard have a similarly long life? I believe it will. After four years it was a distinguished wine with a deep colour, a bouquet that had not yet opened up and a good amount of fruit, strength and aftertaste, together with the beginnings of suppleness. The Count had decanted it two hours previously. The 1978 is also an outstanding, supple wine with plenty of concentrated fruit. Fruit was also present in the bouquet and taste of the 1977; for Soutard this was an elegant, very charming year. The 1976 was a quick developer and will be pleasantly drinkable in the early 1980s; the 1975 can be awaited with equal pleasure. The 1979 tasted charming, and rather elegant; the 1980 was a fairly light, very pleasant luncheon wine, while the 1981 and 1982 will develop into splendid Saint-Emilions. Production varies between 78 and 110 *tonneaux*.

Left:
Mme Capdemourlin has run the château since the death of her husband Jean in 1967. Capdemourlin is a member of the Académie du Vin de Bordeaux as well as the Union des Grands Crus de Bordeaux.

Below:
Not so much a château, more a country house.

Right:
The spotlessly maintained cask cellar. Cap de Mourlin 'Jacques' has its own cellars.

Together, the two Cap de Mourlins produce 45 to 100 tonneaux each year.

Cap de Mourlin 'Jean' has two second wines: Château La Rose Faurie and Château Mayne-d'Artugon.

Château Cap de Mourlin

Grand Cru Classé
Saint-Emilion

Château Cap de Mourlin shows how complicated things can sometimes be in Saint-Emilion. Until the vintage of 1983 there were two châteaux of this name, both *grands crus classés* and both the property of a Capdemourlin. The only difference in their labels lay in their owners' first names: one named Jean, the other Jacques Capdemourlin. Of the two the 'Jean' property constituted the original estate, where the château stands and a vineyard of 23 acres. The 'Jacques' property was a 20-acre estate with just a cellar. Wine from the two properties is vinified, bottled and sold separately. The château is occupied by the widow of Jean Capdemourlin, who did a tremendous amount for the wine of Saint-Emilion. He was very much the pace-setter in the first classification and represented his district many times as *premier jurat* of the Jurade de Saint-Emilion. Since the 1983 harvest both Cap de Mourlins are reunited again under the direction of Jacques Capdemourlin.

Short cask-ageing period

Some acreage seems to have been lost when the two vineyards were reunited. Their combined area should have been just over 43 acres, but it only added up to 34: I assume some land must have been sold. The vines consist of 65% merlot, 30% Cabernet Franc and 5% Cabernet Sauvignon. Concrete vats are used for fermenting and wooden casks — a third of them new — for maturing the wine. Its time in the casks is limited to eight to ten months.

Change of style

I have not yet been able to taste the 1983 wine, but I have made the acquaintance of several vintages of both Cap de Mourlin 'Jean' and Cap de Mourlin 'Jacques'. The 'Jean' wines were notable for their amiable character. They were pure, elegant Saint-Emilions without excess of any kind, not of colour, aroma or strength. Their balance was good and they could be drunk fairly soon after their harvest — three or four years. The wines from 'Jacques' generally had more colour, tannin and flesh. As Jacques Capdemourlin has been directing this vineyard since 1983, I anticipate that we may henceforth expect his style of wine.

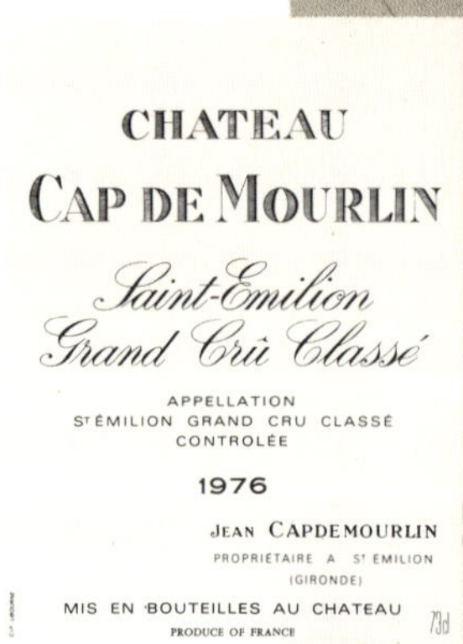

Far left:
The château, its vineyards and cellars have belonged to the Moueix family since 1931.

Below:
Grape pickers' baskets ready for the impending harvest.

Château Fonroque is the property of Jean-Jacques Moueix who works for the firm of Jean-Pierre Moueix. This company leases Fonroque from its owner. To make matters more complicated, Jean-Jacques does not live at Fonroque but at Château Trotanoy in Pomerol.

The manager of Fonroque is Michel Gillet, who oversees all the Moueix estates. He joined the firm of Jean-Pierre Moueix in 1979.

Fonroque's wine is kept for a year at the château, and is then moved to the cellars of Jean-Pierre Moueix at Libourne where maturing is completed over an 8- to 12-month period.

Château Fonroque

Grand Cru Classé
Saint-Emilion

Fonroque is one of the châteaux controlled by the firm of Jean-Pierre Moueix. The company rents the château from its owner, Jean-Jacques Moueix, and his sister, neither of whom lives on the estate. The château, dating from 1850, is about three-quarters of a mile north of Saint-Emilion. The vineyard is a single plot of 47 acres. It faces west so that the vines profit to the full from the good early morning sun. The grapes are therefore usually picked at optimum ripeness. Some parts of the vineyard contain quite a lot of clay; this is one of the reasons why Moueix has planted a high percentage — 70% — of Merlot. The Cabernet Franc accounts for the remaining 30%. The high average age of the vines is 35 years.

Late bottling

Fonroque is as quality conscious as the other Moueix estates. The grapes ferment in concrete vats and then mature in oak casks. At least 20% of the stock of casks is renewed each year. The maturation period usually lasts between 16 and 24 months — but can be half a year longer. Christian Moueix normally bottles Château Fonroque last of all his wines because, he says, it is a wine with a lot of tannin 'qui supporte bien le vieillissement en barrique'. The wine is clarified with beaten egg white and, in principle, it is never filtered. Production varies greatly. In 1974 there was a record grape harvest, giving 130 *tonneaux*; in contrast, after the frost of 1977 Fonroque yielded only 38 *tonneaux*.

Rustic and reserved

The Fonroque wine is a somewhat rustic Saint-Emilion of good quality. Normally it has a deep colour that only very gradually takes on the brownish lustre of maturity. The bouquet is a long time developing and even after many years is never very generous or forthcoming. The taste of a Fonroque does not possess the well-rounded character that you almost automatically expect of a modern Saint-Emilion; it is rather severe, firm and full of tannin. Even Fonroque from a supple vintage like 1976 still has a lot of reserve. It is simply a very individualistic Saint-Emilion that demands one thing above all else of its buyers: years of patience. A bottle of Fonroque from a good vintage can without qualm be laid down for a decade.

Left: Capdemourlin father and son in their spotless, tiled cuverie.

Below: The restored tower, in and around which receptions are held.

Right: The fouloir-égrappoir that both de-stalks and crushes the grapes.

Château Balestard-la-Tonnelle

Grand Cru Classé
Saint-Emilion

Balestard-la-Tonnelle is a very old wine estate, as is evident from a verse from the 15th-century French poet François Villon which contains the line: 'De boire ce divin nectar, qui porte le nom de Balestard.' The whole poem is reproduced on the label of the château, which derived its name from a canon of Saint-Emilion called Balestard. The 'Tonnelle' was added later and refers to a small tower surrounded by a terrace that stands a few hundred yards from the château and is used for receptions. Balestard-la-Tonnelle, after standing empty for 30 years, has been occupied since 1964 by its owner, Jacques Capdemourlin. He and his wife have furnished the château very tastefully; and the wine, too, is now suitably accommodated. The wholly renovated cellar and *cuvier*, with their spotless tiled floors, are a joy to see.

A small expansion

Jacques Capdemourlin uses concrete fermentation vats, wooden casks for maturing, and stainless-steel storage tanks. The wine is alternated between the casks and the tanks during the maturation period of about two years. Capdemourlin bottles his own wine and also sells it directly. Annual production is normally between 34 and 60 *tonneaux*. The vineyard covers 26 acres planted with 70% Merlot, 15% Cabernet Franc, 10% Cabernet Sauvignon and 5% Malbec.

A wine of breeding

Of the three Saint-Emilion *grands crus* made by Jacques Capdemourlin — Petit-Faurie-Soutard, Cap de Mourlin and Balestard-la-Tonnelle — the last is the best, a wine that in addition to its colour, strength and its rounded quality, clearly possesses breeding. Despite its substantial character, it is not heavy or tiring. This 'solid' aspect of Balestard-la-Tonnelle is balanced by a pleasant vitality of bouquet and taste and by a modest finesse. An outstanding example of a good, characteristic vintage is the 1976. In 1975 and 1987, too, Capdemourlin produced very successful wines, and neither the 1977 nor the 1982 were disappointments. I did have some difficulty with the 1970 and 1971 vintages, in which the alcohol seemed to overwhelm the finer nuances. In general, Balestard-la-Tonnelle wine should not be drunk until at least four to five years after the vintage, a fact that certainly is true also for the successful vintages of 1979, 1981 and 1982.

Far left:
The château seen from the rear.

Below:
The estate's original name — Mazerat — can still be seen on the front of the château; it was changed around 1920 to l'Angélus after a part of the vineyard.

Right:
Hubert de Boüard (son of Jacques) has studied oenology under Professor Ribereau-Gayon and now works at l'Angélus.

According to Jacques de Boüard, 'There's never enough of l'Angélus', which explains the very high prices.

Château l'Angélus

Grand Cru Classé
Saint-Emilion

The wine of Château l'Angélus is one of the best-known, most expensive and most sought-after Saint-Emilions. The owners, the de Boüard family, deserve credit for this, for the tremendous reputation of their wine was established in only half a century. Until 1924 the estate was called Château Mazerat, acquiring its present name when the de Boüards took over. The brothers Jacques and Christian, who at present run the estate, have a 69-acre vineyard planted with 50% Cabernet Franc, 45% Merlot and 5% Cabernet Sauvignon: the Cabernet grapes predominate here, which is exceptional for Saint-Emilion. Average annual production lies somewhere between the 80 *tonneaux* of 1977 and the 145 of 1979 and 1982.

The case for new casks

During my visit to Château l'Angélus in 1979 there were no wooden casks to be seen. The wine here not only ferments in concrete vats but matures in them too, for 18 to 24 months. This policy, however, has been drastically changed. By sheer chance I took part in a tasting at the château with the brilliant oeonologist Professor Pascal Ribéreau-Gayon. He offered three 1973 wines for tasting. Not knowing what they were, I suggested that the first was somewhat dull, too flat. The second had rather more mettle, more backbone, but made a rather dry impression and was not very pleasing. I found the third was the best. You could smell and taste the vanilla of new oak casks. Then all was revealed: all three had been from l'Angélus! The first wine was the normal l'Angélus, the second one had been aged in used oak casks and third in new ones. The point Professor Ribérau-Gayon had wanted to make was that only new casks could bring about an improvement. This and other experiments convinced the proprietors of the use of new oak casks; since the 1979 vintage all wine is aged from six to nine months in new *barriques*.

Improved quality

L'Angélus is a full, rich, unaggressive Saint-Emilion. By some means or other, the roundness of this wine absorbs the harshness of the tannin. That the wine has a good dose of tannin is due in part to the high percentage of Cabernet. Of recent vintages the 1978 had a lot of body, power and suppleness. The 1977 was rather lighter, but still firmer than the 1973 that I tasted. The 1976, strangely enough had more to it than the 1975 — just a little more fruit, depth and length. Personally I found all these wines somewhat smooth and lacking refinement of bouquet and taste. Their undeniable early charm remained superficial. Rather more firmness, 'bite' and subtle gradation would make the personality of l'Angélus more attractive for me — as do the vintages from 1979 onwards, including the truly magnificent 1982.

Below left:
Apparatus used to reduce the temperature of the wine during fermentation.

Below right:
The château, partly hidden by trees, with a pile of fresh stakes for a replanting project in the foreground.

Far right:
The château, always shaded by trees in summer, has been the home of estate manager Philippe Carmagnac since 1975.

The wine of Clos des Jacobins is bottled at the château by a mobile unit owned by Cordier.

Château Clos des Jacobins

Grand Cru Classé
Saint-Emilion

Clos des Jacobins is one of the châteaux situated on the road from Saint-Emilion to Libourne. Others are Grand-Pontet, Figeac and Grand-Barail-Lamarzelle-Figeac. Clos de Jacobins is a Cordier estate, the personal property of Jean-Georges Cordier. The vineyard, on a gentle slope, covers 20 acres. The cellars are built right next to the château, which is occupied by Philippe Carmagnac, the young manager. As at other Cordier estates, these are immaculately maintained.

Filtering after clarifying

The vineyard is planted with 47% Merlot, 45% Cabernet Franc and 8% Cabernet Sauvignon. White-painted concrete vats with plastic linings are used for fermentation. After this process is completed the wine is transferred to oak casks for about 15 months; one-third of the casks are replaced each year. The wine is clarified with fresh egg white and is filtered just before bottling to remove the last impurities. Production at Château Clos des Jacobins (odd that both 'château' and 'clos' are used) averages around 40 *tonneaux*, with a maximum of about 65.

Constant quality

I have tasted a number of vintages from Clos des Jacobins. After nine years the 1970 seemed mature at first, but had not yet fully realised all its potential. The 1973 had a fairly deep colour, a mild, amiable bouquet and a pleasant, supple taste. Apart from just a little acidity, the wine was quite ready. The 1974 offered rather more calibre, but fewer subtleties; bouquet and taste were rather indeterminate. The 1975 wine had much more colour and tannin and was well concentrated. I thought the taste was almost creamily rounded and well on the way to being drinkable. The deep colour of the 1976 indicated the beginning of mildness; youthful fruit was still discernible alongside its supple and substantial qualities. The 1977 had a pleasant bouquet and taste, and was ready for drinking in 1980. The 1978 was almost black in colour and had a mild, generous, reasonably complete taste: wine you could almost chew. The 1982 also had a very dark colour and a fairly smooth, firm taste. All the vintages were comparatively mild, supple, full-bodied, without angularity, and the quality seemed quite consistent. This makes Clos des Jacobins attractive for restaurateurs and for a wide public. If they only possessed more character and subtlety I would have rated them more highly.

Far left:
The château viewed from its small, flower-filled garden.

Below:
The main gate of Grand-Pontet that fronts the Saint-Emilion-to-Libourne main road.

Some of the vines in Grand-Pontet's vineyards are 80 years old.

Most of the estate's wine is shipped to Britain and the United States.

Assemblage *or blending of the vats of wine from the different grape varieties and vineyard plots is not done until three months before bottling.*

Château Grand-Pontet

Grand Cru Classé
Saint-Emilion

In 1415 an army captain named d'Estieu enchanted by Saint-Emilion, bought some land there and established the wine estate of Grand-Pontet. The château remained the property of the captain and his descendants for exactly 550 years. One of the most famous owners was Gabriel Combrouze, mayor of Saint-Emilion from 1896 to 1944, and deputy for the Gironde *département* from 1906 to 1924. After 1965 Grand-Pontet belonged to Barton & Guestier, part of the Canadian Seagram concern; and since 1980 it has been the property of the Pourquet and Bécot families, who are related (their interests include Château Beau-Séjour Bécot in Saint-Emilion). Part of the small château is occupied by the cellarman Georges Mallié.

Short maturation period

The vineyard covers 37 acres on a gentle slope and is planted with 65% Merlot, 25 to 30% Cabernet Franc and 5 to 10% Cabernet Sauvignon. At the highest point of the vineyard there is a cellar dug out of the hillside where up to 200,000 bottles can be stored. The *cuvier* stands next to the château. Concrete fermentation vats are used here. The wine is matured in oak casks, all of which come from Beau-Séjour Bécot. The maturation period is rather short for a *grand cru classé*: from 8 to at most 14 months. The wine is not filtered. Grand-Pontet's average annual yield is around 60 *tonneaux*.

Supple and unproblematic

I have got to know four Grand-Pontet vintages well. The oldest was from 1970. After some nine years it had a deep, brownish-red colour. The bouquet was ripe and not very interesting. The taste also seemed mature, with considerable strength, some fat, and a slightly roasted character. The total effect was of a fairly pleasant but rather undistinguished wine. The three other vintages confirmed this impression. I found the 1976 a supple, 'easy' wine with the merest hint of caramel in the taste. The 1977, too, had a lot of suppleness, together with a little *terroir* and some fruit in the bouquet. *Terroir* was similarly present in the mouth-filling 1978 which, drawn from the cask, already tasted amazingly supple. The quality of the wine has improved since 1980 — especially since the 1981 vintage. Grand-Pontet now has more style, more backbone, more character. It is a Saint-Emilion to watch.

Left:
A bottle of 1976. The date 1767 has been chiselled into one of the walls in the cask cellar — two centuries of wine making at Château Grand-Mayne.

Below:
The main entrance to the estate, with the outlines of the château in the distance and the tall trees that surround it.

Right:
Owner Jean-Pierre Nony is clearly aware of the camera as he tests the nose of his wine.

For its second-quality wines the estate uses the labels Château Cassevert and Château Beau-Mazerat.

Much Grand-Mayne goes to Belgium, particularly Antwerp and Ghent.

Château Grand-Mayne

Grand Cru Classé
Saint-Emilion

The name Grand-Mayne appeared for the first time in the *Bordeaux et ses vins* of 1922. In earlier editions it had been listed as Du Mayne or Le Mayne. The château was completed between 1736 and 1767, just before Soutard. The architects of the two châteaux were brothers, and Soutard still possesses documents relating to Grand-Mayne. Since 1934 Grand-Mayne has belonged to the Nony family. The present owner is Jean-Pierre Nony. He arrived at the estate in 1972 after various studies, including oenology. It became his sole property in 1975 and he has lived in the château since his marriage in 1977.

Old and new

The interior of the ivy-clad château calls up memories of the past. The rooms are rather dark, some of the paintings are very old, the floors are wooden, the beams thick. The modern *cuvier* is in sharp contrast. There the traditional wooden vats have been replaced by 16 stainless-steel tanks in which, since the 1975 vintage, Grand-Mayne's annual production of 29 to 113 *tonneaux* has been fermented. The wine is matured for about 15 months in oak casks. Nony replaces one-fifth of them each year with new ones. After fining with powdered albumin the wine is often also filtered: as in 1976 when the wine, from very ripe grapes, was cloudy. The total area of the vineyard is 47 acres and the grape varieties are 50% Merlot, 40% Cabernet Franc and 10% Cabernet Sauvignon.

Agreeable wines

Although I remember the 1964 as a full, sturdy wine, I am concerned here only with the vintages since 1975, when stainless steel was introduced. Grand-Mayne's 1975, unlike many other wines of that year, was ready for drinking about four years after its vintage. The taste had plenty of suppleness, a racy undertone, a fair amount of strength and not a great deal of tannin. The bouquet was rather soft and flat. The 1976 had a more elegant bouquet, with more fruit and a measure of refinement. This wine also had a very supple, pleasant taste that nevertheless seemed rather to lack strength. The 1977 — silver medal winner at the Paris show — was a very nice wine with a charming flavour and an impression of soft fruit. The 1978 — gold medal winner in Paris — had a deep colour, a concentrated bouquet and an accessible, particularly supple taste, with 13° of alcohol. The 1980 here was well-structured for its vintage, and both the 1981 and 1982 offered a very decent quality. Grand-Mayne is not a wine that impresses by its finesse or power, but is a sound, well-made Saint-Emilion that deserves its place among the *grands crus classés*.

Below:
The stylish château looks out over a very attractive parkland. In 1978 several trees — 200 years old and more — had to be felled because they had died.

Far right:
One of the cellar workers pours out a glass from the wood to taste the young wine. A pipette is used to extract the wine from the cask.

Château Laroze

Grand Cru Classé
Saint-Emilion

Tall trees almost hide Château Laroze from passers-by. Some of the trees, like the château, are more than 200 years old. Laroze came into being through the joining of two estates, Camus-la-Gommerie and De Lafontaine. The widowed Mme Gurchy combined these in 1883 and called them Laroze-Gurchy. The present château at Laroze was formerly that of Camus-la-Gommerie. Later a further 32 acres was added to the existing 37 acres of vineyard. The estate is still owned by the heirs of Mme Gurchy. The present administrator (and co-owner) is Georges Meslin. He and his wife live in the château. After bottling, the Laroze wine is stored in Libourne, where Georges Meslin has his own wine business, next to the glass factory.

Reserve fermentation tanks

The winery buildings at Château Laroze stand some distance from the house, behind a small wood. A few tanks outside the entrance to the cellar are used for fermentation when the harvest is exceptionally large, as in 1970; but normally the wine is fermented in concrete vats. The *chai* where the wine matures in oak casks is illuminated by only a few small lights and is rather dim even during the day. One-fifth to one-third of the stock of casks are replaced each year. Since 1979 the château has had a modern bottling unit: this is surprisingly rare in Saint-Emilion, where even many of the *grands crus classés* have to hire a bottler. Average annual production is about 120 *tonneaux.*

Predominantly Cabernet

Laroze's 74 acres are planted with 50% Merlot, 40% Cabernet Franc and Cabernet Sauvignon. The earliest Laroze wine I have drunk is the 1971. Ten years after its harvest it had a soft, mature bouquet, not of a pronounced breadth or depth. The taste was almost mild, but had a firm core. I thought the 1976 a pleasant, supple wine, at the same time sturdy and quite elegant. The 1977 proved lighter, without being actually thin. As far as taste is concerned I was charmed by the 1978, a lively, delicious wine with some nuance and a deep colour. The 1979 in its youth seemed to promise much. Château Laroze does not have a tremendously exciting bouquet, but usually tastes very good.

Left:
The estate's manager, Jean-Marie Carrère.

Below:
The château has a horizontal Vaslin grape press.

Right:
Château Grand-Barrail.

Carrère hopes to be able to buy new casks, once the financial position of the estate allows.

The château produces between 60 and 215 tonneaux *each year, not counting the second wine known as Lamarzelle-Figeac.*

Jean-Marie Carrère is the owner of a handsome collection of semi-precious stones.

Château Grand-Barrail-Lamarzelle-Figeac

Grand Cru Classé
Saint-Emilion

As the name suggests, Grand-Barrail-Lamarzelle-Figeac resulted from the merging of a number of estates. As far as I have been able to discover, these were Clos La-Marzelle-Grand-Barrail, La-Marzelle-Figeac and Clos La-Marzelle. The 99-acre vineyard lies around Château Grand Barrail, built in 1886 with one side in Arabic style, and no two windows alike on the other. Edmond Carrère of Monbazillac bought the vineyard and château in 1956 — the year of the devastating frost. He came to an agreement with the former owner that she should live permanently in the château. I therefore met the *gérant* Jean-Marie Carrère, Edmond's son, in the small house built on to the cellars of the old Clos La-Marzelle (later renamed Château Lamarzelle). The simple furnishing suggested that the Carrères had not so far done too well out of their estate. The frost in 1956 and a number of middling harvests in the 1960s are doubtless to blame for this.

Space shortage

Lack of financial means is also the main reason, according to Jean-Marie Carrère, why Grand-Barrail-Lamarzelle-Figeac uses hardly any casks: 'Casks are too dear and in any case we don't have the room.' The wine therefore matures in the same concrete and metal vats in which it ferments.
Although the famous Château Figeac with its very gravelly soil is close by, Grand-Barrail has hardly any gravel, except in one small plot. Its subsoil is quite sandy, with some clay and limestone. In the lower-lying parts stagnating rainwater sometimes forms a problem. During my stay in Saint-Emilion I saw water puddles standing for weeks on end between the vines. Grand-Barrail's grapes are 60% Merlot, 30% Cabernet Sauvignon and 10% Cabernet Franc.

Not very inspiring

During a great tasting organized by the French journal *Gault-Millau* the Grand-Barrail-Lamarzelle-Figeac 1967 scored remarkably highly. I have never been able to understand why — unless it was a different wine from the uninteresting 1967 I tasted. The almost complete absence of oak-wood and the discouraging vineyard conditions make this Saint-Emilion an easy-going wine that should be drunk early. In 1979, for example, I found the 1971 — an excellent year for Saint-Emilion — already over-mature. Grand-Barrail is a mellow wine, usually with a lot of body and colour — and that is about the sum of it.

Bottom:
Maître de chai *Jean Beyley has worked at La Tour Figeac since 1963, when he moved from Château Maison-Blanche in Montagne-Saint-Emilion.*

Right:
The white château in the 'hunting lodge' style so characteristic of Bordeaux.

Château La Tour Figeac has no second-quality wine.

The wine is usually exported in wooden cases, but distributed in cartons within France itself.

Bottling is done with a mobile unit that can handle 20,000 bottles a day.

It is estate policy to keep some of the vintage in bottles at all times — in 1979, for instance, there were still substantial reserves of the 1974, 1975 and 1976.

Château la Tour Figeac

Grand Cru Classé
Saint-Emilion

The vineyard of La Tour Figeac was once part of the *premier grand cru classé* Château Figeac, but was separated from it in 1879, leaving an area of 100 acres. Three years later this too was divided up, so that La Tour Figeac now has just under 34 acres of wine-growing land: mostly sand (*sables*) with just a small, higher zone of gravel (*graves*). The estate lies between Figeac and Cheval Blanc, on the boundary with Pomerol, as is shown by a sign saying 'Pomerol-Toulifaut' immediately beyond the trimly maintained château. The tower from which La Tour Figeac takes its name stood here on the estate until well into the 18th century. It was rebuilt around 1960 when the château was completely restored. At the end of 1973 La Tour Figeac changed hands. It is now owned by a *société civile*, consisting of one French and two German families. The German Rettenmaiers hold a majority of the shares but the château is occupied by a Frenchwoman. Michel Boutet is the manager; he is also responsible for the German-owned Canon-la-Gaffelière.

Minimum ten months in cask

Glazed concrete fermentation tanks are used at La Tour Figeac. Afterwards the wine — from 60% Merlot and 40% Cabernet Franc — is matured in oak casks. During my visit the cellarman Jean Beyly told me that the estate cannot afford any new casks, though he expected some improvement in the situation, an opinion echoed by Michel Boutet. The maturation period at La Tour Figeac is rather short: about ten months at most. Sometimes, as with the 1973 vintage, the wine does not go into the casks at all but is kept in the fermentation vats or storage tanks. Average annual production is about 65 *tonneaux*.

Balance and terroir

I have very good memories of the 1975 La Tour Figeac. The wine had a really beautiful bouquet (modestly described by the cellarman as 'bien agréable au nez') and a good taste that was firm without being clumsy. It had a deep-red, velvety colour and a long, tannic aftertaste with some *terroir*. I though it a great, soundly balanced Saint-Emilion. The 1976 also tasted pleasant, although lighter in all respects. This wine, too, was very harmonious and well made. Again I detected some *terroir* in the aftertaste. The 1977 was lighter still, although it had a vigorous core to it and a little *terroir*. It was becoming an elegant La Tour Figeac which, like the 1976, was ready for drinking around 1980. The 1978, on the other hand, was a wine that could be laid down for about five years after its vintage, if not longer. The same is true for the 1981 and 1982, while the 1979 deserves attention too.

Below:
Maître de chai *Jacques Chambaud with his first vintage — he started at La Dominique in 1969.*

Right:
The front of Château la Dominique, with shutters closed against the fierce midday sun. The entrance to the cellars is on the right. The château is home to Michel Musset, estate director since 1971.

Cleanliness is definitely a virtue at La Domninique, with the shining stainless-steel fermenting tanks standing on a spotless tiled floor.

The Delor company is a loyal and major customer of Château la Dominique. It is part of a tradition to bottle some wine in the big sizes such as magnum (150 cl), double magnum (300 cl), jeroboam (450 cl) and imperial (600 cl). The oldest ordinary-sized bottle in the cellar dates from 1926.

La Dominique markets its second-quality Saint-Emilion under the Clos des Vergnes label, although production of this wine averages only two tonneaux.

Château la Dominique

Grand Cru Classé
Saint-Emilion

Château la Dominique is next-door neighbour to Château Cheval Blanc and their vineyards adjoin for about half a mile. Altogether La Dominique has a vineyard of some 44 acres with a subsoil of gravel, clay and ferruginous sand. The vines are 76% Merlot, 8% Cabernet Franc, 8% Cabernet Sauvignon and 8% Malbec. The first owner of the estate made his fortune in what is now the Dominican Republic — hence the name of the château. The present owner, Clément Fayat, who bought La Dominique in 1969, is a prosperous building contractor. It was he who built the new cellar at Château Figeac. Since he took over La Dominique many improvements have been made in the château and the cellars. In 1972, for example, nine stainless-steel fermentation tanks were acquired. The wood from the old vats was used for the cellar doors.

No filtering

After fermentation, the wine — between 26 and 100 *tonneaux* a year — is transferred to oak casks. Part of the stock of casks is replaced each year: how many new ones are bought depends on the quality of the wine and the scale of the production. The 1978 wine went into casks of which one-eighth were new; for the smaller 1977 vintage a quarter were replaced. At Château la Dominique they are against filtering. The wine is thoroughly clarified, usually with a minimum of five fresh egg whites per cask. After maturing for about two years, the wine is bottled and part of it is then stored in the roomy château cellars. When I visited the estate the stock was 350,000 bottles. I saw a lot of wine from 1969, and from all the subsequent vintages. Fayat has obviously discovered that wine in the cellar is worth more than money in the bank.

Compact strength

It is hardly surprising that La Dominique's wine should tend towards Pomerol, for like Cheval Blanc, it lies on the boundary with that district. It is a mouth-filling, mild-tasting, fairly broad wine that tends to be chosen not for its subtleties but for its agreeably compact strength and early drinkability. The 1976, for example, was quite mature three years after its vintage. I doubt, however, whether La Dominique has always had this characteristic. Michael Broadbent, Master of Wine and one of the world's best tasters, described the 1955 some 15 years after its vintage as a wine 'with a seemingly endless life ahead of it'. Whether La Dominique is vinified differently from before, I do not know. Of the otherwise good 1978 I noted: 'Not so concentrated as other 1978s; rather a loose structure.' And of the 1976: 'mild taste with just enough backbone to prevent it falling apart.' Of older vintages 1970 and 1971 can be recommended, of more recent ones 1981 and 1982.

Left:
Corbin seen from its back garden.

Below:
Mme Blanchard-Giraud.

Right:
The château is fully appointed but only occupied during the actual vintage time.

Château Corbin

Grand Cru Classé
Saint-Emilion

A chestnut-bordered drive leads up to Château Corbin, one of the oldest estates of Saint-Emilion. The foundations of the château date from the 14th century and according to tradition, Corbin was the centre of a territory held by Edward, Prince of Wales, better known as the Black Prince. At that time it formed a single estate with all the other Corbins of Saint-Emilion, including Grand-Corbin-Despagne, Grand-Corbin, Corbin-Michotte and Haut-Corbin. The only reminder of this illustrious past is the ancient tower in the garden behind the château. This dates from the time of the Black Prince; the present château was built at the end of the 19th and the beginning of this century.

A capable lady

The château is owned by a *société civile*, Domaines Giraud, which also has other properties, among them Certan-Giraud in Pomerol. Supervision of the wine-making is the responsibility of Mme Blanchard-Giraud, a capable and charming lady who, despite her elegant appearance, feels thoroughly at home among the concrete fermentation tanks and the oak casks. She is assisted by her *régisseur*, Max Viaud. The 18 to 75 *tonneaux* that Corbin produces matures for about 20 months in the cask. About 10% of the casks are renewed each year. The wine is fined with fresh white of egg and for the past few years it has also been filtered, to prevent the formation of tartaric acid crystals.

Rather reserved

When Mme Blanchard's parents bought the château in 1920 the vineyard area comprised only 20 acres. Between the 1920s and 1940s they planted another 17 acres. The proportions of the grape varieties are one-half Merlot, one-quarter Cabernet Franc and one-quarter Cabernet Sauvignon. They give an austere-hued wine that some would describe as a classic Bordeaux. Corbin has a rather reserved character and a good deal of tannin. It lacks the mild, rounded traits that characterize many Saint-Emilions, and is, in fact, quite a hard wine (although without the severity of a Médoc) that only becomes really agreeable after several years. Yet it never quite acquires an open, generous roundness. I have drunk the strong, perhaps somewhat too alcoholic 1966 with pleasure. A more recent vintage that turned out well is the 1975: very concentrated, a lot of tannin, great class. The 1976 is a fairly supple vintage for Corbin, although I thought the aftertaste was a little dry. The 1977 is a lighter wine that will develop more quickly than normal. I have the impression that a Corbin from a really good vintage is very much better than one from a less brilliant year. Because of this lack of consistency I would always be inclined to buy Corbins from the sunniest vintages.

Far left:
Mme Despagne poses by the kitchen door of the château that is her home. Her son Guy supervises the estate and lives next door at Château Reine Blanche, which has its own vineyard covering 12 acres.

Below:
Château Grand-Corbin-Despagne viewed from the direction of Château Corbin.

The estate yields between 70 and 140 tonneaux a year, and all wine is bottled with the château's own equipment. Mme Despagne's other son, Gérard, lives at Château Maison-Blanche in Montagne-Saint-Emilion where he makes a very good wine indeed (see 'Other Châteaux of Interest').

Château Grand-Corbin-Despagne

Grand Cru Classé
Saint-Emilion

Grand-Corbin-Despagne is a near neighbour of Château Corbin; the two estates lie almost opposite each other on either side of a metalled road. The buildings are painted a creamy white, probably to temper the effect of the hot midday sun. It was on such a sunny, hot afternoon that I was received in the large, cool château kitchen by Mme Despagne, a widow, and her son Guy. Mme Despagne lives in the château itself and Guy occupies Reine Blanche next door. The Despagne family has owned Grand-Corbin-Despagne for about 200 years. The estate is quite large for Saint-Emilion — 62 acres. The vineyard consists of a number of plots, mostly beside and behind the château, planted with 60% Merlot, 25% Cabernet Franc and 15% Cabernet Sauvignon plus Malbec. (The vines pictured on the label do not belong to Grand-Corbin-Despagne).

Recent rebuilding

There was extensive rebuilding at the château in 1978 to make room for nine big stainless-steel fermentation tanks; a number of concrete vats have also been retained. Used oak casks are employed for maturing the wine. The *collage* or fining is done with fresh egg white. Grand-Corbin-Despagne is not filtered unless absolutely necessary: Guy Despagne told me quite openly that part of the 1977 vintage had been lightly filtered because it needed to be bottled early.

Vigorous and reliable

Grand-Corbin-Despagne enjoys a good reputation because of its reliable quality. About 70% of the wine is sold via the normal trade channels, the rest directly to individuals. Demand for the 1975 was so great that the private customers were limited to 12 bottles each. Four years after its vintage this 1975 had a deep, soft colour, a strong bouquet and a warm, racy taste that was also nicely rounded. A small criticism was the 'stalkiness' I detected in the taste and aftertaste. I thought the 1976 was also a successful wine, although a little less engaging than many of its contemporaries because of its rather hard core and persistently lingering tannin. The 1977 was a fairly light, short wine but the 1978 had many delightful qualities — compactness, opaque colour, blackcurrant bouquet, and taste with the right proportions of strength, fruit and tannin: in short, a Grand-Corbin-Despagne that can be termed a *grand vin.* One should look out for the 1981 and 1982 too.

A lot of Château Croque-Michotte is drunk in Belgium and it enjoys a substantial reputation in Switzerland as well.

All wine is packed in wooden boxes, which facilitate the long-term storage of labelled bottles under perfect conditions at the château itself. This is always done with a part of the vintage.

The concrete fermenting tanks at Croque-Michotte were installed not so long ago, at the beginning of the 1970s.

Left:
One of the simply appointed salons at the château.

Below:
In visual terms the château is not especially remarkable.

Château Croque-Michotte

Grand Cru Classé
Saint-Emilion

The name Croque-Michotte suggests that this used to be a place where travellers could stop for refreshment: 'Croque' comes from *croquer*, 'to crunch', and 'Michotte' from a word meaning bread roll, or loaf. Croque-Michotte owes much of its reputation as a wine estate to Samuel Geoffrion. He was a knowledgeable wine grower, regarded as the *éminence grise* of Saint-Emilion, who did much replanting and achieved excellent results with his painstaking vinification methods. His daughter, Mme Rigal, regularly stays at the château. The wine and the vineyard are the responsibility of Jean Brun, who is also the very capable *régisseur* at Trottevieille, Franc-Mayne, Laniote and elsewhere.

Old trees, gleaming tanks

Outwardly time seems to have stood still at the château, with its small park of tall, venerable trees. But appearances are misleading, for in the cellars everything is run on efficient, modern lines. Since the 1978 vintage five gleaming stainless-steel fermentation tanks have been in use, and in other respects too Jean Brun has things very well organized.
The vineyard covers 30 acres on the boundary of Saint-Emilion and Pomerol. It is 80 to 90% Merlot, supplemented by Cabernet. Production varies between 30 and 70 *tonneaux*. For maturing the wine oak casks are used; between one-sixth and one-fifth of them are replaced annually. At Croque-Michotte the wine remains in contact with the wood for a relatively short time: 6 to 12 months. The château's policy is to reserve a part of each vintge in the bottle; a separate *chai* across the road is stacked highed with cases of earlier vintages.

A lot of glycerine

Croque-Michotte wine has a personality all of its own; Jean Brun describes his product as 'un peu particulier'. A characteristic feature is the generous amount of glycerine it always seems to possess. Because of this the wine gives an impression of suppleness and fat, and it has plenty of alcohol as well. Beyond the smooth, mild exterior you discover something rougher in the taste. It lacks the refinement of a truly great wine. The 1978 was a very characteristic vintage: dark, concentrated, thick with fruit and almost fat in taste. The 1977 was a success for its year. I was rather less lucky with the 1975 which four years after its vintage had a bouquet and taste in which ripeness, a 'burned' element, and a tinge of sweetness all mingled. Croque-Michotte goes best with unsophisticated dishes, although I thought the 1973 was delicious with *foie gras* of goose with chanterelles and a truffle sauce. This Saint-Emilion, which also made good wine in 1979, 1981 and 1982, should be given time to mature — about five years at least.

Left:
Alain Querre raises his glass while brother François pours one for himself. François lives at the château, Alain and his artist wife occupy a country house some distance away.

Below:
Vintage at Monbousquet.

Right:
The château dates from 1864.

No Monbousquet wine was made in 1963, 1965 or 1968. The château is a member of the Académie du Vin de Bordeaux. Alain Querre's customers include some 2,000 French restaurants and tens of thousands of private individuals.

Château Monbousquet

Saint-Emilion

Although Monbousquet is not included in the *grands crus classés*, it is a Saint-Emilion that you come across in many of the better French restaurants, for it is very well known and has a good reputation. The estate is more than four centuries old and lies in the commune of Saint-Sulpice-de-Faleyrens, the flattest and lowest part of Saint-Emilion, leading down to the Dordogne. Looking at the thriving 74-acre vineyard today, it is hard to imagine that a generation ago it was almost completely derelict. When Daniel Querre bought the estate in 1945 there were only 10 acres of vines in miserable condition. He immediately set out replanting the property, and also carried out improvements in the cellars. The result was a sublime 1947 — nearly 100% Merlot — that still made a great impression in 1978 at a blind tasting in Fort Worth, Texas. It even scored higher than the Lafite-Rothschild of the same year.

Hardly any Cabernet Sauvignon

Daniel Querre's successors are his sons Alain, François and Jean. It is Alain — also the director of a wine firm — who is mainly involved with Monbousquet. The production of 110 to 160 *tonneaux* still ferments in oak vats. It then matures for 18 months in casks, also of oak. Some of these casks, usually a quarter, are replaced each year. The wine is filtered.
Besides the 50% Merlot and 40% Cabernet Franc in the vineyard there is 10% Cabernet Sauvignon. However, this last grape is not used for Monbousquet, since, in Alain Querre's view, it tends to upset the character of his best wine. Today the Cabernet Sauvignon is mainly used in the estate's second wine, Bouquet de Monbousquet.

A pleasant taste

At Château Monbousquet they deliberately make a very pleasant-tasting, supple wine soon ready for drinking. It is a mild, almost velvety Saint-Emilion that usually can be drunk without problem about three years after vintage. At the same time it has enough tannin for long bottle ageing: thus, after 17 years, the 1962 was still vital and pleasing, even though this wine came from a fairly light vintage. At the same tasting I also became acquainted with the fine 1964, the mild, mellow 1966, the elegant 1967, the surprisingly strong 1970 (to which all the wine from the pressing was added, which was quite exceptional for Monbousquet) and good, rounded wines from 1975, 1976 and 1978. The 1979, 1981 and 1982 certainly deserve attention too. Monbousquet may not be one of the richest, most refined Saint-Emilions, but it is expertly made and a delight to drink.

Far left:
Pétrus Desbois and his wife during a formal lunch at the château.

Below:
The truly impressive château with one of the 13th-century towers remaining from the old maison forte *on which the present building is constructed. The motto* vini templum *(temple of wine) justly stands over the cellar entrance.*

Saint-Georges enjoys a microclimate with less rainfall than either Saint-Emilion or Libourne, so the grapes ripen earlier.

In one of the reception rooms hangs a gigantic painting by Georges Mathieu entitled 'Hommage à Saint Georges

Château Saint-Georges

Saint-Georges-Saint-Emilion

Château Saint-Georges is a worthy representative of a group of districts bordering on Saint-Emilion itself: Montagne-Saint-Emilion, Lussac-Saint-Emilion, Puisseguin-Saint-Emilion, Parsac-Saint-Emilion and Saint-Georges-Saint-Emilion. The last is by far the smallest and its wine, like that of Parsac, is often sold under the Montagne-Saint-Emilion *appellation*. The most important exception to this general rule is Château Saint-Georges: its label carries the Saint-Georges-Saint-Emilion *appellation*. This is justifiable as it represents nearly one-third of the total wine yield of the district. In addition, the château itself is on a regal scale, a veritable wine palace that stands on a hill dominating all the country around. It was built in 1770 by Victor Louis, architect of the Grand Théâtre at Bordeaux.

Three years in the cask

Château Saint-Georges was bought in 1881 by the father of Pétrus Desbois, the present owner. Father and son worked tremendously hard and, despite difficult periods, they steadily increased the renown of their wine. At present the vineyard covers 123.5 acres planted with Merlot (50%), Cabernet Sauvignon (30%), Cabernet Franc (10%) and Malbec (10%). Until 1978 wooden fermentation vats were used. These have been replaced by stainless-steel tanks. To cope with its production of between 139 and 260 *tonneaux*, the château has at its disposal large cellars and a constant stock of about 3,000 casks for maturing the wine. This very large number is necessary because Saint-Georges wine remains in the cask for two and a half to three years. Normally half of each vintage goes into new casks.

Nobility and mellow strength

The Château Saint-Georges wine has the same nobility as the environment in which it is made. It has mildness, strength, breeding — and in good years an iron constitution. After 15 years the 1964 was still very vital, and the 1947 was amazingly youthful. Incidentally, neither wine had travelled — I drank them during a formal lunch at the château itself. More recent Saint-Georges vintages give the impression that Pétrus Desbois still makes his wines as expertly as ever. His 1982, 1981, 1979, 1978 and 1975 have a great future, and my recollections of the 1980, 1976, 1973, 1971 and 1967 are most agreeable. Château Saint-Georges can never be ranked as a *grand cru* or *grand cru classé* because it lies outside the actual Saint-Emilion district. This does not worry Desbois at all. He told me, 'My only classification is my name. That has to be enough.'

A few production figures show just how much the yield can vary in Pomerol:
1976 — 371,700 cases
1977 — 150,500 cases
1978 — 302,400 cases
1979 — 542,100 cases

Pomerol itself has around 1,750 acres of vineyards; neighbouring Lalande-de-Pomerol boasts approximately 2,050 acres, including the district of Néac whose wines can be sold under their own name, but are usually found under the Lalande-de-Pomerol label. There is also a commune called Lalande-de-Pomerol, to the northwest of Pomerol itself. The village of Néac, with its church spire, is on the northeastern edge of Pomerol.

Below:
Map of Pomerol showing the most important châteaux.

Right:
Grape harvest in Pomerol. These vendangeurs are using plastic baskets instead of the traditional wooden trugs.

Pomerol

The wine district of Pomerol is bounded on the west by Route Nationale 10bis, in the north by the little river Barbanne, in the east by Saint-Emilion and in the south by the town of Libourne. The district boundaries may be clear enough, but the commune itself is less neatly arranged. Pomerol is not a single village but a collection of tiny hamlets, all with the name Pomerol preceding their own. As you drive around you come across Pomerol-Catusseau, Pomerol-Toulifaut, Pomerol-Cloquet, Pomerol-Maillet, Pomerol-Petit Moulinet, Pomerol-Grand Moulinet and others — and Pomerol-Centre, where there is a large church with a tall steeple that is visible from practically all parts of the district. It was built in the 19th century to replace a Romanesque church, founded in the 12th century by the Knights of St John, which had become unsafe.

Charity to pilgrims

The Knights of St John were one of three such religious orders formed at the time of the Crusades to give help and shelter to travellers, pilgrims and the sick. Their symbol was the Maltese cross. These *Hospitaliers* did much for Pomerol, where their charitable activities included building a hospital. They chose this district because of its position in one of the pilgrim routes leading to the shrine of Santiago de Compostela in Spain. Silent witnesses to this period are a number of stone signposts marked with the Maltese cross that are still to be seen in Pomerol. The Knights of St John also gave a stimulus to wine-growing, which had originally been introduced to the district by the Romans; so it is not surprising that the local wine fraternity is called Les Hospitaliers de Pomerol, and that their members' red cloaks are adorned with the Maltese cross.

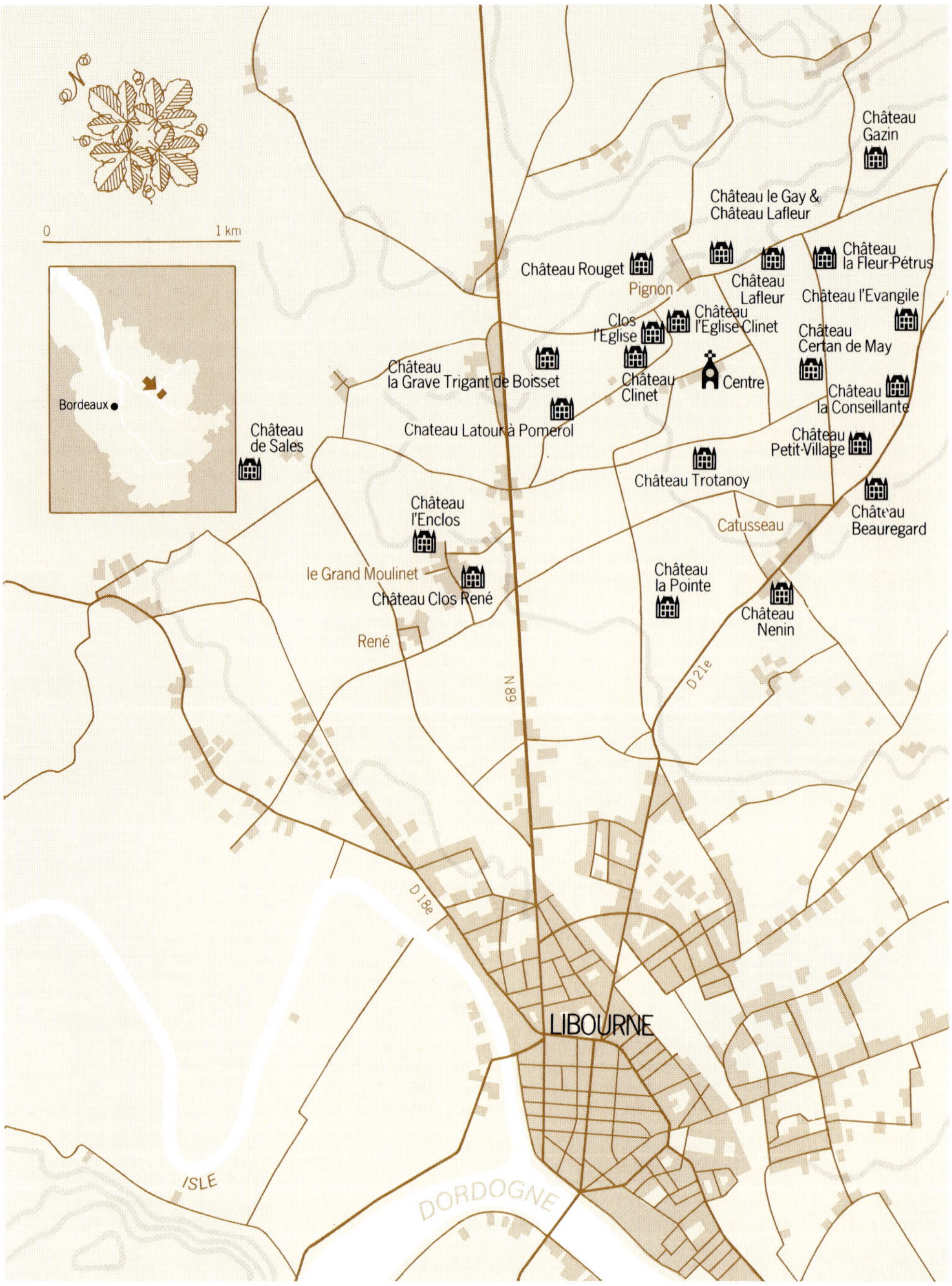

Left:
The church in Pomerol-Centre dates from the 19th century and can be seen from all over the district.

Below:
Three signs point to Pomerol, but each road leads to a different hamlet.

Rural character

As in Saint-Emilion, the grape prevails here, to the exclusion of other crops. The district has about 1,730 acres of vineyards, divided among some 180 growers. There are hardly any grand châteaux hereabouts, nor the droves of tourists who pour into Saint-Emilion every weekend. Even the neighbouring town of Libourne does not seem to disturb the rural aspect or tranquillity of Pomerol.

Clay, sand, gravel and iron

Pomerol has various kinds of soil. On the southwest there is a layer of gravel that runs through to the châteaux of Cheval Blanc and Figeac in Saint-Emilion. On the western side, beyond Route Nationale 89, the terrain is mainly sandy. Between the two lies a plateau formed mainly of clay, with some gravel and a fairly high iron content (*crasse de fer*). Excellent wines can be grown in all these types of soil. The sandy soil in the west is the most difficult, but here châteaux like De Sales, Clos René and l'Enclos show that integrity and expertise can bring good results. The Merlot grape predominates everywhere, followed by the Cabernet Franc, and then the Cabernet Sauvignon. At some châteaux the last-named variety, pre-eminent in the Médoc, is not even grown. A little Malbec is planted here and there.

Ready for early drinking

Soil and grapes yield wines that are often deep in colour and almost luxuriously creamy. They are seldom cumbersome, heady wines and their minimum alcohol content, at only 10.5°, is half a degree less than the simplest Saint-Emilions. Austere, harsh flavours are hardly ever present even in young Pomerols, but a considerable dose of glycerine occurs in them naturally. These wines can therefore be drunk quite early, often within five years, which makes them attractive for the ordinary buyer who often does not have his own cellar. Although ready for drinking so soon, good Pomerols can be laid down for a long period — they do not *have* to be drunk young. Pomerols, however, are more than just a charming type of Bordeaux. The better kinds have an unmistakable style, and sometimes an individual aroma suggestive to some people of truffles, to others of brown sugar (though neither association figures in my own tasting notes).

Jean-Pierre Moueix

In Pomerol one wine concern is more closely associated with the district than all the others: Jean-Pierre Moueix. It is named after its founder, who set it up shortly after the Second World War.
Jean-Pierre Moueix learned wine-selling in the 1930s by travelling abroad for his father, who owned Château Fonroque in Saint-Emilion. Through purchases, renting and sharecropping (*métayage*), Jean-Pierre

Left:
Stones bearing the Maltese cross — like this one from the park at Château Beauregard — are found at several places in Pomerol. They marked the way for pilgrims heading for Santiago de Compostela.

Below:
Market stalls in Libourne's main square.

Right:
Healthy, ripe grapes that will yield a full and luxurious wine in a few years' time.

Château la Croix contains many reminders of the pilgrimage to Santiago de Compostela, and the château still offers shelter to pilgrims in need. The owner, Jean-François Janoueix, has done the pilgrimage himself and is an active member of La Société des Amis de Saint-Jacques de Compostelle, founded in 1950.

The origin of the name Pomerol is a complete mystery.

The Paris-Bordeaux railway runs right through the district.

During my stay in Pomerol I was unable to find a single restaurant, and even the café in Catusseau did not serve meals. Still, Libourne is close by and provides excellent catering (e.g. Loubat and l'Etrier*); nor is Saint-Emilion very far away (*Hostellerie de Plaisance *and* Logis de la Cadène*).*

Many areas in Pomerol have a layer of rock-hard, ferruginous soil with a depth ranging from 20 inches to 7 feet in places. This crasse de fer *prevents rainwater draining away, forcing many growers to construct drainage systems. Jean-Pierre Moueix is one of the growers who has invested large sums in drainage.*

Moueix succeeded in becoming the biggest Pomerol producer. He did this without making concessions on quality: each Moueix estate delivers the best possible product in its category. Among the Moueix châteaux are Pétrus, Trotanoy, La Fleur-Pétrus, Latour à Pomerol, La Grave Trigant de Boisset, Lagrange, Feytit-Clinet and Lafleur-Gazin. In addition the firm has interests in various Saint-Emilion châteaux, such as the aforementioned Fonroque, and Magdelaine, Moulin du Cadet and La Clotte. Since Jean-Pierre, who has a famous art collection, has to some extent withdrawn from the business it has been excellently run by his son Christian.

No classification system

Pomerol is exceptional among the great Bordeaux districts in having no system of classification; and for the moment it is unlikely to have one. Christian Moueix expressed the opinion I had already heard from many other local people when he said: 'As the biggest owners in Pomerol, we would not want classification.' For such a system always creates problems — of rivalry and of keeping up to date. It is not needed here because there are so few wine estates compared to Saint-Emilion, the Médoc, or Graves. Of course, there are differences between the Pomerol châteaux. Everyone agrees that Pétrus makes the best wine — and this is reflected in its price. Most wine critics and importers would place Vieux Château Certan, Trotanoy, La Conseillante and l'Evangile in a group immediately below Pétrus. After that, ranking becomes more difficult. I would be inclined to add Petit-Village, La Fleur-Pétrus, Latour à Pomerol, l'Eglise-Clinet and Certan de May to this select group. However, this is to anticipate the personal impressions of 21 leading Pomerol châteaux that appear on the following pages. Only the two top estates, Pétrus and Vieux Château Certan, are not included: these are described in my book *The Great Wine Châteaux of Bordeaux*.

Only organic manure is used at the Moueix estates, and that includes Trotanoy. The drive up to this château is lined with tall cypresses, and the entrance to the cellars is framed with roses. The château is a member of the Académie du Vin de Bordeaux.

After 12 months' maturing, Trotanoy wine is moved to the Jean-Pierre Moueix cellars at Libourne for another 8 to 12 months of ageing.

Around one-third of the Trotanoy vintage is shipped to the United States every year.

The cellars at Trotanoy are used for vinifying and maturing wine from another Moueix estate, Château Lagrange, which has no facilities of its own (see page 197).

Below: Trotanoy wine has decidedly more grandeur than the château itself, a pleasant country house whose rear windows look out over part of the vineyard. The château dates from 1890 and is occupied by Jean-Jacques Moueix, the owner of Château Fonroque in Saint-Emilion (page 113). Jean-Jacques works for the Jean-Pierre Moueix wine firm.

Far right: Christian Moueix, director of the Jean-Pierre Moueix company, seen here during an open-air lunch in his own garden, designed by a Parisian landscape gardener. Jean-Pierre and his family live in a delightful spot just outside Libourne, with a view of the Dordogne.

Château Trotanoy

Pomerol

The origin of the name Trotanoy is said is lie in the soil of the vineyard. This consists partly of gravel, partly of clay. During drought the gravel becomes so hard, and after rain the clay turns so slippery, that both are too difficult (*trop anoi* in old French) to work. This does not prevent Château Trotanoy producing wine, even excellent wine, every year. In Pomerol it ranks with Pétrus, Vieux Château Certan, La Conseillante and l'Evangile as a leading estate; but since it has the smallest production of the five its wine is rare. The 18-acre vineyard yields at most 35 *tonneaux* (1974), and usually much less. Only 10 *tonneaux* was harvested in 1977; 17 in 1975; and 24 in 1978. The 1982 harvest was 27 *tonneaux*. Recent replanting has produced the proportions of 85% Merlot and 15% Cabernet Franc. This represents an increase of 5% in the Merlot, reflecting the policy of the firm of Jean-Pierre Moueix, owners since 1953.

Special treatment

At Trotanoy concrete fermentation vats are used, with oak casks for maturing. Half of the casks are replaced for each vintage. The maturation period lasts 20 to 24 months and during this time the wine is regularly transferred. It is fined with fresh egg whites, and there is no filtering. It is interesting to note that Trotanoy, with Pétrus and Magdelaine (Saint-Emilion), is given special treatment among the Moueix estates in that the grapes are picked only in the afternoon, having built up more sugar as a result of the morning sun.

Very complete

Trotanoy wine compares with the best of the Médoc. At blind tastings it is often placed with, or even above, renowned *deuxièmes crus*. This was my experience with the aromatic, velvety 1973, and also with the 1961. At one famous tasting session, when the Dutch practitioner, Dr Jan-Dirk Taams, sampled 1961 wines, Trotanoy, the only Pomerol included, scored higher than, for example, Lascombes, Montrose and Léoville-Barton. The wine had a wholly individual bouquet, its velvety quality reinforced by an element that reminded me very slightly of seaweed. I have not come across this in other vintages, all of them generally agreeable and enriched by fine nuances, soft fruit, an unmistakable strength and a sound balance. Among the best Trotanoy vintages are 1967 (amazingly beautiful), the 1970 (can mature for many years yet), the 1971 (delightful), the 1975 (very strong), the 1976 (charming) and the 1978 (a lot of power). The 1979, 1981 and the almost black 1982 seem very promising too. Without doubt, Trotanoy is one of the most complete Pomerols, a wine that even Christian Moueix occasionally mistakes for the much more famous, and more expensive, Pétrus.

Right:
Side view of Château l'Evangile, built between 1850 and 1902.

Below left:
A few bottles of the delicious and expensive Pomerol wine.

Below right:
Louis Ducasse insisted that his family had no links with the man who gave his surname to Château Grand-Puy-Ducasse in the Médoc commune of Pauillac. Louis Ducasse spent 45 years working for a wine firm before taking over as manager at l'Evangile.

Château l'Evangile

Pomerol

That Château l'Evangile belongs to the élite of Pomerol is doubted by no one, least of all Louis Ducasse, for many years its *gérant* and co-owner. On my first visit to the estate he welcomed me with the words: 'I'm not interested in whom you have already visited in Pomerol, but I'll tell you one thing straight away: l'Evangile is the first *premier grand cru* after Pétrus, because of its quality, its price, its reputation; l'Evangile is half-brother to Château Pétrus.' Whether l'Evangile in fact produces a better wine than, for example, Trotanoy, La Conseillante or Vieux Château Certan I would venture to doubt. The claim could only be established by holding a series of blind tastings. Nevertheless, the château's 33-acre vineyard does border on that of Pétrus.
Little is known of the history of this estate because all the records went up in flames during the French Revolution. The Ducasse family has owned it for more than a century.

Varied subsoil

Louis Ducasse (who died in 1982; his heirs now run the estate) used to say that his vineyard could be termed almost perfect. Four different soil types occur: sand, clay, pure gravel and ordinary earth; and thanks to this variety wine from l'Evangile has been consistent in quality over the years. Ducasse quoted the year 1968 as an example, when, as he put it, the strength of the clay compensated for the lightness of the sand. In 1975, on the other hand, the soft sand corrected the severity of the gravel.
Consistent though the quality of l'Evangile may be, this is not true of the quantity. Figures for five successive vintages show this: nearly 76 *tonneaux* produced in 1974, 30 in 1975, 46 in 1976, about 20 in 1977, and about 32 in 1978.

Maximum colour and tannin

At l'Evangile the grapes — two-thirds Merlot, one-third Cabernet Franc — ferment in concrete vats. A special feature is the wooden grid that is placed in the vat a few inches below the surface of the liquid. During fermentation the pulp of grape skins and pips floats upward against the grid. The must also rises but passes through the pulp and the grid. The result is that the fermenting grape juice continually 'feeds' on the pulp, extracting both colour and tannin.

Great demand

After fermentation, the wine goes into oak casks for 22 to 28 months. One-fifth of the casks are replaced each year. The estate's cellarman Zucchi (not employed full-time — he works for other estates, including Beauregard) uses the white of fresh eggs for clarifying the wine. Chemical products are never used, nor is the wine filtered. After bottling, all bottles are packed in wooden cases and sold both through the trade and directly. There is a heavy demand for l'Evangile: the château has never enough of any vintage.

Flowery bouquet

I have not drunk any really old l'Evangile vintages. The earliest was the 1970, nearly a decade after its vintage. The wine had a strong colour, clung to the glass, and had a mild bouquet with some finesse. Its taste

Left:
Part of the cellar — around one-fifth of the casks are replaced annually.

Below:
The front of the château.

was elegant without great depth — and it was quite ready for drinking. I thought the aftertaste a little short. The 1971 actually appealed to me more, although it was lighter: a refined bouquet and a pleasant, satin-smooth taste with sufficient strength for long maturing. I often find a slightly flowery fragrance in the bouquet of l'Evangile wines, especially if the wine still retains its youthful vitality. I had this impression from the 1974, for example, a vintage that was not otherwise much to my liking. I thought it was rather thin and the aftertaste had a slightly bitter tinge. This flowery fragrance was present to a modest degree in the bouquet of the 1975, an athletic wine with a lot of colour, a concentrated taste with both charm and finesse, and a long aftertaste. This was l'Evangile at its best.

Recent vintages

Three years after its birth the 1976 already had quite a mature, almost brownish, hue. Again there was a vague suggestion of flowers, although the bouquet did not have great depth. The taste struck me as really mature, with great strength and plenty of alcohol, yet with a certain refinement and elegance. This wine was further developed than other Pomerols of the same year. Louis Ducasse described it as 'une jolie femme bien habillée'. I was charmed by the 1977, a fairly light wine. The bouquet was fine (flowers again) and there was finesse, too, in the taste; a very agreeable wine for early drinking. The almost opaque 1978 was a complete contrast. It offered a flowery perfume and had a beautiful, concentrated taste with many nuances and a very good finish. It seems that wines of the same excellent standard were made in 1981 and 1982. The 1979 is somewhat light.

Belgium is Château la Conseillante's biggest export market, and this goes for practically all Pomerol estates. La Conseillante is also shipped to West Germany, Britain, Switzerland, the United States and Japan. Estate manager Bernard has even had brochures printed in Japanese.

Below left:
The gate that leads to the unpretentious château.

Below right:
Maître de chai *Lucien Chaucherie 'chews' the still purple cask wine. He and his family have been living and working on the estate for 30 years, as have two other employees of the château.*

Right:
Three sizes of La Conseillante wine: half bottle, bottle and magnum.

Château la Conseillante

Pomerol

There are few Pomerol châteaux of which I have such pleasant memories as La Conseillante. This was the first wine estate I visited in the district, many years ago. The bus carrying our party arrived late at the château. Nevertheless we had a cordial reception from the then owner, Louis Nicolas, who had even put on a striped suit and waistcoat, despite the heat. In the shadow of the trees tables were set ready with fresh flowers, grapes, crackers, cheeses and bottles of still young, fresh, marvellous La Conseillante 1967. The château is on the boundary of Pomerol and Saint-Emilion and from the steps we could see Château Cheval Blanc. Louis Nicolas observed: 'Cheval Blanc is the best Saint-Emilion because it lies so close to Pomerol.'

A demanding mistress

The Nicolas family lives at the château of La Conseillante only in the summer and during the vintage. The property dates from the 18th century, but there was already a vineyard here in the 15th century. The origin of the name La Conseillante is uncertain. It may be a corruption of the French *conseiller*, 'councillor', from the time of the

Normally about one-tenth of each vintage is not sold immediately but allowed to mature in the bottle.

Château la Conseillante belongs to two prestigious organizations in Bordeaux, the Académie du Vin de Bordeaux and the Union des Grands Crus de Bordeaux.

Below:
Bernard Nicolas inspects his grapes almost every day before harvesting begins. Besides being a wine grower he is an insurance underwriter and dep ty mayor of Libourne.

Right:
Inside the labyrinthine cellars. The ceiling is insulated, so it stays cool even in the height of summer.

Bordeaux *parlement*. On the other hand, the name of a Mademoiselle La Conseillante occurs in the Libourne archives. Whatever its origins, the estate was bought in 1874 by the first Louis Nicolas, whose initials still appear on the labels. Today Château la Conseillante is directed by Bernard Nicolas, who also has a flourishing insurance business and is the deputy mayor of Libourne. He is quite obsessed with his wine and lives at the château during the grape harvest: 'I don't even get into my car. My best friend can invite me out for dinner, but I don't go. For two weeks I live with my wine; since my great-grandfather's time La Conseillante has always been our mistress. Voilà mes vacances!'

Modern fermentation tanks

A new era began at La Conseillante in 1971 when the château, advised by the famous oenologist, Professor Emile Peynaud, acquired a new *cuvier*, with stainless-steel fermentation tanks. (There are few signs yet of stainless steel in Pomerol, unlike the other Bordeaux districts.) At La Conseillante this completely modern vinification contrasts with the traditional ageing of the wine. Oak casks, half of them new, are used to mature the wine for 20 to 24 months. Clarifying is done with fresh egg white, and Bernard Nicolas never filters his wine. The château's vineyard extends over 32 acres and produces an average 50 *tonneaux* annually. La Conseillante is the only leading Pomerol estate where the Merlot does not predominate. The proportions here are 45% Merlot, 45% Cabernet Franc and 10% Malbec.

Fine bouquet, silky taste

This relatively high percentage of Cabernet Franc and low (for Pomerol) percentage of Merlot, undoubtedly contributes to the particular La Conseillante personality. In comparison to other great Pomerols it is less rich in colour, less fat. Its most characteristic features are a very fine, mild bouquet with sometimes a hint of sweetness, and an extremely distinguished, silky taste of great purity. There are usually attractive nuances in both bouquet and taste, the wine fills the mouth well, its taste lingers, and it has an excellent balance. For generations La Conseillante has been regarded as one of the best Pomerols — and this is still the case today.

Good vintages

I have been able to taste and drink La Conseillante's wines on many occasions. Some 13 years after its vintage the 1962 — strikingly elegant for a Pomerol, like the 1959 — was still amazingly vital. The mild, ripe taste even became livelier as time passed (I did not decant the wine). The 1967 has remained a good friend, a very charming wine with a touch of sweetness in taste and bouquet. The 1970 and 1971 were both successes. The 1974 surprised me with its colour and firmness, coming across as rather more vigorous than the 1975. Its slight lack of rounded qualities and of refinement was characteristic of its year. The 1975 greatly charmed me with its bouquet, full of finesse, its delicious taste and its long aftertaste. I thought the 1976 was a great Pomerol, gracious and harmonious. Finally, the 1978 was also becoming a very distinguished wine, a great La Conseillante. And how I would love to have 1981 and 1982 in my personal cellar.

No exclusive arrangements

After experiments with cardboard boxes, bottles of La Conseillante are now shipped in wooden cases. Bernard Nicolas has no exclusive contracts with *négociants*, and he does not feel responsible for selling the wine, saying: 'My only concern is to make as good a wine as possible.' He therefore applies the wise principle of quality before quantity, which is in keeping with the family motto: 'Faire peu, mais faire bon'.

Far left:
In the cuverie; *the tanks are made of concrete.*

Below:
The château was built around 1850. All its shutters are painted egg yellow.

Right:
The chai *where the pickers from the Moueix estates eat.*

The château is a member of the Académie du Vin de Bordeaux.

Château la Fleur-Pétrus

Château Pétrus may stand out for its turquoise shutters but those of La Fleur-Pétrus nearby are even more striking — egg-yellow. This estate's label is unusual, too: it has a flag, as though this were a shipping line, and it was designed by a former owner. Since 1952 the estate, with its 18-acre vineyard, has belonged to Jean-Pierre Moueix. After fermentation, the wine is taken to the Moueix cellars in Libourne for maturing in oak casks (about 30% of them new) for 20 to 24 months. The *chai* at La Fleur-Pétrus thus remains empty; it fulfils a useful function only during the grape harvest, when the pickers from the Moueix estates have meals there.

Very gravelly soil

The vineyard at La Fleur-Pétrus is very gravelly and is therefore quite different from the clay of Pétrus. The gravel, or *graves*, makes the grapes — 75% Merlot and 25% Cabernet Franc — ripen quickly and can be picked relatively early. The estate's production is never very large, varying between the 15 *tonneaux* of 1977 and the 31 of 1976.

More complex than most

In my opinion La Fleur-Pétrus is the best Pomerol from the Jean-Pierre Moueix estates, after Pétrus and Trotanoy. I have always enjoyed tasting and drinking this wine. The 1976 is a very characteristic La Fleur-Pétrus vintage. Despite the record volume that year, the wine already had its good features. The colour was deep and dark, the bouquet exciting; three years after the vintage it was not yet fully released, but it already offered great freshness, perhaps derived from the gravel, with a hint of blackcurrants. In addition the wine had a lot of taste and was pleasantly complex. La Fleur-Pétrus might lack some of the rounded character of other Pomerols, but not firmness or tannin. Its finish, the 'end taste', was long. I have tasted these same characteristics in other vintages. La Fleur-Pétrus is a distinguished Pomerol, with more subtlety than most but at the same time less mild, less immediately accessible. It is a wine that demands patience and should be laid down for at least five to ten years. Other recommendable vintages from this château are 1982, 1981, 1979, 1978, 1975, 1974 and 1973; the 1971 was a beauty and both the 1980 and 1977 can be rated as very successful for their year.

Left:
These fermentation tanks at Château Gazin may look like wood, but are in fact made of concrete and merely faced with gleaming oak for effect.

Below:
The château itself lies on a lower level than the vineyard.

Right:
Etienne de Bailliencourt, the owner of Château Gazin.

Gazin wine is fined with fresh egg white but not filtered.

In 1969 Gazin sold 12 acres to Château Pétrus; later on 1⅓ acres were sold to Certan-Giraud for far more than the original 12 acres.

Gazin belongs to the Académie du Vin de Bordeaux and the Union des Grands Crus de Bordeaux.

Château Gazin

Pomerol

Château Gazin is on the site of a former farm that belonged to the Knights Templars and used to be called Domaine des Tempeliers. A reminder of this past is a fireplace with the cross of the order. The origin of the name Gazin is uncertain. At the end of the 1960s the château went through a difficult period. After the death of its owner, three of his four heirs were in favour of selling the estate. Eventually a compromise was reached by which 12 acres of vineyard were sold to Château Pétrus: the land adjoined Pétrus and had the same kind of clay soil. The selling price was apparently 24 million old francs. Eventually the new owner of Gazin was the one heir who had opposed the sale: Etienne de Balliencourt. He does not live on the estate as he has a flourishing wine business in the Oise *département*, north of Paris. He visits Gazin about once a month.

Simulating tradition

The Gazin vineyard now covers 64 acres and is planted with 50% Merlot vines, 25% Cabernet Franc and 25% Cabernet Sauvignon. In good years, like 1982, production reaches almost 100 *tonneaux*. But it can be as low as 35 (in 1977). From the 1979 vintage onwards a harvesting machine was used, making Gazin the first Pomerol estate to employ one. Inside the *cuvier* are what appear to be traditional oak fermentation vats. In fact these are stage props: concrete vats are hidden behind the woodwork. I cannot understand why Etienne de Balliencourt has gone in for this piece of trickery. Even at Pétrus they are not ashamed of concrete. After fermentation, the wine matures for about two years in (genuine) wooden casks, nearly always used ones: the château regularly buys casks from Cheval Blanc.

Room for refinement

When the château still possessed its 12 acres of 'Pétrus' land the wine contained much more tannin than nowadays. The 1967, for example, seemed to me quite different from the 1971. The 1967 wine was still astonishingly concentrated and 'unopened' long after its vintage; the 1971 was mature and mellow. It also had a deep brownish-red colour, a bouquet with *terroir*, somewhat reminiscent of damp brushwood, and a good, firm taste without much depth and containing a trace of bitterness. This bitter element was stronger in the taste and aftertaste of the lighter and rather smoother 1974. The 1976 was supple and had an engaging bouquet; the 1977 had an agreeable taste but was somewhat short and dry; and the 1978 was fairly intense in both bouquet and taste. I regard Gazin as a generally balanced, pleasant, firm yet supple Pomerol, somewhat lacking however in breeding and refinement. This also goes for recent vintages.

Left:
Marie Robin and her sister Thérèse are joint owners of Château le Gay and Château Lafleur. Here she is at the cellar door of Château Lafleur, an otherwise uninteresting building.

Below:
Marie Robin in front of the Château le Gay cellars. Her bicycle leans against the railings.

Far right:
Château le Gay is at its most charming in the spring, when the Bengal roses bloom. There are flowers indoors too, on the faded wallpaper.

Between them, Châteaux le Gay and Lafleur produce on average 40 tonneaux a year.

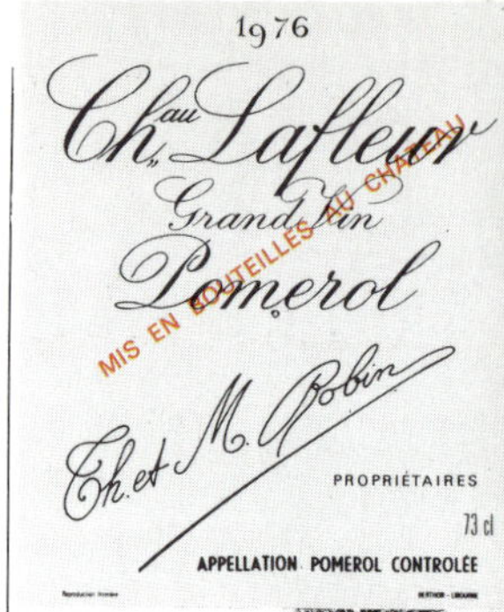

Château le Gay & Château Lafleur

Two unique Pomerol proprietors are the sisters Thérèse and Marie Robin. These two elderly spinster ladies own the châteaux of Le Gay and Lafleur. The two estates lie a few hundred yards apart on the north side of the Pomerol plateau. During the winter the sisters live in Libourne, and the rest of the year at Château le Gay. The entrance to this little estate is graced by some exuberant Bengal rose bushes, but the interior of the château is far from luxurious. The ladies lead a rather secluded life and hardly ever receive visitors.

Le Gay: quick development

Le Gay, with just under 20 acres, is the larger of the two properties. It is planted half with Merlot and half with Cabernet Franc. After fermenting in concrete vats, the wine matures for about two years in the damp cellar beneath the château. New casks are never used. The wine from Le Gay develops more quickly than the Lafleur. It has no very pronounced personality, nor much depth or power. The 1978 — tasted from the cask — had a deep, purple colour, a mild fruit bouquet and a similarly mild taste that became dry as it lingered in the mouth. Not long afterwards I tasted the 1970, which had a deep colour, nothing memorable about the bouquet, and a fairly full, almost elegant taste, still with a fresh trace to it.

Lafleur: more colour and strength

The Château Lafleur wine is made in the identical manner from the same grape varieties. The soil, however, is somewhat better and so is the wine. Although Le Gay ripens first, Lafleur is sold earlier; and the wine has more colour, strength and tannin. I recall the 1971 which seven years after its vintage seemed almost as severe as a Médoc. The bouquet had already developed nicely but the taste was still very young: it had to be decanted. The 1978 confirmed my opinion, for this too was a powerful wine, still undeveloped and almost black in colour. The vineyard at Lafleur covers only 10 acres. I am convinced that with more careful vinification much better wines could be made at both Lafleur and Le Gay. The potential for very good Pomerols seems to be there, but unfortunately it is not fully utilized.

Left:
Grapes on their way to the château. This shot was taken at the 5-acre vineyard that surrounds the château itself, where the soil is rather clayey and muddy. Elsewhere on the Pomerol plateau the estate owns 12 acres of gravelly land, and the two types of soil combine to give the wine much of its character.

Below:
Front view of the château.

Far right:
A bunch of grapes in wrought iron. Latour's grape varieties are 80% Merlot and 20% Cabernet Sauvignon.

The estate is a member of the Académie du Vin de Bordeaux.

Château Latour à Pomerol

Château Latour à Pomerol is on one of the flanks of the plateau where nearly all the better estates lie. The château itself, dating from the 19th century, is in fact more of a country house — but this is quite usual in Pomerol. The last owner but one was Mme Edmond Loubat, to whom Château Pétrus also belonged. In 1917 she made a particularly important change at Latour à Pomerol, buying the Clos des Grandes Vignes, a vineyard a few hundred yards further up the slope, near the church. The grapes from this 10-acre plot were henceforth used for Latour à Pomerol. Mme Loubat's acquisition produced a distinct improvement in the quality of her wine. She died in 1961 and the estate passed to her niece, Mme Paul Lacoste, who rented it out to the firm of Jean-Pierre Moueix.

Stringent selection

Christian Moueix saw to it that a very strict system of selection was introduced. Only the very best of the *cuves* would be used for Latour à Pomerol; and since 1961 the wine from each plot has been vinified separately. After the grapes have been picked they are fermented in concrete vats at the château. The wine is then taken to Jean-Pierre Moueix's cellars to mature for about two years in oak casks, of which approximately one-third are replaced each year. The yield from the nearly 20 acres of vineyard varies usually between 15 and 30 *tonneaux*.

Closest to Pétrus

Of all the Pomerols, Latour is probably the one that comes nearest to the colour and the strength of Pétrus. The Latour à Pomerols I have encountered have had a deep colour, a broad, substantial taste and a large amount of mild tannin, which gives them a long aftertaste. These are also wines that continue to provide an impression of ripe fruit in their bouquet and taste for a long time; in very sunny years such as 1976 the effect is almost sweet. Because of its fruit and its rounded quality, Latour à Pomerol can generally be drunk within about three years of its vintage, but it will go on developing for much longer. One criticism might be some deficiency of elegance, finesse, breeding. The wine therefore does not quite attain the standard of the top group just behind Pètrus: Vieux Château Certain, Trotanoy, La Conseillante, l'Evangile. Nevertheless I regard Latour à Pomerol as one of the best wines of the district, a splendid partner for rich game or a mature cheese.

Approximately two-thirds of the vineyard area of Clos l'Eglise lies around the château itself, while the rest is some distance away, split into two plots. Bottling has been contracted out to specialists since the 1979 harvest. Some of the bottles are packed in wooden cases.

Below left:
Bottles of the 1969 vintage, which was quite successful for its year. The wife of a vineyard worker keeps her eye on the case.

Below right:
Michel Moreau who, with his brother Francis, leases Clos l'Eglise from their family.

Right:
From the rear at least, Clos l'Eglise, with its buttresses, looks rather like a chapel.

Clos l'Eglise

Pomerol

Clos l'Eglise looks like an ordinary house, but wine is stacked behind the closed shutters; the interior walls have been knocked out to make a *chai*. The château is near l'Eglise-Clinet and dates from the 18th century. Until the vintage of 1977 Clos l'Eglise had only 10 acres of productive vineyard. A further 3¾ acres (a field where a horse had grazed) was added in 1978. In 1978 Clos l'Eglise reached a harvest of about 19 *tonneaux*, whereas formerly no more than 17 *tonneaux* had been the norm. In 1982 the little estate produced about 30 *tonneaux*, and a mere 11 in 1977. As elsewhere in Pomerol, the Merlot dominates with 60%, followed by 20% of Cabernet Franc, 10% Cabernet Sauvignon and 10% Malbec.

Stainless steel tanks

Clos l'Eglise belongs to the Moreau family and since 1 January 1977 the brothers Michel and Francis Moreau have rented it from the family. The same situation applies at the slightly bigger, but less well-known, Château Plince. The Moreau brothers are surveyors by profession, but they are very committed to their wines. Since 1975 Clos l'Eglise had concrete fermentation vats, but these were replaced by stainless steel tanks in 1983. As a rule, the wine matures about 15 months in oak casks. About a tenth of the casks are replaced each year. Fining is done with beaten white of egg, and generally there is no filtering.

Clos l'Eglise is one of the lighter Pomerols and, in terms of personality, rather 'introverted': in my experience it is never exuberant or particularly full or rich. Nevertheless it can be a most attractive wine. I have enjoyed drinking the 1967 and the 1969 was successful for its year. Among the more recent vintages the 1976 was unfortunately disappointing — which they acknowledge at the château itself. I noted that the 1977 had a fairly light flavour with little depth, but possessed fruit, a pleasant bouquet and a reasonably deep colour. The 1978 had much more colour and class, although it was less impressive than, for example, its neighbour l'Eglise-Clinet. In my view, it was a wise decision of the Moreau brothers to buy a good number of new casks every year: their wine will undoubtedly gain in strength and class from the extra tannin. In general Clos l'Eglise should not be drunk too young; usually it should be kept for five to eight years before drinking.

The present-day Château l'Eglise-Clinet was apparently formed by a merger between the Domaine de Clinet and a part of the Clos l'Eglise vineyard, said to have taken place in 1882.

Below: Château l'Eglise-Clinet on a wet day; the building dates from 1850. The churchyard of Pomerol is in the middle background, and Pomerol's former church, originally erected by the Templars in the 12th century, once stood next to the property.

Far right: One of the château dwellers.

Château l'Eglise-Clinet

Pomerol

Château l'Eglise-Clinet is a modest house with cellars that faces the churchyard at Pomerol. It is occupied by its owner, Mme Durantou. She is not personally involved with the wine for since 1942 Pierre Lasserre has had a *métayage* arrangement — that is to say he tends the vineyard and makes the wine in return for half the vintage. Lasserre himself owns Clos René. Although l'Eglise-Clinet wine is made in the same way by the same people, it always fetches a 25 to 30% higher price than the Clos René product. The reason is that the former vineyard has better soil, and a few plots with very old vines. These were miraculously spared during the devastating frost of 1956 and give l'Eglise-Clinet wine some extra depth and class. Grape varieties are Merlot (60%), Cabernet Franc (30%) and Malbec (10%), planted in a total area of only 11 acres, plus a field of little under 1 acre that was added in 1979.

Modest yield

Traditional methods are used at l'Eglise-Clinet, with concrete fermentation vats (some of them glass-lined) and maturation for 20 to 24 months in oak casks. A few of the latter — 10% at most — are replaced each year. Pierre Lasserre clarifies his wine with beaten white of egg and never filters it. Obviously the yield here never reaches dramatic proportions. In many recent vintages it was less than 20 *tonneaux*. Only exceptionally does l'Eglise-Clinet produce as much as 30 to 32 *tonneaux*.

Attractive wine

The wine of this small estate particularly appeals to me. Its quality surpasses that of bigger, better-known Pomerol châteaux. Château l'Eglise-Clinet is a wine in which creamy, rounded qualities are harmoniously combined with a sophisticated style. Its colour is deep, its bouquet has subtleties, its taste has vitality and refinement. It is notable not for any mouth-filling breadth, but for a firm elegance and a good balance. Among the best years of the '70s are 1971, 1975 and 1978. The 1973 was rather lighter and in 1979 was ready for drinking. The wine from the difficult year 1977 was greatly to my liking. It had a good deep colour, just a small amount of acid, and the refinement so characteristic of this château. The first wines of the '80s look very promising.

Left:
The château on a summer's day, with the cellars on the right. The main building includes offices, a reception room and the pickers' kitchen.

Below:
Busy pickers take a break, and . . .

Right:
. . . put their backs into it.

At Petit-Village the wine is fined with fresh or powdered egg white, and lightly filtered before bottling.

Château Petit-Village

Pomerol

It is said that the first small community of Pomerol was founded on the site where Château Petit-Village now stands, but no traces of it remain. Instead there are a few unobtrusive buildings and an immaculately tended vineyard of 27 acres. The estate occupies a slight rise in the land near Pomerol-Catusseau. During heavy rain the water runs off Petit-Village and down to this little hamlet. The vineyard is triangular in shape, most of it in a single plot. The château belongs to the Groupement Foncier des Domaines Prats, in other words the brothers Jean-Marie, Yves and Bruno Prats, Bruno being responsible for the estate and its wine.

More Merlot

After the frost of 1956 almost the whole vineyard at Petit-Village had to be replanted, and a relatively large percentage of Cabernet Sauvignon was decided on. This, however, has now been brought down from 28% to 10%,with 86% Merlot and 10% Cabernet Franc. In an average good year Petit-Village produces some 47 *tonneaux*, but how greatly this can vary is shown by the 27 *tonneaux* of 1977 and the 66 (a record) of 1974. The 1982 harvest produced 60 *tonneaux*. Steel tanks lined with a neutral material are used for fermentation. The wine is matured for about 19 months in oak casks; at least half of these are replaced each year and sometimes — as for the 1978 vintage — all of them.

Not so 'petit'

The story goes that Leopold, King of the Belgians, after tasting Petit-Village, said to his butler: 'Strike out the word "petit", for this is truly a great wine.' The anecdote could well be true, for Petit-Village is among the top Pomerols. It usually has plenty of colour, strength and taste. In its early youth it often has an intense aroma and taste of fruit: the young 1978, for example, was strongly evocative of wild strawberries. Over the years this fruit gives way to a mellow charm. In a young Petit-Village you also taste the (new) oak of the casks quite distinctly. This disappears with the years, but it does give the wine some backbone. Recent successes have been the great and powerful 1982, the fat, luscious 1981, the, for its year excellent 1979, the beautiful and compact 1978, the almost sweet 1976, and the concentrated 1975. The exquisite qualities of Petit-Village explain why for years the demand for it has greatly exceeded the supply.

Left:
Owner Paul Clauzel in action with pipette.

Below:
The colour photo shows Beauregard; the black-and-white inset is an exact copy of the original. This fascinating replica can be found at Port Washington on Long Island, in the USA; it is known as 'Mille Fleurs' and is the creation of an American architect who visited the original Château Beauregard during the First World War. It obviously left its mark on him.

Right:
Wooden trugs in readiness for the grape harvest.

Beauregard's less prestigious wines are sold under the Domaine des Douves label.

Château Beauregard

Pomerol

Although it was a family called Beauregard who gave the château its name in the 17th century, the name could equally well refer to the idyllic view from the salons of the garden with its magnificent cedars. The château itself is also well worth viewing. Most Pomerol châteaux are fairly simple country houses. Beauregard, however, is in a distinctly grander manner. It was designed by a pupil of Victor Louis, the noted Bordeaux architect. The building is partly surrounded by a moat, and the rear terrace and steps are flanked by square pavilion towers. Since 1920 Beauregard has belonged to the Clauzel family, owners of La Tour de Mons in the Médoc. Paul Clauzel is the occupant and *gérant*.

Underground storage tanks

The Beauregard vineyard covers 39.5 acres and is planted with Merlot (49%), Cabernet Franc (42%), Cabernet Sauvignon (6%) and Malbec (3%). Production varies between 25 and 65 *tonneaux*. The wine ferments in concrete vats and is then matured in oak casks for 15 to 20 months. Paul Clauzel replaces one-quarter of the casks every three years. After fining, the wine is transferred to glass-lined underground tanks so that, according to Clauzel, 'the risk of drying out is avoided'. The wine is generally not filtered before bottling.

Pronounced fruit

To some extent Beauregard lacks the velvety, creamy roundness that characterizes so many Pomerols. Instead, in its bouquet and taste it often conveys a strong impression of fruit. In other respects the wine is not notably fragrant, nor refined or deep, but it makes a pleasing and positive impression. In addition, it is nearly always excellently balanced. Beauregard may not be a member of Pomerol's nobility, but the name always guarantees a good product. My tasting notes indicated the 1967, 1970 and 1971 as superb. I have drunk and served the 1973 with complete satisfaction. The 1975 was excellent, as was the slightly less tannic 1976. The 1977 could be termed a success for its year and the 1978, 1981 and 1982 were, for this estate, outstanding. A good Beauregard needs about five years at least to develop.

Although there is a small stock of bottles at Château Clinet, most are kept at Château Jonqueyres, in Entre-Deux-Mers. This is the headquarters of Georges Audy's wine business and has a large, vaulted cellar.

All bottles of Château Clinet for export are shipped in wooden cases.

Bottom: This château is not fronted by a trim park but by an ordinary gravel forecourt. Members of Audy's staff live here.

Below: Clinet's cellarman and his wife. He has just tapped a glass of young wine.

Right: The owner, Georges Audy. He likes riding and fast cars.

Château Clinet

Pomerol

Château Clinet is a near neighbour of Clos l'Eglise. It is an unpretentious building occupied by members of the staff of the owner, Georges Audy. A small storage cellar is built next to the château; the *cuvier* is a couple of hundred yards further along the same lane. It is equipped with concrete fermenting vats. The Audy family has owned Château Clinet since 1900; other properties of theirs are Château La Croix du Casse in Pomerol and Château Jonqueyres in Entre-Deux-Mers, where Georges Audy lives and where his own wine firm is based.

A lot of Cabernet Sauvignon

A noticeable feature of Clinet is the relatively high percentage of Cabernet Sauvignon, for Pomerol, in the 17-acre vineyard: 25%, with 60% Merlot and 15% Cabernet Franc. This generous amount of Cabernet Sauvignon makes Clinet an untypical Pomerol. Or, as Audy said to me: 'Everyone thinks that my wine is a Pauillac. The 1950 was once taken for a Lafite at a blind tasting.' Because the wine has a lot of tannin to start with, Audy matures it for no more than about one year in used casks. In any case Audy is not an advocate of long maturation, 'because after a year the wine begins to dry out'. But Clinet wine stays in the fermentation tanks for quite some time and is only transferred to the casks in March or even later. This estate always uses fresh egg white for fining. Occasionally the wine is lightly filtered just before bottling; this happened with the 1976, which Audy considered was almost better than his 1975.

Slightly rustic

Obviously Clinet is not a wine with the generous roundness of a true Pomerol. Usually it has a dark, austere colour, a bouquet that is slow to develop and a rather hard taste. Clinet does not offer a great deal of finesse; the impression of a slightly 'peasant' character has remained with me. However, the 1978 was a particularly successful wine, strong and intense. I thought the rather severe, but fairly light 1977 was no more than reasonable, but the 1976 had a deep colour, a robust although rather flat bouquet, and an uncommonly powerful, full, lasting taste — a memorable wine. In 1979, the 1975 was not yet ready but was also a good wine: Georges Audy won a gold medal with it at the Concours Agricole in Paris.
Production at Clinet varies between about 11 and 42 *tonneaux*. The latter yield — a record — was obtained in 1982.

Below:
The charming and well-kept château, with one of the cellars on the left. On the main front the bell that is rung to call people into meals from the vineyard.

Far right:
Inside the cuvier with its concrete fermentation vats. The estate produces 10 to 35 tonneaux each year, and around one-quarter of this goes to the United States.

Right:
Measuring the alcohol content.

At La Grave Trigant de Boisset, the wine is fined with fresh egg white and never filtered.

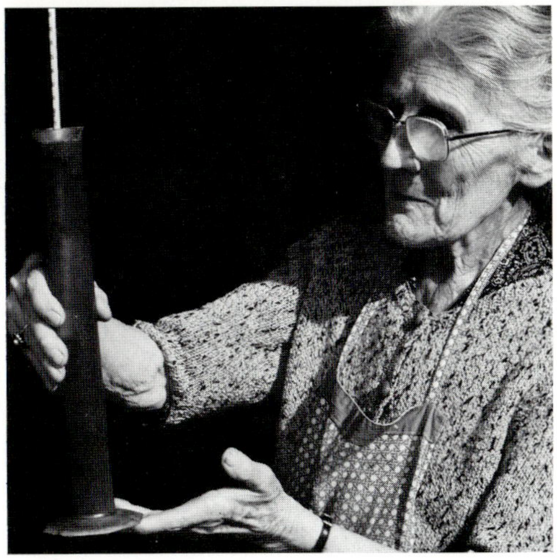

Château la Grave Trigant de Boisset

Pomerol

Whether Monsieur Trigant de Boisset did well to add his name to Château La Grave may be doubted. The difficult title this produced has probably not helped the estate to become better known. Today the reputation of La Grave Trigant de Boisset is still overshadowed by many other Pomerol estates, even though the quality of its wine is often better. The original name of the château indicates that the subsoil contains a lot of gravel. It also appears to have a relatively high iron content, one of the factors that help to determine the personality of the wine. Since 1971 the château, which is surrounded by a small park, has been the personal property of Christian Moueix, director of the wine firm Jean-Pierre Moueix.

Expansion

The vineyard originally covered 12 productive acres, which was increased in the early 1980s to nearly 20 acres after Christian Moueix's new plantings in 1978. Merlot occupies 90% of the area, Cabernet Franc 10%. After extensive experiments Moueix came to the conclusion that in Pomerol the Merlot gives the best results, assisted by a much smaller percentage of Cabernet Franc. This policy is applied on all the Moueix properties — in its most absolute form at Château Pétrus, which has only Merlot.
At La Grave Trigant de Boisset the wine is fermented in concrete vats. After fermentation is completed, it is transferred to Libourne for maturing and bottling at the Jean-Pierre Moueix cellars. The maturation period lasts 16 to 24 months and wooden casks are used; a quarter of these are replaced each year.

Sun-baked ripe grapes

When tasting this wine I have always sensed that the vineyard at La Grave Trigant de Boisset must receive the maximum possible amount of sunshine. Bouquet and taste often convey an impression of very ripe, sun-drenched, almost roasted grapes. This was very marked in the 1976 — but that of course was the product of an exceptionally dry and sunny year. Its colour was deep, its bouquet suggested ripe fruits and burned almonds, and the taste was rich, again with ripe qualities. It was a reasonably fat wine, although less overwhelmingly so, and rather more subtle than, for example, the Latour à Pomerol of the same year. The 1975, too, was noticeable for its pronounced bouquet and its ripe strength. La Grave Trigant de Boisset usually has a good amount of tannin, but of a mild nature so that the wine can be drunk fairly early — mostly after about four years. One of the very best recent wines of this estate is undisputably the 1982.

Left:
Pierre Esben has been estate manager at Nenin since 1967.

Below left:
The administrative office is not without style.

Below right:
The handsome château seen from its park. One thousand bottles of each vintage are kept for consumption at the château.

Right:
A selection of older Nenin vintages — the wording on the label has been altered slightly in the meantime. The estate produces 45 to 80 tonneaux every year, not counting its second wine, Saint-Roch.

The estate is a member of the Académie du Vin de Bordeaux and the Union des Grands Crus de Bordeaux.

Château Nenin

Pomerol

Nenin is one of the bigger Pomerol estates. It is set in a park of 25 acres and has a productive vineyard area of 67 acres. Recently it has been in difficulties. As a result of the death in 1973 of the owner — M. Despujol, whose family had built the château in 1866 — the heirs to the estate were faced with enormous death duties to be paid within eight years. The present *gérant*, François Despujol, has thus been unable to afford new wooden casks, even though Nenin always fetches high prices. Furthermore, since he has not been able to make a living from Nenin he has a factory making wine cases in Libourne and two Citroën agencies.
Despite these heavy financial burdens Nenin does not look at all neglected. The château is well maintained, the *chai* has been rebuilt and since 1974 15 acres of vineyard have been bought.

Fresh white of egg

Despite the unavailability of new casks, there have been no cut-backs on vinification. The wine ferments in concrete vats, matures for two years in casks and is never filtered, but clarified with fresh egg white. Nenin uses at least four, and usually five or six, whites of egg to each cask: because, according to the manager, Pierre Esben, 'if you use fewer than four whites of egg, the effect is almost nil; this has been shown scientifically.'

Over-valued

The basis of Nenin wine is 50% Merlot, 30% Cabernet Franc and 20% Cabernet Sauvignon. The last-named variety, not greatly used in Pomerol, was planted by Despujol's grandfather to make his wine different from that of its neighbours. I have noticed that Nenin sends some people into raptures, others not. I count myself in the latter category. For me Nenin is a rather over-valued Pomerol. The best example I have drunk was the 1966. All the other vintages seemed to me to lack substance, depth and roundness. The wine can be called 'good', but not more than that. Nenin often has a severe, strong taste that can sometimes be a little rough, a sombre colour and a not especially distinguished bouquet. Its tannin content means laying the wine down for a long period. Among the better recent vintages are the 1975, 1976, 1979, 1978 and 1982; the 1974 is somewhat short, the 1977 rather meagre. The British royal household seems not to share my opinion, ordering a whole *tonneau* every year.

Left:
The insulated cellar. The wine is fined in the cask with fresh egg white.

Below:
La Pointe looks out over a magnificent park with a huge lawn and stately trees. The cellars lie behind the château.

Far right:
Owner Bernard d'Arfeuille with some of the 1977 vintage, here in wooden cases stacked on pallets (cartons are also used) ready for shipping. Most La Pointe wines go to Belgium.

La Pointe is so called because the vineyard lies where two roads from Pomerol join at the boundary of Libourne.

Château la Pointe

Pomerol

Château la Pointe is situated just outside Libourne and is surrounded by a park with old, tall trees. It is built in the Directoire style of the late 18th century and has a beautiful tiled entrance hall. Bernard d'Arfeuille and his family have lived there since 1960. His wife and children are the owners; his son Stephane is the *gérant*. Bernard also has a wine business in Libourne.

The château has a large, modern reception room that is, unfortunately, more functional than beautiful. Also very contemporary are the stainless-steel fermentation tanks that were installed alongside the concrete vats in 1976.

Sandy soil

Oak casks are used for maturing the wine. Stephane d'Arfeuille replaces some of these every year, the number depending on the existing need and the available means. Maturation lasts for 16 to 20 months. The wine is filtered just before bottling. Normal production at La Pointe is 50 to 125 *tonneaux*, most of which goes to Belgium. The vineyard covers 62 acres. It grows 80% Merlot, 15% Cabernet Franc and 5% Malbec. The soil consists principally of sand with gravel, on a layer of ferruginous clay.

Best in sunny years

As a result of this rather sandy soil La Pointe wine sometimes rather lacks strength. Only in really sunny, good vintages such as the 1967, 1970, 1971, 1975, 1981 and 1982 does the château manage to make sinewy, richly coloured wines: these are good, with a strong aromatic flavour, though not of exceptional refinement.

Unfortunately I have not encountered this type among four fairly recent vintages I have tasted. The 1976 rather lacked substance, the 1977 was on the light side and only moderate, the 1978 possessed not much character and the 1979 seemed rather light. Has the vinification been made more supple at La Pointe since the arrival of the stainless-steel tanks in 1976? Does the wine spend a shorter time now in contact with the skins and pips (the *cuvaison*)? In my opinion the 1976, 1977, 1978 and 1979 had less depth and length than the same years from many other similarly well-known châteaux. All in all, the current wine from Château la Pointe is not notable for quality — although earlier vintages have shown that the potential for a good, and perhaps even very good wine are certainly there — especially if there is plenty of sunshine.

Below:
Mme Barreau displays a case of her exquisite 1976. She has been assisted since 1974 by her son Jean-Luc: before he came Certan de May was too much for Mme Barreau to run alone, and so it was leased for many years to nearby Château Petit-Village.

Far right:
The main door of the château whose shining appearance is due to a spring clean in 1979.

Part of the vineyard lies behind the château, the rest is situated to the northeast, on the other side of the road.

Château Certan de May

Pomerol

The Certan de May family, of Scottish origin, took part in the Crusades and settled in Pomerol in the 16th or 17th century. It is said that this family was the first to receive from the king this right to cultivate grapes on their own land. A lot of Certan de May wine was delivered to the royal court. The estate came to be called Vieux Château Certan. As a result of the February revolution of 1848, the then owner, also named Certan de May, fled the country. When he returned the estate had passed into other hands, except for a small building facing Vieux Château Certan, and a part of the vineyard. Certan de May decided to go on making wine here and established a château that was long known as Petit-Certan, or simply Certan. On the present label 'Château Certan' is printed in large letters with 'Certan de May' in smaller type underneath. Usually, however, the estate is referred to as Château Certan de May.

Modern equipment

The owner of Certan de May is Mme Odette Barreau whose family bought the château in 1925. She is capably assisted by her son Jean-Luc, who attended the viticultural college at Château la Tour Blanche in Sauternes. Although the vineyard is only 12 acres in area, Certan de May is very well equipped. The cellars are bright, clean and modern, and since 1976 fermentation has been done in up-to-date stainless-steel tanks. About a quarter of the wooden casks in which the wine is matured for 20 months are replaced each year. There is no filtering at Certan de May. The wine is clarified with the beaten whites of fresh eggs. Production lies between about 9 (1977) and 26 (1982) *tonneaux*. Château Certan de May is often one of the last Pomerol estates to harvest its grapes.

An exceptionally good Pomerol

The wine of Certan de May — from 65% Merlot, 25% Cabernet Franc and 10% Cabernet Sauvignon plus Malbec — combines firmness and grace in its taste. I consider it a particularly good Pomerol, perhaps not quite reaching the level of its neighbour opposite, Vieux Château Certan, but far better than many others. The 1978 appealed to me greatly. It was a wine with a deep colour, a firm, elegant taste and a correspondingly impressive aftertaste. Wines of a comparable level were made in 1979, 1981 and 1982.

Left:
François-Jean Brochet has owned Rouget since 1974. He and his uncle Marcel Bertrand (the previous owner and still involved in the business) keep large reserves of old vintages at the château and claim that it is 'better than money in the bank'.

Below:
The ivy-covered château is surrounded on all sides by vineyards and magnificent parkland.

Right:
The end of the afternoon as pickers arrive with their last grapes.

Rouget's second-quality wine is called Château Cantereau.

The soil of the vineyard is mainly gravel with some patches of clay and sand.

Château Rouget

Pomerol

Château Rouget is on the north side of the Pomerol plateau, hidden behind a small park. It is one of the oldest Pomerol *crus*, dating from the Middle Ages. The man who built the present château in about 1750 was Pierre Bayonne, first mayor of the commune of Pomerol. In the present century it is Marcel Bertrand who has left his mark on Rouget. He bought the estate in 1925 and made it over to his nephew François-Jean Brochet in 1974. After 50 years Marcel Bertrand has not lost his interest in Rouget and it was he who received me there. The ivy-covered château is only occupied for part of the year. Its interior is graced with Renaissance, Louis XIV and Louis XV furniture, paintings that include Dutch works, and other antiques. Time seems to have come to a halt long ago in Château Rouget.

Large stock of old wine

At Château Rouget wooden fermentation vats are still used, as well as some concrete ones. Wooden casks are employed for maturing the wine; I was told that about one-third of these are replaced each year. No casks or bottles are to be seen at Rouget itself; because of shortage of space a separate storage cellar has been rented next to the racecourse at Libourne. I was staggered by the enormous quantity of bottles that stood there in the dark, stacked up or in cases. I saw wines from 1928 and 1929, large stocks of 1962 and 1964, and thousands of bottles of 1970s vintages.

A wine that needs to age

Rouget is a wine that can, and should, be laid down for a long period. The 1962, for example, was actually still quite youthful, even acidic in taste, 17 years after its vintage; and the 1964 had an almost opaque colour, an intense bouquet and a very firm, strong, long-lasting taste. Marcel Bertrand said: 'The 1962 and 1964 are the only wines I drink at present. The others are much too young.' Rouget is in fact a usually hard, inaccessible wine until five to ten years after its vintage. Only then does any mellowness begin slowly to appear. I have always found the balance of Rouget wines to be good, but generally they rather lack finesse. They come from a 44-acre vineyard planted with a third each of Merlot, Cabernet Franc and Cabernet Sauvignon. Production varies between 40 and 60 *tonneaux*.

Below left:
Getting the grape pickers' meal ready — there are big chunks of meat for the hungry workers.

Below right:
Young and old at mealtime, starting with a nutritious soup.

Left:
Mme Marc, who runs l'Enclos. She and her joint owners also have a small 1-hectare vineyard called Clos du Chaplain in Lalande-de-Pomerol.

Right:
The grapes arrive in big plastic tubs.

Château l'Enclos

Pomerol

Unlike other Pomerol châteaux, l'Enclos leads a rather secluded existence. There are no signs to attract passers-by, and in spring and summer the façade is hidden by a thick curtain of foliage. Like Clos René, the estate lies in the hamlet of Grand-Moulinet, on the west side of the Libourne-Périgueux road. For about a century it has belonged to the Carteau family, the present owners being Mme Carteau, and her two daughters, Mme Saint-Martin and Mme Marc, as well as her granddaughter Catharine Marc. Since the death of her husband in 1971, Mme Marc has been the *gérante*; she lives at the château, which dates from 1898 and was built on the foundations of a much older house.

One-year-old casks

The vineyard at l'Enclos covers about 26 acres. The vines are 80% Merlot, 19.75% Cabernet Franc and 0.25% Malbec. After being picked, crushed and de-stalked, the grapes ferment in concrete vats. The wine then matures for about 17 to 20 months in oak casks. The number of new casks varies from year to year, but is always small. However, casks that have held wine for one year are regularly bought: half of the 1981 vintage developed in such containers. At l'Enclos the traditional egg white is still used for clarifying the wine, but sometimes it is also lightly filtered. This depends on the nature of the wine. Recent production figures for l'Enclos show 32 *tonneaux* in 1978, 39 in 1979, 23 in 1980, 23 in 1977, 25 in 1981 and about 50 in 1982.

A lot of fruit

Britain's Queen Elizabeth drank l'Enclos wine during her state visit to the Netherlands in 1958. In 1972, when I first discovered this Pomerol, I tasted the 1970, which was still in the cask. It was a formidable wine, almost black in colour, the bouquet with a pleasant nuance, and a rounded, full flavour with an abundance of fruit. In 1979 this wine still had a great deal of fruit, and its youthful reserve had not entirely disappeared. The 1975 had a very similar character, with a broad Pomerol taste that left behind an impression of ripe blackcurrant. At a comparative tasting this wine proved to be slightly less concentrated than the 1975 from Château de Sales, but nonetheless very successful. I also recall the 1976 with pleasure. Three years after its vintage this firm wine was beginning to release its bouquet and its taste was becoming more velvety. In his celebrated book *The Wines of Bordeaux*, Edmund Penning-Rowsell justifiably places the wine of l'Enclos 'in the same excellent class' as Clos René. With recent vintages — for example the splendid 1982 — the quality of l'Enclos is unmistakeably proven again.

Château de Sales

Pomerol

Left:
The vast reception hall of Château de Sales looks magnificent today, but during the French Revolution the building was almost totally stripped of its furnishings.

Right:
Bruno de Lambert. In 1979 his father Henri was elected president of the Conseil Interprofessionel du Vin de Bordeaux (CIVB).

Château de Sales produces some 175 tonneaux per year, plus 45 tonneaux of its second wine, Château Chantalouette.

Château de Sales is by far the biggest estate in Pomerol with a vineyard of nearly 118 acres. The size of this *vignoble* induced the owners quite early on to adopt as efficient a mode of planting as possible. From 1948 replanting was done at wider spacings to allow tractors to be used, and of course after the great frost in 1956 when three-quarters of all the vines had to be replaced. At Château de Sales some of the rows of vines are 930 yards long: a rarity in little Pomerol. Again, in contrast to most others, the pleasant park that surrounds the château is quite large.

Below:
The rear of the château, which was given its present form during the 17th and 18th centuries.

No new oak

The château is occupied by Henri de Lambert, who rents the estate from his wife's family — the owners for five centuries. Henri de Lambert is assisted by his son Bruno, a qualified oenologist. At Château de Sales they work in a traditional way but are not afraid of progress. Fermentation is done in concrete vats, the wine is lightly filtered before bottling, and fining is by fresh white of egg: in all these respects the customary methods are followed. Where this château is clearly different is in the maturing of the wine. Henri de Lambert considers that his wine (from about 66% Merlot, 17% Cabernet Franc and 17% Cabernet Sauvignon grapes) already has sufficient tannin. He therefore does not think new oak casks desirable: 'Besides, people today are not able or willing to wait decades for a wine; wines from de Sales can usually be drunk within five to fifteen years.' While maturing, which takes from 18 to 30 months, the wine is alternated between used casks and the concrete vats.

Reliable quality

The Château de Sales method produces a wine that in its youth is not over-aggressive, and becomes pleasantly supple quickly. Consequently it is never a wine to overwhelm the senses. It does, however, have style, a certain elegance and often, too, a complete taste that is not devoid of mild tannin or firmness. Moreover, Château de Sales has over the years shown itself to be a reliable wine, a Pomerol that hardly ever disappoints. Vintages that I have greatly enjoyed are the 1964, 1971, 1973, 1975, 1978 and 1979. The 1981 and 1982 deserve attention too. For Henri de Lambert himself the most characteristic feature of his wine is its bouquet, which 'possesses a great delicacy, of the standard of a *très grand Pomerol*'.

Far left:
Owner Pierre Lasserre. Besides the vintages mentioned in the text, his 1947 and 1971 were also of excellent quality.

Below:
The château.

Right:
One of the cask cellars.

The wine sold as Château Moulinet-Lasserre is identical to Clos René.

Clos René

Pomerol

The Pomerol district is bisected by the N89 road, which connects Libourne with Périgueux. To the east of this busy route lies the Pomerol plateau with practically all the well-known châteaux. To the west the ground is flatter and the soil sandier, often resulting in a lighter kind of wine. But here, too, some châteaux manage to produce wines that can match those from the other part. Cases in point are Château de Sales, and also Château l'Enclos and Clos René. This last estate, named after the nearby hamlet of René, although situated in Grand-Moulinet, has been in the hands of the same family for six generations. The present owner, Pierre Lasserre, told me that each generation had extended the estate a little. Despite this it is still modest in size: 26 acres, with another 1¼ acres to be planted. In front of the white-painted château, which dates from 1880, there is a delightful garden, and lemon trees grow behind the *cuvier*. It is a typical Pomerol estate where the inhabitants live comfortably but not grandly.

The wine-making

The wine ferments in concrete vats, some above and some below ground. For maturing the wine Pierre Lasserre and his right-hand man, grandson Jean-Marie Garde, use oak casks. Of these, 5 to 10% are new each year. Maturing generally lasts for 20 to 24 months. At Clos René the wine is still fined with egg white, but a single filtering is sometimes made. The wine is made from 60% Merlot, 20% Cabernet Franc and 10% Malbec. Production varies between about 25 and 70 *tonneaux*.

Positive impression

The various Clos René vintages I have tasted left a positive impression. The wine does not have, or make claim to, true greatness, but often it tastes very good and is always soundly made. The 1978 had a deep colour, and it was a wine that filled the mouth and had a nice aftertaste. The 1977 was striking for its amazingly dark colour. Two years after the vintage its bouquet was not yet very developed, the taste rather acidic but not unpleasant. At the same tasting the 1976 proved to be already quite developed, with a soft colour, a genial bouquet and a delicious taste that emerged pleasantly despite the tannin present. The 1975 was more intense, less open; here my notes included: 'Plenty of strength of flavour, but no generous roundness. A trifle bitter and a lot of tannin in the aftertaste. Still very closed up. Very good.' To sum up, the better attributes of Clos René suggest a wine that could be termed not rich but comfortably well-endowed. A very successful recent vintage was the 1982, while the 1979 was not very interesting.

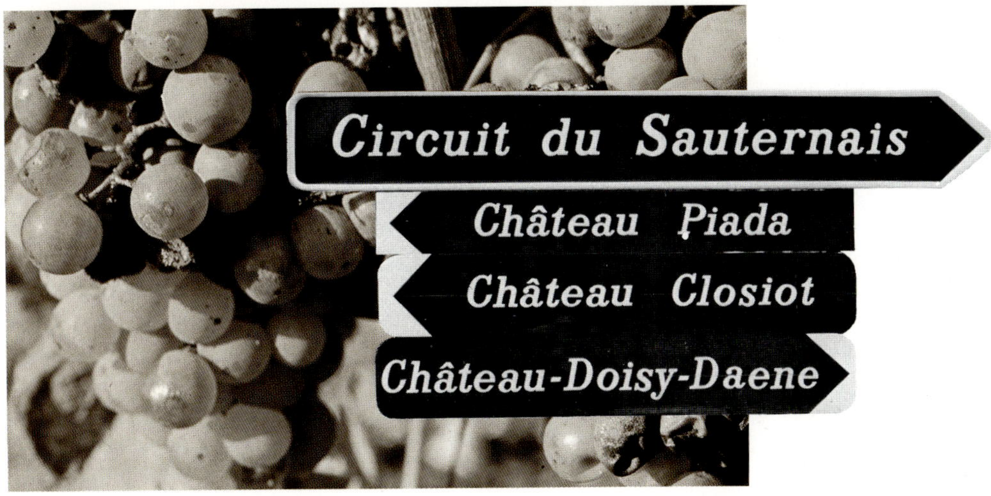

Left:
The Circuit du Sauternais *takes tourists around many different châteaux, both famous and obscure.*

Far left:
Grapes partly affected by pourriture noble.

Below:
Map of the Sauternes region showing the châteaux discussed in this section, and the communes of Barsac, Preignac, Fargues, Bommes and Sauternes itself. The Ciron flows into the Garonne between Barsac and Preignac, and is the cause of mist in the autumn.

Red wines mature gradually, Sauternes wines frequently develop at high speed. Young Sauternes taste very much of their Sauvignon grape and are a shade bitter, but change quickly within 6 to 12 months, becoming mature, softer, heavier and more unctuous.

Serving a Sauternes with a first course and then changing over to red wine can cause problems because the sweetness of the Sauternes will linger in the mouth, ruining the red wine's taste. So take the advice of Alexandre de Lur Saluces, who suggests following the Sauternes course with a bowl of clear bouillon, which will clean the palate ready for the red wine that follows.

Sauternes

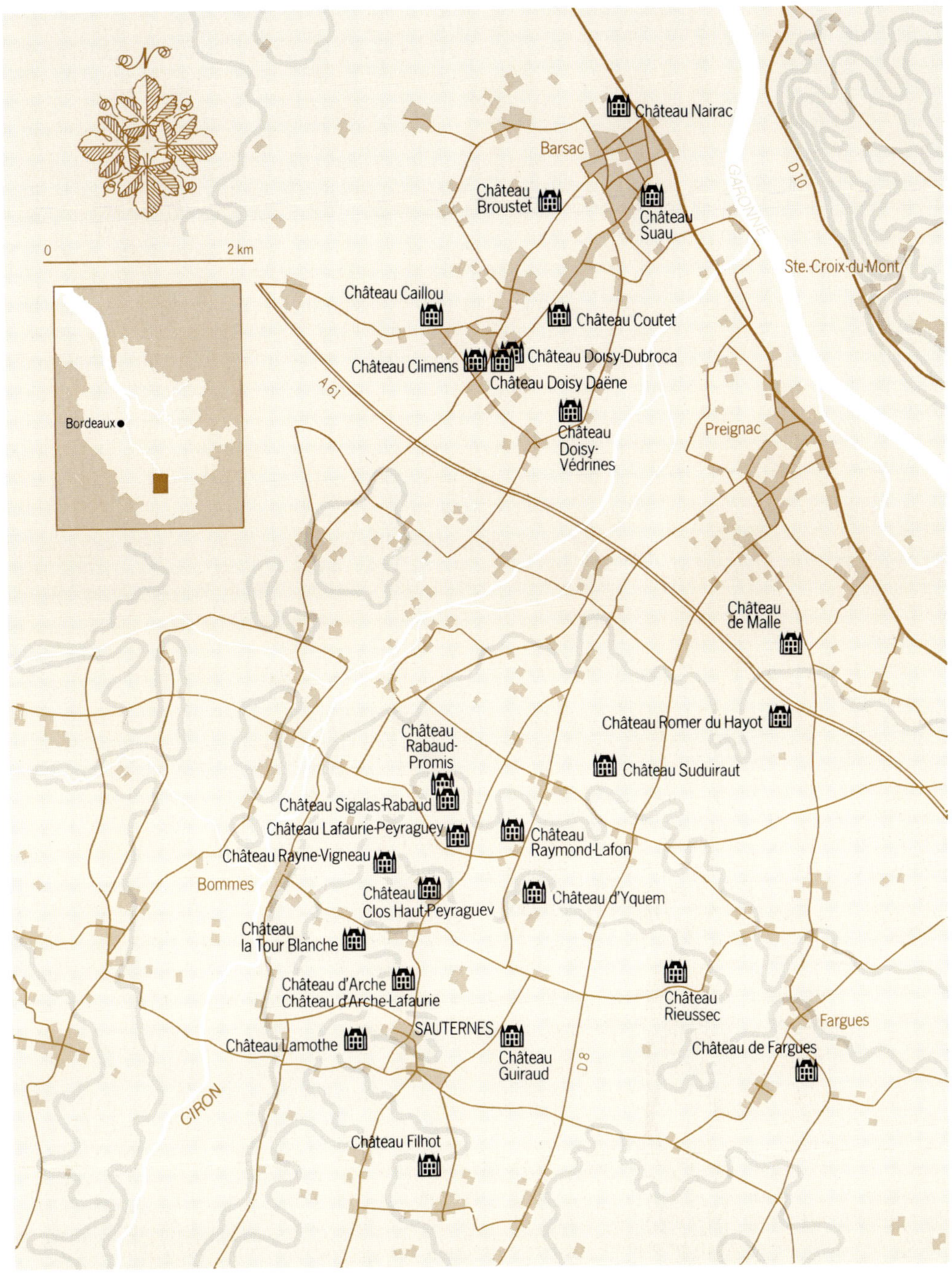

The Sauternes district lies about 25 miles southeast of Bordeaux and forms an enclave in the Graves. It comprises 4,940 acres of vineyards, distributed among the communes of Barsac (1,730 acres), Preignac (1,360 acres), Fargues (370 acres), Bommes (740 acres) and Sauternes (740 acres). Of these five Barsac is the oldest wine village: the grape was introduced here by the Romans. Despite this early cultivation, Sauternes wines were of only local importance for centuries. This changed in the 16th and 17th centuries. At that time the sweet, heavy wines, such as the Spanish muscadels, were regarded as the absolute best. The demand for them was so great that wine growers elsewhere in the world — including the Sauternes — started to imitate them. The Dutch in particular were interested in these French imitations, not least because they were much cheaper than the sumptuous Spanish originals. Holland became the biggest customer for Sauternes wines, which were called *vins de Langon* after the river port from which they were shipped. The Dutch usually added a stiff dose of alcohol to these wines to make them at least as potent as their Spanish models.

American praise

It was only after the decline of the Dutch wine trade that the Sauternes growers gradually started working towards a product of their own. The muscat grape disappeared almost completely to make way for varieties that did better in this soil and climate. They also discovered that picking the grapes late made the wines taste sweeter and richer, and in addition capable of developing for a longer period. By the 18th century Sauternes wines had already acquired a personality of their own, led by Château d'Yquem. Thomas Jefferson, the future American president, visited the district in 1787 and was so delighted with Sauternes that he described it as the best wine in France after Champagne and Hermitage Blanc. Yet many years were to pass before the wines of Sauternes achieved their definitive character.

Left:
The imposing church of Barsac, the oldest wine commune in the Sauternes district. The remains of a Roman villa have been found next to the church. The Romans had an interesting way of finding out whether or not the soil was suitable for wine growing. According to Pierre Dubourdieu of Château Doisy-Daëne they used soil tasters who knew exactly which elements were required for good wines. They took soil samples and let water run through them, then they tasted the water. Apropos of water: Barsac church has two lines high up on the wall next to the main door. These show the flood levels reached by the river Garonne when it burst its banks in 1770 and 1930.

Sauternes must contain at least 12.5° alcohol.

Sauternes forms an ideal partner for most desserts provided the latter are not oversweet, since too much sugar can even spoil the flavour of this sugar-rich wine. Sauternes' greatest enemies among desserts are ice cream, pastries with whipped cream, and chocolate. Its best friends, on the other hand, are all kinds of fruit tarts (like the delightful tarte aux poires *made by the* Les Vignes *restaurant in Sauternes), almond tart, fruit soufflés,* sabayon au Sauternes *and any juicy fruit (pears, peaches, melons, etc.). It also goes with most blue-veined cheeses such as Roquefort or Gorgonzola.*

Pourriture noble

The French Revolution and the years immediately following ruined the Sauternes. For a generation Sauternes wine vanished. According to tradition, the rebirth of region and wine began in 1836, thanks to a German wine grower called Focke. He owned two châteaux in the district where he practised the *pourriture noble* ('noble rot') system he had known on the Rhine. This produces over-ripe, very sweet grapes that give a noble, golden wine rich in sugar. Focke was successful and his method was adopted by more and more growers. At Château d'Yquem they have their own version of the discovery of *pourriture noble*. They say that in 1847 the grapes at d'Yquem were by accident harvested later than usual and the resulting wine differed greatly from the customary product; so much so that the château did not sell it. In 1859, however, Grand Duke Constantine, brother of Tsar Alexander II, tasted the wine. He was so delighted with it that he offered 20,000 gold francs for one *tonneau*, many times the price d'Yquem normally commanded. Only then did d'Yquem deliberately aim at *pourriture noble*, after which, according to this château, the others followed suit. How *pourriture noble* actually came to be introduced, when and by whom, will remain uncertain. The fact is that after 1859 Sauternes suddenly became wildly popular, both in Russia and the rest of Europe.

Microclimate

Pourriture noble is a natural phenomenon that arises due to the special microclimate of the Sauternes. The area has a slightly higher mean annual temperature than the other Bordeaux districts, with rather less rain and fewer storms. The most important factor, however, is the frequency of early morning mists in autumn. These arise because during the summer the water of the Garonne heats up, and around Sauternes an ice-cold spring, the Ciron empties into this relatively warm water. In the morning hours this confluence gives rise to damp mists that shroud the vineyards. Generally the sun breaks through at the end of the morning, so the grapes are bathed in afternoon warmth. This interaction between dampness and sunshine forms a perfect bioclimatic situation for *Botrytis cinerea*, the bacterium that causes the grape to rot. (Note that this is not the dreaded and devastating *pourriture grise*.) During the weeks while the process is at work the grapes often lose half of their moisture and their sugar content increases proportionately. *Botrytis* also adds glycerine to the flesh of the fruit and removes acid. At the same time the grape's own scent disappears, to be replaced by a special aroma that characterizes all good Sauternes; the French describe this as *rôti*, and it reminds some people of stewed plums.

Late, long harvest

Because *pourriture noble* only occurs in fully ripe grapes, picking has to start in the Sauternes after the harvest in the other Bordeaux district is already in. There is a considerably increased risk of bad weather and thus a greater chance of failure. Adding to this risk is the fact that the picking takes much longer than usual — not all the grapes rot at the same rate. The pickers nearly always have to go through the vineyard several times in order to clip off only the right grapes from the bunches with their special pointed shears. Most of the pickers come from the district itself, for the majority of château owners will not entrust this task to inexperienced students or other casual labour. Obviously, a long harvest is an expensive one. Another price-raising factor is the low yield per hectare. Legally this must be no more than 25 hectolitres per hectare — the lowest in the whole of Bordeaux — but in practice even this is not normally reached. At châteaux like d'Yquem and Raymond-Lafon, for example, a mere 9 hectolitres per hectare is achieved, or one glass per vine per year. Little wonder, then, that a good Sauternes can never be really cheap. On the other hand, Sauternes, with the exception of d'Yquem, is not excessively dear; it is the world's most undervalued great white wine.

Years of crisis

In the present century Sauternes sold well until the end of the 1950s, but then the problems began: a series of bad harvests and a world taste that was becoming steadily 'drier'. Sauternes wines fell from favour and the prices collapsed. The district has not yet fully recovered from this crisis; and it is significant that nearly all owners of *crus classés* have a second occupation, for they cannot live from their Sauternes alone. As a rule, too, the production of dry white wine (the Bordeaux *appellation*) and sometimes even red wine has perforce to lighten the financial burden. In spite of all this, one *cru classé*, Château Myrat, disappeared completely and during the 1970s many well-known châteaux changed owners, including Rieussec, Climens, Doisy-Dubroca, Rayne-Vigneau, Nairac and Coutet. In such a situation you would have expected the growers to work closely together in order to turn the tide. Strangely enough, there has been practically no purposeful collective action; and this despite the unanimous conclusion of two independently arranged investigations, to the effect that Sauternes could be sold without difficulty at the desired prices provided the wine growers cooperated with one another.

Considerable differences

Because Sauternes has been going through a somewhat inglorious period and many of the growers have considerable difficulty in making ends meet, there are great variations in quality. Some châteaux try to sell as much wine as possible at an acceptable price, while others aim at the highest quality, whatever the cost. Between these two extremes there is a middle group that for financial reasons cannot reach the very top, but aims, despite all the limitations, to make a good product. The quality of Sauternes is mainly

Left:
The Office Viticole de Sauternes and Barsac *in Barsac is chiefly used as a sales office for wines from the region, and the range is truly massive. The* Office Viticole *also has its own wine, a Sauternes which it sells under the* Terre Noble *label. Some 360 growers produce between 94,500 and 533,000 cases of Sauternes every year; 5.3% of the growers own more than 36 acres and make 37% of the wine, while three-quarters of the growers have less than 12.5 acres each, producing just under 30% of the total.*

Below:
The church of Sauternes stands next to one of the best restaurants in the area, Les Vignes. *The inside looks rather like a log cabin, but the restaurant serves honest and well-prepared regional dishes at reasonable prices, all washed down with Sauternes by the bottle, half-bottle or glass. For those who want a more refined, luxurious atmosphere, there is the* Larozze *restaurant in nearby Langon.*

Sauternes is much more than just a dessert wine, it can be a perfect accompaniment to many starters, hot or cold. Examples include foie gras d'oie *(a classic partner),* vichyssoise, quenelles de brochet, blanquette de veau, *melon with ham and various cocktails containing fruit. Sauternes can also accompany main courses such as turbot served with a* sauce mousseline, *a particular favourite of the region. Other serving suggestions include* canard aux pêches *and* dinde farcie aux marrons. *Finally, Sauternes should be served with any dishes that are made with the wine itself.*

determined by the quality of the grapes. These have to be thoroughly affected by the *pourriture noble* and ideally should contain enough sugar to reach a potential 19° to 21° of alcohol. In practice fermentation stops naturally at 13° to 14°, leaving about 80 to 100 grams (2¾ to 3½ ounces) of residual sugar in every litre of wine, which gives it its sweet taste. Some châteaux, however, pick the grapes before the *pourriture noble* has had its maximum effect. The sugar content then has to be increased artificially (by adding sugar to the grape juice, for example), otherwise a meagre wine is produced. Of course there are other factors that influence the final quality, including the vinification, selection (good or less good qualities of grapes or wine from the *cuves*), and the maturing of the wine: should it be in concrete, metal or man-made materials? In oak casks? New or used ones? For how long should the wine be left? And so on. Naturally, the type of soil and the grape varieties are also tremendously important. The terrain in the three southern communes (Sauternes, Bommes and Fargues) is quite hilly; under a top layer of sand and gravel there is a lot of clay and limestone. In the two northern communes (Preignac and Barsac) the landscape is flatter, the soil more calcareous, sometimes reddish in colour. Wines from Barsac — often the most elegant of the whole Sauternes — can be sold either under the *appellation* Barsac or as Sauternes. In all the Sauternes communes the Sémillon (for alcohol, roundness, suppleness) is the most widely planted grape variety, followed by the Sauvignon (freshness, breeding). A third, much less prevalent, variety is the Muscadelle with its slightly musky aroma.

Classification

Sauternes were the only white wines classified in 1855. There has been no subsequent revision of this classification, except that some châteaux have changed names, merged, or been split up.

Grand premier cru classé
d'Yquem (Sauternes)

Premiers crus classés
La Tour Blanche (Bommes)
Lafaurie-Peyraguey (Bommes)
Clos Haut-Peyraguey (Bommes)
Rayne-Vigneau (Bommes)
Suduiraut (Preignac)
Coutet (Barsac)
Climens (Barsac)
Guiraud (Sauternes)
Rieussec (Fargues)
Sigalas-Rabaud (Bommes)
Rabaud-Promis (Bommes)

Deuxièmes crus classés
Myrat-Barsac (defunct)
Doisy-Daëne (Barsac)
Doisy-Védrines (Barsac)
Doisy-Dubroca (Barsac)
d'Arche (Sauternes)
Filhot (Sauternes)
Broustet (Barsac)
Nairac (Barsac)
Caillou (Barsac)
Suau (Barsac)
De Malle (Preignac)
Romer du Hayot (Preignac)
Lamothe, Despujols (Sauternes)
Lamothe, Bastit-Saint-Martin (Sauternes)

All the existing *crus classés* plus a few other châteaux are described on the following pages.

The wine

Drinking a fine Sauternes is an experience. It has a beautiful colour, sometimes tinged with green, often with the warm glow of gold. Its bouquet can be very luxurious, with the striking *rôti* of the *pourriture noble*, as well as impressions of honey, jasmine, dessert apples, nuts, ripe bananas and apricots. For me the taste of some Sauternes is the height of luxury: a broad, stylish richness of intense power, and a long aftertaste. It is served cool, but not ice-cold. The advice Pierre Meslier, *régisseur* of d'Yquem and owner of Raymond-Lafon, gave me was: 'Drink Sauternes fresh, but as warm as possible, at 12° to 13°C (54 to 55°F). The wine is then just cool enough without the bouquet and taste being frozen.'

Below:
Château Suau.

Right:
Daniel Biarnès with his daughter-in-law, the wife of his son Roger who currently runs the property. Daniel acquired Château Suau — or at least its vineyards in 1960.

Château Suau

2e Cru Classé
Barsac

Château Suau is rather hidden away in the village of Barsac. The name of this *deuxième cru classé* does not appear on signposts and in any case a high wall conceals it from passers-by in the narrow road. Yet Château Suau once belonged to the de Lur Saluces family of d'Yquem. In 1840 the estate passed into the possession of another family, then at the end of the century Emile Garros, manager of the de Lur Saluces properties, became the owner. The château itself, a substantial *maison bourgeoise*, still belongs to his descendants. The vineyard, however, was acquired by Daniel Biarnès in 1960. No doubt this separation of château and vineyard tends to discourage visits. The vineyard lies behind the little château park. It covers only 17 acres, more than two-thirds of it planted with Sémillon and almost one-third Sauvignon plus a little Muscadelle.

Cellars elsewhere

Vinification is carried out at the Biarnès family's headquarters (they own several estates) at Château Navarro in Illats. This lies in wooded country near the village of Cérons north of Barsac. The must ferments in concrete vats and then stays in oak casks — most of them used ones — for at least one year. Roger Biarnès, Daniel's son, supervises this, assisted by his wife Nicole and others. At time of writing not all the wine — rather more than one-half of the approximately 17 *tonneaux* of an average harvest — is bottled at the château. Much of it goes in casks to the firm of Delor, by far the biggest customer.

Not very convincing

Even in outstanding years Château Suau is not a really striking wine. The bouquet is rather flat, without richness or depth, and the taste is not very convincing. It has the elegance of a Barsac, yet at the same time makes a rather bland impression. Although the wine is lacking in breed and refinement, it comes over as pure and quite pleasant — making a good aperitif.

Centre left:
The single-storey Château Broustet is covered in ivy. On the left is the chai.

Far left:
Eric Fournier, manager of the estate, ships most of his wines to Britain.

Below left:
Inside the chai *where the wine both ferments and matures in wood.*

Below right:
Statue in the garden.

Broustet also produces a dry white wine (Camperos, appellation *Bordeaux) as well as some red wine for the staff.*

Château Broustet

2e Cru Classé
Barsac

Since 1885 Château Broustet has belonged to the Fournier family who also own the famous Château Canon in Saint-Emilion. It was the great-grandfather of Eric Fournier, Broustet's *gérant*, who bought the estate — but not because of its wine, vineyard or reputation. He wanted it as a storage area for his cooper's shop nearby. This was one of the most important in the region, freighting out large numbers of casks by both rail and river. That Broustet was acquired in the first instance for its ground and buildings is indicated by the fact that it was not until 1900, 15 years after the purchase, that the vineyard was planted. Four years later came the first vintage. Today the estate has 37 acres of vineyard. The Sémillon, with 63%, predominates, followed by the Sauvignon with 25% and an unusually high proportion of Muscadelle — 12%. The average yield at Broustet is very small as there has been a series of failed vintages. There was no Château Broustet to sell for 1974, 1976 or 1977. The 1976 seemed promising, but the estate had to contend with serious vinification problems. Broustet's second wine is called Château de Ségur, also with the Barsac *appellation*.

Fermentation in the cask

Broustet has no actual château. Apart from the long, low, neat cellars and the accommodation for the staff there is just a fairly modern annexe for the Fourniers. They do not go in for outward show here. The quality of the wine, however, receives full attention. After fermentation in concrete vats, the wine remains for 12 to 18 months in oak casks, of which 10% is renewed every year. A contractor does the bottling.

Well-balanced

Of the vintages tasted the 1975 appealed to me greatly: a fairly light golden colour, a flawless bouquet, a beautiful taste and a good long aftertaste. The wine was luxurious in a restrained sort of way, and not syrupy. The 1978 also presented itself very well: full of elegance, not too sweet, clean of taste and with a fine aftertaste. Both wines were well-balanced. The first impressions of the 1979 and 1980 are also favourable. An earlier vintage that I enjoyed drinking was the 1971.

Far left:
The front of the château; part of the vineyard is directly behind it.

Below:
The Heeters certainly do not live in luxury, but the château and park make a well-cared-for impression.

Opposite, below:
Nicole Heeter-Tari, seen here in her favourite room in the château, her kitchen.

Opposite, above:
Everything is in readiness for the grape harvest.

Château Nairac gets its name from a Protestant wine family from Bordeaux; it is a name that crops up again and again in old books about the city, especially in the 18th century. Paul Nairac, for example, was a politician — député *for Aquitaine — merchant and shipowner. For many years the family lived very comfortably in the Cours de Verdun in Bordeaux, then they commissioned the architect Victor Louis to build them a château in Barsac around 1770. The Nairacs fled France in the wake of the French Revolution, and one of them, Charles Auguste Nairac, settled in the Dutch town of Barneveld where he eventually became burgomaster (1841-83).*

Château Nairac

2e Cru Classé
Barsac

'I am by nature a perfectionist. Therefore we try every year to produce the best wine that nature gives us. Besides, we are still an unknown second *cru*: we cannot afford to make mistakes.' These were the words of Tom Heeter, owner of Château Nairac. His philosophy is admirably clear: at Nairac they are determined to make a really great wine, whatever the cost. Tom and his charming wife Nicole acquired the estate in 1972. She is a Tari, of the wine-growing family who own the *grands crus* Giscours and Branaire-Ducru in the Médoc; he comes of a family of American industrialists in Dayton, Ohio. They got to know each other at Château Giscours where Tom — obsessed by wine — had arrived to work as a trainee. In August 1971 Tom's father-in-law happened to see a small advertisement offering Château Nairac for sale at a relatively low price. The purchase was immediately agreed but it was 1972 before the transaction was completed: the owner had received a more attractive offer in the meantime and tried — in vain — to wriggle out of the first agreement.

Many new casks

One of the first acts of the new owners was to take the advice of Professor Peynaud, the world-famous oenologist. For making the best possible wine he prescribed new oak casks every year, as at Château d'Yquem — an expensive investment but, as it proved, quite justified. Casks, whether used or new, start with the advantage that they are excellent for fermenting small quantities of juice — one reason being that the temperature does not rise so much as with

The Nairac family also settled in Mauritius, where they still play a prominent rôle in public life. Tom and Nicole Heeter have had several members of the family staying with them.

Nairac's wine production varies greatly year by year — in 1977 not a single drop was made, whereas 22 tonneaux *was made the year before.*

Instead of one large cellar, the estate has several small chais *that house the vats in which the wine both ferments and matures.*

All Château Nairac wine is shipped in wooden cases. The 1978 vintage matured in casks whose bungholes were stopped with empty quarter-bottles!

Tom Heeter bottles a lot of his wine in magnums, according to him an ideal size of bottle for dinner parties of 15 or more. A relatively large proportion also goes into half-bottles, and it is typical of the rare perfectionism found at Château Nairac that special scaled-down labels are printed for these bottles.

Nairac is a member of the Académie du Vin de Bordeaux *and of the* Union des Grands Crus de Bordeaux.

bigger amounts. The policy at Nairac, in fact, was to aim at bringing in only small quantities of grapes, enough for four to five casks, each day of the harvest. Casks, being smaller than vats, also allow strict selectivity and very fine-tuned blending. Or, as Tom Heeter put it: 'If I buy 65 casks for a vintage, this in principle gives me 65 elements from which to compose my wine.' New casks have an advantage over used ones in that they give the wine tannin, the basis of longevity, in a natural way. Tannin also helps the wine to clarify. Furthermore, there are certain essences that only new oak can impart to the wine. Once the decision had been taken, Tom Heeter experimented with different types of oak to find the best possible quality for the Nairac casks.

Quality control

There would be no sense in using new oak casks for wine of poor quality. Vines at Nairac are therefore very severely pruned so that the essential substances in the fruits become very concentrated. Heeter and his *chef de culture* see to it that the harvest comes in 'clean'; the pickers' baskets are examined one by one and imperfect grapes are removed. A team of 20 to 25 pickers is employed. In good years like 1975 and 1976 the pickers go through the vineyard about three times to gather the grapes at the right moment, but in bad years more circuits are necessary. The 1974 vintage, for example, required the pickers to go round eleven times. When the grape juice has fermented the process is not halted in the usual way by sulphur dioxide, but by opening the cellar doors at the opportune moment and letting the fresh air do it. At the beginning of the subsequent maturing period — of one and a half to three years depending on the vintage — the casks are constantly topped up to avoid oxidization. Heeter allows his wine to clear by natural means, but he does filter lightly before bottling. Little sulphur is used in the wine; less than 250 milligrams is added in sound years, compared with a legal maximum of 400 milligrams per litre.

Culinary interest

Tom and Nicole Heeter have enlarged the vineyard area, including 6 acres bought from Château Climens. They now have about 40 acres altogether. They have also renovated the château, which was very necessary as it had stood empty for 60 years. They have lived there with their three children since the spring of 1974. A great deal of attention has been paid to the kitchen, for cooking is Nicole's great passion. She knows all the great chefs of the French southwest and with them has compiled a collection of recipes entitled *La Grande Cuisine au Barsac-Sauternes.* A memorable meal was served to a party of journalists on 9 April 1978 at Château Nairac; they were given *pigeonneaux confits au Château Nairac, ris d'agneau aux truffes fraîches, fromages* and *les desserts de Tom,* accompanied in succession by Nairac 1973, Latour 1964, d'Yquem 1928, Climens 1928, d'Arche 1928, Rayne-Vigneau 1928, Rieussec 1928 and Suduiraut 1928. The first two and last three wines came from Tom Heeter's private cellar. The meal was prepared by the famous restaurateur Jean-Marie Amat. He is the best chef of Bordeaux and for far around — and for years a good customer of Nairac, his favourite Barsac.

Much style

For anyone who knows the story of Nairac, the class of its wine hardly comes as a surprise. The 1975 is a very characteristic vintage. I have tasted it many times, for example with *tarte au citron* and *tarte aux fraises* in Amat's restaurant. The wine had a light colour with a tinge of green, an excellent bouquet with obvious finesse and a splendid taste, gracious and rich at the same time. Nairac wines are generally harmonious, extraordinarily pure and never cloyingly sweet. They have great style. The 1976 has rather more strength and luxury than the 1975; the 1974 is lighter and fresher, but cannot be regarded as representative as a difficult vintage caused the Sauvignon to dominate it (with 80 to 90%), whereas the vineyard is planted with 90% Sémillon, only 6% Sauvignon and 4% Muscadelle. Not a drop of Nairac was made in 1977, or 1978 but 1979 gave a small (only 40% accepted) but good harvest, 1980 a wine à la 1975, 1981 a small but correct vintage, and 1982 a suberb Barsac.

Château Coutet

1e Cru Classé
Barsac

The history of Coutet begins in the Middle Ages, when a house was built on the site where the present château stands. In the 13th century this residence was fortified; the square tower on the courtyard dates from this period. About a century later Coutet acquired its own chapel and this too has been preserved. Before the French Revolution the estate belonged to the Filhot family. The Coutet label is a reminder of this fact, for it is very much like that of Château Filhot. Coutet passed into the possession of the de Lur Saluces family via a marriage. In about 1930 they sold it to Henry-Louis Guy, an industrialist from Lyons. His daughter inherited the estate from him and after her death it was bought, in 1977, by Marcel Baly, director of the Société Alsacienne, a well-known concern in France.

The biggest Barsac estate

With its 99 acres of land, 94 acres of it vineyard, Château Coutet is the largest wine estate in Barsac. The vineyard is in the shape of a big, untidy oblong surrounding the château, its cellars and delightful park. The little château has two small round towers on one side, and a lawn with flowerbeds, bright with tulips in spring.

Opposite page, left:
Cleaning one of the small hydraulic presses.

Opposite page, below:
The spacious inner courtyard with its ancient tower, chapel and well.

Opposite page, right:
At vintage time the suitably rotted grapes are picked, leaving the less-affected good fruit for the second round or tri.

Below right:
Proprietor Marcel Baly is also a director of Société Alsacienne (road haulage and hotels).

Right:
Part of Coutet's vineyard, with the château by the trees in the distance.

Château Coutet's reception area features a beautiful display cabinet with old bottles and photographs of Maurice Chevalier, who visited the estate while celebrating his 70th birthday in the Sauternes in 1953. Why there particularly? At Coutet the story goes that Sauternes wine helped the young Chevalier to get started on his long, illustrious career. Feeling nervous before an important stage appearance, he went to a restaurant, ordered a full bottle of Sauternes — and downed the lot. He sang and danced as never before, the show was a huge success and the critics enthusiastic; so Maurice Chevalier never forgot that Sauternes helped him become a star.

Château Coutet

Obviously the cellars at Coutet are large, and about 20 men work in them through the year, including the *régisseur* Bertrand Baly, the son of the owner. I was told that in the course of the 80's the percentage of Sauvignon would be increased to 25 to 30%, because 'our customers' tastes are tending increasingly towards a wine with more fruit.' The firm of Alexis Lichine buys nearly all the Coutet each year. A relatively large quantity is shipped to Australia.

A hundred new casks a year

Although wooden vats stand in the *chai* at Coutet these are not used for fermenting the wine, for this is done in casks. Normally about a hundred of the maturing casks are replaced each year, a big investment. This means that a third to a half of the vintage is matured in new oak, for two years. A dry white Graves, called Le Reverdon, is made from grapes containing too little sugar. The quantity depends very much on the vintage; the average is about 70 *tonneaux* a year. Formerly, in the time of the de Lur Saluces, Coutet also made a red *vin ordinaire*. This came from low-lying vineyards near the Garonne and Ciron that no longer belong to the château.

Unforgettable Cuvée Madame

Occasionally, in superior vintages, the very best and richest grapes are vinified separately. The wine thus produced is called Cuvée Madame — a name given in honour of Mme Rolland, the former owner, by her husband. Since not more than a few thousand bottles are involved, this rare wine is hardly ever sold through the trade but reserved for receptions at Coutet or those held by the Alexis Lichine firm. I therefore consider myself fortunate to have been able to taste Cuvée Madame on one occasion. This happened by accident at a dinner at Château Coutet for a group of Dutch wine merchants. Coutet 1971 was listed on the menu, but the waitresses served Coutet Cuvée Madame 1971. This had certainly not been intentional — someone had picked up the wrong wine in the cellar. My table companion, Patrick Léon of Alexis Lichine, told me that the 1971 was the most beautiful Cuvée Madame ever made. On 15 and 16 October 1971, 60 pickers went through the vineyard gathering the most perfect fruit. The juice from these filled six new oak casks, which produced 1,408 bottles and 177 magnums. Production costs at the time were 80 francs per bottle. For me this 1971 was an experience, a monumental wine, with an aftertaste that was a minute-long explosion of richness. Patrick Léon pushed his sorbet away, saying, 'This is my dessert, you can eat this wine.' I did the same. The Cuvée Madame is one of the most beautiful Sauternes I have ever drunk. Coutet also produced a little Cuvée Madame in years like 1970, 1975 and 1976 — but these were not of the same calibre as that glorious 1971.

Noble and refined

Cuvée Madame is, of course, a quite exceptional wine. But the ordinary Coutet also merits attention. My notes on the 1971 (which I tasted in 1979) record: 'Gold-green, medium-deep colour, fine bouquet with a touch of freshness and a not-too-pronounced *Botrytis* scent; noble taste with elegance and refinement, beautiful aftertaste, harmonious.' I often associate the taste of Coutet with fruit (especially apricots) and honey. The 1976 will perhaps achieve the class of the 1971, or at least approach it. The 1975 will reach full development earlier, but is also a lovely wine, the finesse lingering long in the mouth. The 1972, I am pleased to record, can be regarded as outstanding for its year. The 1978 vintage produced a fairly light Coutet, with less of the *Botrytis* scent than normal, but fruity and distinguished. Very agreeable wines were made in 1979 and 1980. In comparison with Barsac's other famous wine, Climens, Coutet usually is slightly less generous, but a little more refined.

Château Climens

1e Cru Classé
Barsac

For many generations Climens has been regarded as one of the leading wines of Barsac. In the journal *Le Producteur* of 1840 we read: 'The first wines of Barsac are without doubt those of Climens and Château Coutet.' And in many other books and articles Climens is named as one of the best, if not the best, of the Barsacs. The class of the Climens wine is described in no small measure by the situation of the vineyard. For a long time the words 'Haut-Climens' appeared on the label: the estate is on the highest point of the commune. The Garonne used regularly to overflow its banks, as can be ascertained from the old church at Barsac: two lines on the wall near the door show how far the water reached on 7 April 1770 and, just over three feet below, on 6 March 1930. Yet this part of Barsac was never flooded by the river.

A quality-conscious owner

The Climens vineyard, besides lying higher than those of the other Barsac estates, has excellent natural drainage, and the subsoil lends itself perfectly to grape-growing. All this would still not guarantee a truly great wine if the owner were not a man with the will and the talent fully to utilize this natural potential. Lucien Lurton, who comes from a well-known wine-growing family, places quality far above quantity. This is also demonstrated by his other wines, such as Château Brane-Cantenac in the Médoc. Lurton bought Climens in 1971. Daily management was left in the hands of Madame Janin; the Janin family has been associated with Climens for more than a century.

Opposite page, above:
The château's shutters stay closed for as long as it remains unoccupied.

Opposite page, below:
The handsome courtyard at Château Climens.

Left:
This young cellarworker is proud of the 1976.

Below right:
A joint effort — bringing in the grapes.

Right:
Climens wine is generally only sold when it has been allowed to mature for two or three years in the bottle. The 1975 vintage for instance was not marketed until 1979.

Climens is just on the boundary of Barsac; its vineyard practically borders the autoroute *that links Bordeaux with Toulouse.*

The 1929 vintage is the most spectacular that maître de chai *Janin can remember. The grapes were practically roasted, and although there were no signs of* pourriture noble, *the sugar content of the grapes was such that the juice was almost like jam in the presses.*

Low yield

The yield at Climens is low. The vineyard, planted with 85% Sémillon grapes and 15% Sauvignon, covers 74 acres. In the record year of 1976 it gave 55 *tonneaux*, which represents a yield of 16.5 hectolitres per hectare; 25 hectolitres is the permitted amount in the Sauternes. Other recent vintages gave lower yields: 14.7 hl/ha (1982), 15.6 hl/ha (1981), 13.5 hl/ha (1980), 15 hl/ha (1979) and 9.6 hl/ha (1978).
The château has not been lived in since the departure of its last residents, the German occupiers during the Second World War. Lucien Lurton had so far lacked the means to restore the interior, though he has seen to a number of exterior items, including the roof and the two low towers. The building is no architectural marvel: its lines are austere and its design uninspired. The courtyard at the rear, with its shadowy trees, possesses more charm. Lucien Lurton has a small collection of old wine presses and has brought a few of them to Climens. The largest stands near the entrance to the *chai*.

A 1964 of distinction

There are no vats at Climens for the wine ferments in oak casks. About one-fourth of these are replaced each year. The wine matures in the cask for at least two and sometimes two and a half years, and is lightly filtered before bottling. In the dim, roomy cellars I was given six recent vintages to taste. I also had the privilege of drinking some earlier Climens vintages from the private cellar.
The first Climens I got to know was the 1964. In the Sauternes this year is generally recorded as a failure (d'Yquem did not make a drop), but Climens produced a brilliant wine, with richness, distinction and a golden colour.

Sublime balance

Another wine I well remember is the 1967, a little less rich than the 1964, but still princely. The first vintage of the Lucien regime was the 1971. I thought it a typical Climens — a wine without sumptuous sweetness, but with a lot of breeding. A striking characteristic of this particular vintage was the slightly 'roasted' impression that the aftertaste left behind: the same *pain grillé* that you encounter in some of the top white Burgundies.
The 1973 — enjoyed in the company of Lucien's brother André, with a dessert of peaches, grapes and pears — was not markedly sweet either, and the same can be said of the fairly light, fresh 1974. Château Climens produced brilliant, well-made wines in 1975 and 1976; the small vintage of 1977 was rather lighter and a little more severe than normal. The 1978 can be taken as a Climens at its best: a bouquet full of nuances (herbs, flowers, fruit), a pleasing taste full of cultured luxury, and a sublime balance. The château also made very successful wines in 1979, 1981 and 1982. The 1980 is rather light.

Most Doisy-Dubroca wines are shipped to the United States via a négociant in Bordeaux.

For a few years at the end of the 19th century the château was known as Doisy-Graves, although it already belonged to the Dubroca brothers.

Either the outpout — and the vineyard — of Doisy-Dubroca were once much larger than today, or somebody is telling stories. Presentday annual yields are around the 3 tonneaux *mark, but* Bordeaux et Ses Vins *of 1893 refers to an annual output of 30* tonneaux. *Even the 1969 edition recorded 50* tonneaux.

Below:
One shutter is open but the small château is empty and in a poor state of repair.

Right:
Château Doisy-Dubroca with its usually empty cellars behind, and the tiny vineyard to the left of, the unoccupied house.

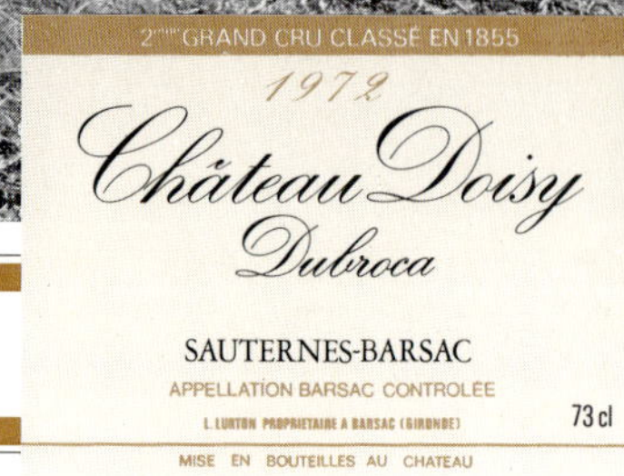

Château Doisy-Dubroca

2e Cru Classé
Barsac

There are three châteaux in the commune of Barsac with 'Doisy' in their names: Doisy-Daëne, Doisy-Védrines and Doisy-Dubroca, all *deuxièmes crus*. They emerged through the division of Château Doisy in the first half of the 19th century.

Château Doisy-Dubroca is the smallest of the three, with a vineyard of only 8 acres, not all of it productive. Château and vineyard are situated next to Doisy-Daëne and look out on Doisy-Védrines. Here, even more than elsewhere in the Sauternes, the description 'château' is very euphemistic. Doisy-Dubroca is a rather small, dilapidated, empty country house in the middle of a bleak garden with just a few trees. There are fairly large cellars behind the house but these are not used. The owner, Lucien Lurton, makes the wine at this other Barsac château of Climens. In 1880 this Doisy estate was bought by the Dubroca family. One of the sons later married a Mademoiselle Climens and since then the two estates have remained attached. So when Lurton bought Climens in 1971 he also became the owner of little Doisy-Dubroca.

Early development

The Doisy-Dubroca vineyard is mainly planted — 90% — with the Sémillon. Production is obviously small; 1982 brought a record six *tonneaux*, but 1977 yielded only one *tonneau* and 1978 just 3½. At the end of the 1970s a number of young vines were still to become productive so that the yield would eventually increase a little. In the Climens cellars, with Lucien Lurton and his assistants, I tasted five recent Doisy-Dubroca vintages. Comparison with Climens was obvious: I found the Doisy-Dubroca to be a little lighter, and also less fragrant, less rich, less deep, less pronounced and shorter; but not unattractive. In their early youth the Doisy-Dubrocas were already particularly mild and agreeable. The 1975 was well ahead, with a broad bouquet full of mild spiciness. The other years I tasted were the 1978 (good), 1977 (lighter, not bad), 1976 (just bottled, unsettled and difficult to taste), and 1971 (golden colour, good taste but just a little thin). More recent good vintages are 1979 and 1981. Lucien Lurton ferments the Doisy-Dubroca wine in oak casks; the wine is then matured for two and a half years, also in the cask. A quarter of the casks are renewed every year.

Below:
Pierre Dubourdieu in his château and with his wine. The most spectacular wine he has made so far was the Vin de Noël *— the very last grapes for this vintage were picked by journalists (!) on 15 December 1979. It is strong (14.7°) and has an elegantly rich flavour. Dubourdieu's dry Doisy-Daëne has been a great commercial success for some 30 years (90,000 bottles a year) and the demand always far exceeds supply. This fresh, clean wine — Bordeaux* appellation *— is made from 30 to 40% Sauvignon, 20 to 25% Sémillon, 10 to 15% Muscadelle and the rest is Riesling plus Chardonnay. Doisy-Daëne's vineyard covers a total of 35 acres.*

Right:
The entrance to the château.

Château Doisy-Daëne

2e Cru Classé
Barsac

Doisy-Daëne, one of the three Doisy estates in Barsac, takes its name from an Englishman, who was the first buyer of this part of the original Doisy estate. Today it belongs to Pierre Dubourdieu, a well-known personality in the Sauternes world. He is an intellectual who loathes the syndicalism of the French wine scene, and who makes his wine in an unconventional way.

Very little sulphur

After picking, the grapes are usually pressed six or seven times in modern presses; the juice then ferments in tanks lined with stainless steel. Fermentation is stopped by letting the temperature fall to 4°C (39°F). The wine is then filtered and some of it is transferred to oak casks (40 of which are replaced each year). Wine in the casks is regularly exchanged with wine in the tanks. After blending there is a second *filtrage*, and a third before bottling. The whole process takes about 18 months and has the advantage that very little sulphur needs to be used to stabilize the wine — usually from one-twentieth to one-tenth the usual amount.

Hundred per cent Sémillon

Doisy-Daëne wine — 40 *tonneaux* of it in normal years — comes entirely from the Sémillon grape. Despite the absence of the Sauvignon, Doisy-Daëne could not be called a heavy wine; Pierre Dubourdieu manages to give his wine sufficient freshness. Yet I do find that the wine lacks some depth and complexity. A Doisy-Daëne from a good vintage possesses a good, full, aromatic taste with just the right amount of *fraîcheur*, but is often without the fine nuances that make a truly great wine so exciting. However, I have greatly enjoyed Doisy-Daëne on many occasions, including old vintages, for it matures extremely well. I recall the still completely vital 1961, the 1942, which had a slight scent of mint, and the 1943, which 35 years after its vintage was still a fantastic wine. So a Doisy-Daëne from a reasonable vintage can be laid down for a long time. Dubourdieu himself has about 10,000 bottles from 30 to 50 years old.

Centre left:
The château with its old circular tower, which now contains two luxury bathrooms.

Far left:
Pierre Castéja and his wife.

Below:
The chais at Château Doisy-Védrines.

One of the château windows has the outline of a human heart engraved in it. It is believed that one Mme de Védrines used her diamond ring to engrave a permanent token of her affections for some lover. This must have happened before the French Revolution.

The estate has around 250 head of sheep who provide a lot of useful manure.

Château Doisy-Védrines

2e Cru Classé
Barsac

Château Doisy-Védrines dates from the 16th century and was probably built on the ruins of a mill. The round tower of the château is said to be a relic of that period. The building is tastefully and comfortably furnished, better than most Barsac châteaux. This does not mean, however, that the owner, Pierre Castéja, has been earning a great deal of money from his wines all these years, though, as he told me: 'In 1947 Doisy-Védrines sold at higher prices than Mouton-Rothschild. We lived in paradise then.' Times changed and prices fell, so sharply that Pierre Castéja was obliged in 1964 to plant part of the vineyard with black grapes: 'I had gradually ruined myself with Sauternes and wanted to spread my risks.' Today 25 acres of his vineyard are planted for red wine, 49 for white. The red wine is called Château la Tour Védrines. In addition Castéja created a red brand wine, also under the Bordeaux appellation: Chevalier de Védrines. There is a dry white version of this, for which a little Doisy-Védrines is sometimes used. These brand wines have enabled Castéja to maintain his château. He is also managing director of the wine firm Roger Joanne.

Very variable yield

The wine of Château Doisy-Vedrines — the original and largest of the three Doisy estates — comes from 80% Sémillon and 20% Sauvignon grapes. The juice from the de-stalked, pressed grapes ferments in oak casks. Maturing takes about two years. Roughly one-third of the casks are replaced each year. In a sound year — like 1979 and also 1982 — production reaches 30 *tonneaux*. In 1973, however, the vineyard was struck twice by hailstorms, in 1974 not a drop was produced, and in 1975 like in 1977 no more than 10 *tonneaux*.

Characteristic aftertaste

Quality as well as yield fluctuates. The light vintages such as 1969 and 1977 were not at all to my liking. I thought the 1970 was better, with a good, lively taste and the vigorous aftertaste very characteristic of this château. The bouquet, however, was slightly musty and that of the 1971 was not brilliant, although the latter's taste fortunately had more to offer. Doisy-Védrines never has that real sumptuousness of its type, although its taste is fuller than many other Barsacs. Naturally the high Sauvignon content usually gives the wine a certain *fraîcheur.* One of the best recent vintages is the 1975: Pierre Cstéja puts it on a par with the 1961 and 1945. I thought it successful, with a vigorous and elegant bouquet, and a fine, reasonably complex, although not really generous taste with a touch of freshness to it. Other successful recent vintages are 1976, 1979, 1980 and the splendid 1982.

Left:
Cellarmaster Marc Lucbert who looks after the 7 to 50 tonneaux produced annually by Caillou.

Below:
The main drive runs right through the vineyard. The château has its own striking clock which the locals can hear better than the one on the tower of Barsac church. The two clocks do not always strike together, and rendez-vous are often made by 'Caillou time'.

Right: Owner Joseph Bravo.

Château Caillou

2e Cru Classé
Barsac

One of the most striking buildings in the Barsac landscape is the slender, whitewashed little château of Caillou with its twin pointed turrets. The building dates from the end of the 19th century. It is not of any great architectural worth — the present owners describe it as 'a bit theatrical' — and the large stone wine bottle in the garden at the front is wholly in keeping. When the grandfather of owner Joseph Bravo bought the estate in 1909 there was only 7½ acres of vineyard left. Bravo succeeded in extending this to about 37 acres. The vineyard surrounds the château and is largely enclosed by a wall. The grape varieties are Sémillon (90%) and Sauvignon (10%).

Direct sales

Both concrete and steel vats are used for fermentation. The wine subsequently spends about three years in the cask. This period is not always the same for all the wine of a given vintage. Sometimes a vintage is bottled in parts; for example, some of the 1976 vintage was not bottled until 1979. About one-tenth of the casks are replaced each year. Château Caillou is seldom noted outside France because since 1936 Joseph Bravo has sold his wine mainly to private individuals in France by mail order and other means. At present both the commercial and the technical direction is in the hands of Bravo's son Jean-Bernard, and his daughter Marie-José supervises the vineyard work.

Modest personality

During my visit to Caillou there were quite a lot of old vintages stored in the clean, roomy cellars. I saw bottles from the 1921, 1934, 1947, 1959, 1962, 1967 and other vintages. I have excellent memories of the 1962: a gold-coloured wine, luxuriantly elegant in taste, beautiful and still completely vital. More recent Caillou vintages somewhat lack this richness. I found that even a generally rich year like 1976 was rather light and without depth. There is a certain finesse in the recent vintages, albeit to a limited extent. Caillou today seems a rather modest Barsac, without a well-defined character or striking taste — but soundly made.

The name Rieussec probably comes from the French ruisseau *or brook; there is a little stream at the bottom of the vineyard.*

A full quarter of the Rieussec vintage is put into half-bottles.

The pleasant dry white 'R' sells well, but production is low: only 15,000 bottles in 1977 and 25,000 the year after.

Albert Vuillier's brother is a wine grower too, and owns Château Paradis-Casseuil in Entre-Deux-Mers.

Rieussec has changed hands many times, and various owners are recorded in Bordeaux et ses vins *down the years.*

The concrete fermentation vats are freshly painted every year — Albert Vuillier is a stickler for cleanliness.

Below:
Inside the chai, *with the large maturing casks.*

Far right:
Albert Vuillier, who bought the estate in 1971.

Opposite page, above:
With all its various buildings, Rieussec is practically a village, with the ivy-covered tower on the left being the most distinctive feature.

Opposite page, below:
The semi-underground cellar where the wine completes the maturing process in the wood.

Château Rieussec

1e Cru Classé
Fargues

Rieussec and its vineyard lie on the highest hill in the whole of the Sauternes, after d'Yquem. The grapes ripen slightly earlier here than elsewhere in the district, and the estate is rather less affected by night frosts (although the 1977 vintage was totally lost through freezing temperatures in spring and autumn). No château as such was ever built at Rieussec because before the French Revolution the estate belonged to a monastery in Langon. The place was seldom lived in, except by a few labourers, until in 1971 the present owner, Albert Vuillier, and his wife Chantal, moved into the simply appointed residential quarters adjoining the *cuvier*. At the weekends they regularly travel to their other property, three hours' drive away, near the Pyrenees, where cereals and rapeseed are grown.

Gradual expansion

The vineyard at Rieussec occupies 160½ acres out of a total area of 190 acres. The Sémillon predominates with 80%, followed by 19% Sauvignon and just 1% Muscadelle. In Vuillier's time there has just been one occasion when the pickers were able to gather all the grapes in one go: the 1975 vintage. In 1976, too, the grapes were very sound and twice through the vineyard was sufficient. In 1974 the pickers had to go round four times, and in 1971 six times. These figures give an idea of the enormous variations in costs that confront the Sauternes château owner who aims at quality.

Two sizes of cask

At Rieussec the wine is fermented in tanks of concrete or stainless steel. Three-quarters of it is then transferred to the traditional oak casks (called *barriques*), and a quarter to the very large oak containers called *foudres*. How long the wine matures depends on its potency. A strong wine is only bottled after about two and a half years, a lighter one after some 12 months. Vuillier selects stringently not only when picking and fermenting, but also afterwards. In the spring, for example, he often has still not yet decided which casks of the previous vintage are to be used for the Rieussec *grand vin*. Less successful wine is marketed under the Clos Labère name; the *appellation* is Sauternes. Rieussec also produces an excellent dry white wine, called 'R', from grapes with a lower sugar content. Its quality was demonstrated when the French journal *Gault-Millau* in May 1979 published the result of a blind tasting. The 'R' was placed ahead of 14 other white Bordeaux, including some from the Graves.

From the visitors' book

'Today, 13 April 1936, I am finally at Rieussec, which I have admired for half a century.' François Mauriac, the celebrated French novelist and playwright, wrote these words in the visitors' book at the château. Rieussec's wine still merits admiration today. It is one of the most reliable *premiers crus*, very consistent in quality. I have come across this wine many times and have never been disappointed. One of the older vintages that I recall with much pleasure is the 1959. Some 20 years on this Rieussec was a feast for the senses: its amber colour had a golden

Château Rieussec

glow, its broad bouquet a spicy depth, its brilliant, rich taste the benefit of all its years of development. The 1969, very full for its year, and the excellent 1971, the first wine by Vuillier, were extremely agreeable.

Ripe apricots

An element of taste that I have repeatedly found in Rieussec is that of ripe apricots. It was present in the 1971, for example, and in the lighter 1973. Rieussec is not one of those really heavy, robust wines. Its richness always has a somewhat restrained character, its taste something refreshingly lively. An exception to this rule was the 1976. The wine from that dry and sunny year had a deep-golden colour, and a concentrated, very forthcoming taste that filled the mouth. The 1975 also had a good colour and four years after its vintage was already very developed — a fat, rounded wine with a lot of strength. The 1979 conformed more to the Rieussec rule: Albert Vuillier expects this to stand comparison with his 1971. I thought the 1979 indeed tasted very fine with plenty of bouquet. Anyone who knows the good wines of Rieussec can understand how someone came to write in the visitors' book: 'And on the seventh day God created Rieussec.' The 1980 is a wine with good *rôti* and structure, but it needs keeping in order to lose some of its acidity. I find the 1981 not a great success, but the 1982 — the little that was made of it — is a big, impressive Sauternes.

Below:
Château de Malle has been in the same family for 500 years.

Below right:
The Italian garden is full of statuary. The Sauternes wine fraternity holds regular meetings at Château de Malle.

Far right:
Comte Pierre de Bournazel in his château.

Centre right:
One of the château's magnificent salons.

The estate also produces a dry white Bordeaux (Chevalier de Malle), a red Graves (Château de Cardaillan) and a second, simpler Sauternes marketed as Domaine de Sainte Hélène.

Château de Malle

2e Cru Classé
Fargues

This château is the only historical monument of the Sauternes. Tourists are welcome here from Easter to mid-October. The château, with its pepperpot towers, was built in the 17th century by Jacques de Malle, a distant forebear of the present owner Comte Pierre de Bournazel. Visitors to the château can see numerous art objects and paintings, a splendid chapel, imposing fireplaces, antique furniture and Europe's largest collection of silhouettes, dating from the 18th century. These are life-size figures cut out in wood and used both for theatrical performances and for screening off the fierce heat of roaring open fires. Behind Château de Malle there lies an elegant Italian garden peopled with statues. The wine-making goes on out of the public sight, in large cellars behind one of the wings.

Wood and fruit

The transition from monument to winery comes as a shock: the charm of the past suddenly gives way to the modern reality of stainless-steel fermenting tanks. Some of the wine ferments in these, some in new oak casks. Tanks and casks also serve for maturing the wine, which sometimes takes three years (Château de Malle 1975, for example). Discussing his system, Pierre de Bournazel, an engineer and oenologist, told me: 'As a wine grower you usually have to choose between fruit and wood in a wine; we want both.' The liqueur-like wine comes from 64 acres of vineyard, planted with 75% Sémillon, 22% Sauvignon and 3% Muscadelle. Production varies from nothing in 1977 to about 40 *tonneaux* in a year like 1981.

Enchanting character

The wine of Château de Malle has the same refinement as the environment in which it is produced. It is usually distinguished and enchanting, never heavy or over-emphatic, and made with craftsmanship. Perhaps no one would call de Malle an absolutely brilliant wine, but at a dinner at the château the 1975 had enough personality to be an excellent accompaniment both to the *foie gras de canard* and the cheese. Even Château de Malle from great years can be drunk fairly early — after four to five years. It will go on developing well after this time, as is shown by an amazingly vital, fresh 1971 drunk in 1979. In the same year the 1970 proved to be too old, too maderized. Of the recent vintages the wines from 1976, 1978, 1979 and 1980 deserve a recommendation.

Below:
The present Château de Fargues stands in front of the remains of the old château.

Far right:
An approaching shower, a rainbow and the village of Fargues (left) with the Château de Fargues which can be seen to the right of the rainbow just behind the outer wall of the former château.

The 23.5-acre vineyards of de Fargues form a minute part of the 408-acre estate, which is mainly planted with pine trees.

Almost 50% of all de Fargues wines is exported to San Francisco.

Château de Fargues

Cru Bourgeois
Fargues

Before the de Lur Saluces family acquired Château d'Yquem it already owned another estate in the district: Château de Fargues. The lordship of Fargues came to the family because five centuries ago, in 1472, a de Lur Saluces married Isabeau de Montferrand. The drive to Château de Fargues begins by the old church of the hamlet of Fargues. It is lined by pine trees and bounded on one side by the local football pitch. The château is a long, low building. A gateway separates the *chai* from the living quarters. Behind the present château are the remains of an old, much bigger castle — not much more than a wall now with crumbling battlements and gaps where there were once windows.

Difficult circumstances

The Château de Fargues vineyard covers only 23.5 acres of an estate totalling 408 acres, so there is plenty of space for the herd of cows that provides manure for d'Yquem as well as Fargues itself. For a long time red wine as well as white was produced at de Fargues. Only under Alexandre de Lur Saluces, the present owner, has all attention been concentrated on making a white, dessert wine of high quality. This has not been easy. Alexandre told me that de Fargues had cost him a fortune; the more so since the wine was completely unknown and initially could only with great difficulty be sold for reasonable prices. Pierre Meslier, *régisseur* of d'Yquem, also supervises de Fargues. When I tasted the wines of d'Yquem and de Fargues he said of the latter: 'For this one I deserve the greater compliment.' The wine of de Fargues is made under much more difficult circumstances. The vineyard lies at the eastern limit of the *appellation* and the grapes generally ripen ten days later than at d'Yquem. There is thus a greater chance of rain and cold — and the days are shorter. More harvests fail at de Fargues than at d'Yquem and the average yield is lower. The 23.5 acres produce not more than 10,000 bottles a year, which means 7.5 hectolitres per hectare, whereas d'Yquem reaches 9 hectolitres.

A minor d'Yquem

The wine of de Fargues, which ferments and matures in new wooden casks, comes from 80% Sémillon grapes and 20% Sauvignon. It could be regarded as a minor d'Yquem, with less colour, strength and richness than its celebrated relative, but still exceptionally fine, with freshness in its early years and later a mature mellowness. Some of the best vintages are 1975, 1980 and 1982. Château de Fargues is a *cru bourgeois*, but deserves a place among the *crus classés*.

Below:
The château, seen here surrounded by its sandy and gravelly vineyard, which produces between 13 and 20 tonneaux *per year. There are modest plans to expand.*

Far right:
The cuverie *in Barsac, with its stainless-steel fermentation tanks. Everything is kept spotlessly clean.*

Centre left:
Owner André du Hayot sells his wine mainly in Belgium, the United States and France.

Château Romer du Hayot

2e Cru Classé
Fargues

In the official classification this estate is listed as Château Romer, but a few years ago the owner, André du Hayot, added his own name. The vineyard forms an enclave in Château de Malle land, next to the *autoroute* and with woodland on three sides. Although the vineyard covers only 25 acres it has for years been divided between two owners: Mme du Hayot (and later her son André) and Roger Fargues. Not long before his death in 1977, Fargues leased his portion to André du Hayot, who since then has worked the whole vineyard, selling the total vintage as Château Romer du Hayot. Roger Fargues' son has inherited the leased portion from his father.

Grapes to Barsac

An unpretentious country house stands next to the vineyard. This is where Roger Fargues lived. The du Hayots also lived in the neighbourhood, in the 13th-century Château Pléteygeat, but this was demolished to make way for the *autoroute*. The grapes from Romer du Hayot — 70% Sémillon, 30% Sauvignon — are taken to Château Guiteronde in Barsac, where the vinification is carried out for all the estates owned or worked by André du Hayot, a total of 160 acres. Steel tanks are used for fermenting the wine. It matures for a short period of about six months in oak casks (of which a third are new). This is a fairly recent development. Until 1980 the wine did not come into contact with wood at all.

Lightweight

Romer du Hayot is often rather a light wine. This applies to the colour, which tends towards green, and continues through the often meagre bouquet and the fresh, not generally very rich taste. The best wine I have tasted from this estate was the 1975. It had more breeding than the 1976 and a sound taste with elegant nuances. The aftertaste was nicely balanced; yet wine from a good year like 1971 was short and severe, with too much sulphur. With some Romer du Hayot vintages I noted that it was the 'middle taste' that mainly appealed to me: the bouquet, the initial taste and the aftertaste did not amount to much, but in between the wine offered quality. I experienced this most strongly with the 1976, and with the rather attractive 1978 (which also had a light aroma of almonds). Altogether, Château Romer du Hayot must be considered a lightweight among the *crus classés*, a fact that is confirmed by more recent vintages.

Below:
The château is not exactly a paragon of spruceness, but there is a nice view from the tower.

Far right:
All bottles are hand-washed before bottling. All Rabaud-Promis wine is put into full bottles — you cannot buy a half-bottle from this particular estate.

Centre right:
Cellar worker standing next to one of the hydraulic presses.

Paul Lanneluc (assisted by his son-in-law Philippe Déjean) has four other estates including Châteaux Cantelaude (Médoc) and Croix-Puyblanquet (Saint-Emilion).

Château Rabaud-Promis

1e Cru Classé
Bommes

In the 1855 classification Château Rabaud was the last of the *premiers crus*. In 1903 Henri de Sigalas sold part of this estate to Adrien Promis, so there were two châteaux with Rabaud in their name: Sigalas-Rabaud and Rabaud-Promis. In 1929 the two properties were reunited, but in 1952 they were separated again. With its 74 acres, Rabaud-Promis is twice the size of Sigalas-Rabaud; but it has added Château Pexoto to its territory, an estate that was listed among the second *crus* in the 1855 classification. Despite this extension, Rabaud kept its *premier cru* status — such is French wine law. The reverse would not apply: a second *cru* that bought land from a *premier cru* would not be promoted.

Impression of neglect

Château Rabaud-Promis must once have been worth seeing. The little château on its hill was built by the architect Victor Louis, whose work is found all over the Bordeaux region. Today, however, Rabaud-Promis looks desolate and neglected. Only a small part of it is occupied, by staff and by the co-owners and managers, M. and Mme Philippe Déjean; otherwise the shutters are permanently closed. I noted that the little tower had lost its top; apparently there is neither the will nor the money to restore it. There is a splendid view from this tower, for up to 30 miles around.

Underground tanks

Although the vineyard is planted in a very traditional way with 80% Sémillon, 18% Sauvignon and 2% Muscadelle, this does not apply to the vinification. The wine ferments in concrete vats and is then transferred to large, underground tanks, also of concrete. The wine is only bottled as the demand arises; so in 1979 there was still wine from the 1972 and all subsequent vintages in the tanks. Of these wines the 1972 was musty and unpleasant, the 1973 obviously oxidized, and the 1974 in possession of an odd tang. Later it was decided that these three vintages were to be sold under the secondary brand name of Domaine de l'Estrémade. Only the 1975 and 1976 were, in my view, satisfactory: balanced wines with a respectable bouquet and a correct taste. The question, however, is what these wines will be like after a long sojourn underground. The only Rabaud-Promis I tasted from the bottle was the 1971. This had a light taste and bouquet, and the aftertaste was distinctly stale and fusty. Practically all Rabaud-Promis is sold to private individuals in France; just a little goes to Germany. The rest of the world obviously has no interest in this *premier cru* — and with reason.

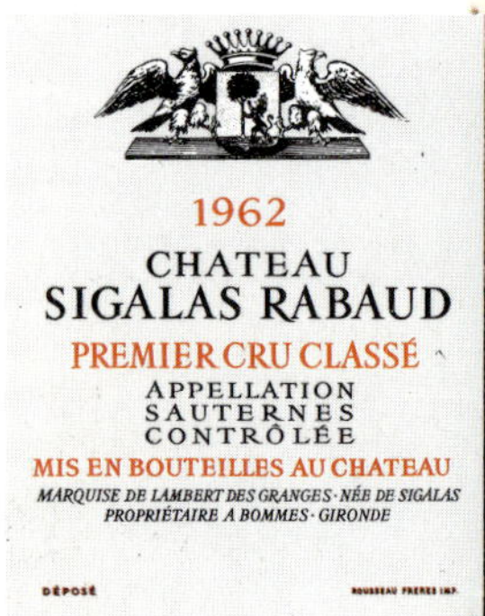

Left:
The Marquis de Lambert des Granges, the owner.

Below left:
Maître de chai *Jean-Pierre Lamarque displays one of the many diplomas the château has won for its wines.*

Below right:
The château with its gravel courtyard.

Right:
Cases of earlier vintages in their wooden cases beneath one of the paintings that adorn the huge maturing cellars.

Sigalas-Rabaud has two secondary brands: Château Perroy and Jean Blanc.

Not a single drop of Sigalas-Rabaud was made in 1974.

Château Sigalas-Rabaud

1e Cru Classé
Bommes

The *chai* at Sigalas-Rabaud is the original cellar of the Château Rabaud estate, which was later divided into Rabaud-Promis and Sigalas-Rabaud. It can accommodate 800 casks. Today this space is far from filled as Sigalas-Rabaud has only some 35 acres of the original vineyard. Next to the cellar and the *cuvier* there is a modest château, no longer occupied. In 1952 the estate became the property of the Marquise de Lambert des Granges, née Sigalas. Her husband, the Marquis de Lambert des Granges, directs the estate. The *chai* is notable for eight large paintings commissioned by the owners from regional artists.

Few casks

The entirely south-facing vineyard is planted with 60% Sémillon and 40% Sauvignon. Concrete and stainless-steel vats are used for fermenting. The latter are also employed for maturing the wine: the Marquis seldom keeps his wine in wooden casks. This method, together with the high Sauvignon content, results in a light wine. The expert Patrick Grubb, Master of Wine at Sotheby's of London, once even compared the Sigalas-Rabaud style to that of the great Rheingau estates in Germany.

Much finesse

When I tasted the still young 1978, from the tank, the sweet taste came almost as a surprise after the unusually fresh Sauvignon bouquet — a strange experience for me. I thought this wine was very clean, clear in taste and light in constitution.
In 1977 Sigalas-Rabaud produced a relatively large amount of wine — 25 *tonneaux*. Abundant years generally yield no more than about 20 *tonneaux*, and even this is rare. This 1977 was also light, with a little spiciness, and not without merit for its year. The 1975 proved to be a wine with exceptional finesse in both taste and bouquet: a delicate, almost tender Sauternes, yet one with a long aftertaste, the sign of a great wine. The vintages of 1976 and 1979 deserve attention too. Sigalas-Rabaud is an extremely elegant, subtle wine in which the Sauvignon is at first strongly dominant. This *premier cru* needs time for the Sémillon to develop; it gains in richness with the years. One of the best wines from this château that I have drunk was the 1967, 12 years after its vintage.

Below:
Lafaurie-Peyraguey from its vineyard. Parts of the castle date from the 13th century, the main building from the 17th.

Far right:
A vendangeur pedals home with tub, shears and all — yet another day's picking over.

Centre right:
The entrance to the main building is leafy and shaded. Estate manager Pierre Patachon and his wife occupy one of the wings. Patachon has been at the château since 1945, which was also one of his best years. Others include 1947, 1979, 1950, 1955, 1961, 1966, 1970, 1975 and 1976.

The output of Lafaurie-Peyraguey varies between nothing and 309 tonneaux.

Château Lafaurie-Peyraguey

1e Cru Classé
Bommes

Lafaurie-Peyraguey is among the oldest Sauternes châteaux. From front and rear it looks like a small fortress, and some of the fortifications date from the 13th century. The main building, where cellar master Michel Laporte, has his apartment, is reached by way of a shady inner courtyard, which is always peaceful — except at vintage time. Most Sauternes châteaux are not equipped for receiving visitors, but Lafaurie-Peyraguey certainly is, with a large, tastefully appointed reception room in the main building. The explanaton is that the estate is owned by the Cordier family, who not only run the wine firm of that name and its branches, but also own celebrated châteaux such as Gruaud-Larose and Talbot in the Médoc.

Change in vinification

In the roomy cellars beside and behind the main building the wine is fermented and matured in oak casks. A third of these are new. The maturing period covers two years. The wood from which these casks are made differs from the usual *limousin* oak. Lafaurie-Peyraguey has chosen the oak type of *merrain* that possesses a higher tannin content, which gives the wine more backbone and durability. This method of maturation was introduced, or rather reintroduced, from the vintage of 1978. In 1967 the system had been abandoned for one in which the wine was transferred from the casks to glass-lined metal tanks for a year. The wine — covered with a layer of nitrogen — retained much of its freshness and remained rather light. Obviously Cordier has discovered that the customer prefers a somewhat fuller Sauternes. Perhaps Lafaurie-Peyraguey will make wines again like the fantastic 1921, which half a century after its birth still made a great impression. The 1922 was equally splendid.

Emphasis on Sémillon

The fact that recent vintages up until 1978 were fairly light, was also due to the high percentage of Sauvignon. This used to be 30%. Nowadays the 50 acres of vineyard area are planted with 90% Sémillon, 5% Sauvignon and 5% Muscadelle. In my experience, the wines from the late '60s and early '70s were generally reliable but not always very exciting. A little more richness, depth and class would have been welcome. The wines usually had a generally pale golden colour with a tinge of green, modest but pure nose, and a taste that rarely struck by its sensuous sweetness or fullness. On the other hand, the wines kept very well. The wine from 1969 — a mediocre year — still tasted very vital ten years after its birth. The 1970 I have enjoyed thoroughly on quite a few occasions, as I did with the 1975. The Lafaurie-Peyraguey 1978 proved to be a delicious wine with a lot of style, and very good wines were made in 1979 and 1980 too. From the cask I had a glimpse of the 1982: a firm well-structured Sauternes with a long future ahead of it.

Below:
The actual château does not form part of the wine estate.

Far right, inset:
An old wine diploma.

Far right:
The vines of Rayne-Vigneau can yield between 130 and 165 tonneaux *in a good year. There is also a dry white wine — Rayne Sec — which has been made since 1976 (about 25* tonneaux*).*

Rayne-Vigneau is administered by the négociants *Mestrezat-Preller.*

Château Rayne-Vigneau

1e Cru Classé
Bommes

The renown of Rayne-Vigneau — called Vigneau-Pontac at the time — was established in 1867 when it triumphed over all other wines, including many from Germany, at the great exhibition in Paris. But glory passes — and just over a century later the 247-acre estate, in a totally ruinous condition, was sold for a sum of not more than three million francs. The château alone remained in the possession of its occupant, the Vicomte de Roton. The estate is now owned by a *société civile*, some of whose shareholders are involved in other properties in Bordeaux (such as Chasse-Spleen, Reysson, Duplessis-Hauchecorne), in the firm of Mestrezat-Preller, and other concerns. With the transfer of ownership Rayne-Vigneau entered an era of large-scale operation. Since 1971 many more acres have been planted and the cellar capacity has been doubled.

Precious stones

Cellars and château dominate the landscape from a wide, imposing hill. The vines occupy the slopes on all sides. They consist of an estimated 50% Sémillon and 50% Sauvignon. The vineyard consists of 165.5 acres. The soil is particularly rich in gravel — and other stones: the former owner found an enormous number of precious and semi-precious stones in the vineyard. His collection comprises some 20,000 agates, sapphires, cornelians, chalcedony and other stones. Examples are on display in a showcase in the *chai* at Rayne-Vigneau.

No greatness

After picking, the grapes go into modern horizontal presses — often six times. Fermentation takes place in tanks with stainless-steel inner walls. The estate matures its wine in oak casks, for 12 to 18 months, depending on the character of the vintage. About 50 casks are replaced by new ones each year. Rayne-Vigneau is not a startlingly great wine. I have really good recollections only of the 1971, the bouquet of which was rather indeterminate, but the taste very full and most pleasant. The 1975 and 1976 both suffered from flat bouquets (the former had just a little spiciness, the latter too much sulphur) and uninteresting tastes. I tasted these wines blind along with the same vintages from other *crus classés*: some of the second *crus* scored higher than this first *cru* from Bommes. I was not impressed by later vintages either. At the moment it rather seems as if yield counts for more at Rayne-Vigneau than quality — in contrast to a century ago.

Below:
The very modest plain château produces 18 to 22 tonneaux *a year.*

Far right:
The fouloir-égrappoir *working at full speed: the de-stalked and de-seeded grapes fall directly down into the press.*

Centre right:
Cellar workers beside a big stack of bottles. Most Clos Haut-Peyraguey is consumed in France itself — as much as two-thirds — and substantial amounts are shipped by Dourthe to Germany.

Château Clos Haut-Peyraguey

1e Cru Classé
Bommes

Clos Haut-Peyraguey lies against the hill that is crowned by Rayne-Vigneau. Not far away is Château Lafaurie-Peyraguey, from which it was separated in 1878. Compared to its neighbours, Clos Haut-Peyraguey is a miniature château: a low, modest building round a small forecourt. Its most striking feature is the tower-like structure in the centre block, where a member of the staff and his family live. The *gérant*, Jacques Pauly, lives a few hundred yards away, at Château Haut-Bommes. The Pauly family bought the little estate in 1914. Jacques Pauly owns a two-thirds share of the estate as well as supervising it.

Alternation between vat and cask

Pauly has planted his vineyard — 37 acres — with 83% Sémillon, 15% Sauvignon plus 2% Muscadelle. The juice from these grapes is fermented in concrete vats. After fermentation has stopped the wine is transferred for five months to mainly used oak casks. During the summer the wine is returned to the vats — these produce less evaporation during the warm months, according to Pauly — and then spends at least 15 months in the casks. Château Clos Haut-Peyraguey generally achieves a reasonable yield per hectare: about 22 hectolitres in 1975, 1976 and 1977, and 21 hectolitres in 1981. Only one-fifth of the 1974 vintage was acceptable; the rest was not sold as Clos Haut-Peyraguey.

Slim Sauternes

Clos Haut-Peyraguey is one of the slimmer Sauternes — I have never tasted a truly substantial wine from this small estate. The colour is usually light with a greenish sheen, the bouquet not very concentrated, the taste never thickly sweet, yet far from unpleasant. One feature I noticed in a number of the wines is to some extent characteristic (the 1975 and 1976 are examples): a slightly bitter-fresh aftertaste. That the wine is expertly made here is shown by the 1977. Despite its difficult year it had an elegant, clean taste, light but of a good standard. Château Clos Haut-Peyraguey is not the richest or most exciting of Sauternes, but despite all the handicaps of a small estate it produces a pure, light wine that certainly has its merits, one that has more to offer than others of its kind from other small properties, such as Romer du Hayot, Suau and the two Lamothe châteaux.

Far left:
Estate director Pierre Pascaud backed by two old casks, now purely decorative.

Below:
One of the château's richly appointed salons, full of splendid antiques.

Opposite page, below:
The gate that leads to the château's forecourt; the building itself is invisible from the road and stands at the end of a long drive, hidden by trees.

Opposite page, left:
The cellars are flanked by these circular towers.

Opposite page, right:
Suduiraut from its gardens, designed by Le Nôtre.

The estate produces between 15 and 70 tonneaux *of sweet, rich wine. It also markets a rather dry white wine under the Château du Broustaret label, plus a small quantity of red wine just for the staff.*

Suduiraut's visitors' book goes back to 17 October 1890.

The coat-of-arms of the Suduiraut family — who owned the château for centuries — can be found in the triangular gable ornamentation above the rear entrance. It shows boars' heads and fleurs de lis.

The balcony on the front of the château was taken from the Hôtel de Richelieu in Paris.

Château Suduiraut is a member of the Académie du Vin de Bordeaux *and the* Union des Grands Crus de Bordeaux, *as are Rayne-Vigneau, Climens, Rieussec, Broustet and Nairac; châteaux d'Yquem, Lafaurie-Peyraguey, Coutet, d'Arche and de Malle belong to the* Académie *only. Both these institutions enjoy much prestige in Bordeaux itself, although the average consumer places more value on the* cru classé *status, even though this unrevised classification dates from 1855.*

Château Suduiraut

1e Cru Classé
Preignac

Château Suduiraut is in all respects a splendid estate. It covers nearly 500 acres, a tripartite entity of château, park and vineyard. In these princely surroundings a princely wine is made. Apart from one weak period, Suduiraut has for generations been regarded as one of the best *grands crus* of the district, directly after d'Yquem. Its great reputation was demonstrated in November 1978 when more than 400 cases from the château cellars were very successfully auctioned at Christie's in London. The record sum of £500 was paid for a half-bottle of the 1820. The château took the initiative towards the auction for publicity reasons — things had been rather quiet around Suduiraut, and money was probably needed for carrying out essential improvements. That the estate went through a period of financial difficulty is shown by the fact that it was for some time offered for sale — without success.

A park à la Versailles

The present château, large, almost pompous and with little ornamentation, acquired its present form in the 17th century. The park behind it also dates from this time. It was apparently designed by no less a person than André Le Nôtre, the great French landsape architect who also created the gardens at Versailles. Only one wing of the original château remains. The Duc d'Epernon, emulating Nero, is said to have burned this and other châteaux in the Bordeaux region. The carved head of the grimacing nobleman can be seen high up on one of the outer walls.

Directed from Paris

For generations the estate belonged to the Suduiraut family, until the end of the 19th century. For a time it was called Cru du Roy, because a daughter of the house married a du Roy. This is why the words 'Ancien cru du Roy' appear on the labels.
On the day of the armistice in 1940, Léopold Fonquernie, a prosperous industrialist from northern France, became the owner. He did a great deal to restore the somewhat faded reputation of Suduiraut to its former lustre. Today it is his daughters who mainly direct the estate, from their office in Paris. The château is usually only occupied at holiday times. Day-to-day management is the responsibility of the *régisseur*, Pierre Pascaud.

Back to casks

The 172-acre vineyard is planted with 80% Sémillon, the rest being Sauvignon. The two varieties are picked together, pressed and vinified. The juice ferments in plastic-lined concrete vats. From 1968 to 1979 at Suduiraut the wine was also stored in these vats and in tanks, but the estate has now abandoned this system. Today the wine again matures in oak casks for 18 to 20 months. According to Pascaud, the casks give a better wine with more colour. Only 50 new casks are bought each year, but Pascaud

Château Suduiraut

hopes that this situation will improve. The Suduiraut cellars are the biggest in the district. The first-year *chai* with its wooden ceiling can hold no fewer than 400 casks.

Flowers and honey

I have the impression that from 1972 to 1975 Suduiraut encountered a very difficult period. The 1972 was not very exciting, and neither the 1973 or 1974 even sold as Suduiraut. But the 1975, with its elegance, finesse and peach-like taste was again a very good wine. Then came the 1976, with an almost decadent, sumptuously honeyed bouquet and taste. The 1978, too, had many good qualities; Pierre Pascaud said of it: 'This is the first wine of my career with a really perfect analysis.' It is impressive not only for its complete soundness, but also for the strong suggestion of flowers in both bouquet and taste. The 1979 was even more rich.

Earlier vintages

In good years Suduiraut is a wine with a truly golden colour, a broad, expansive, flowery scented bouquet and a rich, subtle taste with evocations of honey and ripe fruit — a Sauternes at its best. Of the earlier vintages I thought the 1967 and 1966 were very fine. The most apt description of the 1959 was given by Master of Wine Michael Broadbent in the British magazine *Wine* (no longer, alas, in existence): 'One of the things about Suduiraut which strikes me is its depth of colour. Whatever the vintage, it always appears to look deeper and older than it really is. For example, this 1959 looks to me almost like a 1950 or '52. The bouquet is very rich and honeyed, and on the palate it is a sweet, quite hefty wine. It has been served beautifully chilled, exactly right, and I personally think it most attractive and refreshing.' This Suduiraut was served during a meal at the Connaught Hotel in London. Broadbent added that to partner the wine he asked for fresh wild strawberries to replace the very sweet bread-and-butter pudding that was on the menu. I believe he was quite right, for even a rich Sauternes such as Suduiraut cannot compete with the abundant sugar of this kind of dessert.

Below:
The winery buildings with stainless-steel fermenting tanks at left.

Far right:
Ulysse Gayon, to whom this monument is erected in the château's courtyard opposite the wine cellars, was a fervent champion of the famous bouillie bordelaise, *a blend of copper sulphate, slaked lime and water used to protect the vines after they have set fruit from attack by disease and insects. The mixture is sprayed thinly over the plants, giving the leaves a sickly green colour.* Bouillie bordelaise *has been used for generations without the slightest harm to either wine or its consumers.*

Centre right:
Roger Serra is director of the college and the winery that belongs to it. He has been at La Tour Blanche since 1962, initially as Professor of Viticulture, then in his present capacity (since 1973).

Château La Tour Blanche produces 20 to 55 tonneaux *of Sauternes per year.*

At the time of writing some 60% of the students at the college were from the département *of Gironde, 10% from neighbouring* départements *and the rest from further afield.*

Château la Tour Blanche

1e Cru Classé
Bommes

La Tour Blanche is the only Sauternes château with a rugby pitch in the grounds. The last private owner, a M. Osiris, left the property to the French state on condition that an oenological college was established there. The Ecole de Viticulture et d'Oenologie has been at the château since 1910. Some 70 students, most of them resident, are taught by 9 or 10 lecturers; the course lasts two years. The students are closely involved in the making of La Tour Blanche, the second wine Cru Saint-Marc (from young vines) and the dry white Chevalier de Thiroy (pure Sauvignon, 25 hectolitres of it a year). Since 1973 Roger Serra has been the director of both college and winery.

Modern equipment

Because Château la Tour Blanche comes under the French Ministry of Agriculture, the profits from wine sales are ploughed back into the college, which therefore has modern equipment that includes stainless-steel fermentation tanks. In 1979 the cellars were considerably extended. When the fermentation process is complete, Roger Serra matures his wine for 18 to 24 months in oak casks. A quarter to a third of these are generally replaced each year. Cellars and *cuvier* are situated behind the original château, a *maison bourgeoise.* It is difficult to trace the original form of the latter, surrounded as it is by the angular college buildings. The estate takes its name from an old, solitary tower in the grounds.

Tasting notes

The college has 76.5 acres of vineyard. This is planted in the classical way with 70% Sémillon vines, 27.5% Sauvignon and 2.5% Muscadelle. In the 1855 classification La Tour Blanche was listed first among the *premiers crus,* directly after d'Yquem. Anyone who takes this to imply a strong similarity to d'Yquem will be disillusioned. La Tour Blanche usually has a fairly light colour with a greenish tinge. Taste and bouquet are not very pronounced, rich or powerful. This is no substantial, full, wine rich in sugar, though it does as a rule possess a good balance, a clear taste and a certain refinement. One of my favourite vintages from the '70s is the 1976, a wine with a civilized richness and a long finish. I prefer it above the 1975 and 1979. The estate produces between 23 *tonneaux* (in 1977) and 67 (1979 and 1982) per year. Two-thirds of the wine is usually sold to *négociants*, one-third to private individuals in France.

Below:
The second floor of the château was an addition to the original structure.

Far right:
The château is partly enclosed by a splendid courtyard around which the cellars and other functional buildings are laid out. The visitor can taste Guiraud wine here, and in the summer they open a salle de dégustation *one kilometre away on the D8 road.*

Centre right:
Part of the vineyard that produces from 5 to 75 tonneaux *of Sauternes a year, plus 590* tonneaux *of red wine and just 2 to 3* tonneaux *of dry white.*

Guiraud possesses its own small grass airfield.

Château Guiraud

1e Cru Classé
Sauternes

Château Guiraud, formerly known as Bayle, owes many of its external features to the enormously rich Maxwell family who bought it at the end of the 19th century. The Maxwells devoted a fortune to the estate. A second storey was added to the château, a water tower was built, and also a substantial hunting lodge. (The Maxwells kept a herd of wild boar, mainly so that they could hunt them.) Little is left of this former glory. As I walked around the extensive grounds I could not help reflecting that a great deal of investment is now needed. It would not be easy to run Guiraud profitably. The estate is very large and the interest in Sauternes these days is limited. Guiraud covers a total of 289 acres, of which 178 acres are vineyard. A sign of difficult times is perhaps the 37 acres that have been planted with black grapes (36% Merlot, 42% Cabernet Sauvignon, 10% Cabernet Franc, 12% others). These give a graves-like red wine with the Bordeaux Supérieur *appellation*; it is called Le Dauphin de Château Guiraud. Some dry white Sauvignon labelled 'G' de Château Guiraud, is also produced. Undoubtedly the income from these additional wines is essential if the estate is to go on making Sauternes.

Metal storage tanks

After the grapes have been pressed in modern horizontal presses, the must is pumped into oak casks. About a half of these are replaced by new ones each year. Fermentation takes place in the casks. When the maturing process has been completed, after two and a half to three years, the wine goes partly into bottles, partly into metal tanks. The latter are used to avoid having vast stocks of bottles; the wine inside keeps its perfectly fresh quality.

High proportion of Sauvignon

The Guiraud vineyard has a strikingly high percentage of Sauvignon: almost 51%. The remaining is nearly all Sémillon with a very little Muscadelle. This large dose of Sauvignon makes the Guiraud wines fresher, less sweet than most Sauternes. It has sometimes been my experience with Guiraud that the wine was sweeter in its bouquet than in taste, as with the 1976. In general I find Château Guiraud to be a reasonably reliable wine. The 1977 and 1972 vintages were certainly not bad; the 1972 in fact had a noticeably good bouquet. The 1971 was very respectable, but the 1970 was poor. My favourite wine from the 1970s is the 1975: an exquisite taste with subtlety, elegance and the right balance between sweetness and freshness; and a very impressive aftertaste. I also like the 1979 a lot. Paul Rival was the owner of Château Guiraud from 1935 until July 1981. It now belongs to the Canadian shipowner Hamilton Narby, who not only lives here permanently, but also made many necessary investments. This makes Guiraud certainly a wine to watch.

Château d'Yquem

Premier Grand Cru Classé
Sauternes

Château d'Yquem is the very top Sauternes — and has been for generations. In the 1855 classifications it was placed above all the other châteaux in a category of its own: *premier grand cru classé.* Today this position is still fully justified. Château d'Yquem not only makes the best wine of the district, commanding the highest prices, but for many it is the personification of Sauternes. Often indeed it is the only Sauternes château that people know. In no other Bordeaux district is there a château with such a pre-eminent position. You need a very sound and solid introduction before being received at Château d'Yquem, though thousands of visitors are shown round there every year. And besides these, many wine lovers make their way up the long drive simply to gaze at the château; which is well worth the effort, the grandness of d'Yquem also extends to its place of birth.

The de Lur Saluces

The château was built partly in the 16th, partly in the 17th century on the spot where several centuries previously a castle with a keep had stood. In 1592 the estate came into the possession of the Sauvage d'Yquem family. It became the property of the de Lur Saluces family in 1785 when Joséphine d'Yquem married Comte Louis Amédée de Lur Saluces. By chance the estate was visited two years later by the American ambassador, and future president, Thomas Jefferson. He described Sauternes as the best French wine (after Champagne and Hermitage Blanc), and wrote: 'the best is made by Mr de Lur Saluces'. Jefferson ordered wine from d'Yquem for his embassy and for the White House: and he introduced it to his friend George Washington. The present owner is Comte Alexandre de Lur Saluces, who succeeded his uncle in 1968. Alexandre and his charming wife Berengère

Opposite page, left:
Inside one of the cask cellars.

Opposite page, below:
The imposing château — at the foot of the tower on the left, a gate takes the visitor to the inner courtyard; d'Yquem stands at the top of a large hill and the upper floors offer a stupendous view of the surrounding countryside.

Opposite page, far right:
A bottle of d'Yquem with its simple label, showing only the name, the owner and the year, while all the other statutory declarations are contained in a narrow strip underneath.

Below:
A veteran of d'Yquem vintages, shown here during the 1979 harvest that started on 15 October and ended on the 29 November.

Right:
Comte Alexandre de Lur Saluces — the family name dates from the year when Jean de Lur married Catherine Charlotte de Saluces. Catherine's ancestors hailed from the Italian village of Saluggia, northwest of Turin.

The Château de Fargues has been in the de Lur Saluces family since 1742, and the family has also owned the châteaux Coutet, Filhot, Piada and de Malle at one time or another. Château de Malle (described on page 170) can still be counted as part of the family possessions, for its owner Pierre de Bournazel and Alexandre de Lur Saluces are in fact cousins, although they rarely meet.

All the staff at Château d'Yquem get 56 litres of wine every month including a red that is made specially for them.

When Alexandre Dumas, cold and tired after a long journey, arrived at an inn with some friends, he is said to have cried: 'Bring us fire; bring us oysters, bring us d'Yquem!' According to Alexandre de Lur Saluces, this is a reference to a fact that oysters and Sauternes can make excellent table companions. 'But,' he adds, 'it must be old Sauternes' and as an example he gave the outstanding combination of oysters and a Château Climens of 1919.

At Château d'Yquem they also make a dry white wine known simply as 'Y', and bearing the Bordeaux Supérieur *appellation. Its grapes come from the same vineyards as d'Yquem and are picked in the same painstaking fashion, but the blending is different, with half Sauvignon and half Sémillon grapes. During or just after fermentation they decide whether the wine is to be d'Yquem or 'Y' (or an anonymous bulk wine without either of these names). 'Y' has an alcohol strength of 13.8 to 14.2° — it has a medium dry, pleasant flavour but no outstanding personality. Its costly production and scant yield (30,000 bottles a year on average) make this an expensive wine at any time.*

have a daughter and two sons — the new generation is already in the wings.

Castle on a hill

The large château with its three round towers is splendidly situated on a hill that gives a magnificent, panoramic view on all sides. It is not occupied: Alexandre de Lur Saluces has a house in Bordeaux. Staff live in the grounds, in low buildings behind the big *chais*. The estate has nearly 50 full-time staff, including Pierre Meslier, *régisseur* since 1962, and Guy Latrille, who started at d'Yquem in 1962 and has been *maître de chai* since 1970. Also on the strength are a carpenter and a mechanic. The château has a fine inner courtyard with a deep, old well surrounded by roses. By tradition an open-air concert is given every May in this courtyard, one of the events of the Bordeaux festival.

Its own microclimate

Château d'Yquem has altogether 427 acres of land; 297 acres of this is entitled to the Sauternes *appellation*, but not more than 252 acres has been cultivated. The rest is regarded as less suitable for a really great wine. The productive area is usually just under 202.5 acres. The grape varieties are 70% Sémillon and 30% Sauvignon, but for d'Yquem a ratio of 80% Sémillon and 20% Sauvignon is used: the surplus Sauvignon goes into the dry white wine called Ygrec (*see* note at the top of this page). According to Alexandre de Lur Saluces, the hill on which d'Yquem stands has its own microclimate, with rather more early morning mist in autumn, and more warmth from the afternoon sun. The land is excellently drained. Alexandre's ancestor Romain-Bertrand put down a system of drainage pipes measuring a total of 60 miles. The vines are pruned with extraordinary severity, and only organic fertilizer is used. Some parts of the vineyard are so steep that the tractor cannot negotiate them — d'Yquem always keeps two horses.

One by one

The great secret of d'Yquem is that the grapes are picked one by one at exactly the right moment, namely when their sugar content is such that they could in theory produce wine of an alcohol content of 19° to 20°, no more and no less. When fermentation stops naturally at 13° to 14° of alcohol, unconverted sugar is left — 80 to 100 grams per litre. Selecting the optimally ripe, and hence rotted grapes from the rest requires trained pickers who know exactly what to look for. Château d'Yquem brings in a small army, often 140 to 150 strong. But the pickers must not only be trained — and therefore expensive, they have to be available for a long time. The grape harvest at d'Yquem usually lasts six to eight weeks. Normally the pickers go through the whole vineyard from four to six times. Comte Alexandre once calculated that his pickers walk a combined total of between 750 and 3,750 miles each year. Sometimes even six times is not enough. In 1964, for example, the vineyard was worked through 13 times: an insanely expensive procedure, for that year not a drop of wine was good enough to be called d'Yquem. In 1930, 1951, 1952, 1972 and 1974 no d'Yquem was produced.

One glass per vine

The vintage at d'Yquem is always one of the last in the district. In 1972 a visiting French government minister was dumbfounded to find that on 7 December at 7 o'clock in the evening the pickers were still at work. That year in fact, harvesting went on until 14 December (wholly in vain!). And in 1978 the last grapes were not brought in until 8 December. Occasionally Château d'Yquem has an unexpectedly quick harvest. In 1976 everything was picked within three weeks, between two rainy spells. How little the *vendangeurs* can pick in a day is shown by the fact that six to ten of them have to keep busy all day in order to fill a single wine cask. In the same time a single picker in the Médoc will gather enough for nearly two casks. Including failed harvests, d'Yquem's yield over the last 20 years has been extremely low: 9 hectolitres per hectare (compared with a permitted 25). This comes to about 1.3 decilitres per vine. Of this 20 to 25% is lost through evaporation, absorption into new oak wood and other causes. So about 1 decilitre remains, or one glass per vine per year!

New oak casks exclusively

Once picked, the grapes go into three vertical hydraulic presses — which are very flexible and gentle. The juice is trapped in a cement vat with glazed tiles and then within an hour and a half it is transferred to new oak casks. Fermentation takes place in these — always controlled, always gradual — and lasts for two to six weeks. The wine then matures for at least three years. Château d'Yquem has three large *chais*, for the first, second and

Château d'Yquem

third years of maturation. Because the new wood absorbs a lot of wine, and because some also evaporates, the casks are topped up twice a week throughout the maturing period, and unwanted oxidization is prevented. Every three months Guy Latrille transfers the wine to clean casks. The development of the wine in all the casks is checked continually, by analysis and by tasting. Only the best is used for d'Yquem — some is always rejected. In the outstanding year 1967 only 80% of the total vintage was found good enough, and in 1977 it was only 30%. Château d'Yquem allows itself the use of only the tiniest amounts of sulphur: 40 milligrams per litre at the very most, less than one-tenth of the permitted maximum. The wine is never filtered.

Nine négociants

Bottling is done on a fully automatic unit that not only guarantees exactly the same amount of wine in each bottle, but also breaks very few of them. 'Formerly,' said Alexandre de Lur Saluces, 'twelve bottles a day were broken, now only two.' In recent years d'Yquem's policy has been to put no more than 60,000 bottles a year on the market. These are sold exclusively to nine *négociants* in Bordeaux. This quantity often does not nearly meet the demand for d'Yquem, and Comte Alexandre receives hour-long telephone calls from American importers begging him to send more bottles.

Russian grand duke

The unique character of Château d'Yquem was apparently first made known to the wider world after Grand Duke Constantine, the brother of the Tsar, had tasted the 1847 wine at the château in 1859. This vintage was richer than all the other d'Yquems, because it so happened that the grapes had been picked later than usual that year and were affected by *pourriture noble* to a remarkable degree. The Russian was so enchanted by this wine that he offered 20,000 gold francs for one *tonneau* of it, many times what it normally fetched. Since 1859 *pourriture noble* has been the deliberate aim and object at the estate.

Rembrandt yellow

In terms of pure class, style and richness, a d'Yquem from a good year leaves all other Sauternes behind. I shall never forget my first taste of d'Yquem. It was the still young 1970, which years later I was to taste again. That one sip opened up a whole unknown world of luxury, at once extravagantly rich and impressively civilized, and completely natural: you drank the essence of the grape. It struck me very forcibly then that d'Yquem is the kind of wine that you have to taste for yourself to believe that it can really exist. The most beautiful description of

Opposite page, above:
A part of the immaculate vineyard.

Opposite page, below left:
Golden grapes — many are already affected by pourriture noble.

Opposite page, below right:
Grapes arriving at the press.

Below:
The floor is kept spotless during pressing.

Far right:
Régisseur *Pierre Meslier (left) with* maître de chai *Guy Latrille.*

Right:
Josephine Baker tasting d'Yquem at the 1959 Anuga Fair in Cologne. Photograph from the château's own collection.

d'Yquem's production varies sharply, as a fairly random example of five successive years shows (in tonneaux):
1974 — nothing
1975 — 90
1976 — 105
1977 — 25
1978 — 12.5
The 1976 harvest was relatively plentiful, and the grapes were picked in just three weeks which meant that the three wine presses were kept going till two or three o'clock in the morning in order to cope with all the picked fruit.

d'Yquem's wine frequently has an alcohol content of 14° or more.

d'Yquem came from André Simon who saw the wine as 'distilled dew and honey with the fragrance of all the fresh wild flowers of the field greeting the dawn'. I can also understand those people who have compared the sumptuous qualities of the wine with the paintings of Rubens or the music of Brahms. A Dutch painter once described the colour of d'Yquem as 'Rembrandt's yellow, a colour whose secret we have lost.'

Successful vintages

Château d'Yquem matures excellently. The 1919, which I drank nearly 60 years after its genesis, was still vital, and years like 1921, 1928 and 1929 are legendary. A wine that lasted less well was the 1937. The 1942, by contrast, still had a lot of fruit after some 35 years. A very great year for d'Yquem was 1945, and 1949 was almost as good. The 1947 was very enjoyable — I tasted it 30 years after its vintage. It was quite brown, but by no means past its best: elegant and luxuriantly sweet in taste. Other d'Yquem successes were 1950, 1953, 1955, 1959 and 1961. The 1963, 1965 and 1968 wines were not worthy of the name d'Yquem; but the 1967 was particularly successful. It came from very sound grapes — only three pickings were needed — and possessed a rich, subtle bouquet with suggestions of honey and jasmine, and I found the rich, broad taste intensely enjoyable. The 1969 vintage produced a fairly light, racy wine. The 1970 was a true wine of the gods, brilliantly balanced, with sumptuousness and breeding. The 1971 had the scent of blossom, was more elegant and would develop quicker. The wine of 1975 — the next great vintage — is a very beautiful wine, somewhat more elegant than the 1970. A wine like the 1975 was made in 1980, while the 1981 resembles the honeyed 1976, a wine with lots of style. In 1978 the yield was very limited (42 casks) but the quality is good. A fat, rich wine was produced in 1979. The 1982 is very, very great indeed. Anyone who tastes a great vintage of Château d'Yquem can well imagine why Alexandre de Lur Saluces remarked: 'The price of Château d'Yquem is normal. It is all the other châteaux that are too cheap.' The pinnacle of perfection cannot be reached with economy.

There is a permanent staff of about 20 at Château Filhot.

Very strict quality control is exercised, so much so that in 1963, 1964, 1965 and 1968 not a single drop of wine was deemed good enough to bear the Filhot name. It is not hard to appreciate the kind of financial sacrifices the owners had to make in order to maintain their quality image.

Major customers of Filhot wines are Australia, Britain, the United States, Germany and Japan.

The 1975 Filhot won a gold medal at the 1977 Concours Générale Agricole de Paris, *a deserved accolade for an exquisite wine.*

Below, this page and opposite: The magnificent château is one of the most imposing in the entire Sauternes region, and was built between 1780 and 1850.

Far right:
Henri de Vaucelles. The wooden casks seen here are not used to mature the wine — fibreglass tanks are employed for that.

Château Filhot

2e Cru Classé
Sauternes

Probably the first printed text in which the commune of Sauternes is mentioned is the Abbé Barein's *Variétés Bordeloises* of 1786. He writes: '. . . in Sauternes at present very good white wines are made which are known abroad under the general name of *vins de Langon*, although Sauternes neither forms part of this town, nor falls under its jurisdiction. . . . M. de Filhot, *conseiller au Parlement de Guienne*, has very great possessions in this parish and the wines he grows are of very good quality.' Château Filhot has been in existence for a long time and was an important estate at an early date. When the prosperous Filhot family bought it in 1709 it was called Maison Noble de Verdoulet. The new owners began straight away to replant the vineyard, for it had been almost totally devastated by the frost of 1705. Gabriel Barthélémy Romain de Filhot (born in 1735, president of the Bordeaux *Parlement*, and owner of Coutet from 1788) ended his life on the scaffold in 1794. One of his daughters inherited the estate. In 1827 she married Antoine de Lur Saluces, chamberlain to Napoleon. Under the regime of the Marquises de Lur Saluces the château and vineyard were further extended, partly by the acquisition of the adjoining Château Pineau du Rey. This is mentioned separately in the 1855 classification, but the wine was usually sold with that from Filhot as *Vins de Sauternes* or, at a later stage, as Château de Sauternes.

Period of crisis

Château Pineau du Rey has since disappeared. The vineyard was rooted up in about 1880; the few plots that were later replanted now give only a dry white wine (Château Pineau du Rey, Bordeaux *appellation*). All that remains of the château itself is a 17th-century tower. Filhot too experienced difficult times, losing some 150 acres between 1850 and 1950, but it survived. In 1935 it was bought by the husband of the Comtesse Thérèse Durieu de Lacarelle (*née* de Lur Saluces) and under her direction the estate began to be rebuilt. Her name still appears on the label. Through her daughter's marriage, Filhot passed into the possession of the de Vaucelles family. The estate is now run by Comte Henri de Vaucelles. With its 766 acres, it is the biggest estate in the whole of the Sauternes.

Almost a palace

The château at Filhot, set in an extensive, English-looking park, is almost a palace. It has two wings that are longer than the main building and are set at an angle to it. Henri de Vaucelles lives in one of them with his family, and his brother has an apartment there. The central section of the other wing is missing. The courtyard has a small ornamental pond with a fountain and the entrance is guarded by two stone lions. The wine cellars, which used to be near the vineyard, lie a couple of hundred yards away, near the west entrance. The area planted

The many paintings at Château Filhot include a portrait of Gabriel Barthélémy Romain de Filhot (1735-94), president of the Bordeaux Parlement, *who also bought Château Coutet in 1788 — the labels of the two châteaux are practically identical. The house also contains an almost Impressionist painting of Thérèse de Lur Saluces who became the Comtesse Durieu de Lacarelle (1884-1976) after her marriage. It was she who bought the much-neglected Château Filhot from her brother in 1935 and worked hard and successfully to put the estate back on its feet.*

Far right:
A greenhouse where geraniums and other plants spend the cold seasons.

Right:
One of the silently roaring lions that watch over the château.

with vines has grown steadily to replace what was lost in Filhot's difficult period. In 1935 only 49 acres remained; today there are 148. Some parkland is reclaimed for the vine every year if possible. In good years like 1976, 1979, 1981 and 1982 Filhot produces about 100 *tonneaux*, significantly less in bad ones. The rainy year 1974 produced just 30 *tonneaux*, and 1977, with its night frosts, only 5 *tonneaux*. Henri de Vaucelles told me that Filhot was usually the first of all the Sauternes vineyards to be hit by freezing temperatures. this is due to its position right on the southern boundary of the *appellation*. The grapes ripen more slowly there; in 1978, for example, picking went on right up to 28 November.

No maturing in the wood

In the gigantic Filhot cellars, built for twice the present size of vineyard, the juice is fermented in a battery of fibreglass tanks. The wine also remains in these for the maturing period of about two years, protected from oxidization by a layer of paraffin wax. There are no wooden casks at all at Filhot. This in itself makes the wine less firm than many other *crus classés*, a characteristic further emphasized by the considerable percentage of Sauvignon used: 37%, with 60% Sémillon and 3% Muscadelle. Filhot is therefore a rather slender Sauternes, delicate but with vital suppleness — a wine that keeps its fruit for a long time and seldom tastes very sweet. The 1970 and 1971 vintages were successful, and I did not dislike the 1972. It was a light, elegant wine with a fine bouquet in which the Sauvignon was still dominant seven years after the vintage. The 1976 was a total contrast to the 1972. I found it richer, more complete and honeyed than other recent vintages — a splendid wine. The 1975 was less sumptuous, but greatly appealed to me: a delightful bouquet with blossom and fruit (a lot of the Sauvignon), and an exquisite taste with fine intimations of fruits, not excessively sweet, and with an impeccable balance. The 1979, too, is developing into a good wine. However, the most memorable Filhot for me was the 1928. With Jean-Eugène Borie and Monique Borie (of Ducru Beaucaillou) I was served it by Jean-Claude Vrinat of the famous *Taillevent* restaurant in Paris.
Half a century after its vintage the wine had the colour of tawny port, but still tasted astonishingly young. Its taste was striking for not having very much sugar: apparently this Filhot characteristic is long established.

Left:
The main gate to the château.

Below left:
Château d'Arche stands at the top of a hill. Three wines are made on the estate: d'Arche, d'Arche-Lafaurie and Lamothe (Bastit-St-Martin); the vineyard covers a total of 270 acres.

Below right:
Bottles of the good 1976 vintage. I also noticed the words crême de tête *on the label of exceptional vintages, as on the 1971.*

Far right:
Only d'Arche-Lafaurie wines used to be stored here.

Château d'Arche (including d'Arche-Lafaurie and Lamothe-Guignard)

2e Cru Classé
Sauternes

Château d'Arche overlooks the neighbouring village of Sauternes. The estate is one of the oldest in the district — its main building dates from 1530 — and derives its name from the Comte d'Arche, who bought it in the 18th century. The vineyard covers 69 acres and is planted in the traditional way with 80% Sémillon, 15% Sauvignon and 5% Muscadelle. The wine is fermented in concrete vats, and then matured in wooden casks for at least two years. Roughly one-tenth of these casks are replaced each year.

Not brilliant, but attractive

The Château d'Arche wines are usually reasonably firm in taste; there is refinement there, but it is not immediately obvious. In my expereince they never have brilliant personalities, but are nevertheless attractive. The green and gold of the 1975 were not especially deep in tone. The bouquet was still modest, but with fine nuances. The taste had a certain style, without an excess of richness or strength; there was still some freshness present. This was not a wine that you fall for straight away, yet it had solid attractions; and the same was true of other vintages, such as the distinctly lighter 1973. A wine that will probably surpass the 1975 is the 1980.

Château d'Arche-Lafaurie

One other wine is made in the large cellars of d'Arche. It is called Château d'Arche-Lafaurie. This is Château d'Arche's second wine, made from constituents of lesser quality. It generally tastes lighter and more nervous. It is sold, rightly or not, as a second *cru*. Total production for the estate reaches an average of 50 *tonneaux*. The property is owned by the Bastit-Saint-Martin family and leased by Pierre Perromat.

Château Lamothe

A third wine used to be made in the cellars of Château d'Arche, a second *cru* called Château Lamothe (formerly Lamothe-Bergey). Part of the Lamothe estate was sold in 1961 by its then owner, Bastit-Saint-Martin, to Jean Despujols (*see* opposite page). The remaining 27 acres were bought in 1981 by the Guignard family, who also own Château de Rolland in Barsac. They will continue to use the name Château Lamothe. Hopefully, the wine — first Guignard vintage was 1981 — will be better than in the Bastit-Saint-Martin period. It then was light in colour, flat in nose, and simple in taste with a somewhat vulgar kind of sweetness. The percentages of grape varieties resemble those of Château d'Arche

The château employs just one workman, and then only from the end of April till after the harvest. For the rest of the time the Despujols do it all themselves, apart from the pruning which they contract out.

When I tried the 1975 vintage at home I was amazed to find it had a plastic capsule, something you would never expect of a cru classé.

Below:
The tower of Château Lamothe — at any rate the Lamothe that belongs to Jean Despujols — with the harvest in full swing. Production fluctuates from 10 to 20 tonneaux.

Far right:
Jean Depujols and his wife Stanis. Their two children show no interest in following in their parents' footsteps, perhaps one reason why Jean Despujols was toying with the idea of selling Lamothe.

Right:
Lamothe's wine labels are not always the same from year to year.

Château Lamothe

2e Cru Classé
Sauternes

As mentioned on page 188, Bastit-St Martin sold part of his Château Lamothe estate, consisting of 20 acres of vineyard and the living quarters of the modest château, and about half of the cellar space. The owner of the second Château Lamothe thus brought into being was Jean Despujols, who was already a wine grower by profession. He had owned an estate elsewhere in the Sauternes, but saw no further profit in it after the Garonne overflowed, flooding his home for three weeks.

High yield

It is Jean Despujols's wife who is mainly concerned with the wine, and a specialist firm is brought in to prune the vines. Jean himself is a hunting and shooting fanatic — so much so that he has a camouflaged hide among the ancient oaks behind the house from where he shoots birds. An older curiosity is the remains of a Roman fort, also behind the château. Despujols's Lamothe achieves a yield that few other *crus classés* can equal: in 1975, 1976 and 1978 this was 21 to 22 hectolitres per hectare. Only in 1977 was it lower, at 12 hectolitres per hectare. I can well understand that with such a small estate you have to produce a relatively large quantity of wine to make a living, but this policy is never conducive to quality.

Fibreglass and cement

In the neat, small cellars the wine ferments in vats either of fibreglass or cement. It matures for about two years: for the first year in used oak casks, for the second in the vats. According to Despujols, this treatment keeps the freshness in the wine. Besides its Sauternes, Lamothe also produces about 200 litres of dry white wine.

Lack of class

The four Château Lamothe vintages I have tasted did not altogether impress me favourably. The 1978 was not unpleasant, but very flat. The 1977 smelled of sulphur and also had a suggestion of vegetable in the taste. The 1976 was rather lacking in class, had a slight smell of sulphur, and its taste was somewhat thin for its year. The 1975 had a very subdued bouquet, but fortunately its taste had more to offer: it was reasonably full and pure, but too blandly sweet. In my view neither Lamothes — Bastit-St Martin nor Despujols — deserve their place among today's *crus classés.*

Below:
The château could be taken for an English country house.

Far right:
A case displaying its delicious — and expensive — contents, the glorious Raymond-Lafon of 1975. Note the oval label peculiar to the château.

Right:
Mme Meslier gives all her guests a hearty welcome. She is an excellent cook and also looks after the administration of the estate.

The wines of Château Raymond-Lafon mature in either oak casks or stainless-steel tanks. The chai is partly below ground level, and a small natural spring near one of the walls makes for good humidity.

Pierre Meslier prefers the old hydraulic presses to the more modern horizontal ones; a disadvantage of the latter is that the grape juice has to be fined before it can ferment. This is not necessary with the gentler, more sensitive hydraulic pressoirs: hence the quality of the subsequent wine is superior.

Before becoming régisseur of d'Yquem, Pierre Meslier had the same job at châteaux Lascombes and Prieuré-Lichine in the Médoc, then both the property of Alexis Lichine (the latter firm now owns Prieuré-Lichine only).

Château Raymond-Lafon

Château Raymond-Lafon is an English-style house that looks out on the d'Yquem vineyard in the front and on those of Sigalas-Rabaud and Rabaud-Promis at the back. It dates from 1850. The man who built it, Raymond Lafon, wanted to make only wine of the very best quality; and the same was true of the château's second owner. Until the beginning of this century Raymond-Lafon wine was often sold at nearly the same prices as d'Yquem. However, the property declined and in 1972 only 8½ acres were still in cultivation. But in that year Raymond-Lafon acquired a new owner, Pierre Meslier, the manager of Château d'Yquem. He has succeeded in a relatively short time in building up a great new reputation for the estate.

Lower yield than d'Yquem

Paris-born Meslier and his charming wife Francine, have achieved wonders at Raymond-Lafon.
Without much capital behind them they bought not only the château but also extra land, so that Raymond-Lafon now covers 37 acres. The most important fact, however, is that right from the start Meslier aimed at only the best. In the Sauternes that means working with very low yields. He hopes in the future to reach 9 hectolitres per hectare — the yield at d'Yquem. It is less than this at the moment. From the 1978 vintage he produced around 5,000 bottles, about the same from the 1977, 15,000 from the 1976, 10,000 from the 1975 — and nothing at all from the 1974. These statistics indicate that the Mesliers have been through a number of difficult years, the more so since their wine is a little-known *cru bourgeois* for which not everyone wants to pay a *cru classé* price. Meslier aims at fixing the price of his wine at half that of d'Yquem. Even if he succeeds Raymond-Lafon will still be relatively cheap, for half the price certainly does not imply half the quality.

Pleasant taste, complete wine

The 1975 is a Raymond-Lafon at its finest. The wine has a golden colour, a gratifying, rich bouquet and a pleasant taste full of stylish luxury. You can enjoy the aftertaste for minutes on end. After d'Yquem, Raymond-Lafon is perhaps more complete than any *grand cru.* At present Pierre Meslier can only allow himself 33% new casks a year, but it will be more in the future if things go well. The wine matures for more than three years in the cask. The vineyard is planted in a fairly classic manner with 80% Sémillon and 20% Sauvignon. Thanks to very severe selection, the château has produced a number of delicious wines since the 1975. I mention the rich 1976, the sumptuous 1979, the excellent 1980 (resembles the 1975), the very good 1981 (resembles the 1976) and the simply magnificent 1982 (of which only a third of the harvest will be sold as Raymond-Lafon).

Right:
A familiar sight during the vintage in the Médoc: members of a wine cooperative bring in their grapes for pressing. The queue is often a long one, for each batch of berries has to be weighed and tested for sugar content before processing. This particular scene is at La Rose Pauillac, the wine cooperative of Pauillac itself (see page 192).

Vintages

The following brief vintage evaluations are not to be taken as absolutes, but are intended as a general guide to the average quality of the wine in the various districts. Any wine lover will know that mediocre years can produce good wines and vice versa, a fact borne out by the many tasting notes contained in this book.

Médoc and red Graves

1961 A hot summer: without doubt the year of the century — the wines phenomenal.
1962 A generous harvest that has matured perfectly; no further maturing necessary.
1963 Very mediocre apart from a few exceptions.
1964 Fine summer followed by heavy rain during the harvest, so very irregular, although the better wines are balanced and fragrant.

Continued page 192

Other interesting châteaux

There are of course good wines made in Bordeaux besides those mentioned on the preceding pages. This chapter therefore gives short descriptions of other interesting châteaux. They include estates from the Médoc, Graves, Sauternes, Sainte-Croix-du-Mont, Entre-Deux-Mers, Saint-Emilion, Pomerol, Fronsac, Bourg and Blaye. The selection I have made is strictly personal, based on tastings and, in many cases, visits, and does not aim at comprehensiveness. No mortal could ever manage to taste the wines of all the Bordeaux châteaux — there are more than 3,000 — every year. Most of these châteaux have been included because I think they make good wine. Some are here, however, because they are very well known, which does not of itself guarantee immaculate quality — but you will discover this for yourself in the following pages.

Médoc

Château d'Arche, *Ludon*
This modest old château lies in the heart of the village of Ludon and has 15 acres of vineyard. The grape varieties are Cabernet Sauvignon (50%), Cabernet Franc (10%), Merlot (35%) and Petit Verdot (5%). Annual production is 20 to 36 *tonneaux.* The owner, Frédéric Duchesne, has stainless-steel fermentation tanks, but still works in the old, craftsmanlike way. His wine is fined with fresh egg white and matures for about two years in oak casks (10 % of them new). The wine is lightly filtered before bottling. I have tasted many excellent d'Arche vintages, including a memorable 1964, a very good 1967 and a fruity 1970. The wines of Château d'Arche usually require keeping for some time (the 1971 was an exception) and offer reliable, solid quality. The château houses a pleasant museum with antique wine-making tools and equipment.

Château la Gurgue, *Margaux*
This château is in the centre of the village of Margaux, behind a wrought-iron gateway and at the end of a narrow drive. Since 1978 it has belonged to the Société Bernard Taillan and the Société Bonniéroire Vinicole, which are also joint owners of Chasse-Spleen. These new owners have invested a great deal in La Gurgue. This was overdue: in 1978 the vineyard was giving a poor yield of only 8 to 10 hectolitres per hectare because of its bad condition. Under the energetic direction of Mme Bernadette Villars (also *régisseur* of Chasse-Spleen) La Gurgue acquired four stainless-steel fermentation tanks, completely renovated working areas and a reorganized and cleaned-up vineyard. This covers 30 acres, planted with about 50% Cabernet Sauvignon, 35% Merlot, and 5% Petit Verdot. The wine matures for 20 months in oak casks (one-third new). La Gurgue is becoming a wine well worth following.

Château Tayac, *Cru Bourgeois, Soussans* (appellation *Margaux)*
In the cellars of Château Tayac André Favin makes sound Margaux. It comes from a 86.5-acre vineyard where the vines are 73% Cabernet (principally Sauvignon) and 25% Merlot and 2% Petit Verdot. Production varies between 110 and 185 *tonneaux*. Favin uses concrete and stainless steel fermentation vats and matures his wine for about two years in oak casks (of which one-third are new). The actual château at Tayac stands empty, opposite the cellars. A secondary brand is Château Labory de Tayac.

Château Lestage, *Cru Bourgeois, Listrac*
The imposing Château Lestage is hidden in a park of tall old trees. The proprietors — Jean Chanfreau and his three sisters — also own Château Fonréaud, in Listrac. I think the Lestage is the better of the two wines. It is made from 58% Merlot, 38% Cabernet Sauvignon and 4% Petit Verdot. The wine ferments in concrete vats and also matures in them. The production of the 136-acre vineyard varies between 140 and 310 *tonneaux* of fairly supple wine that achieves its charm early.

Château Clarke, *Cru Bourgeois, Listrac*
On 16 June 1979 all Bordeaux was at Château Clarke for the annual Fête de la Fleur. For most of the nearly 700 guests it was their first view of the wholly renovated and enlarged estate. It was bought in 1973 by Baron Edmond de Rothschild, who has a one-sixth holding in Lafite-Rothschild, and the majority of the shares of the Savour Club wine organization. The baron has invested many million francs of his private fortune in Château Clarke. The vineyard has been increased nearly twelvefold, to 346 acres. This area is gradually becoming productive: in 1977 it yielded 20 *tonneaux*, in 1978 it was 125 and in 1982 no less than 500. The sound, elegant wine comes from 49% Cabernet Sauvignon grapes, 37% Merlot, 10% Cabernet Franc and 4% Petit Verdot. Stainless-steel tanks serve for fermenting the wine, oak casks (a fifth of them new each year) for the 10 months maturation..

Château Duplessis-Fabre, *Cru Bourgeois, Moulis*
In 1974 Duplessis-Fabre went to the same five buyers as Fourcas-Dupré. The vineyard was then only 2½ acres in area, now it is 30. And it will grow with another 25 to 30 acres. Manager and co-owner Guy Pagès still has a lot to do at this château, but his wine is already very agreeable. In the future the grape varieties will be 60% Cabernet Sauvignon, 28% Merlot, 10% Cabernet Franc and 2% Petit Verdot. At time of writing the Cabernet Sauvignon content was a little smaller and that of the Merlot slightly bigger. The wine is vinified at Fourcas-Dupré.

Château Lachesnaye, *Cussac*
Since 1961 Lachesnaye has belonged to the Bouteiller family, of the *grand cru* Pichon-Longueville and the adjacent Lanessan. Since 1961, too, the Lachesnaye vineyard has been replanted little by little. It now covers 49 acres of a 320-acre estate. The wine is made at Lanessan, in concrete fermentation vats and under the supervision of Hubert Bouteiller. The 10 to 23 *tonneaux*

1965 Possibly the worst vintage of the century.
1966 A beautiful summer resulting in robust wines. A very good year.
1967 Bigger vintage than 1966 — the wine has matured more quickly and is softer.
1968 Uninteresting wines with a few surprisingly good ones.
1969 Passable wines in general; they have matured reasonably well.
1970 An outstanding vintage both for quality and quantity; powerful wines, worth waiting for.
1971 Very good, fairly strong and attractive wines, rather underrated after 1970.
1972 Acceptably acidic wines that are gradually maturing into elegant, agreeable vintages.
1973 Soft wines that lack breeding but have lots of charm; very big vintage.
1974 Large and irregular vintage yielding wines with less body and charm than the 1973.
1975 An outstanding vintage with full-bodied, concentrated wines that need time to develop; some are even better than 1970.
1976 An underrated year in the wake of the formidable 1975; generous, soft wines that should be drunk before the 1975 vintage; they are not unlike the 1962 wines.
1977 Disappointingly poor grape harvest with many mediocre, thin wines interspersed with pleasant surprises; better and less acid than 1972.
1978 In terms of quality this very good year ranks just below 1975; the wines are just a little less concentrated.
1979 An abundant harvest with generally good wines, not unlike 1973.

Other interesting châteaux

mature for 12 to 18 months in used wooden casks. Half the grapes are Cabernet Sauvignon, half Merlot.

La Rose Pauillac, *Pauillac*
The Pauillac wine cooperative is one of the best in the Médoc. Its brand name is La Rose Pauillac (and not *Château* La Rose Pauillac as some importers and restaurateurs call it). Some 125 mainly small wine growers are associated with the cooperative, which was set up in 1933. Together they produce, on average, about 550 *tonneaux*. The wine is reliable in quality and reasonably firm, but without a lot of personality, refinement or depth. Sometimes I find it rather too smooth in taste. It is matured for two years, partly in concrete vats, partly in used casks.

Château Bellegrave, *Pauillac*
Bellegrave, situated in the hamlet of Saint-Lambert just south of Pauillac, is a small, traditional wine estate producing firm, deep-coloured, almost rustic wines that can be, and should be, given time to mature. The vineyard covers not quite 10 acres (80% Cabernet Sauvignon, 15% Merlot and 5% Petit Verdot plus Malbec). The Dutchman Henry van der Voort (died 1968) became the owner in 1901; for a long time most of the wine went to the Netherlands. His grandson Yves de Boisredon now exports a lot to America.

Château Haut-Bages-Monpelou, *Cru Bourgeos, Pauillac*
For almost a century the vineyard of this château was part of the estate of Château Duhart-Milon, fourth *grand cru classé*. In 1947 the two estates were separated. Here Emile Castéja makes a vigorous, not particularly substantial Pauillac with a very refined character. Of the 37-acre vineyard, 15 acres is in production, giving 10 to 35 *tonneaux* annually. The wine matures 18 to 20 months in cask and the grape varieties are 75% Cabernet and 25% Merlot.

Château Livran, *Saint-Germain-d'Esteuil*
Amateur painter Robert Godfrin took over Livran in 1961, becoming owner of a château that was built in 1777 on the site of a feudal castle, which had stood near a former Roman river port. Livran has 109 acres of vineyard (to be increased to about 125 acres), planted with 50% Merlot, 25% Cabernet Sauvignon and 25% Cabernet Franc. The annual yield is 100 to 220 *tonneaux*. Because of its great suppleness and rather bland taste, Livran is drinkable very early. Godfrin uses two labels, one with a white and the other with a black background. Château la Rose Goromey is a second brand.

Château Carcanieux, *Cru Bourgeois, Queyrac*
In June 1978 Carcanieux was bought by Marcel Muyres and Erik Sauter. This improved the quality of the wine for *gérant* Sauter (who is also a wine importer at Maastricht in the Netherlands) understands his trade. I have tasted well-structured wines like the 1978, 1979, 1981 and 1982. This is one of the better *crus bourgeois*. The very gravelly Carcanieux vineyard covers 64 acres, 52 being productive. It is planted with 60% Cabernet Sauvignon, 25% Merlot and 15% Cabernet Franc. The 55 to 110 *tonneaux* of annual production ferments in metal resin-lined tanks. The wine then matures for 6 to 18 months in oak casks (in the future a quarter of these will be replaced each year) and also in the casks. Exactly the same wine from this estate is called Château Les Lattes. Secondary brand: La Licorne.

Other Médoc châteaux that deserve mention for their very respectable, often good wine are: Arnauld (Arcins); Montbrun (Cantenac); Canuet (Margaux); Ligondras (Margaux); Malescasse (Lamarque); La Closerie du Grand Poujeax (Moulis); Branas Grand Poujeaux (Moulis); Ducluzeau (Listrac); Cap Léon Veyrin (Listrac); Pibran (Pauillac); Tourteran (Saint-Sauveur); Ramage la Batisse (Saint-Sauveur); La Tour Saint-Joseph (Cissac); Du Breuil (Cissac); Le Bourdieu (Vertheuil); Brame-les-Tours (Saint-Estèphe); La Haye (Saint-Estèphe); Soudars (Saint-Seurin-de-Cadourne); Pey-Martin (Ordonnac); La Tour Haut-Caussan (Blaignan); Des Tourelles (Blaignan); Saint-Bonnet (Saint-Christoly); Saint-Christophe (Saint-Christoly); Saint-Christoly (Saint-Christoly); La Croix Landon (Bégadan); Landon (Bégadan); De By (Bégadan); La Clare (Bégadan).

Graves

Château la Tour Bicheau, *Portets*
The Daubas family has owned La Tour Bicheau since 1836. Three-quarters of the 49-acre vineyard is planted with black grapes — Merlot, Malbec and Cabernets. Concrete vats are used for fermenting. The wine then matures for 18 months in very large wooden casks. It is lightly filtered just before bottling. This is a vital, usually fruity red Graves, of good quality. La Tour Bicheau also produces some dry white wine. In normal years the total yield is 60 to 85 *tonneaux*.

Château Cabannieux, *Portets*
Châteaux Cabannieux is situated in the highest part of Portets, on a very gravelly plateau, and its vineyard covers 62 acres. In 1973 the estate was bought by the Barrière and Dudignac families; the Dudignacs live at the château. Both red and white wine is made — the red is the more interesting. It is made from 65% Merlot and 35% Cabernet. Concrete fermentation vats are employed, and used wooden casks for maturing the wine for about a year. Production of red and white wine combined is 35 to 75 *tonneaux*.

Château Millet, *Portets*
Henri de la Mette bought Millet in 1936 and since then much has been altered and improved. The graceful château has been restored and the vineyard expanded to its present 141 acres. Neither Henri nor his son Thierry will reveal the proportions of the grape varieties they use. Most of the production is of red wine, which is matured for at least two years in wooden casks, of which 40 are replaced each year. Total production varies from 17 *tonneaux* (after

Left:
'Unique in the world' proclaims the sign in a vineyard near Barsac.

Far left:
The Sauternes commune of Preignac. The scene is deceptively tranquil — a busy main road runs right through the town.

Opposite page:
Owner Dominique Guillot de Suduiraut in front of Château Magence in the Graves commune of Saint-Pierre-de-Mons. The château is also his home, and is described on this page.

Saint-Emilion and Pomerol

1961 An exceptional year with well-rounded, full-bodied wines that could be laid down for ten years.
1962 A good year and a pleasant surprise after the succesful 1961.
1963 Mediocre in every way.
1964 A generally better year than in the Médoc, with robust, less subtle wines.
1965 A very poor year.
1966 Perhaps rather heavy, but maturing very well.
1967 Frankly charming wines that should be drunk before the 1966.
1968 Another poor year but with some pleasant surprises.
1969 A year that promised more than it delivered, with wines that are on the light side.
1970 Really exceptional year with excellent,
Continued page 194

the frosts of 1977) to more than 300 (1974). The red wine is distinguished by its dark colour and a pleasant, mellow taste that is pleasing at an early date. As its second wine the estate produces a Bordeaux Supérieur under the name Château du Clos Renon.

Château Ferran, *Martillac*
Château Ferran Blanc is a very successful dry white Graves. It sometimes has a vague aroma of toasted bread and a lightly spicy, mildly fresh taste. Unfortunately not much of it is made, for Ferran's vineyard is only 15 acres, part of it planted with black grapes. White Ferran goes mainly to Britain and America. M. Berau-Sudreau, the owner, makes it from 75% Sémillon, 15% Sauvignon and 10% Muscadelle grapes.

Château Magence, *Saint-Pierre-de-Mons*
White and red Magence both enjoy great popularity in and around Bordeaux: many restaurants, including some very famous ones, carry both wines. The white has an extraordinarily clean, crisp, very slightly tingling taste; in the red the Cabernet Sauvignon is very obviously present. The owner of the low, simple château is Dominique Guillot de Suduiraut. He has long used stainless-steel fermentation tanks: Magence was the third Bordeaux estate, after Latour and Haut-Brion, to adopt them. The vineyard is planted with 35 acres of white grapes (three-fifths Sémillon, two-fifths Sauvignon) and 15 acres of black (two-thirds Cabernet Sauvignon, one-sixth Cabernet Franc and one-sixth Merlot). At Magence is the headquarters of the SICA Les Vignobles de Bordeaux, a collaborative group of estates from Saint-Pierre-de-Mons (the Graves' biggest wine commune) and district.

Château Toumillon, *Saint-Pierre-de-Mons*
'Toumillon' apparently comes from *'tout meilleur'*, 'everything better'. In the 18th and early 19th century this château belonged to owners from Antwerp. One of the most enterprising of these was Charles Brannens, who in 1807 set out for America to sell his wine in Philadelphia and New Orleans. The present owner, Jean Sevenet, has 35 acres of vineyard, planted with white (59%) and black (41%) grapes. The white wine does not appeal to me much, but the red does. It is a dark, somewhat rustic, very tannic Graves — the very good 1975 is an example. The wine is not matured in casks but in resin-lined vats and tanks.

Other Graves châteaux worthy of attention for their red or white wine are: Couhins-Lurton (white, Villenave-d'Ornon, property of André Lurton;; Haut-Bergey (red, Léognan); Graville-Lacoste (white, Pujols); Montalivet (red, Pujols); De Cantegrive (red, Padensac); Pontac-Monplaisir (white, Villenave-d'Ornon); Le Tuquet (white and red, Beautiran); Crabitey (red, Portets); from Piron (white, Saint-Morillon).

Sauternes

Château Piada, *Barsac*
Château Piada lies on the north side of the village of Barsac. It is one of the oldest estates in the whole Sauternes. Like many other châteaux it once belonged to the de Lur Saluces family of Château d'Yquem. Owner Jean Lalande makes his sweet white wine from about 27 acres, and a dry white wine from some 32 acres. The latter is called Clos du Roy.

Château Gravas, *Barsac*
Château Gravas, a property of 25 acres, is in the centre of the Barsac *appellation*, between Coutet and Climens. The 16th-century château and its vineyard belong to Pierre Barnard. The wine, made mainly from Sémillon grapes, is often served by the Parisian chef Gérard Pangaud: a compliment, for Pangaud is something of a Sauternes connoisseur.

Château Saint-Amand, *Preignac*
If you drive from Barsac towards Preignac, Saint-Amand is one of the first châteaux you see, not far from the Ciron. This little river separates the two communes and in the autumn gives rise to the early morning mists in which the *Botrytis cinerea* thrives. Saint-Amand is the property of Louis Ricard, an authoritative local wine grower. His 49-acre vineyard is planted with two-thirds Sémillon and one-third Sauvignon grapes. The wine matures at least 18 months in wooden casks. Part of the vintage is sold exclusively by the firm of Sichel under the name Château de la Chartreuse.

Château Haut-Bergeron, *Preignac*
For four generations the Lamothe family has worked Haut-Bergeron. The vineyard covers 45 acres and adjoins that of Château d'Yquem. The grapes are 80% Sémillon, 10% Sauvignon and 10% Muscadelle. The wine is matured for two years in wooden casks. It enjoys a good reputation and regularly wins medals. Robert Lamothe, the owner, lives in the 19th-century château.

Other Sauternes châteaux with successful wines I have tasted are: Liot (Barsac); Haut-Bommes (Bommes, the same owner as Clos Haut-Peyraguey); and Pajot (Sauternes).

Saint-Croix-du-Mont
Opposite the Sauternes, on the far side of the Garonne, there are two small districts where pleasant, liqueur-like white wines are made. Though less rich and refined than their counterparts across the river, they usually offer attractive value for money. These districts are Sainte-Croix-du-Mont (the larger, with about 1,240 acres of vineyards) and Loupiac (see below). Details of four châteaux of Sainte-Croix-du-Mont follow:

Château de Tastes, *Saint-Croix-du-Mont*
This medieval castle, built by the English, stands high above the Garonne. It gives a tremendous view over the Sauternes landscape across the river. Directly beneath the castle there is a gravel terrace where you can sample and drink the local wine. The rock is rich in fossils. Château de Tastes

powerful and sturdy wines that could be laid down for several years.

1971 A very good, fine year with outstandingly enjoyable vintages.
1972 A rather acidic year that has failed to mature exceptionally.
1973 An uneven vintage; the wine could have been fuller but is still tolerably refined.
1974 Another irregular year but with wines superior to those of 1973.
1975 An eminent vintage with really big wines that will last well.
1976 Fruity, soft wines that mature less slowly than the 1975.
1977 A disastrous year with a miserable grape harvest, but better quality than the 1972.
1978 A depressing summer gave way to a brilliant autumn that produced very good wines in the end.
1979 An abundant harvest yielding satisfying wines of respectable quality.

Other interesting châteaux

belongs to the Prats brothers (Cos d'Estournel, De Marbuzet, Petit-Village, etc.). Because of the present crisis in the sweet white wine market they have reduced the vineyard area to 2½ acres, planted exclusively with Sauvignon. It is to be hoped that they will start replanting as soon as interest in Sainte-Croix-du-Mont increases again, for the wine of Château de Tastes — I recall a splendid 1949 — has great style.

Château Loubens, *Sainte-Croix-du-Mont*
Loubens wine is the best-known of its district. The château, once a fort, is built over a complex of deep cellars hewn out of the rock, where the wine matures in oak casks. From its 69 acres the estate produces white, sweet Sainte-Crois-du-Mont, a dry white Bordeaux (Fleuron Blanc) and a little red wine.

Château des Mailles, *Sainte-Croix-du-Mont*
M. Larrieu, the owner, produces an elegant, fine wine. For me his *crême de tête* (such as the 1970, tasted in 1979) was a discovery.

Château Lousteau-Vieil, *Sainte-Croix-du-Mont*
The owner of this estate, M. Sessacq, is a very serious wine maker, as testified by wines such as the very good 1975, which was deservedly awarded a gold medal at the annual agricultural show in Paris. Another good wine is made at Château La Rame.

Loupiac

This district is one of the first places where vines were planted in Bordeaux. Its production amounts to about two-thirds that of Sainte-Croix-du-Mont. In the abundant year 1979, for example, Loupiac's yield was some 123,000 cases; Sainte-Croix-du-Mont's 186,000 cases. Some of the châteaux where a feeling for quality prevails are Barbe-Morin, Bel-Air, De Loupiac/De Gaudiet, Malandure, Mazarin, Du Portail Rouge and Peyrondet.

Entre-deux-Mers

The district of Entre-Deux-Mers, contained between two stretches of water, the Dordogne and the Garonne, is the biggest of the Bordeaux wine region. Considerable quantities of mainly dry white wine are made (the *appellation* is Entre-Deux-Mers) and substantial amounts of red wine (*appellations* Bordeaux and Bordeaux Supérieur).

Château Bonnet, *Grézillac*
This is one of the estates of the extremely active André Lurton (see also Château la Louvière, page 94). He works on a big scale here at Grézillac, where he is also the mayor. He has 198 acres of black grapes (70% Cabernet Sauvignon, 20% Merlot, 10% Cabernet Franc) and 148 acres of white (about 45% Sémillon, 30% Muscadelle, 15% Sauvignon, 10% Ugni Blanc). Since 1972 the grapes have been mechanically picked; the two machines save 120 pickers and also do the work much faster. The Bonnet wines have a clean, clear taste and are expertly made. Their supple, fruity nature makes them pleasantly drinkable at a very early stage. Bonnet wines are sold under other names in various markets: Château la Tour de Bonnet, Château Peyraud etc.

Château Launay, *Soussac*
Rémy Greffier is an important wine grower with some 247 acres of vineyard. Château Launay is on one of the highest points of Entre-Deux-Mers and produces a sound, pure wine in which the fruit of the Sauvignon grape usually dominates. The estate has modern cellars with stainless-steel fermentation tanks.

Château Toutigeac, *Targon*
Château Toutigeac is a vast estate of nearly 620 acres, of which 370 acres is at present planted with vines. This area is to be increased in the future. Owner René Mazeau takes great care with the planting and tending of the vineyards and the vinification, as shown by the high-trained vines, the stainless-steel fermentation tanks and many small details of method. The white wine is made exclusively from Sémillon grapes, the red only from Cabernets (half Cabernet Sauvignon, half Cabernet Franc). Both are pleasant, pure wines, fresh, fragrant and, in their youth, with much fruit in their taste. They should be drunk young. The Toutigeac vineyard is closely connected with four other estates of the Mazeau family — De Lagorce, De Hartes, De Costis and De Roustaign. They belong to René's four sons. The wines show a great family likeness. Sometimes they are sold under one another's names: a lot of white Toutigeac, for example, is marketed as Château de Lagorce.

Château la Tour de Beaupoil, *Pessac-sur-Dordogne*
This is an example of a fairly small Entre-Deux-Mers estate (74 acres) with a conscientious approach. In fact, Château la Tour de Beaupoil is the best wine of Château Coursou; the vineyard of La Tour de Beaupoil (but not the château itself) is included in the Coursou estate. The owner, René Dupas, uses no insecticides or weedkillers. He makes both white and red wine, and the latter appeals to me more: usually dark red, with plenty of fruit, very pure and agreeably drinkable in the first year after its vintage. The grape varieties are one-third each of Cabernet Sauvignon, Cabernet Franc and Merlot.

Saint-Emilion

Château Tertre-Daugay, *Grand Cru Classé, Saint-Emilion*
Tertre-Daugay is one of the oldest estates of Saint-Emilion, in the extreme southwest of the plateau. In the 1970s it lost much of its reputation — vineyard and château were, in fact, so badly maintained that a large part of the vineyard had to be replanted by the man who bought the property in 1978, Comte de Malet de Roquefort of Château la Gaffelière. The 38-acre vineyard is therefore only just coming back into production. The grapes are 60% Merlot, 25% Cabernet Franc and 15%

Opposite page, far left:
This bust of a woman — she seems to be wearing a hat of green moss — stands in the park at Château Bonnet in the Entre-Deux-Mers district.

Left, both pages:
Landscape with vines in Entre-Deux-Mers.

Right:
The village of Montagne-Saint-Emilion where the Romanesque church has a square tower with crenellated battlements that afford a superb view of Saint-Emilion and the Dordogne valley.

Sauternes
1961 Not much wine, but of remarkable quality, if somewhat light.
1962 A plentiful harvest with well-balanced rich wines of outstanding quality.
1963 Lots of thin, meagre wine.
1964 An almost total disaster with scattered exceptions (e.g. Climens).
1965 Poor, lightweight and undernourished wines.
1966 Pleasant, fruity vintages but lacking in body; some are even very good.
1967 A good vintage with varying quality — the better wines are excellent.
1968 Eminently forgettable.
1969 By and large of no more than reasonable quality.
1970 Lots of wine and a high level of quality too; the best wines are very powerful.
1971 Rather lighter than the 1970 but nevertheless plenty of outstanding stylish wines.
Continued page 196

Cabernet Sauvignon. For vinifying the wine, stainless-steel fermentation tanks are used and oak maturing casks (one-third new each year); maturing takes 18 months. Without doubt Tertre-Daugay will win back its good name.

Château St-Georges Côte Pavie, *Grand Cru Classé, Saint-Emilion*
Jacques Masson, a bank director in Nantes, owns this small, 13½-acre wine estate. From two-thirds Merlot and one-third Cabernet *maître de chai* Jean-Gabriel Cassin makes a fairly robust, harmonious wine. He matures it for about two years in used wooden casks. Production is 17 to 27 *tonneaux* annually.

Clos la Madeleine, *Grand Cru Classé, Saint-Emilion*
Since 1947 Clos la Madeleine has belonged to M. Pistouley. The little vineyard is of only 5 productive acres, yielding 6 to 12 *tonneaux.* Practically the whole vintage goes to Belgium. The wine matures for 18 months in casks and is made from 50% Merlot, 30% Cabernet Franc and 20% Cabernet Sauvignon. The 20-acre vineyard of Château Magnan-la-Gaffelière is connected with Clos la Madeleine.

Château la Clotte, *Grand Cru Classé, Saint-Emilion*
The firm of Jean-Pierre Moueix of Libourne leases La Clotte under the *métayage* system, tending the vineyard and making the wine in return for a part of the vintage: Moueix receives two-thirds of the wine and sees to its maturation; the owner, Mme Brac, has the remainder, which she matures at the château. The Moueix wine is distinctly the better of the two. It is a fairly mellow but firm wine, of a decent quality although not truly great. The 9-acre vineyard is planted with 85% Merlot and 15% Cabernet Franc. Moueix matures its wine for about 20 months in the wood — about one-eighth of the casks are new. Total production is 7 to 17 *tonneaux.*

Château la Serre, *Grand Cru Classé, Saint-Emilion*
The wine of La Serre is based on four-fifths Merlot and one-fifth Cabernet Franc. For some reason the Cabernet always seems to be more strongly present in the wine than its actual proportion would suggest. La Serre is a reasonably generous Saint-Emilion without much depth or refinement, but nevertheless of a very decent quality. Proprietor Bernard d'Artefeuille also owns La Pointe in Pomerol. His son Luc lives at La Serre. Lined concrete fermentation tanks are used and the wine is matured for 16 months mainly in casks of which one-third are new. About 15 to 32 *tonneaux* a year are produced from this vineyard of nearly 17 acres.

Château Grandes Murailles, *Grand Cru Classé, Saint-Emilion*
This wine takes its name from the monument just outside the walls of Saint-Emilion. The vineyard, in front of the solitary old wall, is small and for this reason the wines from two other *grands crus classés,* Baleau and Clos Saint-Martin, are also sold under the Grandes Murailles name. All three belong to the Reiffers-Malen family. The wine matures in concrete vats, hardly ever in casks. It has a decently complete, lasting taste but rather lacks personality and subtlety. The three estates together cover 52 acres and yield about 100 *tonneaux* annually.

Château Guadet-St Julien, *Grand Cru Classé, Saint-Emilion*
Guadet-St Julien's two vineyard plots lie just outside Saint-Emilion, the château in the little town itself. It is a large house with ancient cellars full of atmosphere, a well 52 feet deep and a pleasant tasting room. The owner is Robert Lignac, whose family has possessed the 15-acre estate for three generations. The average 25 *tonneaux* a year come from 50% Merlot, 25% Cabernet Franc and 25% Cabernet Sauvignon. The wine is matured for two years in oak casks (a quarter of them new). Guadet-St Julien is a fairly hard Saint-Emilion that needs time to develop; I find its quality good.

Château Haut-Sarpe, *Grand Cru Classé, Saint-Emilion*
Haut-Sarpe is one of the most beautiful châteaux of Saint-Emilion. Built in 1895, it was inspired by the Trianons at Versailles and is set in a spacious park with fine old trees. The interior is splendid. Near the château there is a miniature village where the pickers are housed (it has its own café, *Le Glouglou*) and where artists live from time to time. Owner Jean-François Janoueix (of the firm of that name at Libourne) has also fitted out the *cuvier* and cellars in an attractive way. Unfortunately Haut-Sarpe wine does not come up to the expectations evoked by the château. I find it rather fat, and flat, with limited class or richness. The 31-acre vineyard is planted with 60% Merlot, 30% Cabernet Franc and 10% Cabernet Sauvignon grapes. The wine from Château Vieux-Sarpe (28 acres) is somewhat similar. Haut-Sarpe's second brand (from young vines etc.) is called Château Côte Mauvezin Badette.

Château Moulin du Cadet, *Grand Cru Classé, Saint-Emilion*
The modest château of Moulin du Cadet, almost hidden by trees, has a 12-acre vineyard area divided into two plots. One is by the château and has a clay and limestone soil; the other is near Cap de Mourlin and has more sand. The grapes (90% Merlot, 10% Cabernet Franc) and expert vinification by Jean-Pierre Moueix (joint owner with Mademoiselle Moulierac) combine to produce an excellent Saint-Emilion, with strength, charm and refinement; a wine that make you regret that only 10 to 24 *tonneaux* of it are made. It is vinified in the *chais* of nearby Château Fonroque and then it matures for 16 to 22 months in the Moueix cellars at Libourne. An eighth of the maturing casks are replaced each year.

Château Petit-Faurie-de-Soutard, *Grand Cru Classé, Saint-Emilion*
Since January 1977 this estate has been worked by a *société civile* of which Jacques Capdemourlin is the *gérant.* (He has been

1972 An almost complete failure.
1973 Charming, medium-bodied wines that are hardly improved by further maturing.
1974 A generally scanty harvest with the odd pleasant surprise.
1975 A celebrated year with lots of rich, long-lived wines of outstanding balance.
1976 Full-bodied, ample wines with a little less breeding than 1975 but still very good.
1977 A small harvest with wine to match.
1978 *Pourriture noble* often absent; good wines without being truly *rôtis*.
1979 A healthy, sumptuous vintage of mostly good quality; somewhat uneven, however, especially in Barsac.

Left:
Château la Tour du Pin Figeac in Saint-Emilion, which despite its name has neither a tower nor pine trees. The vineyard has two owners, Gérard Bélivier, who owns the left-hand half with the house, and the Moueix family (of the A. Moueix company, not Jean-Pierre Moueix), which owns the cellars on the right. The château is described on this page.

Opposite page, left:
The unusual church of Lalande-de-Pomerol.

Opposite page, right:
Maître de chai *Paul Cazenave looks on while owner Jean-François Janoueix tastes his wine at Château la Croix in Pomerol.* *See page 197.*

mentioned earlier in connection with Château Balestard-la-Tonnelle, also a Saint-Emilion.) Petit-Faurie-de-Soutard has 19 acres of vineyard, planted with 65% Merlot and 35% Cabernet. The 20 to 50 *tonneaux* of wine is matured for about two years in used wooden casks. It is usually dark in colour with a not very pronounced bouquet and a somewhat rustic taste, moderately rounded and with some tannin.

Château Faurie de Souchard, *Grand Cru Classé, Saint-Emilion*
A ditch forms the boundary between Petit-Faurie-de-Soutard and Faurie de Souchard. The latter estate has 27 acres of vineyard and belongs to the Jabiol family (of Château Cadet-Piola). The vines consist of 65.5% Merlot, 26% Cabernet Franc and 2.5% Cabernet Sauvignon. The vintages I tasted had a rather austere colour, a firm, not exuberant bouquet and a somewhat hard, firm but not broad taste. The wine is matured for 12 to 18 months in the cask. About a quarter of the casks are replaced for each vintage. Yield is 15 to 55 *tonneaux* a year.

Château Trimoulet, *Grand Cru Classé, Saint-Emilion*
Michel Jean owns various châteaux in Saint-Emilion and also directs a wine firm. Trimoulet is his 'flagship': an estate of 42 acres that produces between 37 and 100 *tonneaux.* Grape varieties are Merlot (60%), Cabernet Franc (20%), Cabernet Sauvignon (15%) and Malbec (5%). The wine spends only one year in wooden casks (one-quarter to one-third new) but nevertheless has a rather 'woody', severe taste — certainly when it is young. It should therefore be given time to develop.

Château Laniote, *Grand Cru Classé, Saint-Emilion*
Practically all the wine from this small estate goes to Brussels; the remainder is drunk by private individuals or sold by the Paris cheese specialist Androuet. It is not a refined or generous Saint-Emilion, but it has sufficient strength of taste and a deep colour, and it matures excellently. The 12-acre vineyard is planted with three-quarters Merlot and one quarter Cabernet. The owners are the heirs of Freymond Schneider; Jean Brun is the *régisseur.*

Château Franc-Mayne, *Grand Cru Classé, Saint-Emilion*
Château Franc-Mayne, flanked by two tall cedars, stands on the hill up which climb its 20 acres of vines. The soil here contains lime and is almost identical to that of Saint-Emilion's famous plateau. Franc-Mayne's wine used to be very tannic, but is now a little less so: the manager, Jean Brun, has replaced some of the Cabernet Sauvignon with the more supple Cabernet Franc. The vines now consist of two-thirds Merlot and one-third Cabernet Franc with Cabernet Sauvignon. Recent vintages of the wine have had an elegant power and very good quality. The 22 to 33 *tonneaux* of wine produced is matured in used wooden casks.

Château la Tour du Pin Figeac, *Grand Cru Classé, Saint-Emilion*
Two halves of the original property operate under this name. One belongs to Gérard Béliver, the other to Jean-Michel and Bernard Moueix (of the firm of A. Moueix at Libourne). I find the Moueix wine by far the better of the two. The 20 to 40 *tonneaux* of wine comes from 22 acres planted with 65% Merlot and 35% Cabernet Franc. It remains for about 15 months in used wooden casks. The wine possesses quite a mellow taste, full and generous in nature. America is the most important market.

Château Grand Corbin, *Grand Cru Classé, Saint-Emilion*
Grand Corbin belongs to Alain Giraud and covers 35 acres of vineyard. Giraud uses 50% Merlot, 25% Cabernet Franc, 25% Cabernet Sauvignon, and annual production is 20 to 75 *tonneaux.* The wine ferments in concrete and matures in wood, for 20 months; 10% of the casks are replaced each year. Grand Corbin tastes mild, pleasant and just slightly bland. Though agreeable in the mouth it leaves no memorable impressions. It has no great subtlety of bouquet or taste.

Château Puy-Razac, *Saint-Emilion*
There are a number of particularly good Saint-Emilions that are not included among the *grands crus classés.* One example of these is Puy-Razac. I discovered the really delightful, velvety 1974 from this château at the restaurant Loubat in Libourne during a Sunday dinner with *steak au canard de Saint-Emilion.* Puy-Razac has 15 acres planted with 40% Merlot, 35% Cabernet Franc, and 25% Cabernet Sauvignon, and is owned by Guy Tholliez, *chef de culture* at Château Monbousquet. The 10 to 28 *tonneaux* produced is matured in vats, not in wooden casks.

Château Maison-Blanche, *Montagne-Saint-Emilion*
This château is an example of the attractive estates to be found in the satellite districts of Saint-Emilion. It makes long-keeping, full-bodied wines of a very reliable quality. The immaculately maintained, 74-acre vineyard lies round a pleasant little park. The wine matures for at least 15 months in mostly used oak casks. Production is 55 to 150 *tonneaux.* Gérard Despagne, the owner, uses equal parts of Cabernet Franc, Cabernet Sauvignon and Merlot. He also owns the Châteaux Tour Corbin Despagne (Saint-Emilion) and La Rose Figeac (Pomerol).

Other Saint-Emilion châteaux that merit attention for their reasonable, good, or even very good wine, are: Bellevue (Grand Cru Classé), Yon Figeac (Grand Cru Classé), Corbin-Michotte (Grand Cru Classé), Berliquet, Carteau, La Coix Chantecaille, Lapelleterie, Fombrauge, de Ferrand, Gravet, Béard, Rozier, Macquin-Saint-Georges (Saint-Georges-Saint-Emilion) and Belair-Haut-Montaiguillon (Saint-Georges-Saint-Emilion).

Other interesting châteaux

Pomerol

Château Taillefer, *Pomerol*
Taillefer is the headquarters of the firm of A. Moueix as well as a wine estate. Owners Jean-Michel and Bernard Moueix cultivate 49 acres, planted with two-thirds Merlot and one-third Cabernet Franc grapes. Production varies from about 30 to about 100 *tonneaux*. Taillefer's wine stays for 12 to 15 months in used wooden casks before being bottled. It tastes pleasant and supple and can generally be drunk young. A lesser quality of wine is marketed under the name Clos Toulifaut.

Château la Commanderie, *Pomerol*
Since April 1957 Fernand Dé and his sister Marie-Hélène have been the owners of this small, 14½-acre estate; they produce 7 to 26 *tonneaux* of wine from 65% Merlot grapes, the rest being mainly Cabernet Franc. The fermentation tanks are of stainless steel. The wine matures in used wooden casks for 12 to 18 months. A second quality is sold as Château le Priourat.

Château La Croix, *Pomerol*
At La Croix, the property of Jean-François Janoueix, who is also a *négociant*, many reminders of the pilgrims who used to travel to Santiago de Compostela in Spain have been assembled. There is also a collection of hearthplates from all over France. La Croix has about 42 acres of vineyard, growing 60% Merlot, 25% Cabernet Franc and 15% Cabernet Sauvignon grapes. These give an average annual production of some 50 *tonneaux*. To me it seems a typical wine merchant's Pomerol: an easy rather fat taste, without much breeding or finesse. Yet the Elysée Palace bought the 1966 and 1976. Janoueix matures his wine for 18 months in wooden casks, a quarter of which are new. A second brand of lesser quality is Château le Gabachot.

Château Certan-Giraud, *Pomerol*
Until 1956 the ivy-covered Certan-Giraud was called Certan-Marzelle. The Giraud family (of Corbin in Saint-Emilion and other châteaux) changed the name of the château after they had acquired it. The name Certan-Marzelle continues, however, for a third of the vintage is sold as such by one *négociant*. The 16-acre vineyard is planted with two-thirds Merlot and one-third Cabernet Franc. Production is 7 to 26 *tonneaux* a year. The wine matures two years in used casks. Certan-Giraud is a strong, creamily rounded wine that is not among the top Pomerols (because of a lack of refinement) yet of very good quality. The second wine from this estate is sold as Château Clos du Roy. Philippe Giraud lives at the château.

Château Lagrange, *Pomerol*
Lagrange's 20-acre vineyard is on the plateau of Pomerol and produces 1 to 34 *tonneaux* a year. The estate belongs to Jean-Pierre Moueix. The vines consist of 90% Merlot and 10% Cabernet Franc. They are relatively young, so that Lagrange is a fairly light kind of Pomerol with little depth. It is, however, well made, is matured for 16 to 22 months in the wood (16% of the casks are new) and has a vigorous core to its taste. The wine is vinified at Château Trotanoy: the rather humble Lagrange does not have the space.

Château du Domaine de l'Eglise, *Pomerol*
The Domaine de l'Eglise lies around the spot where the old church of Pomerol stood. The unoccupied château looks out on a 17-acre vineyard planted with 75% Merlot and 25% Cabernet Franc. Emile Castéja (of the firm of Borie-Manoux and various estates) bought Domaine de l'Eglise in 1972 and gave it to his son Philippe and his daughter Mme Preben-Hansen. The wine, which matures for 18 months in casks, half of them new, is a firm Pomerol of good quality.

Vraye Croix de Gaÿ, *Pomerol*
This tiny 10-acre property is situated near Le Gay, Lafleur and Lagrange, three châteaux on the plateau at Pomerol. Here Baroness Guichard makes a powerful, intense, yet elegant-tasting wine, producing an average of about 10 *tonneaux*. Because the estate has no château of its own the grapes are taken to Château Siaurac in Néac for vinification. The grapes are 50% Merlot, 40% Cabernet Franc and 10% Cabernet Sauvignon. A third property of Baroness Guichard is the *grand cru classé* Château le Prieuré in Saint-Emilion.

Château la Cabanne, *Pomerol*
Thanks to such wines as the beautiful 1971, La Cabanne has built up an excellent reputation among lovers of Pomerol. The Estager family has owned the 25-acre estate since 1951. Its annual 20 to 55 *tonneaux* of wine is made from 60% Merlot, 30% Cabernet Franc and 10% Malbec. Owner Jean-Pierre Estager matures his wine for 12 to 18 months in oak casks. One-fifth of these are replaced each year.

Château Bourgneuf-Vayron, *Pomerol*
Once at an official dinner a famous French *maréchale* apparently toasted the wine that had been served with the words, 'Il mérite la croix.' The wine that deserved a medal was the Bourgneuf-Vayron. This successful Pomerol comes from 80% Merlot and 20% Cabernet Franc. The vineyard covers 25 acres and yields between 16 and 57 *tonneaux*. The owner, Xavier Vayron, does not use oak casks but says he gets the same effect by frequently racking the wine during its maturation period.

Château Moulinet, *Pomerol*
Armand Moueix has owned Moulinet since 1971. The château, dating from 1902, lies in the northwest corner of Pomerol, near Château de Sales. The vineyard covers 44 acres and its grape varieties are two-thirds Merlot (plus some Malbec) and one-third Cabernet. Annual production varies between 33 and 95 *tonneaux*. Used wooden casks serve for maturing the wine (for 12 to 15 months). Moulinet is a pleasant, not particularly strong Pomerol with some elegance.

Other Pomerol châteaux worthy of note for their wines are: Feytit-Clinet, La Violette,

Left:
Vintage time in Fronsac with the 12th-century Romanesque church in the background. It is hard to imagine that this quiet, dusty village was once the site where Charlemagne built fortifications in the 8th century, and where a descendant of Cardinal Richelieu held sumptuous banquets. Apart from its wine, the only other thing worth visiting Fronsac for is the hill just outside the village which affords a superb panorama over the Dordogne valley.

Far left:
The tasting and sales centre run by the wine growers of Bourg en Blaye, next to the Blaye-Lamarque ferry.

Mazeyres, La Croix de Gay, La Fleur Gazin, Bon Pasteur, Perrucheau and — sometimes — Plince.

Fronsac

The little district of Fronsac lies about two miles west of Libourne and is bounded on two sides by the Dordogne and Isle Rivers. The best wines come from a hilly area and bear the *appellation* Canon-Fronsac; there is also a plain and simple Fronsac designation. A good Fronsac is characterized by a deep, dark colour and a kind of hearty finesse in the taste, often with a slightly bitter aftertaste.

Château Canon, *Canon-Fronsac*
The vineyard of 19th-century Canon covers not quite 25 acres and is planted with 95% Merlot and 5% Cabernet. It belongs to Mademoiselle Horeau and is occupied by Jacques de Coninck. The latter makes the wine, 20 to 30 *tonneaux* annually. Canon is a mild, generous yet not heavy Fronsac of exemplary quality.

Château Junayme, *Canon-Fronsac*
The name Junayme is said to derive from 'Adieu ma jeune aimée', words Godfrey of Bouillon is supposed to have said to his beloved on his departure for the Crusades. The owner, René de Coninck, produces between 60 and 90 *tonneaux* of good wine from Junayme's 39 acres. The grape varieties are Merlot (90%) and Cabernet (10%).

Château Vray Canon Boyer, *Canon-Fronsac*
The story goes that Vray Canon Boyer defeated various *grands crus* from the Médoc at a blind tasting. The wine from this now-empty château, dating from 1750, is indeed of an attractive quality: firm, full of heart, pure. A *société civile* owns the estate, with René de Coninck as *gérant* and Jacques de Coninck as *régisseur.* Production is 20 to 22 *tonneaux* from a vineyard of about 20 acres where the grape varieties are Merlot (90%) and Cabernet (10%). The Fronsacs of La Rivière, Canon-de-Brem, Toumalin and La Duchesse deserve attention too.

Bourg

The hilly district of Bourg is called 'the Switzerland of the Gironde'. The wines, sold as Côtes de Bourg, are unpretentious but often offer pleasing value for money. The reds are preferable to the whites, and are much more common. I have pleasant recollections of the Bourg wines from Guiraud-Cheval-Blanc, Rousselle, De Boyer, Grand Plantier, La Joncarde, Lalibarde, Peyroland, La Plantonne, De Barbe, Moulin Guérit, Moulin de Manbras, and Bujan.

Blaye

White wine plays the main role in the extensive district of Blaye, but the red is better. The latter is usually sold as Premières Côtes de Blaye. These are lighter wines than those of Bourg. I have drunk some delicious wines from various châteaux, such as Haut-Rives, La Tour Gayet, Perenne, Charron-Doudet, Bourdieu, Des Petits Arnauds and Haut-Sociondo.

Index

Figures in *italics* refer to the pages where the main description of the châteaux etc. appears. The word 'château', which occurs in most wine names, is omitted in the index.